Semiparametric and Nonparametric Methods in Econometrics

Springer Series in Statistics

Advisors

P. Bickel, P. Diggle, S. Fienberg, U. Gather, I. Olkin, S. Zeger

For other titles published in this series, go to
http://www.springer.com/series/692

Joel L. Horowitz

Semiparametric and Nonparametric Methods in Econometrics

Springer

Joel L. Horowitz
Northwestern University
Department of Economics
2001 Sheridan Road
Evanston IL 60208
USA
joel-horowitz@northwestern.edu

ISBN 978-0-387-92869-2 e-ISBN 978-0-387-92870-8
DOI 10.1007/978-0-387-92870-8
Springer Dordrecht Heidelberg London New York

Library of Congress Control Number: 2009929719

Printed on acid-free paper

Springer is part of Springer Science+Business Media (www.springer.com)

Preface

This book is intended to introduce graduate students and practicing professionals to some of the main ideas and methods of semiparametric and nonparametric estimation in econometrics. It contains more than enough material for a one-semester graduate-level course and, to a large extent, is based on a course in semiparametric and nonparametric methods that I teach at Northwestern University. In the book, as in the course, I try to emphasize key ideas and provide an intuitive grasp of how things work while avoiding formal proofs, which in this field tend to be highly technical, lengthy, and intimidating. Readers who want to see the proofs can find them in the references that are cited in the book. The book is mainly methodological, but it includes empirical examples that illustrate the usefulness of the estimation methods that are presented. The main prerequisite for this book is knowledge of econometric theory, especially asymptotic distribution theory, at the level found (for example) in the textbooks by Amemiya (1985) and Davidson and MacKinnon (1993) and the *Handbook of Econometrics* chapter by McFadden and Newey (1994).

The literature in semiparametric and nonparametric estimation in econometrics and statistics is huge. A book of encyclopedic length would be needed to cover it exhaustively. The treatment in this book is highly selective. It presents a relatively small set of methods that are important for applied research and that use and, thereby, provide an opportunity for explaining fundamental concepts and results. Because the treatment is selective, some readers will find that their favorite methods are not discussed. However, I hope that this book will provide readers with a background and understanding of key ideas that makes the broader literature more accessible to than it would otherwise be.

This book builds on and greatly extends my 1998 book on semiparametric methods in econometrics. About 50% of the material in this book was not in the 1998 book. The new material includes estimation of nonparametric additive models, including models with an unknown link function, partially linear models, nonparametric instrumental variables estimation, semiparametric proportional hazards models with unobserved heterogeneity, and quantile estimators for nonparametric additive, partially linear, and semiparametric single-index models. In addition, there are brief discussions of local linear and series estimation of conditional mean and quantile functions. Most of the material that was in the previous book is also in this one, but it has been expanded to include estimation methods, especially for single-index models, that were developed after the previous book was finished.

Many people helped to make this book possible. Wolfgang Härdle provided the initial impetus for the 1998 book and, indirectly, this one by inviting me to give a series of lectures at the annual Paris-Berlin Seminar (which, unfortunately, no longer exists). The 1998 book is an expanded version of these lectures. Numerous students read and commented on parts of the new manuscript. I especially thank Brendan Kline for reading the entire manuscript, finding many errors, and providing many suggestions for improvements. Xiaohong Chen also read and provided very helpful comments on parts of the manuscript. John Kimmel, my editor at Springer, encouraged me to write this book and remained patient even when it became clear that the writing was taking much longer than either of us originally intended it to. Finally, I thank Ronna Lerner for her patience and support throughout the lengthy preparation of this book.

Evanston, IL
Joel L. Horowitz

Contents

Chapter 1
Introduction

1.1 The Goals of This Book

Many estimation problems in econometrics involve an unknown function or an unknown function and an unknown finite-dimensional parameter. Models and estimation problems that involve an unknown function are called *nonparametric*. Models and estimation problems that involve an unknown function and an unknown finite-dimensional parameter are called *semiparametric*.

There are many simple and familiar examples of semiparametric estimation problems. One is estimating the vector of coefficients β in the linear model

$$Y = X'\beta + U,$$

where Y is an observed dependent variable, X is an observed (column) vector of explanatory variables, and U is an unobserved random variable whose mean conditional on X is zero. If the distribution of U is known up to finitely many parameters, then the method of maximum likelihood provides an asymptotically efficient estimator of β and the parameters of the distribution of U. Examples of finite-dimensional families of distributions are the normal, the exponential, and the Poisson. Each of these distributions is completely determined by the values of one or two constants (e.g., the mean and the standard deviation in the case of the normal distribution). If the distribution of U is not known up to finitely many parameters, the problem of estimating β is semiparametric. The most familiar semiparametric estimator is ordinary least squares (OLS), which is consistent under mild assumptions regardless of the distribution of U. By contrast, a parametric estimator of β need not be consistent. For example, the maximum-likelihood estimator is inconsistent if U is exponentially distributed but the analyst erroneously assumes it to be lognormal.

The problem of estimating the coefficient vector in a linear model is so simple and familiar that labeling it with a term as fancy as *semiparametric* may seem excessive. A more difficult problem that has received much attention in econometrics is estimation of a binary-response model. Let Y be a random variable whose only possible values are 0 and 1, and let X be a vector of covariates of Y. Consider

J.L. Horowitz, *Semiparametric and Nonparametric Methods in Econometrics*,
Springer Series in Statistics, DOI 10.1007/978-0-387-92870-8_1,

the problem of estimating the probability that $Y = 1$ conditional on X. Suppose that the true conditional probability is

$$P(Y = 1|X = x) = F(x'\beta),$$

where F is a distribution function and β is a vector of constant parameters that is conformable with X. If F is assumed to be known a priori, as in a binary probit model, where F is the standard normal distribution function, the only problem is to estimate β. This can be done by maximum likelihood. F is rarely known in applications, however. If F is misspecified, then the maximum-likelihood estimators of β and $P(Y = 1|X = x)$ are inconsistent except in special cases, and inferences based on them can be highly misleading. In contrast to estimation of a linear model, where a simple and familiar estimator (OLS) is automatically semiparametric, the distribution function F has a nontrivial influence on the most familiar estimator of a binary-response model.

Many other important estimation problems involve unknown functions in nontrivial ways. Often, as is the case in the foregoing examples, the unknown function is the distribution function of an unobserved random variable that influences the relation between observed variables. As will be discussed later in this chapter, however, the unknown function may also describe other features of a model. The methods needed to estimate models that include both an unknown function and an unknown finite-dimensional parameter (semiparametric models) are different from those needed to estimate models that contain one or more unknown functions but no finite-dimensional parameters (nonparametric models). Thus, it is important to distinguish between the two types of models. This book is concerned with estimation of both types.

Nonparametric and semiparametric estimation problems have generated large literatures in both econometrics and statistics. Most of this literature is highly technical. Moreover, much of it is divorced from applications, so even technically sophisticated readers can have difficulty judging whether a particular technique is likely to be useful in applied research. This book aims at mitigating these problems. I have tried to present the main ideas underlying a variety of nonparametric and semiparametric methods in a way that will be accessible to graduate students and applied researchers who are familiar with econometric theory at the level found (for example) in the textbooks by Amemiya (1985) and Davidson and MacKinnon (1993) or the *Handbook of Econometrics* chapter by McFadden and Newey (1994). To this end, I have emphasized ideas rather than technical details and have provided as intuitive an exposition as possible. I have given heuristic explanations of how important results are proved, rather than formal proofs. Many results are stated without any kind of proof, heuristic or otherwise. In all cases, however, I have given references to sources that provide complete, formal proofs.

I have also tried to establish links to applications and to illustrate the ability of nonparametric and semiparametric methods to provide insights into data that are not readily available using more familiar parametric methods. To this end, each chapter contains a real-data application as well as examples without data of applied problems in which semiparametric methods can be useful.

I have not attempted to provide a comprehensive treatment of nonparametric and semiparametric methods in econometrics. The subject is so large that any effort to treat it comprehensively would require a book of encyclopedic length. Accordingly, this book treats only a small set of estimation problems that I have selected because they are central to the field, illustrate important methods and ideas, and are useful for a wide variety of applications. Some other important estimation problems are described briefly, but I have not attempted to list all important problems and topics. Estimation of models for time series is not treated. Nonparametric and semiparametric methods for estimating conditional quantile functions have received much attention in recent years, but their treatment in this book is briefer than the treatment of conditional mean functions. Quantile estimation is technically complex owing to the nonsmoothness of the quantile criterion function. A thorough treatment would be parallel to and as long as this book's treatment of conditional mean functions. The subject of specification testing, which has received much attention recently, is also not treated. Other treatments of nonparametric and semiparametric estimation are provided in the books by Bickel et al. (1993), Pagan and Ullah (1999), and Li and Racine (2007) and the review by Powell (1994). These treatments are also selective, but they cover some of the topics not included in this book.

1.2 Dimension Reduction

One of the most important tasks of applied econometrics and statistics is estimating a conditional mean or quantile function. For example, one may want to estimate the mean annual earnings of workers in a certain population as a function of observable characteristics such as level of education and experience in the workforce. As another example, one may want to estimate the probability that an individual is employed conditional on observable characteristics such as age, level of education, and sex.

The most frequently used estimation methods assume that the function of interest is known up to a set of constant parameters that can be estimated from data. For example, a linear model of the mean of a random variable Y conditional on another variable X is $E(Y|X = x) = \beta_0 + \beta_1 x$, where β_0 and β_1 are constant parameters. The use of such a parametric model greatly simplifies estimation, statistical inference, and interpretation of the estimation results but is rarely justified by theoretical or other a priori considerations. Estimation and inference based on convenient but incorrect assumptions about the form of the conditional mean function can be highly misleading.

As an illustration, the solid line in Fig. 1.1 shows an estimate of the mean of the logarithm of weekly wages, $\log W$, conditional on years of work experience, EXP, for white males with 12 years of education who work full time and live in urban areas of the North Central United States. The estimate was obtained by applying kernel nonparametric regression (see Section A.2 of the Appendix) to data from the 1993 Current Population Survey (CPS). The estimated conditional mean of $\log W$

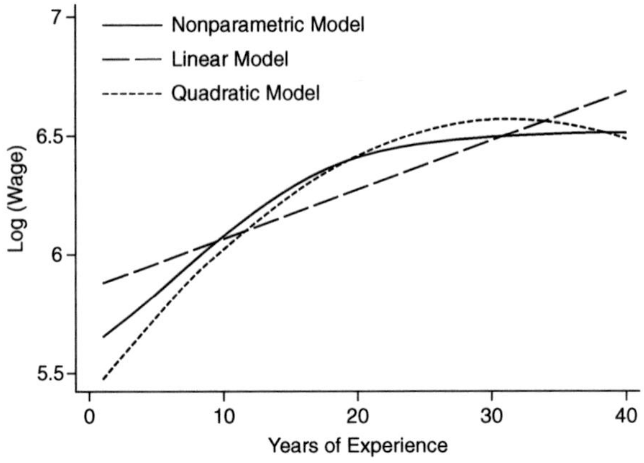

Fig. 1.1 Nonparametric and parametric estimates of mean log wages

increases steadily up to approximately 25 years of experience and is nearly flat thereafter. The dashed and dotted lines in Fig. 1.1 show two parametric estimates of the mean of the logarithm of weekly wages conditional on years of work experience. The dashed line is the OLS estimate that is obtained by assuming that the mean of $\log W$ conditional on EXP is the linear function $E(\log W \mid EXP) = \beta_0 + \beta_1 EXP$. The dotted line is the OLS estimate that is obtained by assuming that $E(\log W|EXP)$ is the quadratic function $\boldsymbol{E}(\log W \mid EXP) = \beta_0 + \beta_1 EXP + \beta_2 EXP^2$. The nonparametric estimate (solid line) places no restrictions on the shape of $E(\log W|EXP)$. The linear and quadratic models give misleading estimates of $\boldsymbol{E}(\log W|EXP)$. The linear model indicates that $\boldsymbol{E}(\log W|EXP)$ increases steadily as experience increases. The quadratic model indicates that $\boldsymbol{E}(\log W|EXP)$ decreases after 32 years of experience. Because the nonparametric estimate does not restrict the conditional mean function to be linear or quadratic, it is more likely to represent the true conditional mean function. In fact, the linear and quadratic models are misspecified. Both are rejected by simple specification tests such as RESET (Ramsey 1969).

Many investigators attempt to minimize the risk of specification error by carrying out a *specification search* in which several different models are estimated and conclusions are based on the one that appears to fit the data best. Specification searches may be unavoidable in some applications, but they have many undesirable properties and their use should be minimized. There is no guarantee that a specification search will include the correct model or a good approximation to it. If the search includes the correct model, there is no guarantee that it will be selected by the investigator's model selection criteria. Moreover, the search process invalidates the statistical theory on which inference is based.

The possibility of specification error in estimation of a conditional mean or quantile function can be essentially eliminated through the use of nonparametric estimation methods. In nonparametric estimation, $E(Y|X = x)$ considered as a function of x is assumed to satisfy smoothness conditions (e.g., differentiability), but no assumptions are made about its shape or the form of its dependence on x. Similarly, a conditional quantile function is assumed to satisfy smoothness conditions but is otherwise unrestricted. Nonparametric estimation techniques and their properties are summarized in the Appendix. Nonparametric estimation of a conditional mean or quantile function maximizes flexibility and minimizes the risk of specification error. The price of this flexibility can be high, however, for several reasons.

First, estimation precision decreases rapidly as the dimension of X increases (the curse of dimensionality). Specifically, the fastest achievable rate of convergence in probability of an estimator of $E(Y\,|\,X = x)$ decreases as the number of continuously distributed components of X increases (Stone 1980). The same is true for a conditional quantile function. As a result, impracticably large samples may be needed to obtain acceptable estimation precision if X is multidimensional, as it often is in economic applications. This is an unavoidable problem in nonparametric estimation.

A second problem with nonparametric estimation is that its results can be difficult to display, communicate, and interpret when X is multidimensional. Nonparametric estimates usually do not have simple analytic forms. If x is one- or two-dimensional, a nonparametric estimate of, say, $E(Y\,|\,X = x)$ can be displayed graphically. When X has three or more components, however, only reduced-dimension projections of $E(Y|X = x)$ can be displayed. Many such displays and much skill in interpreting them may be needed to fully convey and comprehend the shape of $E(Y|X = x)$.

A further problem with nonparametric estimation is that it does not permit extrapolation. For example, in the case of a conditional mean function it does not provide predictions of $E(Y|\,X = x)$ at points x that are outside of the support (or range) of the random variable X. This is a serious drawback in policy analysis and forecasting, where it is often important to predict what might happen under conditions that do not exist in the available data. Finally, in nonparametric estimation, it can be difficult to impose restrictions suggested by economic or other theory. Matzkin (1994) discusses this issue.

A variety of methods are now available for overcoming the curse of dimensionality and other drawbacks of fully nonparametric estimation. These methods offer a compromise between the flexibility of fully nonparametric estimation and the precision of parametric models. They make assumptions about functional form that are stronger than those of a nonparametric model but less restrictive than those of a parametric model, thereby reducing (though not eliminating) the possibility of specification error. They provide greater estimation precision than do fully nonparametric methods when X is multidimensional; the estimation results are easier to display and interpret; and there are limited capabilities for extrapolation and imposing restrictions derived from economic or other theory models. The term *dimension reduction* is often used to describe these estimation methods because they increase estimation precision by reducing the effective dimension of the estimation problem. Chapters 2, 3, 4, and 6 of this book present several leading methods for achieving dimension reduction. Chapter 2 treats semiparametric single-index models. Chapter 3 treats nonparametric additive models and semiparametric partially linear models. Chapter 4 discusses semiparametric estimation methods for binary-response models.

Chapter 6 discusses semiparametric transformation models. Chapter 5 treats a class of nonparametric estimation problems that do not involve dimension reduction.

1.3 Are Semiparametric and Nonparametric Methods Really Different from Parametric Ones?

Suppose one wants to estimate the conditional mean function $E(Y|X = x)$, and $E(Y|X = x)$ is a continuous function of x. Suppose, also, that X is contained in the compact interval $[a,b]$. A continuous function on a compact set can be approximated arbitrarily accurately by a polynomial, so $E(Y|X = x)$ can be approximated arbitrarily accurately on $[a,b]$ by a polynomial. Sometimes it is argued that this fact makes nonparametric estimation unnecessary. According to the argument, it suffices to estimate the coefficients of the approximating polynomial, which can be done by ordinary least squares. Indeed, a class of nonparametric estimation methods called series or sieve estimators works this way. See the Appendix. Thus, it is possible for parametric and nonparametric estimates of a conditional mean function to be identical. Similar results are available for other functions and for semiparametric estimation.

However, parametric estimation and nonparametric series or sieve estimation lead to different inference even if they give identical estimates of a conditional mean function or other function. Inference based on a parametric estimate treats the parametric model as exact, whereas inference based on nonparametric estimation treats it as an approximation. The approximation error is included in confidence intervals and hypothesis tests based on nonparametric methods but not in those based on parametric estimation. Therefore, the apparent precision of parametric estimates is misleading unless the parametric model is known to be correct. The parametric model reflects "information" that is in the parametric specification as well as information that is in the data. For example, in the case of using a polynomial to estimate a conditional mean function, parametric estimation assumes that the true conditional mean function is a polynomial whose degree does not exceed a known, finite value. In contrast, nonparametric estimation allows the possibility that no finite polynomial fits the true conditional mean function exactly. Because inference based on parametric estimation does not take account of approximation error, conclusions that appear to be supported by a parametric model may not be supported by nonparametric methods even if the parametric and nonparametric estimates are identical. This is why the argument described in the previous paragraph is wrong. Similar considerations apply to semiparametric models. Even if a parametric model gives the same estimates as a semiparametric one, the parametric and semiparametric models yield different inference except in special cases.

Chapter 2
Single-Index Models

This chapter describes *single-index* models for conditional mean and quantile functions. Single-index models relax some of the restrictive assumptions of familiar parametric models, such as linear models and binary probit or logit models. In addition, single-index models achieve dimension reduction and, thereby, greater estimation precision than is possible with fully nonparametric estimation of $E(Y|X = x)$ when X is multidimensional. Finally, single-index models are often easy to compute, and their results are easy to interpret. Sections 2.1–2.9 present a detailed discussion of single-index models for conditional mean functions. Conditional quantile functions are discussed in Section 2.9.

2.1 Definition of a Single-Index Model of a Conditional Mean Function

Let Y be a scalar random variable and X be a $d \times 1$ random vector. In a single-index model, the conditional mean function $E(Y|X = x)$ has the form

$$E(Y|X = x) = G\left(x'\beta\right), \tag{2.1}$$

where β is an unknown $d \times 1$ constant vector and G is an unknown function. The quantity $x'\beta$ is called an *index*. The inferential problem in (2.1) is to estimate β and G from observations of (Y, X).

Model (2.1) contains many widely used parametric models as special cases. If G is the identity function, then (2.1) is a linear model. If G is the cumulative normal or logistic distribution function, then (2.1) is a binary probit or logit model. A tobit model is obtained if one assumes that $G\left(x'\beta\right) = E(Y|X = x)$ in the model

$$Y = \max\left(0, X'\beta + U\right),$$

where U is an unobserved, normally distributed random variable that is independent of X and has a mean of zero. When G is unknown, (2.1) provides a specification that

J.L. Horowitz, *Semiparametric and Nonparametric Methods in Econometrics*,
Springer Series in Statistics, DOI 10.1007/978-0-387-92870-8_2,

is more flexible than a parametric model but retains many of the desirable features of parametric models.

A single-index model achieves dimension reduction and avoids the curse of dimensionality because, as will be seen later in this chapter, the index $x'\beta$ aggregates the dimension of x. Consequently, G in a single-index model can be estimated with the same rate of convergence in probability that it would have if the one-dimensional quantity $X'\beta$ were observable. Moreover, β can be estimated with the same rate of convergence, $n^{-1/2}$, that is achieved in a parametric model. Thus, in terms of rate of convergence in probability, the single-index model is as accurate as a parametric model for estimating β and as accurate as a one-dimensional nonparametric mean regression for estimating G. This dimension-reduction feature of single-index models gives them a considerable advantage over nonparametric methods in applications where X is multidimensional and the single-index structure is plausible.

The assumptions of a single-index model are weaker than those of a parametric model and stronger than those of a fully nonparametric model. Thus, a single-index model reduces the risk of misspecification relative to a parametric model while avoiding some drawbacks of fully nonparametric methods such as the curse of dimensionality, difficulty of interpretation, and lack of extrapolation capability.

There is an important exception to the characterization of a single-index model as intermediate or as making weaker assumptions than a nonparametric model. This exception occurs in the estimation of structural economic models. A structural model is one whose components have a clearly defined relation to economic theory. It turns out that the restrictions needed to make possible a structural interpretation of a nonparametric model can cause the nonparametric model to be no more general than a single-index model. To see why, consider a simple structural model of whether an individual is employed or unemployed.

Example 2.1: A Binary-Response Model of Employment Status An important model in economic theory states that an individual is employed if his market wage exceeds his reservation wage, which is the value of his time if unemployed. Let Y^* denote the difference between an individual's market and reservation wages. Consider the problem of inferring the probability distribution of Y^* conditional on a vector of covariates, X, that characterizes the individual and, possibly, the state of the economy. Let H denote the conditional mean function. That is, $E(Y^*|X = x) = H(x)$. Then

$$Y^* = H(X) - U, \tag{2.2}$$

where U is an unobserved random variable that captures the effects of variables other than X that influence employment status (unobserved covariates). Suppose that U is independent of X, and let F be the cumulative distribution function (CDF) of U. The estimation problem is to infer H and F. It turns out, however, that this problem has no solution unless suitable a priori restrictions are placed on H and F. The remainder of this example explains why this is so and compares alternative sets of restrictions.

To begin, suppose that Y^* were observable. Then H could be estimated nonparametrically as the nonparametric mean regression of Y^* on X. More importantly, the population distribution of the random vector (Y^*, X) would identify (that is, uniquely determine) H if H is a continuous function of the continuous components of X. F would also be identified if Y^* were observable, because F would be the CDF of the identified random variable $U = H(X) - Y^*$. F could be estimated as the empirical distribution function of the quantity that is obtained from U by replacing H with its estimator. However, Y^* is not observable because the market wage is observable only for employed individuals, and the reservation wage is never observable. An individual's employment status is observable, though. Moreover, according to the economic theory model, $Y^* \geq 0$ for employed individuals, whereas $Y^* < 0$ for individuals who are not employed. Thus, employment status provides an observation of the sign of Y^*. Let Y be the indicator of employment status: $Y = 1$ if an individual is employed and $Y = 0$ otherwise. We now investigate whether H and F can be inferred from observations of (Y, X).

To solve this problem, let $G(x) = P(Y = 1|x)$ be the probability that $Y = 1$ conditional on $X = x$. Because Y is binary, $G(x) = E(Y|X = x)$ and G can be estimated as the nonparametric mean regression of Y on X. More importantly, the population distribution of the observable random vector (Y, X) identifies G if G is a continuous function of the continuous components of X. It follows from (2.2) that $P(Y^* \geq 0|X = x) = F[H(x)]$. Therefore, since $Y^* \geq 0$ if and only if $Y = 1$, $P(Y^* \geq 0|X = x) = P(Y = 1|x)$ and

$$F[H(x)] = G(x). \tag{2.3}$$

The problem of inferring H and F can now be seen. The population distribution of (Y, X) identifies G. H and F are related to G by (2.3). Therefore, H and F are identified and nonparametrically estimable only if (2.3) has a unique solution for H and F in terms of G.

One way to achieve identification is by assuming that H has the single-index structure

$$H(x) = x'\beta. \tag{2.4}$$

If (2.4) holds, then identification of H is equivalent to identification of β. As will be discussed in Section 2.3, β is identified if X has at least one continuously distributed component whose β coefficient is nonzero, F is differentiable and nonconstant, and certain other conditions are satisfied. F is also identified and can be estimated as the nonparametric mean regression of Y on the estimate of $X'\beta$.

The single-index model (2.4) is more restrictive than a fully nonparametric model, so it is important to ask whether H and F are identified and estimable nonparametrically. This question has been investigatedby Matzkin (1992, 1994). The answer turns out to be *no* unless H is restricted to a suitably small class of functions. To see why, suppose that X is a scalar and

$$G(x) = \frac{1}{1+e^{-x}}.$$

Then one solution to (2.3) is

$$H(x) = x$$

and

$$F(u) = \frac{1}{1+e^{-u}}; \; -\infty < u < \infty.$$

Another solution is

$$H(x) = \frac{1}{1+e^{-x}}$$

and

$$F(u) = u; 0 \leq u \leq 1.$$

Therefore, (2.3) does not have a unique solution, and F and H are not identified unless they are restricted to classes that are smaller than the class of all distribution functions (for F) and the class of all functions (for H).

Matzkin (1992, 1994) gives examples of suitable classes. Each contains some single-index models but none contains all. Thus, the single-index specification consisting of (2.3) and (2.4) contains models that are not within Matzkin's classes of identifiable, nonparametric, structural models. Similarly, there are identifiable, nonparametric, structural models that are not single-index models. Therefore, Matzkin's classes of identifiable, nonparametric, structural models are neither more nor less general than the class of single-index models. It is an open question whether there are interesting and useful classes of identifiable, nonparametric, structural models of the form (2.3) that contain all identifiable single-index submodels of (2.3).

2.2 Multiple-Index Models

A multiple-index model is a generalization of a single-index model. Its form is

$$E(Y|X = x) = x_0'\beta_0 + G\left(x_1'\beta_1, \ldots, x_M'\beta_M\right), \tag{2.5}$$

where $M \geq 1$ is a known integer, x_m ($m = 0, \ldots, M$) is a subvector of x, β_m ($m = 0, \ldots, M$) is a vector of unknown parameters, and G is an unknown function. This model has been investigated in detail by Ichimura and Lee (1991) and

Hristache et al. (2001). A different form of the model called *sliced inverse regression* has been proposed by Li (1991). If the β parameters in (2.5) are identified and certain other conditions are satisfied, then the β s can be estimated with a $n^{-1/2}$ rate of convergence in probability, the same as the rate with a parametric model. The estimator of $E(Y|X = x)$ converges at the rate of a nonparametric estimate of a conditional mean function with an M-dimensional argument. Thus, in a multiple-index model, estimation of $E(Y|X = x)$ but not of β suffers from the curse of dimensionality as M increases.

The applications in which a multiple-index model is likely to be useful are different from those in which a single-index model is likely to be useful. The curse of dimensionality associated with increasing M and the need to specify identifiable indices a priori limit the usefulness of multiple-index models for estimating $E(Y|X = x)$. There are, however, applications in which the object of interest is β, not $E(Y|X = x)$, and the specification of indices arises naturally. The following example provides an illustration.

Example 2.2: A Wage Equation with Selectivity Bias Let W denote the logarithm of an individual's market wage. Suppose we want to estimate $E(W|Z = z) \equiv E(W|z)$, where Z is a vector of covariates such as experience and level of education. Suppose, also, that the conditional mean function is assumed to be linear. Then $E(W|z) = z'\alpha$, where α is a vector of coefficients. Moreover,

$$W = z'\alpha + V, \tag{2.6}$$

where V is an unobserved random variable that represents the effects on wages of variables not included in Z (e.g., unobserved ability). If (W, Z) were observable for a random sample of individuals, then α could be estimated, among other ways, by applying ordinary least squares to (2.6). However, W is observable only for employed individuals, and a random sample of individuals is likely to include some who are unemployed. Therefore, unless attention is restricted to groups in which nearly everyone is employed, one cannot expect to observe (W, Z) for a random sample of individuals.

To see how this problem affects estimation of α and how it can lead to a multiple-index model, suppose that employment status is given by the single-index model consisting of (2.2) and (2.4). Then the mean of W conditional on $X = x$, $Z = z$, and $Y = 1$ is

$$E(W|z, x, Y = 1) = z'\alpha + E\left(V|z, x, U \leq x'\beta\right). \tag{2.7}$$

If V is independent of Z and X conditional on U, then (2.7) becomes

$$E(W|z, x, Y = 1) = z'\alpha + G\left(x'\beta\right), \tag{2.8}$$

where $G(x'\beta) = E(V|z, x, U \leq x'\beta)$. Equation (2.8) is a multiple-index model that gives the mean of log wages of employed individuals conditional on covariates

Z and X. Observe that (2.8) is not equivalent to the linear model (2.6) unless $E(V|z, x, U \leq x'\beta) = 0$. If $E(V|z, x, U \leq x'\beta) \neq 0$, estimation of (2.6) by ordinary least squares will give rise to a *selectivity bias* arising from the fact that one does not observe W for a random sample of individuals. This is also called a *sample selection* problem because the observed values of W are selected nonrandomly from the population. Gronau (1974) and Heckman (1974) used models like (2.7) under the additional assumption that V and U are bivariate normally distributed. In this case G is known up to a scalar parameter, and the model is no longer semiparametric.

In (2.8), α is identified only if X has at least one continuously distributed component that is not a component of Z and whose β coefficient is nonzero. The credibility of such an *exclusion restriction* in an application can be highly problematic. Manski (1994, 1995) provides a detailed discussion of the problems of identification in the presence of sample selection. ■

2.3 Identification of Single-Index Models

The remainder of this chapter is concerned with the semiparametric single-index model (2.1).

2.3.1 *Conditions for Identification of β and* G

Before estimation of β and G can be considered, restrictions must be imposed that ensure their identification. That is, β and G must be uniquely determined by the population distribution of (Y, X). Identification of single-index models has been investigated by Ichimura (1993) and, for the special case of binary-response models, by Manski (1988). Some of the restrictions required for identification are easy to see. It is clear that β is not identified if G is a constant function. It is also clear that as in a linear model, β is not identified if there is an exact linear relation among the components of X (perfect multicollinearity). In other words, β is not identified if there are a constant vector α and a constant scalar c such that $X'\alpha = c$ with probability one.

To obtain additional conditions for identification, let γ be any constant and δ be any nonzero constant. Define the function G^* by the relation $G^*(\gamma + \delta v) = G(v)$ for all v in the support of $X'\beta$. Then

$$E(Y|X = x) = G\left(x'\beta\right) \tag{2.9}$$

and

$$E(Y|X = x) = G^*(\gamma + x'\beta\delta). \tag{2.10}$$

Models (2.9) and (2.10) are observationally equivalent. They could not be distinguished empirically even if the population distribution of (Y, X) were known. Therefore, β and G are not identified unless restrictions are imposed that uniquely specify

γ and δ. The restriction on γ is called a *location normalization*, and the restriction on δ is called a *scale normalization*. Location normalization can be achieved by requiring X to contain no constant (intercept) component. Scale normalization can be achieved by setting the β coefficient of one component of X equal to one. In this chapter it will be assumed that the components of X have been arranged so that scale normalization is carried out on the coefficient of the first component. Moreover, for reasons that will now be explained, it will also be assumed that this component of X is a continuously distributed random variable.

To see why there must be at least one continuously distributed component of X, consider the following example.

Example 2.3: A Single-Index Model with Only Discrete Covariates Suppose that $X = (X_1,X_2)$ is two-dimensional and discrete with support consisting of the corners of the unit square: (0,0), (1,0), (0,1), and (1,1). Set the coefficient X_1 equal to one to achieve scale normalization. Then (2.1) becomes

$$E(Y|X = x) = G(x_1 + \beta_2 x_2).$$

Suppose that the values of $E(Y|X = x)$ at the points of support of X are as shown in Table 2.1. Then all choices of β_2 and G that equate the entry in the second column to the corresponding entry in the third column are correct models of $E(Y|X = x)$. These models are observationally equivalent and would be indistinguishable from one another even if the population distribution of (Y, X) were known. There are infinitely many such models, so β_2 and G are not identified. Bierens and Hartog (1988) provide a detailed discussion of alternative, observationally equivalent forms of β and G when all components of X are discrete. ■

Another requirement for identification is that G must be differentiable. To understand why, observe that the distinguishing characteristic of a single-index model that makes identification possible is that $E(Y|X = x)$ is constant if x changes in such a way that $x'\beta$ stays constant. However, if $X'\beta$ is a continuously distributed random variable, as it is if X has at least one continuous component with a nonzero coefficient, the set of X values on which $X'\beta = c$ has probability zero for any c. Events of probability zero happen too infrequently to permit identification. If G is differentiable, then $G(X'\beta)$ is close to $G(c)$ whenever $X'\beta$ is close to c. The set of

Table 2.1 An unidentified single-index model

(x_1,x_2) (x_1, x_2)	$E(Y\|X = x)$	$G(x_1 + \beta_2 x_2)$
(0, 0)	0	$G(0)$
(1, 0)	0.1	$G(1)$
(0, 1)	0.3	$G(\beta_2)$
(1, 1)	0.4	$G(1 + \beta_2)$

X values on which $X'\beta$ is within any specified nonzero distance of c has nonzero probability for any c in the interior of the support of $X'\beta$. This permits identification of β through "approximate" constancy of $X'\beta$.

It is now possible to state a complete set of conditions for identification of β in a single-index model. This theorem assumes that the components of X are all continuous random variables. Identification when some components of X are discrete is more complicated. This case is discussed after the statement of the theorem.

Theorem 2.1 (Identification in Single-Index Models)**:** *Suppose that $E(Y|X = x)$ satisfies model (2.1) and X is a d-dimensional random variable. Then β and G are identified if the following conditions hold:*

(a) G is differentiable and not constant on the support of $X'\beta$.
(b) The components of X are continuously distributed random variables that have a joint probability density function.
(c) The support of X is not contained in any proper linear subspace of $\mathbb{R}^d$.
(d) $\beta_1 = 1$. ■

Ichimura (1993) and Manski (1988) provide proofs of several versions of this theorem. It is also possible to prove a version that permits some components of X to be discrete. Two additional conditions are needed. These are as follows: (1) varying the values of the discrete components must not divide the support of $X'\beta$ into disjoint subsets and (2) G must satisfy a nonperiodicity condition.

The following example illustrates the need for condition (1).

Example 2.4: Identification of a Single-Index Model with Continuous and Discrete Covariates Suppose that X has one continuous component, X_1, whose support is [0,1], and one discrete component, X_2, whose support is the two-point set {0,1}. Assume that X_1 and X_2 are independent and that G is strictly increasing on [0,1]. Set $\beta_1 = 1$ to achieve scale normalization. Then $X'\beta = X_1+\beta_2 X_2$. Observe that $E[Y|X = (x_1,0)] = G(x_1)$ and $E[Y|X = (x_1,1)] = G(x_1 + \beta_2)$. Observations of X for which $X_2 = 0$ identify G on [0,1]. However, if $\beta_2 > 1$, the support of $X_1 + \beta_2$ is disjoint from [0,1], and β_2 is, in effect, an intercept term in the model for $E[Y|X = (x_1,1)]$. As was explained in the discussion of location and scale normalization, an intercept term is not identified, so β_2 is not identified in this model.

The situation is different if $\beta_2 < 1$, because the supports of X_1 and $X_1 + \beta_2$ then overlap. The interval of overlap is $[\beta_2,1]$. Because of this overlap, there is a subset of the support of X on which $X_2 = 1$ and $G(X_1 + \beta_2) = G(v)$ for some $v \in [0,1]$. The subset is $\{X\colon X_1 \in [\beta_2,1],\ X_2 = 1\}$. Since $G(v)$ is identified for $v \in [\beta_2,1]$ by observations of X_1 for which $X_2 = 0$, β_2 can be identified by solving

$$E[Y|X = (x_1,1)] = G(x_1 + \beta_2) \tag{2.11}$$

on the set of x_1 values where the ranges of $E(Y|X = (x_1,1))$ and $G(x_1 + \beta_2)$ overlap. ■

To see why G must satisfy a nonperiodicity condition, suppose that in Example 2.3 G were periodic on $[\beta_2,1]$ instead of strictly increasing. Then (2.11) would have at least two solutions, so β_2 would not be identified. The assumption that G is strictly increasing on [0,1] prevents this kind of periodicity, but many other shapes of G also satisfy the nonperiodicity requirement. See Ichimura (1993) for details.

2.3.2 Identification Analysis When X Is Discrete

One of the conclusions reached in Section 2.3.1 is that β and G are not identified in a semiparametric single-index model if all components of X are discrete. It does not necessarily follow, however, that data are completely uninformative about β. In this section it is shown that if G is assumed to be an increasing function, then one can obtain identified *bounds* on the components of β.

To begin, it can be seen from Table 2.1 that there is a G that solves (2.11) for every possible value of β_2 in Example 2.3. Therefore, nothing can be learned about β_2 if nothing is known about G. This is not surprising. Even when the components of X are all continuous, some information about G is necessary to identify β (e.g., differentiability in the case of Theorem 2.1). Continuity and differentiability of G are not useful for identification when all components of X are discrete. A property that is useful, however, is monotonicity. The usefulness of this property is illustrated by the following example, which is a continuation of Example 2.3.

Example 2.5: Identification When X Is Discrete and G Is Monotonic Consider the model of Example 2.3 and Table 2.1 but with the additional assumption that G is a strictly increasing function. That is,

$$G(v_1) < G(v_2) \Leftrightarrow v_1 < v_2. \tag{2.12}$$

Inequality (2.12) together with the information in columns 2 and 3 of Table 2.1 implies that $\beta_2 > 1$. This result is informative, even though it does not point-identify β_2, because any value of β_2 in $(-\infty,\infty)$ is possible in principle. Knowledge of the population distribution of (Y, X) combined with monotonicity of G excludes all values in $(-\infty,1]$.

If the support of X is large enough, then it is possible to identify an upper bound on β_2 as well as a lower bound. For example, suppose that the point $(X_1,X_2) = (0.6,0.5)$ is in the support of X along with the four points in Example 2.3 and that $E(Y|X_1 = 0.6, X_2 = 0.5) = G(0.6 + 0.5\beta_2) = 0.35$. This information combined with (2.12) and row 3 of Table 2.1 implies that $\beta_2 < 0.6{+}0.5\beta_2$, so $\beta_2 < 1.2$. Therefore, the available information gives the identified bounds $1 < \beta_2 < 1.2$. Any value of β_2 in the interval (1,1.2) is logically possible given the available information, so the bounds $1 < \beta_2 < 1.2$ are the tightest possible. ■

Now consider the general case in which X is d-dimensional for any finite $d \geq 2$ and has M points of support for any finite $M \geq 2$. Let x_m denote the m th point of support ($m = 1, \ldots, M$). The population distribution of (Y, X) identifies $G(x_m'\beta)$ for each m. Assume without loss of generality that the support points x_m are sorted so that

$$G(x_1'\beta) \leq G(x_2'\beta) \leq \cdots \leq G(x_M'\beta).$$

Achieve location and scale normalization by assuming that X has no constant component and that $\beta_1 = 1$. Also, assume that G is strictly increasing. Then tight, identified bounds on β_m ($2 \leq m \leq M$) can be obtained by solving the linear programming problems

$$\begin{aligned} &\text{maximize (minimize): } b_m \\ &\text{subject to: } x_j'b \leq x_{j+1}'b; \quad j = 1, \ldots, M-1 \end{aligned} \tag{2.13}$$

with strict equality holding in the constraint if $G(x_j'b) = G(x_{j+1}'b)$. The solutions to these problems are informative whenever they are not infinite.

Bounds on other functionals of β can be obtained by suitably modifying the objective function of (2.13). For example, suppose that z is a point that is not in the support of X and that we are interested in learning whether $E(Y|X = z) = G(z'\beta)$ is larger or smaller than $E(Y|X = x_m) = G(x_m'\beta)$ for some x_m in the support of X. $G(z'\beta) - G(x_m'\beta)$ is not identified if X is discrete, but $(z - x_m)'\beta$ can be bounded by replacing b_m with $(z - x_m)'b$ in the objective function of (2.13). If the resulting lower bound exceeds zero, then we know that $G(z'\beta) > G(x_m'\beta)$, even though $G(z'\beta)$ is unknown. Similarly, $G(z'\beta) < G(x_m'\beta)$ if the upper bound obtained from the modified version of (2.13) is negative.

Now consider solving (2.13) with the objective function $(x_m - z)'b$ for each $m = 1, \ldots, M$. Suppose this procedure yields the result $(x_m - z)'\beta < 0$ if $m \leq j$ for some j ($1 \leq j \leq M$). Then it follows from monotonicity of G that $G(z'\beta) > G(x_j'\beta)$. Similarly, if the solutions to the modified version of (2.13) yield the result $(x_m - z)'\beta > 0$ if $m \geq k$ for some k ($1 \leq k \leq M$), then $G(z'\beta) < G(x_k'\beta)$. Since $G(x_j'\beta)$ and $G(x_k'\beta)$ are identified, this procedure yields identified bounds on the unidentified quantity $G(z'\beta)$, thereby providing a form of extrapolation in a single-index model with a discrete X. The following example illustrates this form of extrapolation.

Example 2.6: Extrapolation When X Is Discrete and G Is Monotonic Let G, $E(Y|X = x)$, and the points of support of X be as in Example 2.5. Order the points of support as in Table 2.2. As in Example 2.5, the available information implies that

$$1 < \beta_2 < 1.2 \tag{2.14}$$

but does not further identify β_2. Suppose that $z = (0.3, 0.25)'$. What can be said about the value of $E(Y|X = z) = G(z'\beta) = G(0.3 + 0.25\beta_2)$? This quantity is not

Table 2.2 A second unidentified single-index model

m	x_m	$E(Y\|X = x_m)$	$G(x_m)$
1	(0, 0)	0	$G(0)$
2	(1, 0)	0.1	$G(1)$
3	(0, 1)	0.3	$G(\beta_2)$
4	(0.6, 0.5)	0.35	$G(0.6 + 0.5\beta_2)$
5	(1, 1)	0.4	$G(1 + \beta_2)$

identified, but the following bounds may be obtained by combining the information in Table 2.2 with inequality (2.14):

$$-0.6 < (x_1 - z)'\beta < -0.55,$$
$$0.4 < (x_2 - z)'\beta < 0.45,$$
$$0.45 < (x_3 - z)'\beta < 0.60,$$
$$0.55 < (x_4 - z)'\beta < 0.60,$$

and

$$1.45 < (x_5 - z)'\beta < 1.60.$$

Therefore, monotonicity of G implies that $G(x_1'\beta) < G(z'\beta) < G(x_2'\beta)$, so identified bounds on the unidentified quantity $G(z'\beta)$ are $0 < G(z'\beta) < 0.1$. ■

2.4 Estimating *G* in a Single-Index Model

We now turn to the problem of estimating G and β in the single-index model (2.1). It is assumed throughout the remainder of this chapter that G and β are identified. This section is concerned with estimating G. Estimation of β is dealt with in Sections 2.5 and 2.6.

Suppose, for the moment, that β is known. Then G can be estimated as the nonparametric mean regression of Y on $X'\beta$. There are many nonparametric mean-regression estimators that can be used. See, for example, Härdle (1990), Härdle and Linton (1994), and the Appendix. This chapter uses kernel estimators. The properties of these estimators are summarized in the Appendix.

To obtain a kernel estimator of $G(z)$ at any z in the support of $X'\beta$, let the data consist of a random sample of n observations of (Y, X). Let $\{Y_i, X_i : i = 1, \ldots, n\}$ denote the sample. Here, the subscript i indexes observations, not components of X. Define $Z_i = X_i'\beta$. Let K be a kernel function, and let $\{h_n\}$ be a sequence of bandwidth parameters. Under the assumption that β is known, the kernel nonparametric estimator of $G(z)$ is

$$G_n^*(z) = \frac{1}{nh_n p_n^*(z)} \sum_{i=1}^{n} Y_i K\left(\frac{z - Z_i}{h_n}\right), \qquad (2.15)$$

where

$$p_n^*(z) = \frac{1}{nh_n}\sum_{i=1}^{n} K\left(\frac{z - Z_i}{h_n}\right). \tag{2.16}$$

The estimator (2.15) cannot be implemented in an application because β and, therefore, Z_i are not known. This problem can be remedied by replacing the unknown β with an estimator b_n. Define $Z_{ni} = X_i' b_n$ to be the corresponding estimator of Z_i. The resulting kernel estimator of G is

$$G_n(z) = \frac{1}{nh_n p_n(z)}\sum_{i=1}^{n} Y_i K\left(\frac{z - Z_{ni}}{h_n}\right), \tag{2.17}$$

where

$$p_n(z) = \frac{1}{nh_n}\sum_{i=1}^{n} K\left(\frac{z - Z_{ni}}{h_n}\right). \tag{2.18}$$

It is shown in Sections 2.5 and 2.6 that β can be estimated with a $n^{-1/2}$ rate of convergence in probability. That is, there exist estimators b_n with the property that $(b_n - \beta) = O_p(n^{-1/2})$. This is faster than the fastest possible rate of convergence in probability of a nonparametric estimator of $E(Y|X'\beta = z)$. As a result, the difference between the estimators G_n^* and G_n is asymptotically negligible. Specifically,

$$(nh_n)^{1/2}[G_n(z) - G(z)] = (nh_n)^{1/2}[G_n^*(z) - G(z)] + o_p(1)$$

for any z in the support of Z. Therefore, estimation of β has no effect on the asymptotic distributional properties of the estimator of G. The reasoning behind this conclusion is easily outlined. Let $\tilde{b}_n$ and $\tilde{\beta}$, respectively, denote the vectors obtained from b_n and β by removing their first components (the components set by scale normalization). Let $\tilde{X}_i$ be the vector obtained from X_i, by removing its first component. Define K' to be the derivative of the kernel function K. For any $\tilde{b}$ and $b \equiv (1, \tilde{b}')'$, define

$$A_n(\tilde{b}) = \frac{1}{nh_n}\sum_{i=1}^{n} Y_i K\left(\frac{z - X_i' b}{h_n}\right),$$

$$A_{nz}(\tilde{b}) = -\frac{1}{nh_n^2}\sum_{i=1}^{n} Y_i K'\left(\frac{z - X_i' b}{h_n}\right)\tilde{X}_i,$$

$$\tilde{p}_n(\tilde{b}) = \frac{1}{nh_n}\sum_{i=1}^{n} K\left(\frac{z - X_i' b}{h_n}\right),$$

and

$$\tilde{p}_{nz}(\tilde{b}) = -\frac{1}{nh_n^2}\sum_{i=1}^{n} K'\left(\frac{z - X_i'b}{h_n}\right)\tilde{X}_i.$$

Now observe that $G_n(z) = A_n(\tilde{b}_n)/\tilde{p}_n(\tilde{b}_n)$ and $G_n^*(z) = A_n(\tilde{\beta})/\tilde{p}_n(\tilde{\beta})$. Therefore, a Taylor-series expansion of the right-hand side of (2.17) about $b_n = \beta$ yields

$$G_n(z) = G_n^*(z) + \left[\frac{A_{nz}\left(\tilde{b}_n^*\right)}{\tilde{p}_n\left(\tilde{b}_n^*\right)} - \frac{A_n\left(\tilde{b}_n^*\right)\tilde{p}_{nz}\left(\tilde{b}_n^*\right)}{\tilde{p}_{nz}^2\left(\tilde{b}_n^*\right)}\right](\tilde{b}_n - \beta), \tag{2.19}$$

where $\tilde{b}_n^*$ is between $\tilde{b}_n$ and $\tilde{\beta}$. By using a suitable uniform law of large numbers (see, e.g., Pakes and Pollard 1989, Lemma 2.8), it can be shown that the quantity in brackets on the right-hand side of (2.19) converges in probability to a nonstochastic limit. Therefore, there is a nonstochastic function Γ such that

$$\frac{A_{nz}\left(\tilde{b}_n^*\right)}{\tilde{p}_n\left(\tilde{b}_n^*\right)} - \frac{A_n\left(\tilde{b}_n^*\right)\tilde{p}_{nz}\left(\tilde{b}_n^*\right)}{\tilde{p}_{nz}^2\left(\tilde{b}_n^*\right)} = \Gamma(z) + o_p(1). \tag{2.20}$$

It follows from (2.19), (2.20), and $b_n - \beta = O_p(n^{-1/2})$ that

$$G_n(z) - G_n^*(z) = \Gamma(z)(\tilde{b}_n - \tilde{\beta}) + o_p(\tilde{b}_n - \tilde{\beta}) = O_p(n^{-1/2}).$$

This implies that

$$(nh_n)^{1/2}[G_n(z) - G_n^*(z)] = O_p(h_n^{1/2}), \tag{2.21}$$

which gives the desired result

The foregoing results concerning estimation of G apply with any b_n that is a $n^{-1/2}$-consistent estimator of β. We now turn to developing such estimators.

2.5 Optimization Estimators of β

Estimators of β can be classified according to whether they require solving nonlinear optimization problems. This section discusses estimators that are obtained as the solutions to nonlinear optimization problems. Section 2.6 discusses estimators that do not require solving optimization problems.

2.5.1 Nonlinear Least Squares

If G were known, then β could be estimated by nonlinear least squares or weighted nonlinear least squares (WNLS). Let the data consist of the random sample $\{Y_i, X_i : i = 1, \ldots, n\}$. Then the WNLS estimator of β, b_{NLS}, is the solution to

$$\text{minimize: } S_n^*(b) = \frac{1}{n}\sum_{i=1}^{n} W(X_i)\left[Y_i - G\left(X_i'b\right)\right]^2, \tag{2.22}$$

where W is the weight function. Under mild regularity conditions, b_{NLS} is a consistent estimator of β, and $n^{1/2}(b_{NLS} - \beta)$ is asymptotically normally distributed with a mean of zero and a covariance matrix that can be estimated consistently. See, for example, Amemiya (1985), Davidson and MacKinnon (1993), and Gallant (1987).

The estimator b_{NLS} is not available in the semiparametric case, where G is unknown. Ichimura (1993) showed that this problem can be overcome by replacing G in (2.22) with a suitable estimator. This estimator is a modified version of the kernel estimator (2.17). Carroll et al. (1997) proposed using a local-linear estimator for a more elaborate model that includes a single-index model as a special case. Ichimura (1993) makes three modifications of the usual kernel estimator. First, observe that if G_n is defined as in (2.17), then the denominator of $G_n\left(X_i'b\right)$ contains the term $p_n\left(X_i'b\right)$. To keep this term from getting arbitrarily close to zero as n increases, it is necessary to restrict the sums in (2.17) and (2.22) to observations i for which the probability density of $X'\beta$ at the point $X_i'\beta$ exceeds a small, positive number. Second, observation i is excluded from the calculation of $G_n\left(X_i'b\right)$. Third, the terms of the sums in the calculation of G_n are weighted the same way that the terms in the sum (2.22) are weighted.

To carry out these modifications, let $p(\cdot, b)$ denote the probability density function of $X'b$. Let B be a compact set that contains β. Define A_x and A_{nx} to be the following sets:

$$A_x = \left\{x: p(x'b, b) \geq \eta \text{ for all } b \in B\right\}$$

and

$$A_{nx} = \left\{x: \left\|x - x^*\right\| \leq 2h_n \text{ for some } x^* \in A_x\right\},$$

where $\eta > 0$ is a constant, h_n is the bandwidth used for kernel estimation, and $\|\cdot\|$ is the Euclidean norm. A_{nx} contains A_x and shrinks toward A_x as $h_n \to 0$. Let I denote the indicator function. $I(\cdot) = 1$ if the event in parentheses occurs and 0 otherwise. Define $J_i = I(X_i \in A_x)$ and $J_{ni} = I(X_i \in A_{nx})$. Finally, define

$$G_{ni}(z, b) = \frac{1}{nh_n p_{ni}(z, b)}\sum_{j\neq i} J_{nj}W(X_j)Y_jK\left(\frac{z - X_j'b}{h_n}\right), \tag{2.23}$$

where for any z

$$p_{ni}(z, b) = \frac{1}{nh_n} \sum_{j \neq i} J_{nj} W(X_j) K\left(\frac{z - X_j'b}{h_n}\right). \tag{2.24}$$

The estimator of $G(X_i'b)$ that is used in (2.22) is $G_{ni}(X_i'b, b)$. Thus, the semiparametric WNLS estimator of β is the solution to

$$\text{minimize: } S_n(\tilde{b}) = \frac{1}{n} \sum_{i=1}^{n} J_i W(X_i) \left[Y_i - G_{ni}\left(X_i'b, b\right)\right]^2. \tag{2.25}$$

The minimization is over $\tilde{b}$, not b, to impose scale normalization. Let $\tilde{b}_n$ denote the resulting estimator, and call it the semiparametric WNLS estimator of $\tilde{\beta}$.

Ichimura (1993) gives conditions under which $\tilde{b}_n$ is a consistent estimator of $\tilde{\beta}$ and

$$n^{1/2}(\tilde{b}_n - \tilde{\beta}) \xrightarrow{d} N(0, \Omega). \tag{2.26}$$

The covariance matrix, Ω, is given in (2.28) below. The conditions under which (2.26) holds are stated in Theorem 2.2.

Theorem 2.2: *Equation (2.26) holds if the following conditions are satisfied:*

(a) $\{Y_i, X_i : i = 1, \ldots, n\}$ *is a random sample from a distribution that satisfies (2.1).*
(b) β *is identified and is an interior point of the known compact set* B.
(c) A_x *is compact, and* W *is bounded and positive on* A_x.
(d) $E(Y|X'b = z)$ *and* $p(z, b)$ *are three times continuously differentiable with respect to* z. *The third derivatives are Lipschitz continuous uniformly over* B *for all* $z \in \{z: z = x'b,\ b \in B,\ x \in A_x\}$.
(e) $E|Y|^m < \infty$ *for some* $m \geq 3$. *The variance of* Y *conditional on* $X = x$ *is bounded and bounded away from 0 for* $x \in A_x$.
(f) The kernel function K *is twice continuously differentiable, and its second derivative is Lipschitz continuous. Moreover* $K(v) = 0$ *if* $|v| > 1$, *and*

$$\int_{-1}^{1} v^j K(v)dv = \begin{cases} 1 & \text{if } j = 0 \\ 0 & \text{if } j = 1 \end{cases}.$$

(g) The bandwidth sequence $\{h_n\}$ *satisfies* $(\log h_n) / \left[nh_n^{3+3/(m-1)}\right] \to 0$ *and* $nh_n^8 \to 0$ *as* $n \to \infty$. ■

There are several noteworthy features of Theorem 2.2. First, $\tilde{b}_n$ converges in probability to $\tilde{\beta}$ at the rate $n^{-1/2}$, which is the same rate that would be obtained if G were known and faster than the rate of convergence of a nonparametric density or mean-regression estimator. This result was used in deriving (2.21). Second, the asymptotic distribution of $n^{1/2}(\tilde{b}_n - \tilde{\beta})$ is centered at zero. This contrasts with the case of nonparametric density and mean-regression estimators, whose asymptotic distributions are not centered at zero in general when the estimators have their fastest possible rates of convergence. Third, the range of permissible rates of convergence of h_n includes the rate $n^{-1/5}$, which is the standard rate in nonparametric density and mean-regression estimation. Finally, Theorem 2.2 requires β to be contained in the known, compact set B. Therefore, in principle $S_n(\tilde{b})$ should be minimized subject to the constraint $\tilde{b} \in B$. In practice, however, the probability that the constraint is binding for any reasonable B is so small that it can be ignored. This is a useful result because solving a constrained nonlinear optimization problem is usually much more difficult than solving an unconstrained one.

Stating the covariance matrix, Ω, requires additional notation. Let $p(\cdot\,|\tilde{x}, b)$ denote the probability density function of $X'b$ conditional on $\tilde{X} = \tilde{x}$. Define $p(\cdot|\tilde{x}) = p(\cdot\,|\tilde{x}, \beta)$, $\sigma^2(x) = Var(Y|X = x)$, and

$$G(z, b) = \operatorname*{plim}_{n\to\infty} G_{ni}(z, b).$$

Calculations that are lengthy but standard in kernel estimation show that

$$\begin{aligned} G(z, b) &= \frac{E[E(Y|X'b = z, \tilde{X})I(X \in A_x)W(X)p(z|\tilde{X}, b)]}{E[I(X \in A_x)W(X)p(z|\tilde{X}, b)]} \\ &= \frac{R_1(z, b)}{R_2(z, b)}, \end{aligned}$$

where

$$R_1(z, b) = E\{G[z - \tilde{X}'(\tilde{b} - \tilde{\beta})]p[z - \tilde{X}'(\tilde{b} - \tilde{\beta})|\tilde{X}]W(X)I(X \in A_x)\}$$

and

$$R_2(z, b) = E\{p[z - \tilde{X}'(\tilde{b} - \tilde{\beta})|\tilde{X}]W(X)I(X \in A_x)\}.$$

Moreover,

$$G(z, \beta) = G(z)$$

and for $z = x'\beta$

$$\frac{\partial G(z, \beta)}{\partial \tilde{b}} = G'(z)\left\{\tilde{x} - \frac{E[\tilde{X}W(X)|X'\beta = z, X \in A_x]}{E[W(X)|X'\beta = z, X \in A_x]}\right\}. \tag{2.27}$$

Now define

$$C = 2E\left[I(X \in A_x)W(X)\frac{\partial G(X'\beta,\beta)}{\partial \tilde{b}}\frac{\partial G(X'\beta,\beta)}{\partial \tilde{b}'}\right]$$

and

$$D = 4E\left[I(X \in A_x)W^2(X)\sigma^2(x)\frac{\partial G(X'\beta,\beta)}{\partial \tilde{b}}\frac{\partial G(X'\beta,\beta)}{\partial \tilde{b}'}\right].$$

Then

$$\Omega = C^{-1}DC^{-1}. \tag{2.28}$$

Theorem 2.2 is proved in Ichimura (1993). The technical details of the proof are complex, but the main ideas are straightforward and based on the familiar Taylor-series methods of asymptotic distribution theory. With probability approaching one as $n \to \infty$, the solution to (2.25) satisfies the first-order condition

$$\frac{\partial S_n(\tilde{b}_n)}{\partial \tilde{b}} = 0.$$

Therefore, a Taylor-series expansion gives

$$n^{1/2}\frac{\partial S_n(\tilde{\beta})}{\partial \tilde{\beta}} = -\frac{\partial^2 S_n(\bar{b}_n)}{\partial \tilde{b}\partial \tilde{b}'}n^{1/2}(\tilde{b}_n - \tilde{\beta}), \tag{2.29}$$

where $\bar{b}_n$ is between $\tilde{b}_n$ and $\tilde{\beta}$. Now consider the left-hand side of (2.29). Differentiation of S_n gives

$$n^{1/2}\frac{\partial S_n(\tilde{\beta})}{\partial \tilde{b}} = -\frac{2}{n^{1/2}}\sum_{i=1}^{n} J_i W(X_i)\left[Y_i - G_{ni}\left(X_i'\beta,\beta\right)\right]\frac{\partial G_{ni}\left(X_i'\beta,\beta\right)}{\partial \tilde{b}}.$$

Moreover,

$$G_{ni}\left(X_i'\beta,\beta\right) \xrightarrow{p} G\left(X_i'\beta\right)$$

and

$$\frac{\partial G_{ni}\left(X_i'\beta,\beta\right)}{\partial \tilde{b}} \xrightarrow{p} \frac{\partial G\left(X_i'\beta,\beta\right)}{\partial \tilde{b}}$$

sufficiently rapidly that we may write

$$n^{1/2}\frac{\partial S_n(\tilde{\beta})}{\partial \tilde{b}} = -\frac{2}{n^{1/2}}\sum_{i=1}^{n} J_i W(X_i)\left[Y_i - G\left(X_i'\beta\right)\right]\frac{\partial G\left(X_i'\beta,\beta\right)}{\partial \tilde{b}} + o_p(1). \tag{2.30}$$

The first term on the right-hand side of (2.30) is asymptotically distributed as $N(0, D)$ by the multivariate generalization of the Lindeberg–Levy central limit theorem. Therefore, the left-hand side of (2.29) is also asymptotically distributed as $N(0, D)$.

Now consider the right-hand side of (2.29). Differentiation of S_n gives

$$\frac{\partial^2 S_n(\bar{b}_n)}{\partial\tilde{b}\partial\tilde{b}'} = \frac{2}{n}\sum_{i=1}^{n} J_i W(X_i)\frac{\partial G_{ni}(X_i'\bar{b}_n,\bar{b}_n)}{\partial\tilde{b}}\frac{\partial G_{ni}(X_i'\bar{b}_n,\bar{b}_n)}{\partial\tilde{b}}$$
$$-\frac{2}{n}\sum_{i=1}^{n} J_i W(X_i)[Y_i - G_{ni}(X_i'\bar{b}_n,\bar{b}_n)]\frac{\partial^2 G_{ni}(X_i'\bar{b}_n,\bar{b}_n)}{\partial\tilde{b}\partial\tilde{b}'}.$$

Because $G_{ni}(x'b, b)$ and its derivatives converge to $G(x'b, b)$ and its derivatives uniformly over both arguments, we may write

$$\frac{\partial^2 S_n(\bar{b}_n)}{\partial\tilde{b}\partial\tilde{b}'} = \frac{2}{n}\sum_{i=1}^{n} J_i W(X_i)\frac{\partial G(X_i'\beta,\, \beta)}{\partial\tilde{b}}\frac{\partial G\left(X_i'\beta,\, \beta\right)}{\partial\tilde{b}}$$
$$-\frac{2}{n}\sum_{i=1}^{n} J_i W(X_i)[Y_i - G(X_i'\beta,\, \beta)]\frac{\partial^2 G(X_i'\beta,\, \beta)}{\partial\tilde{b}\partial\tilde{b}'} + o_p(1).$$

The first term on the right-hand side of this equation converges almost surely to C and the second term converges almost surely to zero by the strong law of large numbers. This result together with the previously obtained asymptotic distribution of the left-hand side of (2.29) implies that (2.29) can be written in the form

$$N(0,\, D) = Cn^{1/2}(\tilde{b}_n - \tilde{\beta}) + o_p(1). \tag{2.31}$$

Equation (2.26) is obtained by multiplying both sides of (2.31) by C^{-1}.

In applications, Ω is unknown, and a consistent estimator is needed to make statistical inference possible. To this end, define

$$C_n = \frac{2}{n}\sum_{i=1}^{n} J_i W(X_i)\frac{\partial G_{ni}(X_i'b_n,\, b_n)}{\partial\tilde{b}}\frac{\partial G_{ni}(X_i'b_n,\, b_n)}{\partial\tilde{b}'}$$

and

$$D_n = \frac{4}{n}\sum_{i=1}^{n} J_i W(X_i)[Y_i - G_{ni}(X_i'b_n)]^2\frac{\partial G_{ni}(X_i'b_n,\, b_n)}{\partial\tilde{b}}\frac{\partial G_{ni}(X_i'b_n,\, b_n)}{\partial\tilde{b}'}.$$

Under the assumptions of Theorem 2.2, C_n and D_n, respectively, are consistent estimators of C and D. Ω is estimated consistently by

$$\Omega_n = C_n^{-1} D_n C_n^{-1}.$$

Intuitively, these results can be understood by observing that because G_{ni} converges in probability to G and b_n converges in probability to β,

$$C_n = \frac{2}{n}\sum_{i=1}^{n} J_i W(X_i) \frac{\partial G(X_i'\beta,\beta)}{\partial \tilde{b}} \frac{\partial G(X_i'\beta,\beta)}{\partial \tilde{b}'} + o_p(1)$$

and

$$D_n = \frac{4}{n}\sum_{i=1}^{n} J_i W(X_i)[Y_i - G(X_i'\beta)]^2 \frac{\partial G(X_i'\beta,\beta)}{\partial \tilde{b}} \frac{\partial G(X_i'\beta,\beta)}{\partial \tilde{b}'} + o_p(1).$$

Convergence of C_n to C and D_n to D now follows from the strong law of large numbers.

2.5.2 Choosing the Weight Function

The choice of weight function, W, affects the efficiency of the estimator of $\tilde{\beta}$. Ideally, one would like to choose W so as to maximize the asymptotic efficiency of the estimator. Some care is needed in defining the concept of asymptotic efficiency so as to avoid the pathology of superefficiency. See Bickel et al. (1993) and Ibragimov and Has'minskii (1981) for discussions of superefficiency and methods for avoiding it. Estimators that are restricted so as to avoid superefficiency are called *regular*.

Within the class of semiparametric WNLS estimators, an estimator is asymptotically efficient if the covariance matrix Ω of its asymptotic distribution differs from the covariance matrix Ω^* of any other weighted WNLS estimator by a positive-semidefinite matrix. That is, $\Omega^* - \Omega$ is positive semidefinite. More generally, one can consider the class of all regular estimators of single-index models (2.1). This class includes estimators that may not be semiparametric WNLS estimators. The definition of an asymptotically efficient estimator remains the same, however. The covariance matrix of the asymptotic distribution of any regular estimator exceeds that of the asymptotically efficient estimator by a positive-semidefinite matrix.

The problem of asymptotically efficient estimation of β in a semiparametric single-index model is related to but more difficult than the problem of asymptotically efficient estimation in a nonlinear regression model with a known G. The case of a nonlinear regression model (not necessarily a single-index model) in which G is known has been investigated by Chamberlain (1987), who derived an asymptotic efficiency bound. The covariance matrix of the asymptotic distribution of any regular estimator must exceed this bound by a positive-semidefinite matrix. The model is $E(Y|X = x) = G(x, \beta)$. The variance function, $\sigma^2(x) = E\{[Y - G(X, \beta)]^2|X = x\}$, is unknown. Chamberlain (1986) showed that the efficiency bound is

$$\Omega_{NLR} = \left\{E\left[\frac{1}{\sigma^2(X)} \frac{\partial G(X, \beta)}{\partial b} \frac{\partial G(X, \beta)}{\partial b'}\right]\right\}^{-1}.$$

This is the covariance matrix of a weighted (or generalized) nonlinear least-squares estimator of β with weight function $W(x) = 1/\sigma^2(x)$. For the special case of the linear model $G(x, \beta) = x\beta$, Carroll (1982) and Robinson (1987) showed that this covariance matrix is obtained asymptotically even if $\sigma^2(x)$ is unknown by replacing $\sigma^2(x)$ with a nonparametric estimator. Thus, lack of knowledge of $\sigma^2(x)$ causes no loss of asymptotic efficiency relative to infeasible generalized least-squares estimation.

The problem of efficient estimation of β in a single-index model with an unknown G has been investigated by Hall and Ichimura (1991) and Newey and Stoker (1993). These authors showed that under regularity conditions, the efficiency bound for estimating β in a single-index model with unknown G and using only data for which $X \in A_x$ is (2.28) with weight function $W(x) = 1/\sigma^2(x)$. With this weight function, $C = D$ in (2.28), so the efficiency bound is

$$\Omega_{SI} = \left\{ E\left[\frac{I(X \in A_x)}{\sigma^2(X)} \frac{\partial G(X'\beta,\beta)}{\partial \tilde{b}} \frac{\partial G(X'\beta,\beta)}{\partial \tilde{b}'} \right] \right\}^{-1}. \tag{2.32}$$

This bound is achieved by the semiparametric WNLS estimator if $\sigma^2(X)$ is known or independent of X. The assumption that the estimator uses only observations for which $X \in A_x$ can be eliminated by letting A_x grow very slowly as n increases. Chamberlain (1986) and Cosslett (1987) derived this asymptotic efficiency bound for the case in which (2.1) is a binary-response model (that is, the only possible values of Y are 0 and 1) and G is a distribution function. Chamberlain and Cosslett also derived efficiency bounds for certain kinds of censored regression models. Except in special cases, Ω_{SI} exceeds the asymptotic efficiency bound that would be achievable if G were known. Thus, there is a cost in terms of asymptotic efficiency (but not rate of convergence of the estimator) for not knowing G. Cosslett (1987) gives formulae for the efficiency losses in binary-response and censored linear regression models.

When $\sigma^2(x)$ is unknown, as is likely in applications, it can be replaced by a consistent estimator. Call this estimator $s_n^2(x)$. The asymptotic efficiency bound will be achieved by setting $W(x) = 1/s_n^2(x)$ in the semiparametric WNLS estimator (Newey and Stoker 1993). Therefore, an asymptotically efficient estimator of β can be obtained even when σ^2 (x) is unknown.

A consistent estimator of σ^2 (x) can be obtained by using the following two-step procedure. In the first step, estimate β by using semiparametric WNLS with $W(x) = 1$. The resulting estimator is $n^{-1/2}$ -consistent and asymptotically normal but inefficient. Let e_i be the ith residual from the estimated model. That is, $e_i = Y_i - G_{ni}(X_i' b_n,\ b_n)$. In the second step, set $s_n^2(x)$ equal to a nonparametric estimator of the mean regression of e_i^2 on X_i. Robinson (1987) discusses technical problems that arise if X has unbounded support or a density that can be arbitrarily close to zero. He avoids these problems by using a nearest-neighbor nonparametric regression estimator. In practice, a kernel estimator will suffice if A_x is chosen so as to keep the estimated density of X away from zero.

This concludes the discussion of semiparametric weighted nonlinear least-squares estimation of single-index models. To summarize, Ichimura (1993) has given conditions under which the semiparametric WNLS estimator of β in (2.1) is $n^{-1/2}$-consistent and asymptotically normal. The estimator of β is also asymptotically efficient if the weight function is a consistent estimator of $1/\sigma^2(x)$. A consistent estimator of $\sigma^2(x)$ can be obtained by a two-step procedure in which the first step is semiparametric WNLS estimation of β with a unit weight function and the second step is nonparametric estimation of the mean of the squared first-step residuals conditional on X.

2.5.3 *Semiparametric Maximum-Likelihood Estimation of Binary-Response Models*

This section is concerned with estimation of (2.1) when the only possible values of Y are 0 and 1. In this case, $G(x'\beta) = P(Y = 1|X = x)$. If G were a known function, then the asymptotically efficient estimator of β would be the maximum-likelihood estimator (MLE). The MLE solves the problem

$$\text{maximize:} \quad \log L(b) = \frac{1}{n}\sum_{i=1}^{n}\{Y_i \log G(X_i'b) + (1 - Y_i)\log[1 - G(X_i'b)]\}. \quad (2.33)$$

In the semiparametric case, where G is unknown, one can consider replacing G on the right-hand side of (2.33) with an estimator such as G_{ni} in (2.23). This idea has been investigated in detail by Klein and Spady (1993). It is clear from (2.33) that care must be taken to ensure that any estimate of G is kept sufficiently far from 0 and 1. Klein and Spady (1993) use elaborate trimming procedures to accomplish this without artificially restricting X to a fixed set A_x on which $G(X'\beta)$ is bounded away from 0 and 1. They find, however, that trimming has little effect on the numerical performance of the resulting estimator. Therefore, in practice little is lost in terms of estimation efficiency and much is gained in simplicity by using only observations for which $x \in A_x$. This method will be used in the remainder of this section.

A second simplification can be obtained by observing that in the special case of a binary-response model, $Var(Y|X = x) = G(x'\beta)[1 - G(x'\beta)]$. Thus, $\sigma^2(x)$ depends only on the index $z = x'\beta$. In this case, W cancels out of the numerator and denominator terms on the right-hand side of (2.27), so

$$\frac{\partial G(z, \beta)}{\partial \tilde{b}} = G'(z)\{\tilde{x} - E[\tilde{X}|X'\beta = z, X \in A_x]\}.$$

By substituting this result into (2.28) and (2.32), it can be seen that the covariance matrix of the asymptotic distribution of the semiparametric WNLS estimator of β is the same whether the estimator of G is weighted or not. Moreover, the asymptotic efficiency bound Ω_{SI} can be achieved without weighting the estimator of G. Accordingly, define the unweighted estimator of G

$$\hat{G}_{ni}(z, b) = \frac{1}{nh_n\hat{p}_{ni}(z, b)} \sum_{j \neq i} J_{nj} Y_i K\left(\frac{z - X_j'b}{h_n}\right),$$

where

$$\hat{p}_{ni}(z, b) = \frac{1}{nh_n} \sum_{j \neq i} J_{nj} K\left(\frac{z - X_j'b}{h_n}\right).$$

Now consider the following semiparametric analog of (2.33):

$$\text{maximize: } \log L_{SP}(\tilde{b}) = \frac{1}{n}\sum_{i=1}^{n} J_i\{Y_i \log \hat{G}_{ni}(X_i'b, b) + (1 - Y_i)\log[1 - \hat{G}_{ni}(X_i'b, b)]\}. \tag{2.34}$$

Let $\tilde{b}_n$ denote the resulting estimator of $\tilde{\beta}$. If β is identified (see the discussion in Section 2.3), consistency of $\tilde{b}_n$ for $\tilde{\beta}$ can be demonstrated by showing that $\hat{G}_{ni}(z, b)$ converges to $G(z, b)$ uniformly over z and b. Therefore, the probability limit of the solution to (2.34) is the same as the probability limit of the solution to

$$\text{maximize: } \log L^*_{SP}(\tilde{b}) = \frac{1}{n}\sum_{i=1}^{n} J_i\{Y_i \log G(X_i'b, b) + (1 - Y_i)\log[1 - G(X_i'b, b)]\}. \tag{2.35}$$

The solution to (2.34) is consistent for $\tilde{\beta}$ if the solution to (2.35) is. The solution to (2.35) is a parametric maximum-likelihood estimator. Consistency for $\tilde{\beta}$ can be proved using standard methods for parametric maximum-likelihood estimators. See, for example, Amemiya (1985).

By differentiating the right-hand side of (2.34), it can be seen that $b_n \equiv (1, \tilde{b}_n')'$ satisfies the first-order condition

$$\frac{1}{n}\sum_{i=1}^{n} J_i \frac{Y_i - \hat{G}_{ni}(X_i'b_n, b_n)}{\hat{G}_{ni}(X_ib_n, b_n)[1 - \hat{G}_{ni}(X_ib_n, b_n)]} \frac{\partial \hat{G}_{ni}(X_i'b_n, b_n)}{\partial \tilde{b}} = 0$$

with probability approaching 1 as $n \to \infty$. This is the same as the first-order condition for semiparametric WNLS estimation of β with the estimated weight function

$$\begin{aligned} W(x) &= \{\hat{G}_{ni}(x'b_n, b_n)[1 - \hat{G}_{ni}(x'b_n, b_n)]\}^{-1} \\ &= \{G(x'\beta)[1 - G(x'\beta)]\}^{-1} + o_p(1) \\ &= [Var(Y|X = x)]^{-1} + o_p(1). \end{aligned}$$

It now follows from the discussion of asymptotic efficiency in semiparametric WNLS estimation (Section 2.5.2) that the semiparametric maximum-likelihood estimator of β in a single-index binary-response model achieves the asymptotic efficiency bound Ω_{SI}.

The conclusions of this section may be summarized as follows. The semiparametric maximum-likelihood estimator of β in a single-index binary-response model solves (2.34). The estimator is asymptotically efficient and satisfies

$$n^{1/2}(\hat{b}_n - \tilde{\beta}) \xrightarrow{d} N(0,\ \Omega_{SI}).$$

2.5.4 Semiparametric Maximum-Likelihood Estimation of Other Single-Index Models

Ai (1997) has extended semiparametric maximum-likelihood estimation to single-index models other than binary-response models. As in the binary-response estimator of Klein and Spady (1993), Ai (1997) forms a quasi-likelihood function by replacing the unknown probability density function of the dependent variable conditional on the index with a nonparametric estimator. To illustrate, suppose that the probability distribution of the dependent variable Y depends on the explanatory variables X only through the index $X'\beta$. Let $f(\cdot\,|v,\ \beta)$ denote the probability density function of Y conditional on $X'\beta = v$. If f were known, then β could be estimated by parametric maximum likelihood. For the semiparametric case, in which f is unknown, Ai replaces f with a kernel estimator of the density of Y conditional on the index. He then maximizes a trimmed version of the resulting quasi-likelihood function. Under suitable conditions, the resulting semiparametric estimator of β is asymptotically efficient (in the sense of achieving the semiparametric efficiency bound). See Ai (1997) for the details of the trimming procedure and regularity conditions.

Ai and Chen (2003) have given conditions for asymptotically efficient estimation of β in the moment condition model

$$E[\rho(Z,\ \beta, g(\cdot))|X] = 0, \tag{2.36}$$

where $Z = (Y',\ X_Z')'$, Y is a random vector, X_Z is a subvector of the random vector X, ρ is a vector of known functions, β is an unknown finite-dimensional parameter, and g is a finite-dimensional vector of unknown functions that may include β among their arguments. Model (2.36) is very general and includes single-index models, partially linear models, and many others as special cases. The cost of this generality, however, is that the analysis of (2.36) is both lengthy and complicated. The details are given in Ai and Chen (2003).

2.5.5 Semiparametric Rank Estimators

If G in (2.1) is a nondecreasing function and $Y - G(X'\beta)$ is independent of X, then $X_i'\beta > X_j'\beta$ implies that $P(Y_i > Y_j) > P(Y_j > Y_i)$. This suggests estimating β by choosing the estimator b_n so as to make the rank ordering of $\{Y_i: i = 1, \ldots, n\}$ as close as possible to that of $\{X_i'\beta: i = 1, \ldots, n\}$. The resulting maximum rank correlation (MRC) estimator is

$$b_{n,\ MRC} = \arg\max_b \frac{1}{n(n-1)} \sum_{i=1}^{n} \sum_{\substack{j=1 \\ j \neq i}}^{n} I(Y_i > Y_j) I(X_i'b > X_j'b).$$

The MRC estimator was first proposed by Han (1987), who also gave conditions for consistency of the estimator. Cavanagh and Sherman (1998) proposed a modified estimator

$$b_{n,CS} = \arg\max_b \frac{1}{n(n-1)} \sum_{i=1}^{n} \sum_{\substack{j=1 \\ j \neq i}}^{n} M(Y_i) I(X_i'b > X_j'b),$$

where M is an increasing function. This estimator is consistent under conditions that are weaker than those required for the MRC estimator. It is also easier to compute than the MRC estimator.

Deriving the asymptotic distributions of these estimators is complicated because their objective functions are discontinuous. Sherman (1993) gave conditions under which $n^{1/2}(b_{n,\ MRC} - \beta)$ is asymptotically normally distributed with mean 0. Cavanagh and Sherman (1998) gave conditions for asymptotic normality of $n^{1/2}(b_{n,CS} - \beta)$. The derivation of these results relies on empirical process methods that are beyond the scope of this book. Sherman (1993) and Cavanagh and Sherman (1998) also give methods for estimating the covariance matrices of the asymptotic distributions of $n^{1/2}(b_{n,\ MRC} - \beta)$ and $n^{1/2}(b_{n,CS} - \beta)$, but these are hard to implement. Subbotin (2008) proves that the bootstrap estimates these distributions consistently, which makes the bootstrap a potentially attractive method for carrying out inference with $b_{n,\ MRC}$ and $b_{n,CS}$ in applied research. Rank estimators are not asymptotically efficient and can be hard to compute, but they do not require bandwidths or other smoothing parameters. This may be an advantage in some applications.

2.6 Direct Semiparametric Estimators

Semiparametric weighted nonlinear least-squares and maximum-likelihood estimators have the significant practical disadvantage of being very difficult to compute. This is because they are solutions to nonlinear optimization problems whose objective functions may be nonconvex (nonconcave in the case of the maximum-likelihood estimator) or multimodal. Moreover, computing the objective functions requires estimating a nonparametric mean regression at each data point and, therefore, can be very slow.

This section describes an estimation approach that does not require solving an optimization problem and is noniterative (hence the name *direct*). Direct estimates can be computed very quickly. Although direct estimators are not asymptotically efficient, an asymptotically efficient estimator can be obtained from a direct estimator in one additional, noniterative, computational step. The relative computational simplicity of direct estimators makes them highly attractive for practical data analysis.

Xia et al. (2002) have proposed an iterative scheme called rMAVE (Refined Minimum Average Conditional Variance Estimation) that simplifies the computations of semiparametric weighted nonlinear least-squares and maximum-likelihood estimators. Xia (2006) has given conditions under which rMAVE yields the asymptotically efficient estimator of a single-index model. However, these conditions include starting the rMAVE iterations at a point b_0 that satisfies $\|b_0 - \beta\| = o(n^{-9/20})$. Consequently, rMAVE has no apparent advantages over taking an additional step beyond one of the direct estimators that is described in this section.

Section 2.6.1 describes a well-known direct estimation method under the assumption that X is a continuously distributed random vector. Section 2.6.2 describes a direct estimation method that overcomes an important disadvantage of the method of Section 2.6.1 though at the cost of additional complexity. Section 2.6.3 shows how the direct estimation method can be extended to models in which some components of X are discrete. Section 2.6.4 describes the one-step method for obtaining an asymptotically efficient estimator from a direct estimate.

2.6.1 Average-Derivative Estimators

The idea underlying direct estimation of a single-index model when X is a continuously distributed random vector is very simple. Let (2.1) hold. Assume that G is differentiable, as is required for identification of β. Then

$$\frac{\partial E(Y|X=x)}{\partial x} = \beta G'(x'\beta). \tag{2.37}$$

Moreover, for any bounded, continuous function W,

$$E\left[W(X)\frac{\partial E(Y|X)}{\partial x}\right] = \beta E\left[W(X)G'(X'\beta)\right]. \tag{2.38}$$

The quantity on the left-hand side of (2.38) is called a *weighted average derivative* of $E(Y|X)$ with weight function W. Equation (2.38) shows that a weighted average derivative of $E(Y|X)$ is proportional to β. Owing to the need for scale normalization, β is identified only up to scale, so any weighted average derivative of $E(Y|X)$ is observationally equivalent to β. Thus, to estimate β, it suffices to estimate the left-hand side of (2.38) for some W. The scale normalization $\beta_1 = 1$ can be imposed, if desired, by dividing each component of the left-hand side of (2.38) by the first component.

The left-hand side of (2.38) can be estimated by replacing $\partial E(Y|X)/\partial x$ with a kernel (or other nonparametric) estimator and the population expectation $E(\cdot)$ with a sample average. Hristache et al. (2001), Härdle and Stoker (1989), Powell et al. (1989), and Stoker (1986, 1991a,b) describe various ways of doing this. The discussion in this section concentrates on the method of Powell et al. (1989), which is especially easy to analyze and implement. Section 2.6.2 describes the method of Hristache et al. (2001), which overcomes an important disadvantage of the method of Powell et al. (1989).

To describe the method of Powell et al. (1989), let $p(\cdot)$ denote the probability density function of X, and set $W(x) = p(x)$. Then the left-hand side of (2.38) can be written in the form

$$E\left[W(X)\frac{\partial E(Y|X)}{\partial x}\right] = E\left[p(X)\frac{\partial E(Y|X)}{\partial x}\right] = \int \frac{\partial E(Y|X=x)}{\partial x} p(x)^2 dx.$$

Assume that $p(x) = 0$ if x is on the boundary of the support of X. Then integration by parts gives

$$E\left[W(X)\frac{\partial E(Y|X)}{\partial x}\right] = -2\int E(Y|X=x)\frac{\partial p(x)}{\partial x} p(x)dx = -2E\left[Y\frac{\partial p(X)}{\partial x}\right].$$

Define

$$\delta = -2E[Y\partial p(X)/\partial x]. \tag{2.39}$$

Then δ is observationally equivalent to β up to scale normalization. A consistent estimator of δ can be obtained by replacing p with a nonparametric estimator and the expectation operator with a sample average. Let $\{Y_i, X_i: i = 1, \ldots, n\}$ denote the sample. The estimator of δ is

$$\delta_n = -2\sum_{i=1}^{n} Y_i \frac{\partial p_{ni}(X_i)}{\partial x}, \tag{2.40}$$

where $p_{ni}(X_i)$ is the estimator of $p(X_i)$. The quantity δ_n is called a *density-weighted average-derivative estimator*.

To implement (2.40), the estimator of p must be specified. A kernel estimator is attractive because it is relatively easily analyzed and implemented. To this end, let $d = \dim(X)$, and let K be a kernel function with a d-dimensional argument. Conditions that K must satisfy are given in Theorem 2.3 below. Let $\{h_n\}$ be a sequence of bandwidth parameters. Set

$$p_{ni}(x) = \frac{1}{n-1}\frac{1}{h_n^d}\sum_{j \neq i} K\left(\frac{x - X_j}{h_n}\right).$$

It follows from the properties of kernel density estimators (see the Appendix) that $p_{ni}(x)$ is a consistent estimator of $p(x)$. Moreover, $\partial p(x)/\partial x$ is estimated consistently by $\partial p_{ni}(x)/\partial x$. The formula for $\partial p_{ni}(x)/\partial x$ is

$$\frac{\partial p_{ni}(x)}{\partial x} = \frac{1}{n-1}\frac{1}{h_n^{d+1}}\sum_{j \neq i} K'\left(\frac{x - X_j}{h_n}\right), \tag{2.41}$$

where K' denotes the gradient of K. Substituting (2.41) into (2.40) yields

$$\delta_n = -\frac{2}{n(n-1)}\frac{1}{h_n^{d+1}}\sum_{i=1}^{n}\sum_{j \neq i} Y_i K'\left(\frac{X_i - X_j}{h_n}\right). \tag{2.42}$$

Observe that the right-hand side of (2.42) does not have a density estimator or other random variable in its denominator. This is because setting $W(x) = p(x)$ in the weighted average derivative defined in (2.38) cancels the density function that would otherwise be in the denominator of the estimator of $E(Y|X = x)$. This lack of a random denominator is the main reason for the relative ease with which δ_n can be analyzed and implemented.

Powell et al. (1989) give conditions under which δ_n is a consistent estimator of δ and $n^{1/2}(\delta_n - \delta)$ is asymptotically normally distributed with mean 0. The formal statement of this result and the conditions under which it holds are given in Theorem 2.3. Let $\|\cdot\|$ denote the Euclidean norm. Let $P = (d+2)/2$ if d is even and $P = (d+3)/2$ if d is odd.

Theorem 2.3: *Let the following conditions hold.*

(a) *The support of X is a convex, possibly unbounded, subset of $\mathbb{R}^d$ with a nonempty interior. X has a probability density function p. All partial derivatives of p up to order $P+1$ exist.*

(b) *The components of $\partial E(Y|X)/\partial x$ and of the matrix $[\partial p(X)/\partial x](Y, X')$ have finite second moments. $E[Y\partial^r p(X)]$ exists for all positive integers $r \leq P+1$, where $\partial^r p(x)$ denotes any order r mixed partial derivative of p. $E(Y^2|X = x)$ is a continuous function of x. There is a function $m(x)$ such that*

$$E\left[(1 + |Y| + \|X\|)m(X)\right]^2 < \infty,$$

$$\left\|\frac{\partial p(x+\zeta)}{\partial x} - \frac{\partial p(x)}{\partial x}\right\| < m(x)\,\|\zeta\|,$$

and

$$\left\|\frac{\partial p(x+\zeta)E(Y|X = x+\zeta)}{\partial x} - \frac{\partial p(x)E(Y|X = x)}{\partial x}\right\| < m(x)\,\|\zeta\|.$$

(c) *The kernel function K is symmetrical about the origin, bounded, and differentiable. The moments of K through order P are finite. The moments of K of order r are all 0 if* $1 \leq r < P$. *In addition*

$$\int K(v)dv = 1.$$

(d) *The bandwidth sequence* $\{h_n\}$ *satisfies* $nh_n^{2P} \to 0$ *and* $nh_n^{d+2} \to \infty$ *as* $n \to \infty$.

Then

$$n^{1/2}(\delta_n - \delta) \xrightarrow{d} N(0, \ \Omega_{AD}),$$

where

$$\Omega_{AD} = 4E[R(Y, X)R(Y, X)'] - 4\delta\delta' \tag{2.43}$$

and

$$R(y, x) = p(x)\frac{\partial E(Y|X = x)}{\partial x} - [Y - E(Y|X = x)]\frac{\partial p(x)}{\partial x}. \blacksquare$$

A consistent estimator of Ω_{AD} is given in (2.44) below.

Several comments may be made about the conditions imposed in Theorem 2.3. Condition (a) implies that X is a continuously distributed random variable and that no component of X is functionally determined by other components. Condition (b) requires the existence of various moments and imposes smoothness requirements on $p(x)$, $E(Y|X = x)$, and $E(Y^2|X = x)$. Condition (c) requires K to be a *higher-order* kernel, meaning that some of its even moments vanish. In condition (c), the order is P. Higher-order kernels are used in density estimation and nonparametric mean regression to reduce bias. See the Appendix for further discussion of this use of higher-order kernels. Here, the higher-order kernel is used to make the bias of δ_n have size $o(n^{-1/2})$, which is needed to ensure that the asymptotic distribution of $n^{1/2}(\delta_n - \delta)$ is centered at 0. Finally, the rate of convergence of h_n is faster than would be optimal if the aim were to estimate $p(x)$ or $E(Y|X = x)$ nonparametrically. Under the conditions of Theorem 2.3, the rate of convergence in probability of an estimator of $p(x)$ or $E(Y|X = x)$ is maximized by setting $h_n \propto n^{-1/(2P+d)}$, which is too slow to satisfy the requirement in condition (d) that $nh_n^{2P} \to 0$ as $n \to \infty$. The relatively fast rate of convergence of h_n required by condition (d), like the higher-order kernel required by condition (c), is needed to prevent the asymptotic distribution of $n^{1/2}(\delta_n - \delta)$ from having a nonzero mean.

Kernel density and mean-regression estimators cannot achieve $O_p(n^{-1/2})$ rates of convergence, so it may seem surprising that δ_n achieves this rate. The fast convergence of δ_n is possible because the sum over i on the right-hand side of (2.42) makes δ_n an average of kernel estimators. Averages of kernel estimators can achieve faster rates of convergence than kernel estimators that are not averaged.

A consistent estimator of Ω_{AD} can be obtained from (2.43) by replacing δ with δ_n, the population expectation with a sample average, and R with a consistent estimator. Powell et al. (1989) give the details of the calculation. The result is that Ω_{AD} is estimated consistently by

$$\Omega_{AD,\,n} = \frac{4}{n}\sum_{i=1}^{n} R_n(Y_i, X_i)R_n(Y_i, X_i)' - 4\delta_n\delta_n', \tag{2.44}$$

where

$$R_n(Y_i, X_i) = -\frac{1}{n-1}\frac{1}{h_n^{d+1}}\sum_{j\neq i}(Y_i - Y_j)K'\left(\frac{X_i - X_j}{h_n}\right).$$

2.6.2 An Improved Average-Derivative Estimator

The density-weighted average-derivative estimator of (2.42) requires the density of X to be increasingly smooth as the dimension of X increases. This is necessary to make $n^{1/2}(\hat{\delta}_n - \delta)$ asymptotically normal with a mean of 0. See assumption (a) of Theorem 2.3. The need for increasing smoothness is a form of the curse of dimensionality. Its practical consequence is that the finite-sample performance of the density-weighted average-derivative estimator is likely to deteriorate as the dimension of X increases, especially if the density of X is not very smooth. Specifically, the estimator's bias and mean-square error are likely to increase as the dimension of X increases.

Hristache et al. (2001) proposed an iterated average-derivative estimator that overcomes this problem. Their estimator is based on the observation that $G(x'\beta)$ does not vary when x varies in a direction that is perpendicular to β. Therefore, only the directional derivative of $E(Y|X = x)$ along the direction of β is needed for estimation. If this direction were known, then estimating the directional derivative would be a one-dimensional nonparametric estimation problem, and there would be no curse of dimensionality.

Of course, the direction of β is not known in applications, but Hristache et al. show that it can be estimated with sufficient accuracy through an iterative procedure. At each iteration, the gradient of $E(Y|X = x)$ is estimated using two bandwidths. The bandwidth in the estimated direction of β decreases as the iterations proceed, and the bandwidth in the estimated perpendicular direction increases. The use of two bandwidths enables the iterative procedure to mimic taking a directional derivative with increasing accuracy as the iterations proceed. The contribution to variance from estimation in the estimated perpendicular direction is small because the bandwidth in this direction is large. The contribution to bias is small despite the large bandwidth because $E(Y|X = x)$ varies little in the estimated perpendicular direction.

The details of the estimation procedure are as follows:

1. Specify the values of the tuning parameters ρ_1, $\rho_{\min}$, a_ρ, a_h, h_1, and $h_{\max}$. Methods for doing this are discussed below. Also, set $b_0 = 0$ and $j = 1$.
2. At iteration $j (j = 1,2, \ldots)$, set $S_j = (I + \rho_j^{-2} b_{j-1} b_{j-1}')^{1/2}$, where b_{j-1} is the estimate of β at iteration $j-1$, I is the $k \times k$ identity matrix, and $k = \dim(\beta)$.
3. Let K be a kernel function. Denote the data by $\{Y_i, X_i : i = 1, \ldots, n\}$. For each $i, \ell = 1, \ldots, n$, define the column vector $X_{\ell i} = X_\ell - X_i$. Let $\hat{E}_j(X_i)$ and $\hat{\nabla} E_j(X_i)$ denote the estimates of $E(Y|X = X_i)$ and $\partial E(Y|X = X_i)/\partial x$ at the jth iteration. For each $i = 1, \ldots, n$, these are obtained from the formula

$$\begin{bmatrix} \hat{E}_j(X_i) \\ \hat{\nabla} E_j(X_i) \end{bmatrix} = \left[\sum_{\ell=1}^{n} \begin{pmatrix} 1 \\ X_{\ell i} \end{pmatrix} \begin{pmatrix} 1 \\ X_{\ell i} \end{pmatrix}' K\left(\frac{\|S_j X_{\ell i}\|^2}{h_j^2} \right) \right]^{-1} \sum_{\ell=1}^{n} Y_\ell \begin{pmatrix} 1 \\ X_{\ell i} \end{pmatrix} K\left(\frac{\|S_j X_{\ell i}\|^2}{h_j^2} \right).$$

4. Compute the vector $b_j = n^{-1} \sum_{i=1}^{n} \hat{\nabla} E_j(X_i)$.
5. Set $h_{j+1} = a_h h_j$ and $\rho_{j+1} = a_\rho \rho_j$. If $\rho_{j+1} > \rho_{\min}$, set $j = j + 1$ and return to Step 2. Terminate if $\rho_{j+1} \leq \rho_{\min}$.

Let $j(n)$ denote the total number of iterations. The average-derivative estimate of β is $b_{j(n)}$. This estimate does not satisfy the scale normalization that requires its first component to equal 1, but that normalization can be achieved by division. Alternatively, $b_{j(n)}$ can be normalized to have unit length. This is the normalization that Hristache et al. use. It gives the estimate $\hat{\theta} = b_{j(n)} / \|b_{j(n)}\|$. In Step 3, $\hat{E}_j(X_i)$ and $\hat{\nabla} E_j(X_i)$ are local-linear estimates of $E(Y|X = X_i)$ and its gradient. Local-linear estimation is discussed in the Appendix. In particular, $\hat{E}_j(X_i)$ and $\hat{\nabla} E_j(X_i)$ solve the problem

$$\begin{bmatrix} \hat{E}_j(X_i) \\ \hat{\nabla} E_j(X_i) \end{bmatrix} = \arg \min_{c \in \mathbb{R},\, b \in \mathbb{R}^k} \sum_{\ell=1}^{n} (Y_\ell - c - b' X_{\ell i})^2 K\left(\frac{\|S_j X_{\ell i}\|^2}{h_j^2} \right).$$

Hristache et al. proposed the following choices of tuning parameters. These choices are based on heuristic considerations and simulation evidence:

$$\begin{aligned} &\rho_1 = 1, && \rho_{\min} = n^{-1/3}/h_{\max}, && a_\rho = e^{-1/6}, \\ &h_1 = n^{-1/(4 \vee d)}, && h_{\max} = 2d^{1/2}, && a_h = e^{1/[2(4 \vee d)]}. \end{aligned}$$

We now state the asymptotic properties of the estimator. Make the following assumptions.

HJS1: The kernel, K, is a continuously differentiable, decreasing function on $\mathbb{R}_+$ with $K(0) = 1$ and $K(v) = 0$ for all $v \geq 1$.

HJS2: The model is $Y_i = G(X_i' \beta) + U_i$, where the U_i are independently and identically normally distributed with mean 0 and finite variance σ^2.

HJS3: The function G is twice differentiable with a bounded second derivative.
HJS4: The points $\{X_i: i = 1, \ldots, n\}$ are independently and identically distributed with a continuous, strictly positive density on $[0,1]^d$.

We now have the following theorem.

Theorem 2.4: *Let assumptions HJS1–HJS4 hold. Define* $z_n = (1 + 2\log n + 2\log\log n)^{1/2}$ *and* $\beta^* = n^{-1}\beta' \sum_{i=1}^{n} G'(X_i'\beta)$*. Then for all sufficiently large n,*

$$P\left[\left\|(\hat{\theta} - \theta) - \frac{\gamma}{n^{1/2}}\right\| > \frac{Cz_n^2 n^{-2/3}}{\|\beta^*\|}\right] \leq \frac{3j(n)}{n},$$

where C is a constant and γ *is a normally distributed random vector in* $\mathbb{R}^d$ *with mean 0 and a bounded covariance matrix.* ∎

Hristache et al. actually assume a fixed design (the X_i s are nonrandom), but this requires a rather complicated "design regularity" condition. A random design satisfies this condition with a probability that approaches 1 exponentially as n increases. Normality of the U_i s is not essential. The results can be extended to heteroskedastic, nonnormal U_is that satisfy $\sup_{1\leq i\leq n} E[\exp(\lambda U_i)] \leq D$ for some positive constants λ and D. The requirement that $X_i \in [0,1]^d$ is not restrictive because it can always be satisfied by transforming the X_i s.

Theorem 2.4 states, among other things, that the iterated average-derivative estimator is $n^{-1/2}$-consistent and asymptotically normally distributed with a mean of 0. In contrast to the density-weighted average-derivative estimator of Section 2.6.1, this happens whenever X has a continuous, positive density, regardless of the dimension of X. Increasing smoothness and higher-order kernels are not needed to accommodate high-dimensional X s. The covariance matrix of the asymptotic distribution of the iterated average-derivative estimator is not specified, but this is unimportant because the estimator can be made asymptotically efficient with covariance matrix Ω_{SI} by taking one step toward the minimum of a suitable version of the weighted nonlinear least-squares estimator of Section 2.5. See Section 2.6.4.

2.6.3 Direct Estimation with Discrete Covariates

Average-derivative methods cannot be used to estimate components of β that multiply discrete components of X. This is because derivatives of $E(Y|X = x)$ with respect to discrete components of X are not identified. This section explains how direct (noniterative) estimation can be carried out when some components of X are discrete.

To distinguish between continuous and discrete covariates, let X denote the continuously distributed covariates and Z denote the discrete ones. Rewrite (2.1) in the form

$$E(Y|X = x, Z = z) = G(x'\beta + z'\alpha), \tag{2.45}$$

where α is the vector of coefficients of the discrete covariates. As was discussed in Section 2.3, identification requires there to be at least one continuous covariate. There need not be any discrete covariates, but it is assumed in this section that there is at least one. Let $d_z \geq 1$ denote the number of discrete covariates and components of Z.

The problem of interest in this section is estimating α. The parameter β can be estimated by using the average-derivative estimators of Sections 2.6.1 and 2.6.2 as follows. Let $S_z \equiv \{z^{(i)}: i = 1, \ldots, M\}$ be the points of support of Z. Define $\delta_n^{(i)}$ to be the average-derivative estimator of δ that is obtained by applying the methods of Section 2.6.1 or 2.6.2 to the observations for which $Z = z^{(i)}$. Let $\delta_{n1}^{(i)}$ be the first component of $\delta_n^{(i)}$. Let w_{ni} ($i = 1, \ldots, M$) be a set of nonnegative (possibly data-dependent) weights that sum to one. The estimator of β is

$$b_n = \frac{\sum_{i=1}^{M} w_{ni}\delta_n^{(i)}}{\sum_{i=1}^{M} w_{ni}\delta_{n1}^{(i)}}. \tag{2.46}$$

One possible set of weights is $w_{ni} = n_i/n$, where n_i is the number of observations the sample for which $Z = z^{(i)}$. However, the results presented in this section hold with any set of nonnegative weights that sum to one.

To see how α can be estimated, assume for the moment that G in (2.45) is known. Let $p(\cdot|z)$ denote the probability density function of $X'\beta$ conditional on $Z = z$. Make the following assumption.

Assumption G: There are finite numbers v_0, v_1, c_0, and c_1 such that $v_0 < v_1$, $c_0 < c_1$, and $G(v) = c_0$ or c_1 at only finitely many values of v. Moreover, for each $z \in S_z$,

(a) $G(v + z'\alpha) < c_0$ if $v < v_0$,
(b) $G(v + z'\alpha) > c_1$ if $v > v_1$,
(c) $p(\cdot|z)$ is bounded away from 0 on an open interval containing $[v_0, v_1]$.

Parts (a) and (b) of Assumption G impose a form of weak monotonicity on G. G must be smaller than c_0 at sufficiently small values of its argument and larger than c_1 at sufficiently large values. G is unrestricted at intermediate values of its argument. Part (c) ensures that $G(v + z'\alpha)$ is identified on $v_0 \leq v \leq v_1$.

To see the implications of Assumption G for estimating α, define

$$J(z) = \int_{v_0}^{v_1} \{c_0 I[G(v + z'\alpha) < c_0] + c_1 I[G(v + z'\alpha) > c_1] \\ + G(v + z'\alpha) I[c_0 \leq G(v + z'\alpha) \leq c_1]\} dv.$$

Define $v_a = \max\{v_0 + z'\alpha: z \in S_z\}$ and $v_b = \min\{v_1 + z'\alpha: z \in S_z\}$. Make the change of variables $v = u - z'\alpha$ in the integrals on the right-hand side of $J(z)$.

Observe that by Assumption G, $I[G(u) < c_0] = 0$ if $u > v_b$, $I[G(u) > c_1] = 0$ if $u < v_a$, and $I[c_0 \le G(u) \le c_1] = 0$ if $u < v_a$ or $u > v_b$. Therefore,

$$
\begin{aligned}
J(z) &= c_0 \int_{v_0+z'\alpha}^{v_a} I[G(u) < c_0]du + c_0 \int_{v_a}^{v_b} I[G(u) < c_0]du \\
&+ \int_{v_a}^{v_b} G(u)I[c_0 \le G(u) \le c_1]du + c_1 \int_{v_a}^{v_b} I[G(u) > c_1]du \\
&+ c_1 \int_{v_b}^{v_1+z'\alpha} I[G(u) > c_1]du \\
&= c_0(v_a - v_0 - z'\alpha) + c_0 \int_{v_a}^{v_b} I[G(u) < c_0]du + \int_{v_a}^{v_b} G(u)I[c_0 \le G(u) \le c_1]du \\
&+ c_1 \int_{v_a}^{v_b} I[G(u) > c_1]du + c_1(v_1 - v_b + z'\alpha).
\end{aligned}
$$

It follows that for $i = 2, \ldots, M$

$$
J[z^{(i)}] - J[z^{(1)}] = (c_1 - c_0)[z^{(i)} - z^{(1)}]'\alpha. \tag{2.47}
$$

Since c_0, c_1, and the support of Z are known, (2.47) constitutes $M - 1$ linear equations in the d_z unknown components of α. These equations can be solved for α if a unique solution exists. To do this, define the $(M - 1) \times 1$ vector ΔJ by

$$
\Delta J = \begin{bmatrix} J[z^{(2)}] - J[z^{(1)}] \\ \vdots \\ J[z^{(M)}] - J[z^{(1)}] \end{bmatrix}.
$$

Also, define the $(M - 1) \times d_z$ matrix W by

$$
W = \begin{bmatrix} z^{(2)} - z^{(1)} \\ \vdots \\ z^{(M)} - z^{(1)} \end{bmatrix}.
$$

Then

$$
W'\Delta J = (c_1 - c_0)^{-1} W'W\alpha.
$$

Therefore, if $W'W$ is a nonsingular matrix,

$$
\alpha = (c_1 - c_0)(W'W)^{-1}W'\Delta J. \tag{2.48}
$$

Equation (2.48) forms the basis of the estimator of α. The estimator is obtained by replacing the unknown $G(v + z'\alpha)$ that enters ΔJ with a kernel estimator of the nonparametric mean regression of Y on $X'b_n$ conditional on $Z = z$. The resulting estimator of $G(v + z'\alpha)$ is

$$G_{nz}(v) = \frac{1}{nh_{nz}p_{nz}(v)} \sum_{i=1}^{n} I(Z_i = z)Y_i K\left(\frac{v - V_{ni}}{h_{nz}}\right), \tag{2.49}$$

where h_{nz} is a bandwidth, K is a kernel function, $V_{ni} = X_i' b_n$, and

$$p_{nz}(v) = \frac{1}{nh_{nz}} \sum_{i=1}^{n} I(Z_i = z)K\left(\frac{v - V_{ni}}{h_{nz}}\right). \tag{2.50}$$

The estimator of α is then

$$a_n = (c_1 - c_0)^{-1}(W'W)^{-1}W'\Delta J_n, \tag{2.51}$$

where

$$\Delta J_n = \begin{bmatrix} J_n[z^{(2)}] - J_n[z^{(1)}] \\ \vdots \\ J_n[z^{(M)}] - J_n[z^{(1)}] \end{bmatrix}$$

and

$$\begin{aligned} J_n(z) = \int_{v_0}^{v_1} & \{c_0 I[G_{nz}(v) < c_0] + c_1 I[G_{nz}(v) > c_1] \\ & + G_{nz}(v)I[c_0 \le G_{nz}(v) \le c_1]\}dv. \end{aligned}$$

Horowitz and Härdle (1996) give conditions under which a_n in (2.51) is a consistent estimator of α and $n^{1/2}(a_n - \alpha)$ is asymptotically normally distributed with mean 0. The formal statement of this result is given in Theorem 2.5. Define $V = X'\beta$, $V_i = X_i'\beta$, $v = x'\beta$, and $G_z(v) = G(v + z'\alpha)$. Let $p(v|z)$ be the probability density of V conditional on $Z = z$, let $p(z)$ be the probability that $Z = z$ ($z \in S_z$), let $p(v, z) = p(v|z)p(z)$, and let $p(v, \tilde{x}|z)$ be the joint density of $(V, \tilde{X})$ conditional on $Z = z$. Finally, define

$$\Gamma(z) = -\int_{v_0}^{v_1} G_z'(v)E(\tilde{X}|v, z)I[c_0 \le G(v + z'\alpha) \le c_1]dv.$$

Theorem 2.5: *Let the following conditions hold.*

(a) S_z *is a finite set.* $E\left(\|\tilde{X}\|^2 |Z = z\right) < \infty$ *and* $E\left(|Y| \, \|\tilde{X}\|^2 |Z = z\right) < \infty$ *for each* $z \in S_z$. $E\left(|Y|^2 \|\tilde{X}\|^2 |V = v, Z = z\right)$, $E(|Y|^2|V = v, Z = z)$, *and* $p(v, z)$ *are bounded uniformly over* $v \in [v_0 - \varepsilon, v_1 + \varepsilon]$ *for some* $\varepsilon > 0$ *and*

all $z \in S_z$. For each $z \in S_z$, $p(v, \tilde{x}|z)$ is everywhere three times continuously differentiable with respect to v and the third derivative is bounded uniformly. $Var(Y|V = v, Z = z) > 0$ for all $z \in S_z$ and almost every v.

(b) $W'W$ is nonsingular.

(c) $E(Y|X = x, Z = z) = G(x'\beta + z'\alpha)$. G is r times continuously differentiable for some $r \geq 4$. G and its first r derivatives are bounded on all bounded intervals.

(d) Assumption G holds.

(e) If $d = \dim(X) > 1$, there is a $(d-1) \times 1$ vector-valued function $\omega(y, x, z)$ satisfying $E[\omega(Y, X, Z)] = 0$,

$$n^{1/2}(b_n - \beta) = \frac{1}{n^{1/2}} \sum_{i=1}^{n} \omega(Y_i, X_i, Z_i) + o_p(1),$$

and

$$\frac{1}{n^{1/2}} \sum_{i=1}^{n} \omega(Y_i, X_i, Z_i) \xrightarrow{d} N(0, V_\omega)$$

for some finite matrix V_ω.

(f) K in (2.49) and (2.50) is a bounded, symmetrical, differentiable function that is nonzero only on $[-1,1]$. K' is Lipschitz continuous. For each integer j between 0 and r ($r \geq 4$),

$$\int_{-1}^{1} v^j K(v) dv = \begin{cases} 1 \text{ if } j = 0 \\ 0 \text{ if } 1 \leq j \leq r-1 \end{cases}.$$

(g) As $n \to \infty$, $nh_n^{r+3} \to \infty$ and $nh_n^{2r} \to 0$, where h_n is the bandwidth in (2.49) and (2.50).

Then a_n is a consistent estimator of α. Moreover, $n^{1/2}(a_n - \alpha)$ is asymptotically distributed as $N(0, \Omega_\alpha)$, where Ω_α is the covariance matrix of the $d_z \times 1$ random vector Λ_n whose m th component is

$$\sum_{j=2}^{m} [(W'W)^{-1}W']_{mj} n^{-1/2} \sum_{i=1}^{n} \{I(Z_i = z^{(j)}) p(V_i, z^{(j)})^{-1}$$
$$[Y_i - G_{z^{(j)}}(V_i)] I[c_0 \leq G_{z^{(j)}}(V_i) \leq c_1] - I(Z_i = z^{(1)}) p(V_i, z^{(1)})^{-1}$$
$$[Y_i - G_{z^{(1)}}(V_i)] I[c_0 \leq G_{z^{(1)}}(V_i) \leq c_1] + (\Gamma_{z^{(j)}} - \Gamma_{z^{(1)}}) \omega(Y_i, X_i, Z_i)\}. \blacksquare$$

Condition (a) makes *Z* a discrete random variable with finite support and establishes the existence and properties of certain moments. The need for conditions (b) and (d) has already been discussed. Condition (c) makes $E(Y|X = x, Z = z)$ a single-index model. Condition (e) is satisfied by the estimators of β discussed in Sections 2.6.1 and 2.6.2 but does not require the use of these estimators. Conditions (f) and (g) require *K* to be a higher-order kernel with undersmoothing. As in

Section 2.6.1, conditions (f) and (g) are used to insure that the asymptotic distribution of $n^{1/2}(a_n - \alpha)$ is centered at 0.

The covariance matrix Ω_α can be estimated consistently by replacing unknown quantities with consistent estimators. Γ_z is estimated consistently by

$$\Gamma_{nz} = -\frac{1}{n}\sum_{i=1}^{n} \tilde{X}_i I(Z_i = z) I(v_0 \le V_{ni} \le v_1) I[c_0 \le G_{nz}(V_{ni}) \le c_1] G'_{nz}(V_{ni})/p_{nz}(V_{ni}),$$

where $G'_{nz}(v) = dG_{nz}(v)/dv$. Define $\lambda(y,v,\ z)$ to be the $(M-1)\times 1$ vector whose $(j-1)$ component ($j = 2,\ \ldots,\ M$) is

$$\lambda_j(y,v,\ z) = I(z = z^{(j)})\frac{y - G_{nz^{(j)}}(v)}{p_{nz^{(j)}}(v)} I[c_0 \le G_{nz^{(j)}(v)} \le c_1] - I(z = z^{(1)})\frac{y - G_{nz^{(1)}}(v)}{p_{nz^{(1)}}(v)} I[c_0 \le G_{nz^{(1)}(v)} \le c_1].$$

Let ω_n be a consistent estimator of ω. Then Ω_α is estimated consistently by the sample covariance of the $d_z \times 1$ vector whose mth component ($m = 1,\ \ldots,\ d_z$) is

$$\sum_{j=2}^{m} [(W'W)^{-1}W']_{mj}[\lambda_j(Y_i,\ V_{ni},\ Z_i) + (\Gamma_{nz^{(j)}} - \Gamma_{nz^{(1)}})\omega_n(Y_i,\ X_i,\ Z_i)].$$

Horowitz and Härdle (1996) show how to estimate ω when the estimator of β is (2.46) and the $\delta_n^{(i)}$ are density-weighted average-derivative estimates (Section 2.6.1). To state their result, let $p_{ni}(x)$ be a kernel estimator of the probability density of X conditional on $Z = z^{(i)}$. That is,

$$p_{ni}(x) = \frac{1}{n_i s_n}\sum_{j=1}^{n} I(Z_j = z^{(i)}) K^*\left(\frac{x - X_j}{s_n}\right),$$

where K^* is a kernel function of a k -dimensional argument, n_i is the number of observations for which $Z = z^{(i)}$, and s_n is a bandwidth. Let $x^{(1)}$ be the first component of x. Then the estimator of ω is

$$\omega_n(y,\ x,\ z^{(i)}) = -2\frac{n_i}{n\delta_{n1}^{(i)}}[y - G(x'b_n + z^{(i)\prime}a_n)]\left[\frac{\partial p_{ni}(x)}{\partial \tilde{x}} - \tilde{b}_n\frac{\partial p_{ni}(x)}{\partial x^{(1)}}\right].$$

2.6.4 One-Step Asymptotically Efficient Estimators

In parametric estimation, an asymptotically efficient estimator can be obtained by taking one Newton step from any $n^{-1/2}$-consistent estimator toward the maximum-likelihood estimator. This procedure is called *one-step asymptotically efficient estimation*. The resulting estimator is called a *one-step asymptotically efficient estimator*. This section shows that the same idea applies to estimation of β in a semiparametric single-index model. Specifically, let S_n be the objective function of the semiparametric WNLS estimator (2.25) with $W(x) = 1/s_n^2(x)$. Then an asymptotically efficient estimator of β can be obtained by taking one Newton step from any $n^{1/2}$ -consistent estimator toward the minimum of S_n. In the case of a single-index binary-response model, the step may be taken toward the maximum of the semiparametric log-likelihood function (2.34).

One-step asymptotically efficient estimation is especially useful in semiparametric single-index models because the direct estimators described in Sections 2.6.1–2.6.3 can be computed very rapidly. Therefore, one-step estimators can be obtained with much less computation than is needed to minimize S_n or maximize the semiparametric log-likelihood function.

Consider one-step asymptotically efficient estimation based on S_n . Let X denote the entire vector of covariates, continuous and discrete. Let β denote the entire vector of coefficients of X in (2.1). Let $\tilde{b}_n^*$ be any $n^{-1/2}$ -consistent estimator of $\tilde{\beta}$. It is convenient in applications but not essential to the arguments made here to let $\tilde{b}_n^*$ be a direct estimator. The one-step asymptotically efficient estimator of $\tilde{\beta}$ is

$$\tilde{b}_n = \tilde{b}_n^* - \left[\frac{\partial^2 S_n(\tilde{b}_n^*)}{\partial\tilde{b}\partial\tilde{b}'}\right]^{-1} \frac{\partial S_n(\tilde{b}_n^*)}{\partial\tilde{b}}. \tag{2.52}$$

To see why $\tilde{b}_n$ is asymptotically efficient, write (2.52) in the form

$$n^{1/2}(\tilde{b}_n - \tilde{\beta}) = n^{1/2}(\tilde{b}_n^* - \tilde{\beta}) - \left[\frac{\partial^2 S_n(\tilde{b}_n^*)}{\partial\tilde{b}\partial\tilde{b}'}\right]^{-1} n^{1/2}\frac{\partial S_n(\tilde{b}_n^*)}{\partial\tilde{b}}. \tag{2.53}$$

Observe that just as in the arguments leading to (2.31),

$$\frac{\partial^2 S_n(\tilde{b}_n^*)}{\partial\tilde{b}\partial\tilde{b}'} = C + o_p(1). \tag{2.54}$$

Moreover, a Taylor-series expansion gives

$$\frac{\partial S_n(\tilde{b}_n^*)}{\partial\tilde{b}} = \frac{\partial S_n(\tilde{\beta})}{\partial\tilde{b}} + \frac{\partial^2 S_n(\bar{b}_n)}{\partial\tilde{b}\partial\tilde{b}'}(\tilde{b}_n^* - \tilde{\beta}),$$

where $\bar{b}_n$ is between $\tilde{b}_n^*$ and $\tilde{\beta}$. The second-derivative term in this equation converges in probability to C, so

$$n^{1/2}\frac{\partial S_n(\tilde{b}_n^*)}{\partial\tilde{b}} = n^{1/2}\frac{\partial S_n(\tilde{\beta})}{\partial\tilde{b}} + Cn^{1/2}(\tilde{b}_n^* - \tilde{\beta}) + o_p(1). \tag{2.55}$$

Substitution of (2.54) and (2.55) into (2.53) yields

$$n^{1/2}(\tilde{b}_n - \tilde{\beta}) = -C^{-1} n^{1/2} \frac{\partial S_n(\tilde{\beta})}{\partial \tilde{b}} + o_p(1).$$

As in (2.30)

$$n^{1/2} \frac{\partial S_n(\tilde{\beta})}{\partial \tilde{b}} \xrightarrow{d} N(0, D).$$

Therefore, $n^{1/2}(\tilde{b}_n - \tilde{\beta}) \xrightarrow{d} N(0, C^{-1}DC^{-1})$. Since $C^{-1}DC^{-1} = \Omega_{SI}$ when $W(x) = 1/s_n^2(x)$,

$$n^{1/2}(\tilde{b}_n - \tilde{\beta}) \xrightarrow{d} N(0, \Omega_{SI}).$$

This establishes the asymptotic efficiency of the one-step semiparametric WNLS estimator. The same arguments apply to the one-step semiparametric maximum-likelihood estimator after replacing S_n with the semiparametric log-likelihood function.

2.7 Bandwidth Selection

Implementation of any of the semiparametric estimators for single-index models that are discussed in this chapter requires choosing the numerical values of one or more bandwidth parameters and, possibly, of other tuning parameters. The selection of tuning parameters for the average-derivative estimator of Section 2.6.2 was discussed in that section. This section summarizes what is known about selecting tuning parameters for other estimators.

Härdle et al. (1993) investigated bandwidth selection for the semiparametric weighted nonlinear least-squares estimator of (2.25). They proposed optimizing the objective function over $\tilde{b}$ and the bandwidth h_n. They gave conditions under which this yields an estimate of the bandwidth that minimizes the asymptotic integrated mean-square error of a kernel estimator of G. Thus, the resulting bandwidth estimate is an estimate of the asymptotically optimal bandwidth for kernel estimation of G. This bandwidth does not necessarily have any optimality properties for estimation of β.

As can be seen from the results in Sections 2.4, 2.5, and 2.6, in semiparametric single-index models, the asymptotic distribution of $n^{1/2}(b_n - \beta)$ does not depend on the bandwidth h_n. Therefore, bandwidth selection must be based on a higher-order approximation to the distribution of $n^{1/2}(b_n - \beta)$. Härdle and Tsybakov (1993) used such an approximation to obtain a formula for the bandwidth that minimizes the asymptotic approximation to $E\,\|\delta_n - \delta\|^2$, where δ and δ_n, respectively, are as in (2.39) and (2.42), and $\|\cdot\|$ is the Euclidean norm. This is an asymptotically optimal bandwidth for estimating β. Powell and Stoker(1996) obtained the bandwidth that minimizes the asymptotic mean-square error of a single component of $\delta_n - \delta$.

Two aspects of the results of Härdle and Tsybakov (1993) and Powell and Stoker (1996) are especially noteworthy. First, the asymptotically optimal bandwidth has the form

$$h_{n,opt} = h_0 n^{-2/(2P+d+2)},$$

where P and d are defined as in Theorem 2.3 and h_0 is a constant. Second, Powell and Stoker (1996) provide a method for estimating h_0 in an application. To state this method, let h_{n1} be an initial bandwidth estimate that satisfies $h_{n1} \to 0$ and $nh_{n1}^c \to \infty$ as $n \to \infty$, where $c = \max(\eta + 2d + 4,\ P + d + 2)$ for some $\eta > 0$. Define

$$q_n(y_1, x_1, y_2, x_2) = -\frac{1}{h_{n1}^{d+1}}(y_1 - y_2)K'\left(\frac{x_1 - x_2}{h_{n1}}\right)$$

and

$$\hat{Q} = \frac{2h_{n1}^{d+2}}{n(n-1)} \sum_{i<j} q_n(Y_i, X_i, Y_j, X_j)^2.$$

Let $\delta_n(h)$ denote the density-weighted average-derivative estimator of δ based on bandwidth h. Let $\tau \neq 1$ be a positive number. Define

$$\hat{S} = \frac{\delta_n(\tau h_{n1}) - \delta_n(h_{n1})}{(\tau h_{n1})^P - h_{n1}^P}.$$

The estimator of h_0 is

$$\hat{h}_0 = \left[\frac{(d+2)\hat{Q}}{P\hat{S}^2}\right]^{1/(2P+d+2)}.$$

Another possible approach to bandwidth selection is based on resampling the data. Suppose that the asymptotically optimal bandwidth has the form

$$h_{n,opt} = h_0 n^{-\gamma}$$

for some known γ. For example, in density-weighted average-derivative estimation, $\gamma = 2P + d + 2$. Let $m < n$ be a positive integer. Let $\{Y_i^*,\ X_i^*:\ i = 1,\ \ldots,\ m\}$ be a sample of size m that is obtained by sampling the estimation data randomly without replacement. Then $\{Y_i^*,\ X_i^*\}$ is a random sample from the population distribution of $(Y,\ X)$. Repeat this resampling process J times. Let $b_{mj}(h)$ ($j = 1,\ \ldots,\ J$) be the estimate of β that is obtained from the jth sample using bandwidth $h = \tau m^{-\gamma}$, where τ is a constant. Let b_n be the estimate of β that is obtained from the full sample by using a preliminary bandwidth estimate that satisfies the requirements needed to make b_n a $n^{-1/2}$-consistent estimator of β. Let τ_m be the solution to the problem

$$\text{minimize: } \frac{1}{J}\sum_{j=1}^{J}[b_{mj}(h) - b_n]^2.$$

Then τ_m estimates h_0, and $h_{n,opt}$ is estimated by

$$\hat{h}_{n,opt} = \tau_m n^{-\gamma}.$$

Horowitz and Härdle (1996) used Monte Carlo methods to obtain rules of thumb for selecting the tuning parameters required for the estimator of α described in Section 2.6.3. Horowitz and Härdle (1996) obtained good numerical results in Monte Carlo experiments by setting $h_{nz} = s_{vz} n_z^{-1/7.5}$, where s_{vz} is the sample standard deviation of $X'b_n$ conditional on $Z = z \in S_z$ and n_z is the number of observations with $Z = z$. In these experiments, the values of the other tuning parameters were

$$v_1 = \min_{z \in S_z} \max_{1 \le i \le n} \{X_i'b_n - h_{nz}: Z_i = z\},$$

$$v_0 = \max_{z \in S_z} \min_{1 \le i \le n} \{X_i'b_n + h_{nz}: Z_i = z\},$$

$$c_0 = \max_{z \in S_z} \max_{X_i b_n \le v_0} G_{nz}^*(X_i'b_n),$$

and

$$c_1 = \min_{z \in S_z} \min_{X_i b_n \ge v_1} G_{nz}^*(X_i'b_n).$$

In the formulae for c_0 and c_1, G_{nz}^* is the kernel estimator of G_z that is obtained using a second-order kernel instead of the higher-order kernel used to estimate α. Horowitz and Härdle (1996) found that using a second-order kernel produced estimates of c_0 and c_1 that were more stable than those obtained with a higher-order kernel.

2.8 An Empirical Example

This section presents an empirical example that illustrates the usefulness of semiparametric single-index models. The example is taken from Horowitz and Härdle (1996) and consists of estimating a model of product innovation by German manufacturers of investment goods. The data, assembled in 1989 by the IFO Institute of Munich, consist of observations on 1100 manufacturers. The dependent variable is $Y = 1$ if a manufacturer realized an innovation during 1989 in a specific product category and 0 otherwise. The independent variables are the number of employees in the product category (EMPLP), the number of employees in the entire firm (EMPLF), an indicator of the firm's production capacity utilization (CAP), and a discrete variable DEM, which is 1 if a firm expected increasing demand in the product category and 0 otherwise.The first three independent variables are standardized so that they have units of standard deviations from their means. Scale normalization was achieved by setting $\beta_{EMPLP} = 1$.

Table 2.3 shows the parameter estimates obtained using a binary probit model and the direct semiparametric methods of Sections 2.6.1 and 2.6.3. Figure 2.1 shows a kernel estimate of $G'(v)$. There are two important differences between the semiparametric and probit estimates. First, the semiparametric estimate of β_{EMPLF} is small and statistically nonsignificant, whereas the probit estimate is significant at the 0.05 level and similar in size to β_{CAP}. Second, in the binary probit model, G is a cumulative normal distribution function, so G' is a normal density function. Figure 2.1 reveals, however, that G' is bimodal. This bimodality suggests that the data may be a mixture of two populations. An obvious next step in the analysis of the data would be to search for variables that characterize these populations. Standard diagnostic techniques for binary probit models would provide no indication that G' is bimodal. Thus, the semiparametric estimate has revealed an important feature of the data that could not easily be found using standard parametric methods.

Table 2.3 Estimated coefficients (standard errors) for model of product innovation

EMPLP	EMPLF	CAP	DEM
	Semiparametric model		
1	0.032	0.346	1.732
	(0.023)	(0.078)	(0.509)
	Probit model		
1	0.516	0.520	1.895
	(0.024)	(0.163)	(0.387)

Source: Horowitz and Härdle (1996). The coefficient of EMPLP is 1 by scale normalization.

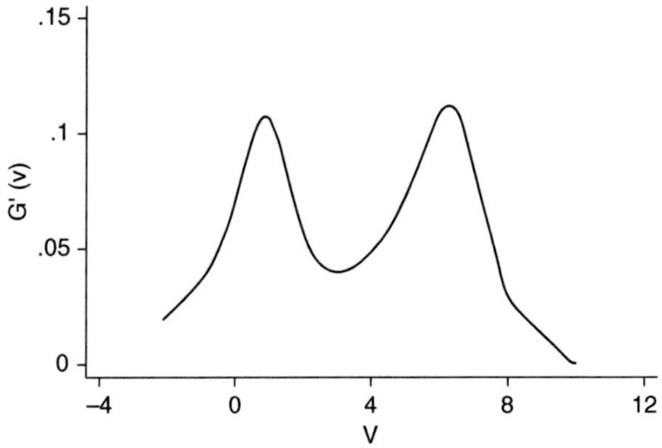

Fig. 2.1 Plot of $G'(v)$ for model of product innovation. Source: Horowitz and Härdle (1996)

2.9 Single-Index Models of Conditional Quantile Functions

Let $Q_\alpha(Y|X)$ denote the α-quantile of Y conditional on X, where $0 < \alpha < 1$. Then $P[Y \leq Q_\alpha(Y|X)|X] = \alpha$. In a single-index model of the conditional quantile function,

$$Q_\alpha(Y|X = x) = G(x'\beta), \tag{2.56}$$

where β is an unknown constant vector and G is an unknown function. It is not difficult to show that G and β are identified under the assumptions of Theorem 2.1. Moreover, if b_n is a $n^{-1/2}$-consistent estimator of β, then G can be estimated with a one-dimensional nonparametric rate of convergence by carrying out a nonparametric quantile regression of Y on $X'b_n$. Nonparametric quantile regression is discussed briefly in the Appendix and in more detail by Chaudhuri (1991a,b), Fan et al. (1994), and Yu and Jones (1998). This section concentrates on $n^{-1/2}$-consistent estimation of β. As is explained in the Appendix, estimating a conditional quantile function requires optimizing a nonsmooth objective function. Consequently, quantile estimation is more complex technically than estimation of conditional mean functions, and it requires regularity conditions that are more elaborate and difficult to interpret intuitively.

As with single-index models of conditional mean functions, β in (2.56) is proportional to $\partial Q_\alpha(Y|X = x)/\partial x$. Let W be a weight function. Define

$$\delta = E\left[\frac{\partial Q_\alpha(Y|X = x)}{\partial x} W(x)\right]. \tag{2.57}$$

Then δ and β are equal up to a proportionality constant. Replacing $\partial Q_\alpha(Y|X = x)/\partial x$ with a nonparametric estimator and the population expectation with a sample average in (2.57) yields an average-derivative estimator of δ and, hence, β up to a proportionality constant. Specifically, let the data $\{Y_i, X_i : i = 1, \ldots, n\}$ be a simple random sample of (Y, X), and let $\partial \hat{Q}_\alpha(Y|X_i)/\partial x$ be a nonparametric estimator of $\partial Q_\alpha(Y|X = x)/\partial x|_{x=X_i}$. Then the average-derivative estimator is

$$\hat{\delta}_{AD} = \frac{1}{n}\sum_{i=1}^{n}\left[\frac{\partial \hat{Q}_\alpha(Y|X_i)}{\partial x}\right] W(X_i).$$

Chaudhuri et al. (1997) have derived the asymptotic distributional properties of $\hat{\delta}_{AD}$. Their result requires the following definition of smoothness of a function. The definition is somewhat technical but basically requires derivatives of the function to be continuous. Let V be an open, convex subset of $\mathbb{R}^d$, where $d = \dim(X)$. Let m be a function from $\mathbb{R}^d$ to $\mathbb{R}$. Define m to have order of smoothness p on V and write

$m \in S_p(V)$ if $p = \ell + \gamma$ for some integer $\ell \geq 0$ and γ satisfies $0 < \gamma \leq 1$, all partial derivatives of m through order ℓ exist, and each order ℓ partial derivative satisfies

$$\left| D^\ell m(x_1) - D^\ell m(x_2) \right| \leq C \, \|x_1 - x_2\|^\gamma$$

for all x_1, $x_2 \in V$, where $D^\ell m$ denotes any order ℓ partial derivative of m and $C > 0$ is a finite constant.

Let p_X denote the probability density function of X and $p_{Y|X}$ denote the density of Y conditional on X. For sequences of numbers $\{c_n\}$ and $\{d_n\}$, let $c_n \asymp d_n$ mean that c_n/d_n is bounded away from 0 and ∞ as $n \to \infty$. Let $[p]$ denote the largest integer that is less than or equal to p. For data $\{Y_i, X_i : i = 1, \ldots, n\}$ define $U_i = Y_i - Q_\alpha(Y|X_i)$. Let ∇ denote the gradient operator. Define $l(x) = \nabla \log [p_X(x)]$.

Now make the following assumptions.

QAD1: The probability density of X is positive on V and $p_X \in S_{p_1}(V)$, where $p_1 = 1 + \gamma$ for some $\gamma \in (0,1]$.

QAD2: The weight function W is supported on a compact set with nonempty interior that is contained in V, and $W \in S_{p_1}(V)$.

QAD3: Define $U = Y - Q_\alpha(Y|X = x)$. Let $p_{U|X}(u|x)$ denote the probability density function of U at u conditional on $X = x$. Then $p_{U|X}(u|x)$ considered as a function of x belongs to $S_{p_1(V)}$ for all u in a neighborhood of 0. Moreover $p_{U|X}(u|x) > 0$ and $\partial p_{U|X}(u|x)/\partial u$ exists and is continuous for all u in a neighborhood of 0 and all $x \in V$.

QAD4: $Q_\alpha(Y|X = x) \in S_{p_4(V)}$, where $p_4 > 3 + 3d/2$.

QAD5: $\hat{Q}_\alpha(Y|X = x)$ is the local polynomial estimator of Chaudhuri (1991a,b) with a polynomial of degree $[p_4]$ and bandwidth h_n satisfying $h_n \asymp n^{-\kappa}$ with $\frac{1}{2(p_4 - 1)} < \kappa < \frac{1}{4+3d}$.

The next theorem states the result of Chaudhuri et al. (1997).

Theorem 2.6: *Let assumptions QAD1–QAD4 hold. Then as $n \to \infty$,*

$$\hat{\delta}_{AD} - \delta = \frac{1}{n} \sum_{i=1}^{n} \left\{ W(X_i) \nabla Q_\alpha(Y|X_i) - [\alpha - I(U_i \leq 0)] \frac{\nabla W(X_i) + W(X_i) l(X_i)}{p_{Y|X}[Q_\alpha(Y|X_i)|X_i]} \right\}$$
$$- \beta + o_p(n^{-1/2}). \blacksquare$$

Theorem 2.6 implies that $n^{1/2}(\hat{\delta}_{AD} - \delta)$ is asymptotically normally distributed with mean 0 and variance equal to the variance of the summand on the right-hand side of (2.58). As in average-derivative estimation of a conditional mean function (Section 2.6), averaging of the nonparametric estimator $\partial \hat{Q}_\alpha / \partial x$ in (2.58) enables $\hat{\delta}_{AD}$ to achieve a $n^{-1/2}$ rate of convergence instead of the slower rate for nonparametric estimation of derivatives. It follows from QAD5 that Q_α must be increasingly smooth as d increases. Thus, the average-derivative estimator of Chaudhuri et al. (1997), like the density-weighted average-derivative estimator of Powell et al.

(1989) for conditional mean functions, has a curse of dimensionality. Methods for choosing W and h_n in applications and for avoiding the curse of dimensionality in average-derivative estimation of conditional quantile functions have not yet been developed.

Khan (2001) has developed a rank estimator of β in (2.56) that is $n^{-1/2}$-consistent and asymptotically normal if G is monotonic. The average-derivative estimator does not require monotonicity, but the rank estimator requires less smoothness than does the average-derivative estimator. In addition, the rank estimator can accommodate discrete components of X, although at least one component must be continuously distributed. Khan's estimator is based on an estimator of Cavanagh and Sherman (1998) and is

$$b_n = \arg \min_{\tilde{b} \in \tilde{B},\, b_1 = 1} \frac{1}{n} \sum_{\substack{i,j=1 \\ i \neq j}}^{n} W(X_i)\hat{Q}_\alpha(Y|X_i)I(X_i'b > X_j'b),$$

where $\tilde{b}$ denotes the vector consisting of all components of b except the first, $\tilde{B} \in \mathbb{R}^{d-1}$ is a compact parameter set, W is a weight function, and $\hat{Q}_\alpha$ is Chaudhuri's (1991a,b) nonparametric estimator of Q_α.

To obtain the asymptotic distribution of Khan's estimator, define

$$\tau_1(x,\ b) = \int W(x)Q_\alpha(Y|X = x)I(x'b > v'b)p_X(v)dv + \int W(v)Q_\alpha(Y|X = v)I(v'b > x'b)p_X(v)dv$$

and

$$\tau_2(x,\ b) = \int I(x'b > v'b)p_X(v)dv.$$

Let $\tilde{\beta}$ be the vector consisting of all components of β except the first. Let N be a neighborhood of $\tilde{\beta}$. Now make the following assumptions.

RAD1: $\tilde{\beta}$ is in the interior of the compact parameter set $\tilde{B}$.
RAD2: $Q_\alpha(Y|X = x) = G(x'\beta)$ and G is a nonconstant, increasing function.
RAD3: $Q_\alpha(Y|X) \in S_p(V)$, where $p > 3d/2$ and V is the support of X.
RAD4: The weight function W is continuous, bounded, and bounded away from 0 on its support, S_W. S_W has the form $S_{W1} \times \tilde{S}_W$, where S_{W1} is a compact subset of the support of the first component of X and has a nonempty interior. $\tilde{S}_W$ is a compact subset of the remaining $d-1$ components of X and has a nonempty interior. S_W is not contained in any proper linear subspace of $\mathbb{R}^d$.
RAD5: The support of X is a convex subset of $\mathbb{R}^d$ with a nonempty interior.
RAD6: X has a probability density function, p_X, that is continuous and bounded on its support. Moreover, $p_X(x) \geq c$ for some constant $c > 0$ and all $x \in S_W$.

RAD7: Let t_0 satisfy $G(t) < G(t_0)$ if $t < t_0$. Assume that

$$T \equiv \max_{\tilde{x} \in \tilde{S}_W,\ \tilde{b} \in \tilde{B}} |\tilde{x}'\tilde{b}| < \infty.$$

Then $[t_0 - 3T, t_0 + 3T] \in S_{W1}$.

RAD8: Define $U = Y - Q_\alpha(Y|X = x)$. Let $p_{U|X}(u|x)$ denote the probability density function of U at u conditional on $X = x$. Then $p_{U|X}(u|x)$ considered as a function of x is Lipschitz continuous for all u in a neighborhood of 0. Moreover $p_{U|X}(u|x)$ considered as a function of u is continuous, bounded, and bounded away from 0 for all u in a neighborhood of 0.

RAD9: For each x in the support of X and all $\tilde{b} \in N$, $\nabla^2\tau_1(x, b) \equiv \partial^2\tau_1(x, b)/\partial\tilde{b}\partial\tilde{b}'$ exists and is Lipschitz continuous. Moreover, $E[\nabla^2\tau_1(X, \beta)]$ is negative definite.

RAD10: For each x in the support of X and all $\tilde{b} \in N$, $\nabla\tau_2(x, b) \equiv \partial\tau_2(x, b)/\partial\tilde{b}$ exists and is continuous. Moreover, $E\,\|\nabla\tau_2(X, \beta)\| < \infty$.

RAD11: $\hat{Q}_\alpha$ is a local polynomial estimator based on a polynomial of degree $[p]$ and bandwidth h_n satisfying $n^{1/2}h_n^p \to 0$ and $(\log n)/(nh_n^{3d})^{1/2} \to 0$ as $n \to \infty$.

The following theorem shows that $n^{1/2}(\tilde{b}_n - \tilde{\beta})$ is asymptotically normal under RAD1–RAD11.

Theorem 2.7: *Let RAD1–RAD11 hold. Then* $n^{1/2}(\tilde{b}_n - \tilde{\beta}) \xrightarrow{d} N(0, D^{-1}\Sigma D^{-1})$, *where* $D = 0.5E[\nabla^2\tau_1(X, \beta)]$, $\Sigma = E[s(Y, X)s(Y, X)']$, *and*

$$s(y, x) = \frac{W(x)}{p_{U|X}(0|x)}\{I[y \le Q_\alpha(Y|X = x)] - \alpha\}\nabla\tau_2(x, \beta). \blacksquare$$

Khan (2001) proves Theorem 2.7, provides an estimator of the covariance matrix $D^{-1}\Sigma D^{-1}$, and shows that under slightly modified assumptions, the conclusion of the theorem holds if some components of X are discrete. Like the average-derivative estimator, the rank estimator requires fully nonparametric estimation of Q_α and has a curse of dimensionality, but the rank estimator's smoothness assumptions are weaker than the smoothness assumptions of the average-derivative estimator.

Chapter 3
Nonparametric Additive Models and Semiparametric Partially Linear Models

This chapter discusses two types of models of conditional mean and quantile functions. The first is a nonparametric additive model. The second is a semiparametric partially linear model. In a nonparametric additive model, the mean or quantile of a random variable Y conditional on a d-dimensional, continuously distributed, random vector of covariates X is

$$E(Y|X=x) = G[\mu + m_1(x^1) + \cdots + m_d(x^d)] \tag{3.1a}$$

or

$$Q_\alpha(Y|X=x) = G[\mu + m_1(x^1) + \cdots + m_d(x^d)], \tag{3.1b}$$

where $Q_\alpha(Y|X = x)$ is the α-quantile of Y conditional on $X = x$. In these specifications, $x^j (j = 1, \ldots, d)$ is the jth component of the d-dimensional vector x; G is a known function, possibly the identity function, called a *link function*; μ is an unknown constant; and $m_1, \ldots, m_d$ are unknown functions with scalar arguments. The inferential problem is to estimate μ and $m_1, \ldots, m_d$ from observations of (Y, X). In a semiparametric partially linear model, there are two vectors of covariates, X and Z. Let d denote the dimension of X. The model is

$$E(Y|X=x, Z=z) = X'\beta + g(Z) \tag{3.2a}$$

or

$$Q_\alpha(Y|X=x, Z=z) = X'\beta + g(Z), \tag{3.2b}$$

where β is a d-dimensional vector of unknown coefficients and g is an unknown function. It is usually assumed that Z is continuously distributed, whereas the components of X may be discrete or continuous. The inferential problem is to estimate β and, possibly, g from observations of (Y, X, Z).

Like single-index models, nonparametric additive and semiparametric partially linear models achieve dimension reduction and, thereby, greater estimation accuracy than is possible in fully nonparametric estimation (Stone 1985). In a nonparametric

J.L. Horowitz, *Semiparametric and Nonparametric Methods in Econometrics*, Springer Series in Statistics, DOI 10.1007/978-0-387-92870-8_3,

additive model, each of the additive components $m_j (j = 1, \ldots, d)$ can be estimated with the one-dimensional nonparametric rate of convergence. Indeed, it is possible to estimate each additive component with the same asymptotic accuracy that would be achieved if all the other components were known and one had to estimate only a single component with a scalar argument. This property is called *oracle efficiency* because, asymptotically (though not necessarily in a finite sample), each additive component can be estimated with the same accuracy that would be achievable if an oracle told us the other components. In the partially linear model, β can be estimated with a $n^{-1/2}$ rate of convergence in probability. This is the same rate that would be achievable if the function g were known.

Single-index, nonparametric additive, and semiparametric partially linear models are nonnested. That is, there are single-index models that are not additive or partially linear, additive models that are not single index or partially linear, and partially linear models that are not single index or additive. Therefore, except in special cases, at most one of these models can be correctly specified in a given application. An analyst must choose among the models, and an incorrect choice causes the resulting model to be misspecified. Nonetheless, each of the models relaxes some of the strong assumptions of standard parametric models. For example, setting G in (3.1) equal to the identity function yields a model that is less restrictive than the standard linear model. Setting G equal to the normal (logistic) distribution function yields a binary-response model that is less restrictive than a probit (logit) model.

Single-index and nonparametric additive models are nonnested because the link function G is known and fixed in (3.1), whereas it is unknown in a single-index model. If G is treated as unknown in (3.1), then single-index models become a special case of the resulting class of nonparametric additive models with *unknown* link functions. Specifically, (3.1) with an unknown link function is a semiparametric single-index model if the m_j s are all linear functions. By nesting single-index and nonparametric additive models, (3.1) with an unknown link function eliminates the need to choose between single-index and additive models and reduces the likelihood of specification error. However, estimation with an unknown G is more difficult than it is for a single-index model or an additive model with a known link.

There is also a connection between additive and partially linear models. To see this, suppose that $d = 2$ and G is the identity function in (3.1), so the model is

$$E(Y|X = x) = \mu + m_1(x^1) + m_2(x^2). \tag{3.3}$$

Also suppose that X^1, the first component of the covariate X, is discrete and can take only J values. Denote these by x^{1j} $(j = 1, \ldots, J)$. Define $\beta_j = m_1(x^{1j})$ and $x_j = I(x^1 = x^{1j})$, where I is the indicator function. Let β and $\tilde{x}$, respectively, be the J-dimensional vectors whose jth elements are β_j and x_j. Then the additive model (3.3) is equivalent to the partially linear model

$$E(Y|X^1 = \tilde{x},\ X^2 = z) = \mu + \tilde{x}'\beta + m_2(z). \tag{3.4}$$

In applications with continuous covariates, it may be difficult to justify assuming that the conditional mean function is linear in some covariates but nonparametric in others. However, (3.4) shows that partial linearity arises naturally if some of the covariates are discrete and do not interact with the continuous covariates. Absence of interaction between discrete and continuous covariates means that the conditional mean function can be written as the sum of a function of the discrete covariates and a function of the continuous covariates.

Sections 3.1, 3.2, and 3.3 of this chapter discuss estimation of model (3.1a). Estimation of model (3.1b) is discussed in Section 3.4. Models (3.2a) and (3.2b) are discussed in Section 3.6. Section 3.5 presents an empirical example.

3.1 Nonparametric Additive Models with Identity Link Functions

This section is concerned with estimating the model

$$E(Y|X = x) = \mu + m_1(x^1) + \cdots + m_d(x^d), \tag{3.5}$$

where μ and the m_j s are defined as in (3.1) and X is a continuously distributed random vector. We describe three kinds of estimators of μ and the additive components m_j when the data consist of the simple random sample $\{Y_i, X_i: i = 1, \ldots, n\}$. The first method is called marginal integration. It is conceptually simple but can be hard to compute and does not work well when d is large. The other two methods are backfitting and a two-step procedure. The two-step procedure and a version of backfitting yield asymptotically normal, oracle-efficient estimators that have good properties even when d is large. The two-step procedure can easily be extended to estimate an additive model with a link function. This is done in Section 3.2.

The property of oracle efficiency is referred to repeatedly in the discussion of additive models and requires a precise definition. Suppose that $m_2, \ldots, m_d$ and μ were known. Then $m_1(x^1)$ could be estimated by carrying out the nonparametric regression of $Y - \mu - m_2(X^2) - \cdots - m_d(X^d)$ on X^1. Call the resulting estimator $\tilde{m}_1(x^1)$. Any estimator that has the same asymptotic distribution as $\tilde{m}_1(x^1)$ is called oracle efficient. If such an estimator can be found, then asymptotically there is no penalty for not knowing $m_2, \ldots, m_d$ and μ when estimating m_1.

It is important to use notation that distinguishes between observations and components of random vectors. Accordingly, in this chapter, X^j denotes the jth component of the random vector X, X_i denotes the ith observation of X, and X_i^j denotes the ith observation of the jth component of X.

3.1.1 Marginal Integration

This section describes a method called *marginal integration* for estimating μ and the additive components m_j in (3.5). To begin, observe that (3.5) is unchanged if each component m_j is replaced by $m_j + \alpha_j$ for some finite constant α_j and μ is replaced by $\mu - \alpha_1 - \cdots - \alpha_d$. Therefore, a *location normalization* that fixes μ and the m_js is needed to identify these quantities. In marginal integration, this is accomplished by setting

$$E[m_j(X^j)] = 0; j = 1,\ 2,\ \ldots,\ d. \tag{3.6}$$

This condition prevents replacing m_j with $m_j + \alpha_j$ for any nonzero α_j and, thereby, identifies μ and the m_js. We now consider estimation of μ and m_1. Other additive components can be estimated by swapping them with m_1.

Let $X^{(-1)}$ be the vector consisting of all components of X except X^1. Let p_{-1} denote the probability density function of $X^{(-1)}$. Then (3.5) and (3.6) imply that

$$\begin{aligned} E(Y) &= E[E(Y|X)] \\ &= \mu + \sum_{j=1}^{d} Em_j(X^j) \\ &= \mu. \end{aligned} \tag{3.7}$$

Moreover,

$$\int E(Y|X = x)p_{-1}(x^{(-1)})dx^{(-1)} = \mu + m_1(x^1),$$

so

$$m_1(x^1) = \int E(Y|X = x)p_{-1}(x^{(-1)})dx^{(-1)} - \mu. \tag{3.8}$$

Equations (3.7) and (3.8) express μ and $m_1(x^1)$ in terms of the population distribution of the observed random variables $(Y,\ X)$. We can estimate μ and m_1 by replacing unknown population quantities on the left-hand side of (3.7) and the right-hand side of (3.8) with consistent estimators. This gives the following estimator of μ:

$$\hat{\mu} = n^{-1}\sum_{i=1}^{n} Y_i.$$

To estimate $m_1(x^1)$, let $\hat{g}(x^1,\ x^{(-1)})$ be a kernel estimator of $E(Y|X^1 = x^1,\ X^{(-1)} = x^{(-1)})$. Specifically, let

$$\hat{g}(x^1,\ x^{(-1)}) = \hat{P}(x^1,\ x^{(-1)})^{-1}\sum_{i=1}^{n} Y_i K_1\left(\frac{x^1 - X_i^1}{h_1}\right)K_2\left(\frac{x^{(-1)} - X_i^{(-1)}}{h_2}\right), \tag{3.9}$$

where

$$\hat{P}(x^1,\ x^{(-1)}) = \sum_{i=1}^{n} K_1\left(\frac{x^1 - X_i^1}{h_1}\right) K_2\left(\frac{x^{(-1)} - X_i^{(-1)}}{h_2}\right),$$

K_1 is a kernel function of a scalar argument, K_2 is a kernel function of a $d-1$ dimensional argument, and h_1 and h_2 are bandwidths. Now observe that the integral on the right-hand side of (3.8) is the average of $E(Y|X^1 = x^1,\ X^{(-1)} = x^{(-1)})$ over $X^{(-1)}$. This can be estimated by the sample average of $\hat{g}(x^1,\ X^{(-1)})$. The resulting *marginal integration* estimator of m_1 is

$$\hat{m}_1(x^1) = n^{-1} \sum_{i=1}^{n} \hat{g}(x^1,\ X_i^{(-1)}) - \hat{\mu},$$

where $X_i^{(-1)}$ is the ith observation of $X^{(-1)}$.

The marginal integration estimator was first proposed by Linton and Nielsen (1995), who derived its asymptotic distributional properties for $d = 2$. Tjøstheim and Auestad (1994) present similar ideas in a different setting. Linton and Härdle (1996) derived the properties of the estimator for any finite d. They proved the following theorem.

Theorem 3.1: *Assume that*

(a) *Var*$(Y|X = x) \equiv \sigma^2(x)$ *is bounded and Lipschitz continuous.*

(b) *The functions* m_j *are* q *times continuously differentiable for some integer* $q > d - 1$.

(c) *Let* p *denote the density of* X. *Then* p *and* p_{-1} *are bounded away from 0 and are* q *times continuously differentiable.*

(d) *The kernel function* K_1 *is bounded, nonnegative, compactly supported, and Lipschitz continuous. It satisfies*

$$\int_{-1}^{1} K_1(z)dz = 1,$$

$$\int_{-1}^{1} zK_1(z)dz = 0,$$

and

$$\int_{-1}^{1} z^2 K_1(z)dz = A < \infty.$$

(e) *The kernel function* K_2 *has the form* $K_2(z) = \prod_{j=1}^{d-1} k_2(z^j)$, *where* k_2 *is bounded, compactly supported, and Lipschitz continuous. It satisfies*

$$\int_{-1}^{1} k_2(v)dv = 1$$

and

$$\int_{-1}^{1} v^j k_2(v)dv = 0; \;\; j = 1, \; \ldots, \; q-1$$

(f) *The bandwidths satisfy* $h_1 = c_1 n^{-1/5}$ *for some constant* $c_1 < \infty$, $n^{2/5} h_2^q \to 0$ *and* $n^{2/5} h_2^{d-1} \to \infty$ *as* $n \to \infty$.
Define

$$B = \int [K_1(z)]^2 dz.$$

Then

$$n^{2/5}[\hat{m}_1(x^1) - m_1(x^1)] \to^d n[\beta_1(x^1), \; v_1(x^1)],$$

where

$$\beta_1 = c_1^2 A \left[\frac{1}{2} m_1''(x^1) + m_1' \int \frac{\partial \log p(x)}{\partial x_1} p_{-1}(x^{(-1)}) dx^{(-1)} \right],$$

and

$$v_1(x^1) = c_1^{-1} B \int \sigma^2(x) \frac{p_{-1}^2(x^{(-1)})}{p(x)} dx^{(-1)}. \blacksquare$$

Under the assumptions of Theorem 3.1, the additive components m_j can be estimated with $n^{-2/5}$ rates of convergence. This is the fastest possible rate of convergence of an estimator of a twice-differentiable conditional mean function of a scalar argument. But the number of derivatives required by Theorem 3.1, $(d-1)$, is larger than two whenever $d > 3$. Thus, the marginal integration estimator suffers from a form of the curse of dimensionality in that more derivatives of the m_js and densities are needed to achieve the $n^{-2/5}$ rate as d increases. In addition, the marginal integration estimator is not oracle efficient. For example, if $\sigma^2(x) = \sigma^2$, where σ^2 is a constant, then

$$v_1(x^1) = c_1^{-1} B\sigma^2 \int \frac{p_{-1}^2(x^{(-1)})}{p(x)} dx^{(-1)}.$$

In contrast, the variance of the oracle-efficient estimator that is obtained from the nonparametric regression of $Y - m_2(X^2) - \cdots - m_d(X^d)$ on X^1 is $c_1^{-1} B\sigma^2 / p_1(x^1) \le v_1(x^1)$, where p_1 is the probability density function of X^1 (Linton 1997).

The marginal integration estimator has a curse of dimensionality because it begins with a full-dimensional nonparametric estimator of the conditional mean of Y. See (3.9). As a consequence, the finite-sample performance of the marginal integration estimator tends to be poor when d is large. If d is large, then there may be few data points within a bandwidth of any given point x, which causes the estimator to have a high variance and become numerically unstable. If a large bandwidth is chosen to reduce this problem, then the estimator may be badly biased.

There have been several refinements of the marginal integration estimator that enable it to achieve oracle efficiency or overcome the curse of dimensionality, but none of these refinements achieves both goals. Linton (1997) has shown that if $d = 2$, then an oracle-efficient estimator can be obtained by taking one step from a suitable marginal integration estimator. Specifically, define $\hat{U}_i = Y_i - \hat{\mu} - \hat{m}_2(X_i^2)$. Then an oracle-efficient estimator of $m_1(x^1)$ can be obtained as the value of β_0 in

$$(\beta_0, \beta_1) = \arg\min_{b_0, b_1} \sum_{i=1}^{n} [\hat{U}_i - b_0 - b_1'(X_i^1 - x^1)]^2 K_1\left(\frac{X_i^1 - x^1}{h_3}\right),$$

where h_3 is a bandwidth parameter. Fan et al. (1998) showed how to achieve oracle efficiency with arbitrary values of d. However, this method requires increasing smoothness of the additive components and density of X as d increases, so it does not avoid the curse of dimensionality.

Kim et al. (1999) proposed a modified marginal integration estimator that achieves oracle efficiency if the additive components and densities have enough derivatives. The modified estimator is also easier to compute than the original marginal integration estimator. To describe the modified estimator, let $m_{-1} = m_2 + \cdots + m_d$, and let p_1 denote the probability density function of X^1. Define

$$w(x) = \frac{p_1(x^1)p_{-1}(x^{(-1)})}{p(x)}.$$

Then

$$E[w(X)m_{-1}(X^{(-1)})|X^1 = x^1] = 0.$$

Therefore,

$$\mu + m_1(x^1) = E[Yw(X)|X^1 = x^1], \tag{3.10}$$

and $m_1(x^1)$ can be estimated by replacing the expectation and w on the right-hand side of (3.10) with sample analogs. The resulting estimate of $m_1(x^1)$ is

$$\hat{m}_1(x^1) = \frac{1}{nh}\sum_{i=1}^{n} Y_i K\left(\frac{x^1 - X_i^1}{h}\right)\frac{\hat{p}_{-1}(X_i^{(-1)})}{\hat{p}(X_i)} - \hat{\mu},$$

where $\hat{p}$ and $\hat{p}_{-1}$ are kernel estimators of p and p_{-1}, respectively. Achieving oracle efficiency requires an additional step. Define

$$\hat{U}_i = Y_i - \hat{\mu} - \hat{m}_2(X_i^2) - \cdots - \hat{m}_d(X_i^d),$$

where $\hat{m}_j$ is the modified marginal integration estimator of m_j, and define

$$S = \{x \in \mathbb{R}^d: \underline{b}_j + h \leq x^j \leq \bar{b}_j - h; \; j = 1, \; \ldots, \; d\},$$

where $\underline{b}_j$ and $\bar{b}_j$, respectively, are the lower and upper bounds of the support of x^j. The oracle-efficient estimator of $m_1(x^1)$ is α_0 in

$$(\alpha_0, \ldots, \alpha_{q-1}) = \min_{a_0, \ldots, a_{q-1}} \sum_{i=1}^{n} \left[\hat{U}_i - \sum_{j=0}^{q-1} a_j \left(X_i^1 - x^1 \right)^j \right] K_1 \left(\frac{x^1 - X_i^1}{h_1} \right) I(X_i \in S),$$

where h_1 is a bandwidth and q is the number of derivatives that the m_js and the densities have. Kim et al. (1999) show that α_0 is oracle efficient if the following conditions are satisfied.

KLH1. The kernel is bounded, symmetrical about 0, supported on $[-1, 1]$, and satisfies

$$\int_{-1}^{1} z^j K_1(z) dv = 0; \; j = 1, \; \ldots, \; q-1.$$

KLH2. The functions m_j ($j = 1, \ldots, d$) and p are $q - 1$ times continuously differentiable, where $q \geq (d-1)/2$.

KLH3. The density function p is bounded away from 0 and ∞ and supported on $[\underline{b}_1, \bar{b}_1] \times \cdots \times [\underline{b}_d, \bar{b}_d]$.

KLH4. $Var(Y|X = x)$ is Lipschitz continuous and bounded away from 0 and ∞.

KLH5. The bandwidths satisfy $h_1 = cn^{-1/(2q+1)}$ for some positive constant $c < \infty$ and $h = o[n^{-1/(2q+1)}]$ as $n \to \infty$.

The result of Kim et al. (1999) shows that an oracle-efficient estimator can be obtained from a marginal integration estimator if q is sufficiently large. But the estimator of Kim et al. requires full-dimensional nonparametric estimation of p, and the curse of dimensionality remains. That is, the number of derivatives that the m_js and p must have increases as d increases. Consequently, the estimator of Kim et al. (1999), like the estimator of Theorem 3.1, is likely to perform poorly when d is large.

Hengartner and Sperlich (2005) found a way to modify the marginal integration estimator so as to overcome the curse of dimensionality, though the resulting estimator is not oracle efficient. To describe their method, let $m_{-1}(x^{(-1)}) = m_2(x^2) + \cdots + m_d(x^d)$. Let π_1 and π_{-1} be sufficiently smooth density functions on

$\mathbb{R}$ and $\mathbb{R}^{d-1}$, respectively. Define $\pi = \pi_1\pi_{-1}$. Hengartner's and Sperlich's idea is to use the location normalization

$$\int m_1(x^1)\pi_1(x^1)dx^1 = 0 \tag{3.11}$$

and

$$\int m_{-1}(x^{(-1)})\pi_{-1}(x^{(-1)})dx^{(-1)} = 0 \tag{3.12}$$

instead of (3.6). The normalization (3.11) and (3.12) makes it possible to use the smoothness of π_1 to reduce the bias of the marginal integration estimator instead of using the smoothness of the m_js. Therefore, the m_js do not need to be as smooth as in marginal integration methods based on (3.6). The avoidance of a need for smoothness of m_js enables Hengartner's and Sperlich's estimator to overcome the curse of dimensionality.

To describe the estimator, let K_1 be a kernel function of a scalar argument and K_2 be a kernel function of a $d-1$ dimensional argument. Let $\hat{p}$ be a kernel estimator of p. Let h_1 and h_2 be bandwidths. Define

$$\tilde{g}(x^1, x^{(-1)}) = \frac{1}{nh_1h_2^{d-1}}\sum_{i=1}^{n}\frac{Y_i}{\hat{p}(X_i)}K_1\left(\frac{x^1 - X_i^1}{h_1}\right)K_2\left(\frac{x^{(-1)} - X_i^{(-1)}}{h_2}\right).$$

Observe that $\tilde{g}(x)$ is a kind of kernel estimator of $E(Y|X = x)$. The estimator of $m_1(x^1)$ is

$$\begin{aligned}\hat{m}_1(x^1) = &\int \tilde{g}(x^1, x^{(-1)})\pi_{-1}(x^{(-1)})dx^{(-1)} \\ &- \int \tilde{g}(z, x^{(-1)})\pi(z, x^{(-1)})dzdx^{(-1)}.\end{aligned} \tag{3.13}$$

This estimator can be understood intuitively by observing that if g replaces $\tilde{g}$ in (3.13), then the location normalization (3.11) and (3.12) implies that the right-hand side of (3.13) equals $m_1(x^1)$. The following theorem, which is proved in Hengartner and Sperlich (2005), gives the asymptotic behavior of the estimator (3.13).

Theorem 3.2: *Assume that*

(a) *The conditional mean function $g(x)$ is s times continuously differentiable in x^1. The conditional variance function $\sigma^2(x)$ is finite and Lipschitz continuous.*
(b) *The density function p is compactly supported, Lipschitz continuous, and bounded away from 0 and ∞ in the interior of the support.*
(c) *The density of $X^{(-1)}$ conditional on X^1 is bounded away from 0 everywhere in the support of X.*

(d) *The density* π *is continuous and bounded away from 0 and* ∞ *on its support, which is contained in the support of* X *. Moreover, the density* π_1 *has* $s+1$ *continuous, bounded derivatives.*

(e) *The kernels* K_1 *and* K_2 *are compactly supported and Lipschitz continuous.* K_1 *satisfies*

$$\int_{-1}^{1} z^j K_1(z)dz = 0; j = 1, \ldots, s-1,$$

$$\int_{-1}^{1} z^s K_1(z)dz = A > 0,$$

$$\int_{-1}^{1} K_1(z)^2 dz = B.$$

(f) *The bandwidths satisfy* $h_1 = n^{-1/(2s+1)}$, $h_2 = o(1)$, *and* $nh_2^d \to \infty$ *as* $n \to \infty$.

Then

$$(nh_1)^{1/2}[\hat{m}_1(x^1) - m_1(x^1)] \xrightarrow{d} N[\beta(x^1),\ v_1(x^1)],$$

where

$$\beta_1(x^1) = A\left[\frac{1}{p_1(x^1)}\frac{d^2}{dx_1^s}m_1(x^1) - \int m_1(z)\frac{d^2}{dz^2}\pi_1(z)dz\right],$$

$$v_1(x^1) = B\frac{\omega(x^1,\ x^1)}{p_1(x^1)},$$

$$\omega(z^1,\ x^1) = \int [\sigma^2(x) + g(x)^2]\frac{\pi_{-1}(x^{(-1)})p_1(x^1)}{p(x)}dx^{(-1)} - \left[\int g(z)\frac{p(z)p_1(x^1)}{p_1(z^1)p(x^1,z^{(-1)})}\pi_{-1}(z^{(-1)})dz^{(-1)}\right]^2,$$

and p_1 *is the density of* x^1.■

Theorem 3.2 imposes no smoothness requirements on π_{-1}. Therefore, this density can be set equal to the Dirac delta function centered at any $x^{(-1)}$. This yields

$$m_1(x^1) = \tilde{g}(x^1,\ x^{(-1)}) - \int \tilde{g}(z,\ x^{(-1)})\pi_1(z)dz$$

for any $x^{(-1)}$ in the support of $X^{(-1)}$.

The assumptions of Theorem 3.2 do not require s to increase as d increases. Therefore, the estimator (3.13) avoids the curse of dimensionality. The estimator is not oracle efficient, however, and it is not known whether oracle efficiency can be obtained by taking an additional step as in Linton (1997) and Kim et al. (1999).

Hengartner and Sperlich (2005) do not explore how the density π should be chosen in applications.

The next two sections describe estimation methods that avoid the curse of dimensionality and, in some cases, achieve oracle efficiency. The method of Section 3.1.3 is extended in Section 3.2 to estimate an additive model with a nonidentity link function.

3.1.2 Backfitting

Backfitting is an estimation procedure for model (3.1) that is implemented in many statistical software packages. To describe the procedure, define

$$W_i^j = Y_i - \mu - \sum_{k \neq j} m_k(X_i^k)$$

for $j = 1, \ldots, d$. Write model (3.1) as

$$W_i^j = m_j(X_i^j) + U_i. \tag{3.14}$$

If W_j^i were known, then oracle efficiency could be achieved by estimating m_j in (3.14) nonparametrically, but W_i^j is not known. To obtain a feasible estimator, let $\hat{\mu}^0, \hat{m}_2^0, \ldots, \hat{m}_d^0$ be preliminary estimates of $\mu, m_2, \ldots, m_d$. Set

$$\hat{W}_{i,\,0}^1 = Y_i - \hat{\mu}^0 - \sum_{j=2}^{d} \hat{m}_j^0(X_i^j).$$

Backfitting now proceeds as follows:

1. Estimate m_1 by nonparametric regression of $\hat{W}_{i,\,0}^1$ on X_i^1. Denote the resulting estimate by $\hat{m}_1^1$.
2. Set $\hat{W}_{i,\,1}^2 = Y_i - \hat{\mu}^0 - \hat{m}_1^1(X_i^1) - \sum_{j=3}^{d} \hat{m}_j^0(X_i^j)$.
3. Estimate m_2 by nonparametric regression of $\hat{W}_{i,\,1}^2$ on X_i^2. Denote the resulting estimate by $\hat{m}_2^1$.
4. Set $\hat{W}_{i,\,1}^3 = Y_i - \hat{\mu}^0 - \hat{m}_1^1(X_i^1) - \hat{m}_2^1(X_i^2) - \sum_{j=4}^{d} \hat{m}_j^0(X_i^j)$.
5. Estimate m_3 by nonparametric regression of $\hat{W}_{i,\,1}^3$ on X_i^3. Denote the resulting estimate by $\hat{m}_3^1$.
6. Continue until all additive components have been estimated. Then return to Step 1 but with $\hat{m}_j^1$ $(j = 2, \ldots, d)$ in place of $\hat{m}_j^0$.
7. Iterate Steps 1–6 until convergence is achieved.

This estimation procedure was first proposed by Buja et al. (1989) and further developed by Hastie and Tibshirani (1990). Backfitting does not require full-dimensional nonparametric estimation, so one might hope that it avoids the curse of dimensionality. However, investigation of the statistical properties of the backfitting procedure is difficult because the estimator is defined as the limit (if it exists) of a sequence of iterations, rather than by an analytic formula. Opsomer and Ruppert (1997) and Opsomer (2000) investigated the properties of a version of backfitting and found, among other things, that the estimator is not oracle efficient. They also required strong restrictions on the distribution of X.

Mammen et al. (1999) and Mammen and Park (2006) have found ways to modify backfitting to achieve estimators that are oracle efficient, asymptotically normal, and free of the curse of dimensionality. The modified estimators are the solutions to systems of linear integral equations. The equations cannot be solved analytically, but the solutions can be approached numerically through sequences of successive approximations that are similar (though not identical) to the sequence used in backfitting. The details are lengthy. Rather than present them here, we explain a simpler, noniterative, two-step estimator that is easy to implement, asymptotically normal, and oracle efficient. The two-step method can be extended easily to models with nonidentity link functions (see Section 3.2) and estimation of conditional quantile functions (see Section 3.4).

3.1.3 Two-Step, Oracle-Efficient Estimation

This section describes an estimation procedure that was developed by Horowitz and Mammen (2004). The procedure does not use d-dimensional nonparametric regression and avoids the curse of dimensionality. Estimation takes place in two stages. In the first stage, ordinary least squares is used to obtain a series approximation to each m_j. Nonparametric series approximations are explained in the Appendix. The first-stage procedure imposes the additive structure of (3.1), thereby avoiding the need for d-dimensional nonparametric estimation. This enables the estimator to avoid the curse of dimensionality. However, it is hard to establish the asymptotic distributional properties of series estimators. To overcome this problem, the Horowitz–Mammen procedure uses the first-stage estimates as inputs to a second stage whose output is an asymptotically normal, oracle-efficient estimator of each additive component. The second-stage estimates, like the first-stage ones, avoid the curse of dimensionality.

To describe the second-stage procedure, let $\tilde{\mu}$, $\tilde{m}_2$, $\ldots$, $\tilde{m}_d$ denote the first-stage series estimates of μ, m_2, $\ldots$, m_d. Then second-stage estimate of m_1 is obtained by carrying out the kernel or local-linear nonparametric regression of $Y - \tilde{\mu} - \tilde{m}_2(X^2) - \cdots - \tilde{m}_d(X^d)$ on X^1. The local-linear estimator has better behavior near the boundaries of the support of X and adapts better to nonuniform designs (Fan and Gijbels 1996), but it does not necessarily have better numerical performance in finite samples. In large samples, the second-stage estimator has the structure of an ordinary kernel estimator or local-linear estimator, so deriving its pointwise rate of convergence and asymptotic distribution is relatively easy.

3.1.3.1 Informal Description of the Estimator

Assume that the support of X is $\mathcal{X} \equiv [-1,\ 1]^d$, and normalize $m_1,\ \ldots,\ m_d$ so that

$$\int_{-1}^{1} m_j(v)dv = 0;\ \ j = 1,\ \ldots,\ d.$$

For any $x \in \mathbb{R}^d$ define $m(x) = m_1(x^1) + \cdots + m_d(x^d)$, where x^j is the jth component of x. Let $\{\psi_k\colon k = 1,\ 2,\ \ldots\}$ denote a basis for smooth functions on $[-1,\ 1]$. A precise definition of "smooth" and conditions that the basis functions must satisfy are given in Section 3.1.3.2. These conditions include

$$\int_{-1}^{1} \psi_k(v)dv = 0; \tag{3.15}$$

$$\int_{-1}^{1} \psi_j(v)\psi_k(v)dv = \begin{cases} 1 \text{ if } j = k \\ 0 \text{ otherwise} \end{cases}; \tag{3.16}$$

and

$$m_j(x^j) = \sum_{k=1}^{\infty} \theta_{jk}\psi_k(x^j)$$

for each $j = 1,\ \ldots,\ d$, each $x^j \in [-1,\ 1]$, and suitable coefficients $\{\theta_{jk}\}$. For any positive integer κ, define

$$\begin{aligned} \Psi_\kappa(x) =& [1,\ \psi_1(x^1),\ \ldots,\ \psi_\kappa(x^1),\ \psi_1(x^2),\ \ldots,\ \psi_\kappa(x^2),\ \ldots, \\ & \psi_1(x^d),\ \ldots \psi_\kappa(x^d)]'. \end{aligned} \tag{3.17}$$

Then for $\theta_\kappa \in \mathbb{R}^{\kappa d+1}$, $\Psi_\kappa(x)'\theta_\kappa$ is a series approximation to $\mu + m(x)$. Section 3.1.3.2 gives conditions that κ must satisfy. These require that $\kappa \to \infty$ at an appropriate rate as $n \to \infty$.

To obtain the first-stage estimators of the m_js, let $\{Y_i,\ X_i\colon i = 1,\ \ldots,\ n\}$ be a random sample of $(Y,\ X)$. Let $\hat{\theta}_{n\kappa}$ be the solution to the ordinary least-squares estimation problem:

$$\underset{\theta \in \Theta_\kappa}{\text{minimize}}\colon S_{n\kappa}(\theta) \equiv n^{-1}\sum_{i=1}^{n} [Y_i - \Psi_\kappa(X_i)'\theta]^2,$$

where $\Theta_\kappa \subset \mathbb{R}^{\kappa d+1}$ is a compact parameter set. The first-stage series estimator of $\mu + m(x)$ is

$$\tilde{\mu} + \tilde{m}(x) = \Psi_\kappa(x)'\hat{\theta}_{n\kappa},$$

where $\tilde{\mu}$ is the first component of $\hat{\theta}_{n\kappa}$. The estimator of $m_j(x^j)$ for any $j = 1, \ldots, d$ and any $x^j \in [-1, 1]$ is the product of $[\psi_1(x^j), \ldots, \psi_\kappa(x^j)]$ with the appropriate components of $\hat{\theta}_{n\kappa}$. There is no curse of dimensionality in this estimator because all the estimated functions have scalar arguments.

We now describe the second-stage kernel (or local constant) estimator of (say) $m_1(x^1)$. Let $X_i^{(-1)}$ denote the ith observation of $X^{(-1)} \equiv (X^2, \ldots, X^d)$. Define $\tilde{m}_{-1}(X_i^{(-1)}) = \tilde{m}_2(X_i^2) + \cdots + \tilde{m}_d(X_i^d)$, where X_i^j is the ith observation of the jth component of X and $\tilde{m}_j$ is the series estimator of m_j. Let K be a probability density function on $[-1, 1]$ and h be a real, positive constant. Conditions that K and h must satisfy are given in Section 3.1.3.2 These include $h \to 0$ at an appropriate rate as $n \to \infty$. The second-stage estimator of $m_1(x^1)$ is

$$\hat{m}_{1,\,K}(x^1) = \left[\sum_{i=1}^{n} K\left(\frac{x^1 - X_i^1}{h}\right)\right]^{-1} \sum_{i=1}^{n} [Y_i - \tilde{m}_{-1}(X_i^{(-1)})] K\left(\frac{x^1 - X_i^1}{h}\right), \quad (3.18)$$

where the subscript K indicates that $\hat{m}_{1,\,K}$ is the kernel second-stage estimator. In fact, $\hat{m}_{1,\,K}$ is simply the Nadaraya–Watson kernel regression of $Y - \tilde{m}_{-1}(X^{(-1)})$ on X^1.

The local-linear version of the second-stage estimator is obtained by replacing the kernel regression with the local-linear regression of $Y - \tilde{m}_{-1}(X^{(-1)})$ on X^1. Accordingly, the local-linear estimator of $m_1(x^1)$ is $\hat{m}_{1,\,LL}(x^1) = \hat{b}_0$, where $\hat{b}_0$ solves the problem

$$\underset{b_0,\, b_1}{\text{minimize}}: S_n(x^1, b_0, b_1) = \sum_{i=1}^{n} [Y_i - b_0 - b_1(X_i^1 - x^1) - \tilde{\mu} - \tilde{m}_{-1}(X_i^{(-1)})]^2 \\ K\left(\frac{x^1 - X_i^1}{h}\right).$$

Section 3.1.3.2 gives conditions under which $\hat{m}_{1,\,K}(x^1)$ and $\hat{m}_{1,\,LL}(x^1)$ are $n^{-2/5}$ consistent, asymptotically normal, and oracle efficient for any finite d when the m_js are twice continuously differentiable. Thus, the second-stage estimators converge at the optimal rate for estimating a twice-differentiable conditional mean function of a scalar argument. This result holds for any finite d, so there is no curse of dimensionality.

3.1.3.2 Asymptotic Properties of the Two-Stage Estimator

This section begins by stating the assumptions that are used to prove that the two-stage estimator is asymptotically normal and oracle efficient.

The following additional notation is used. For any matrix A, define the matrix norm $\|A\| = [trace(A'A)]^{1/2}$. Define $U = Y - \mu + m(X)$, $V(x) = Var(U|X = x)$, $Q_\kappa = E[\Psi_\kappa(X)\Psi_\kappa(X)']$, and $\Upsilon_\kappa = Q_\kappa^{-1} E\{[m(X)]^2 V(X)\Psi_\kappa(X)\Psi_\kappa(X)'\}Q_\kappa^{-1}$ whenever the latter quantity exists. Q_κ and Υ_κ are $d(\kappa) \times d(\kappa)$ positive-semidefinite matrices, where $d(\kappa) = \kappa d + 1$. Let $\lambda_{\kappa,\ \min}$ denote the smallest eigenvalue of Q_κ. Let $Q_{\kappa,\ ij}$ denote the $(i,\ j)$ element of Q_κ. Define $\zeta_\kappa = \sup_{x\in\mathcal{X}} \|\Psi_\kappa(x)\|$. Let $\{\theta_{jk}\}$ be the coefficients of the series expansion of m_j. For each κ define

$$\theta_\kappa = (\mu,\ \theta_{11},\ \ldots,\ \theta_{1\kappa},\ \theta_{21},\ \ldots,\ \theta_{2\kappa},\ \ldots,\ \theta_{d1},\ \ldots,\ \theta_{d\kappa})'.$$

The assumptions are

ADD1: The data, $\{Y_i,\ X_i\colon i = 1,\ \ldots,\ n\}$, are a simple random sample from the distribution of $(Y,\ X)$. Moreover, $E(Y|X = x) = \mu + m(x)$ for almost every $x \in \mathcal{X} \equiv [-1,\ 1]^d$.

ADD2: (i) The support of X is $\mathcal{X}$. (ii) The distribution of X is absolutely continuous with respect to Lebesgue measure. (iii) The probability density function of X is bounded, bounded away from zero, and twice continuously differentiable on $\mathcal{X}$. (iv) There are constants $c_V > 0$ and $C_V < \infty$ such that $c_V \le Var(U|X = x) \le C_V$ for all $x \in \mathcal{X}$. (v) There is a constant $C_U < \infty$ such that $E|U|^j \le C_U^{j-2} j! E(U^2) < \infty$ for all $j \ge 2$.

ADD3: (i) There is a constant $C_m < \infty$ such that $|m_j(v)| \le C_m$ for each $j = 1,\ \ldots,\ d$ and all $v \in [-1,\ 1]$. (ii) Each function m_j is twice continuously differentiable on $[-1,\ 1]$.

ADD4: (i) There are constants $C_Q < \infty$ and $c_\lambda > 0$ such that $|Q_{\kappa,\ ij}| \le C_Q$ and $\lambda_{\kappa,\ \min} > c_\lambda$ for all κ and all $i,\ j = 1,\ \ldots,\ d(\kappa)$. (ii) The largest eigenvalue of Ψ_κ is bounded for all κ.

ADD5: (i) The functions $\{\psi_k\}$ satisfy (3.15) and (3.16). (ii) There is a constant $c_\kappa > 0$ such that $\zeta_\kappa \ge c_\kappa$ for all sufficiently large κ. (iii) $\zeta_\kappa = O(\kappa^{1/2})$ as $\kappa \to \infty$. (iv) There are a constant $C_\theta < \infty$ and vectors $\theta_{\kappa 0} \in \Theta_\kappa \equiv [-C_\theta,\ C_\theta]^{d(\kappa)}$ such that $\sup_{x\in\mathcal{X}} |\mu + m(x) - \Psi_\kappa(x)'\theta_{\kappa 0}| = O(\kappa^{-2})$ as $\kappa \to \infty$. (v) For each κ, θ_κ is an interior point of Θ_κ.

ADD6: (i) $\kappa = C_\kappa n^{4/15+\nu}$ for some constant C_κ satisfying $0 < C_\kappa < \infty$ and some ν satisfying $0 < \nu < 1/30$. (ii) $h = C_h n^{-1/5}$ for some constant C_h satisfying $0 < C_h < \infty$.

ADD7: The function K is a bounded, continuous probability density function on $[-1,\ 1]$ and is symmetrical about 0.

The assumption that the support of X is $[-1,\ 1]^d$ entails no loss of generality as it can always be satisfied by carrying out monotone increasing transformations of the components of X, even if their support before transformation is unbounded. For practical computations, it suffices to transform the empirical support to $[-1,\ 1]^d$. Assumption ADD2 precludes the possibility of treating discrete covariates, though they can be handled inelegantly by conditioning on them. Differentiability of the density of X, assumption 2(iii), ensures that the bias of the estimator converges to zero sufficiently rapidly. Assumption 2(v) restricts the thickness of the tails of the distribution of U and is used to prove consistency of the first-stage estimator. Assumption ADD3 defines the sense in which m_js must be smooth. Assumption ADD4 insures the existence and nonsingularity of the covariance matrix of the asymptotic form of the first-stage estimator. This is analogous to assuming that the information matrix is positive definite in parametric maximum-likelihood estimation. Assumption ADD4(i) implies ADD4(ii) if U is homoskedastic. Assumptions ADD5(iii) and ADD5(iv) bound the magnitudes of the basis functions and ensure that the errors in the series approximations to the m_js converge to zero sufficiently rapidly as $\kappa \to \infty$. These assumptions are satisfied by spline and (for periodic functions) Fourier bases. The bias of series approximations is discussed further in the Appendix. Assumption ADD6 states the rates at which $\kappa \to \infty$ and $h \to 0$ as $n \to \infty$. The assumed rate of convergence of h is asymptotically optimal for one-dimensional kernel mean regression when the conditional mean function is twice continuously differentiable. The required rate for κ ensures that the asymptotic bias and variance of the first-stage estimator are sufficiently small to achieve an $n^{-2/5}$ rate of convergence in the second stage. The rate of convergence of the integrated mean-square error of a series estimator of m_j is maximized by setting $\kappa \propto n^{1/5}$, which is slower than the rates permitted by assumption ADD6(i) (Newey 1997). Thus, assumption ADD6(i) requires the first-stage estimator to be undersmoothed. Undersmoothing is needed to ensure sufficiently rapid convergence of the bias of the first-stage estimator. Horowitz and Mammen (2004) show that the first-order performance of the second-stage estimator does not depend on the choice of κ if assumption ADD6(i) is satisfied. See Theorems 3.4 and 3.5 below. Optimizing the choice of κ would require a rather complicated higher-order theory and is beyond the scope of this discussion.

We now state three theorems that give the asymptotic properties of the two-stage estimator. The theorems are proved in Horowitz and Mammen (2004). Theorem 3.3 gives the asymptotic behavior of the first-stage series estimator under assumptions ADD1–ADD6(i). Theorem 3.4 gives the properties of the second-stage kernel estimator. Theorem 3.5 gives the properties of the second-stage local-linear estimator.

For $i = 1, \ldots, n$, define $U_i = Y_i - \mu + m(X_i)$ and $b_{\kappa 0}(x) = \mu + m(x) - \Psi_\kappa(x)'\theta_{\kappa 0}$. Let $\|v\|$ denote the Euclidean norm of any finite-dimensional vector v.

Theorem 3.3: *Let assumptions ADD1–ADD6(i) hold. Then*

(a) $\lim_{n\to\infty} \left\|\hat{\theta}_{n\kappa} - \theta_{\kappa 0}\right\| = 0$

almost surely,

(b) $\hat{\theta}_{n\kappa} - \theta_{\kappa 0} = O_p(\kappa^{1/2}/n^{1/2} + \kappa^{-2}),$

and

(c) $\sup_{x\in\mathcal{X}} |\tilde{m}(x) - m(x)| = O_p(\kappa/n^{1/2} + \kappa^{-3/2}).$

In addition,

$$(d)\ \hat{\theta}_{n\kappa} - \theta_{\kappa 0} = n^{-1}Q_\kappa^{-1}\sum_{i=1}^{n}\Psi_\kappa(X_i)U_i + n^{-1}Q_\kappa^{-1}\sum_{i=1}^{n}\Psi_\kappa(X_i)b_{\kappa 0}(X_i) + R_n,$$

where $\|R_n\| = O_p(\kappa^{3/2}/n + n^{-1/2})$. ■

Parts (a–c) of Theorem 3.3 establish the uniform consistency and uniform rate of convergence of the series estimator. These are standard properties of series estimators that are derived, for example, by Newey (1997). Part (d) provides an asymptotic representation that is used to derive the properties of the second-stage estimators.

Now let f_X and f_1, respectively, denote the probability density function of X and X^1. Define

$$S'_{n1}(x^1, m) = -2\sum_{i=1}^{n}[Y_i - \mu - m_1(x^1) - m_{-1}(X_i^{(-1)})]K\left(\frac{x^1 - X_i^1}{h}\right).$$

Also define

$$A_K = \int_{-1}^{1} v^2 K(v)dv,$$

$$B_K = \int_{-1}^{1} K(v)^2 dv,$$

$$g(x^1, x^{(-1)}) = (\partial^2/\partial\zeta^2)\Big\{[m_1(\zeta + x^1) + m_{-1}(x^{(-1)})] - [m_1(x^1) + m_{-1}(x^{(-1)})]\Big\} f_X(\zeta + x^1, x^{(-1)})\Big|_{\zeta=0},$$

$$\beta_1(x^1) = C_h^2 A_K f_1(x^1)^{-1}\int g(x^1, x^{(-1)}) f_X(x^1, x^{(-1)})dx^{(-1)},$$

and

$$V_1(x^1) = B_K C_h^{-1}[4f_1(x^1)]^{-2}\int Var(U|x^1, x^{(-1)}) f_X(x^1, x^{(-1)})dx^{(-1)}.$$

Theorem 3.4: *Let assumptions ADD1–ADD7 hold. Then*

(a) $\hat{m}_{1,K}(x^1) - m_1(x^1) = -[2nhf_1(x^1)]^{-1}S'_{n1}(x^1, m) + o_p(n^{-2/5})$, *uniformly over* $|x^1| \le 1 - h$ *and* $\hat{m}_{1,K}(x^1) - m_1(x^1) = O_p[(\log n)^{1/2} n^{-2/5}]$ *uniformly over* $|x^1| \le 1$.
(b) $n^{2/5}[\hat{m}_{1,K}(x^1) - m_1(x^1)] \xrightarrow{d} N[\beta_1(x^1), V_1(x^1)]$.
(c) If $j \ne 1$, *then* $n^{2/5}[\hat{m}_{1,K}(x^1) - m_1(x^1)]$ *and* $n^{2/5}[\hat{m}_{j,K}(x^j) - m_j(x^j)]$ *are asymptotically independently normally distributed.*■

Theorem 3.4(a) implies that asymptotically, $n^{2/5}[\hat{m}_{1,K}(x^1) - m_1(x^1)]$ is not affected by random sampling errors in the first-stage estimator. In fact, the second-stage kernel estimator of $m_1(x^1)$ has the same asymptotic distribution that it would have if $m_2, \ldots, m_d$ were known and kernel estimation were used to estimate $m_1(x^1)$ directly. This is the oracle-efficiency property. Parts (b) and (c) of Theorem 3.4 imply that the estimators of $m_1(x^1), \ldots, m_d(x^d)$ are asymptotically independently normally distributed with $n^{-2/5}$ rates of convergence. These rates do not depend on d, so there is no curse of dimensionality.

The oracle-efficiency result can be understood intuitively by observing that $\hat{m}_{1,\ K}$ would be oracle efficient by definition if $\tilde{m}_{-1}$ could be replaced by m_{-1} in (3.18). The use of $\tilde{m}_{-1}$ contributes bias and variance to $\hat{m}_{1,\ K}$. However, the bias is asymptotically negligible because $\tilde{m}_{-1}$ is undersmoothed (assumption ADD6(i)). Undersmoothing increases the variance of $\tilde{m}_{-1}$, but (3.18) averages $\tilde{m}_{-1}$, and averaging reduces variance. The combination of bias reduction through undersmoothing and variance reduction through averaging makes $\hat{m}_{1,\ K}$ oracle efficient.

Theorem 3.5 extends the results of Theorem 3.4 to the local-linear estimator. We need the following additional notation. For $j = 0,\ 1$, define

$$S'_{nj1}(x^1,\ m) = -2\sum_{i=1}^{n}[Y_i - \mu - m_1(x^1) - m_{-1}(\tilde{X}_i)]\}(X_i^1 - x^1)^j K_h(x^1 - X_i^1).$$

Also define

$$\beta_{1,\ LL}(x^1) = C_h^2 A_K m_1''(x^1) f_1(x^1).$$

The theorem is as follows.

Theorem 3.5: *Let assumptions ADD1–ADD7 hold. Then*

(a) $\hat{m}_{1,\ LL}(x^1) - m_1(x^1) = [2nhf_1(x^1)]^{-1}\{-S'_{n01}(x^1,\ m) + [f_1'(x^1)/f_1(x^1)] S'_{n11}(x^1,\ m)\} + o_p(n^{-2/5})$ *uniformly over* $|x^1| \leq 1-h$ *and* $\hat{m}_{1,\ LL}(x^1) - m_1(x^1) = O_p[(\log n)^{1/2} n^{-2/5}]$ *uniformly over* $|x^1| \leq 1$.

(b) $n^{2/5}[\hat{m}_{1,\ LL}(x^1) - m_1(x^1)] \xrightarrow{d} N[\beta_{1,\ LL}(x^1),\ V_1(x^1)]$

(c) *If* $j \neq 1$, *then* $n^{2/5}[\hat{m}_{1,\ LL}(x^1) - m_1(x^1)]$ *and* $n^{2/5}[\hat{m}_{j,\ LL}(x^j) - m_j(x^j)]$ *are asymptotically independently normally distributed.*■

Theorem 3.4 implies that the second-stage local-linear estimator of $m_1(x^1)$ has the same asymptotic distribution that it would have if $m_2,\ \ldots,\ m_d$ were known and local-linear estimation were used to estimate $m_1(x^1)$ directly. Thus, like the kernel estimator, the local-linear estimator is oracle efficient. Theorem 3.4 also implies that the local-linear estimators of $m_1(x^1),\ \ldots,\ m_d(x^d)$ are asymptotically independently normally distributed with $n^{-2/5}$ rates of convergence and that there is no curse of dimensionality.

3.2 Estimation with a Nonidentity Link Function

This section extends the two-stage method of Section 3.1.3 to estimation of the model

$$E(Y|X = x) = G[\mu + m_1(x^1) + \cdots + m_d(x^d)], \tag{3.19}$$

where G is a known function that is not necessarily the identity function. As in the case of an identity link function, the first estimation stage consists of obtaining a series estimator of the m_js. This is done by using nonlinear least squares to estimate the coefficients of the series approximation. The additive structure is imposed through the series approximation, thereby avoiding the curse of dimensionality. The second estimation stage consists of taking one Newton step from the first-stage estimate toward a local-linear or local constant estimate. In large samples, the second-stage estimator of each additive component has the structure of a local-linear or local constant estimate in which the other components are known. This implies that the second-stage estimator is oracle efficient and asymptotically normal. Yu et al. (2008) give an alternative method for estimating (3.19). This method is more complicated than the one described here but can have better finite-sample accuracy when the covariates are highly correlated.

3.2.1 Estimation

This section describes the estimator of the additive components in (3.19). The results are proved in Horowitz and Mammen (2004). As before, let $\{\psi_k: k = 1, 2, \ldots\}$ denote a basis for smooth functions on $[-1, 1]$. Assume that $\{\psi_k\}$ satisfies (3.15) and (3.16). Define Ψ_κ as in (3.17). Let $\{Y_i, X_i: i = 1, \ldots, n\}$ be a random sample of (Y, X). To obtain the first-stage estimator, let $\hat{\theta}_{n\kappa}$ be a solution to

$$\underset{\theta \in \Theta_\kappa}{\text{minimize}}: S_{n\kappa}(\theta) \equiv n^{-1} \sum_{i=1}^{n} \{Y_i - G[\Psi_\kappa(X_i)'\theta]\}^2,$$

where $\Theta_\kappa \subset \mathbb{R}^{\kappa d+1}$ is a compact parameter set. Thus, first-stage estimation with a nonidentity link function is like estimation with an identity link function except that nonlinear least squares is used instead of ordinary least squares. As with an identity link function, the series estimator of $\mu + m(x)$ is $\tilde{\mu} + \tilde{m}(x) = \Psi_\kappa(x)'\hat{\theta}_{n\kappa}$, where $\tilde{\mu}$ is the first component of $\hat{\theta}_{n\kappa}$, and the estimator of $m_j(x^j)$ for any $j = 1, \ldots, d$ and any $x^j \in [0, 1]$ is the product of $[\psi_1(x^j), \ldots, \psi_\kappa(x^j)]$ with the appropriate components of $\hat{\theta}_\kappa$.

We now describe the second-stage kernel (local constant) estimator of (say) $m_1(x^1)$. As in Section 3.1.3, let $X_i^{(-1)}$ denote the ith observation of $X^{(-1)} \equiv (X^2, \ldots, X^d)$, and define $\tilde{m}_{-1}(X_i^{(-1)}) = \tilde{m}_2(X_i^2) + \cdots + \tilde{m}_d(X_i^d)$, where $\tilde{m}_j$ is the series estimator of m_j. Let K and h be the kernel and bandwidth, respectively. Define

$$S'_{n1}(x^1, \tilde{m}) = -2\sum_{i=1}^{n}\{Y_i - G[\tilde{\mu} + \tilde{m}_1(x^1) + \tilde{m}_{-1}(X_i^{(-1)})]\} \\ G'[\tilde{\mu} + \tilde{m}_1(x^1) + \tilde{m}_{-1}(X_i^{(-1)})]K\left(\frac{x^1 - X_i^1}{h}\right)$$

and

$$
\begin{aligned}
S''_{n1}(x^1,\ \tilde{m}) =& 2\sum_{i=1}^{n} G'[\tilde{\mu} + \tilde{m}_1(x^1) + \tilde{m}_{-1}(X_i^{(-1)})]^2 K\left(\frac{x^1 - X_i^1}{h}\right) \\
& - 2\sum_{i=1}^{n} \{Y_i - G[\tilde{\mu} + \tilde{m}_1(x^1) + \tilde{m}_{-1}(X_i^{(-1)})]\} \\
& G''[\tilde{\mu} + \tilde{m}_1(x^1) + \tilde{m}_{-1}(X_i^{(-1)})]K\left(\frac{x^1 - X_i^1}{h}\right).
\end{aligned}
$$

The second-stage estimator of $m_1(x^1)$ is

$$
\hat{m}_1(x^1) = \tilde{m}_1(x^1) - S'_{n1}(x^1,\ \tilde{m})/S''_{n1}(x^1,\ \tilde{m}). \tag{3.20}
$$

The second-stage estimators of $m_2(x^2),\ \ldots,\ m_d(x^d)$ are obtained similarly.

The estimator (3.20) can be understood intuitively by observing that if $\tilde{\mu}$ and $\tilde{m}_{-1}$ were the true values of μ and m_{-1}, then $m_1(x^1)$ could be estimated by the value of b that minimizes

$$
S_{n1}(x^1,\ b) = \sum_{i=1}^{n} \{Y_i - G[\tilde{\mu} + b + \tilde{m}_{-1}(X_i^{(-1)})]\}^2 K\left(\frac{x^1 - X_i^1}{h}\right). \tag{3.21}
$$

The estimator (3.20) is the result of taking one Newton step from the starting value $b_0 = \tilde{m}_1(x^1)$ toward the minimum of the right-hand side of (3.21).

Describing the asymptotic distributional properties of the second-stage estimator requires modifying some of the notation and assumptions of Section 3.1.3. Define A_K and B_K as in Section 3.1.3, $U = Y - G[\mu + m(X)]$, and $V(x) = Var(U|X = x)$. Redefine $Q_\kappa = E\{G'[\mu + m(X)]^2 \Psi_\kappa(X)\Psi_\kappa(X)'\}$, and $\Upsilon_\kappa = Q_\kappa^{-1} E\{G'[\mu + m(X)]^2 V(X)\Psi_\kappa(X)\Psi_\kappa(X)'\}Q_\kappa^{-1}$. Define $\lambda_{\kappa,\ \min}$, $Q_{\kappa,\ ij}$, ζ_κ, $\{\theta_{jk}\}$, and θ_κ as in Section 3.1.3 but with the redefined Q_κ in place of the version used in Section 3.1.3. In addition, define

$$
\begin{aligned}
S'_{n1}(x^1,\ m) =& -2\sum_{i=1}^{n} \{Y_i - G[\mu + m_1(x^1) + m_{-1}(X_i^{(-1)})]\} \\
& G'[\mu + m_1(x^1) + m_{-1}(X_i^{(-1)})]K\left(\frac{x^1 - X_i^1}{h}\right), \\
D_0(x^1) =& 2\int G'[\mu + m_1(x^1) + m_{-1}(x^{(-1)})]^2 f_X(x^1,\ x^{(-1)})dx^{(-1)}, \\
g(x^1,\ x^{(-1)}) =& (\partial^2/\partial\zeta^2)\Big\{G[m_1(\zeta + x^1) + m_{-1}(x^{(-1)})] \\
& - G[m_1(x^1) + m_{-1}(x^{(-1)})]\Big\} f_X(\zeta + x^1,\ x^{(-1)})\Big|_{\zeta=0}, \\
\beta_1(x^1) =& 2C_h^2 A_K D_0(x^1)^{-1} \int g(x^1,\ x^{(-1)})G'[\mu + m_1(x^1) + m_{-1}(x^{(-1)})] \\
& f_X(x^1,\ x^{(-1)})dx^{(-1)},
\end{aligned}
$$

and

$$V_1(x^1) = B_K C_h^{-1} D_0(x^1)^{-2} \int Var(U|x^1, x^{(-1)}) G'[\mu + m_1(x^1) + m_{-1}(x^{(-1)})]^2 f_X(x^1, x^{(-1)}) dx^{(-1)}.$$

Make the following assumptions in addition to those already made in Section 3.1.3.

ADD3∗: (iii) There are constants $C_{G1} < \infty$, $c_{G2} > 0$, and $C_{G2} < \infty$ such that $G(v) \leq C_{G1}$ and $c_{G2} \leq G'(v) \leq C_{G2}$ for all $v \in [\mu - C_m d,\ \mu + C_m d]$. (iv) G is twice continuously differentiable on $[\mu - C_m d,\ \mu + C_m d]$. (v) There is a constant $C_{G3} < \infty$ such that $|G''(v_2) - G''(v_1)| \leq C_{G3}|v_2 - v_1|$ for all $v_2,\ v_1 \in [\mu - C_m d,\ \mu + C_m d]$.

These assumptions impose smoothness restrictions on the link function G. They are satisfied automatically and, therefore, not needed if G is the identity function.

The properties of the first-stage estimator are given by the following theorem.

Theorem 3.6: *Let assumptions ADD1–ADD6(i) hold. Then*

(a) $\lim_{n \to \infty} \left\| \hat{\theta}_{n\kappa} - \theta_{\kappa 0} \right\| = 0$

almost surely,

(b) $\hat{\theta}_{n\kappa} - \theta_{\kappa 0} = O_p(\kappa^{1/2}/n^{1/2} + \kappa^{-2})$,

and

(c) $\sup_{x \in \mathcal{X}} |\tilde{m}(x) - m(x)| = O_p(\kappa/n^{1/2} + \kappa^{-3/2})$.

In addition,

(d)

$$\hat{\theta}_{n\kappa} - \theta_{\kappa 0} = n^{-1} Q_\kappa^{-1} \sum_{i=1}^{n} G'[\mu + m(X_i)] \Psi_\kappa(X_i) U_i + n^{-1} Q_\kappa^{-1} \sum_{i=1}^{n} G'[\mu + m(X_i)]^2 \Psi_\kappa(X_i) b_{\kappa 0}(X_i) + R_n,$$

where $\|R_n\| = O_p(\kappa^{3/2}/n + n^{-1/2})$.■

The interpretation of this theorem is the same as that of Theorem 3.3. Parts (a–c) of Theorem 3.6 establish the consistency and uniform rate of convergence of the series estimator. Part (d) provides an asymptotic representation that is used in deriving the properties of the second-stage estimator.

The properties of the second-stage kernel estimator are given by the next theorem.

Theorem 3.7: *Let assumptions ADD1–ADD7 and ADD3* hold. Then*

(a) $\hat{m}_{1,K}(x^1) - m_1(x^1) = -[nhD_0(x^1)]^{-1} S'_{n1}(x^1, m) + o_p(n^{-2/5})$, *uniformly over* $|x^1| \leq 1 - h$ *and* $\hat{m}_{1,K}(x^1) - m_1(x^1) = O_p[(\log n)^{1/2} n^{-2/5}]$ *uniformly over* $|x^1| \leq 1$.

(b) $n^{2/5}[\hat{m}_{1,K}(x^1) - m_1(x^1)] \xrightarrow{d} N[\beta_1(x^1), V_1(x^1)]$.

(c) If $j \neq 1$, *then* $n^{2/5}[\hat{m}_{1,K}(x^1) - m_1(x^1)]$ *and* $n^{2/5}[\hat{m}_{j,K}(x^j) - m_j(x^j)]$ *are asymptotically independently normally distributed.*■

Theorem 3.7(a) provides an asymptotic representation of $\hat{m}_{1,\,K}(x^1)$ that is identical to the representation that would be obtained from solving (3.21) with the true additive components m_{-1} in place of the estimates $\tilde{m}_{-1}$. Therefore, Theorem 3.7(a) implies that the second-stage estimator is oracle efficient. Parts (b) and (c) of Theorem 3.7 show that $\hat{m}_{1,\,K}$ is $n^{-2/5}$-consistent and asymptotically normal. The rate of convergence does not depend on d, so there is no curse of dimensionality.

We now describe the local-linear second-stage estimator. Define

$$S'_{nj1}(x^1,\ \tilde{m}) = -2\sum_{i=1}^{n}\{Y_i - G[\tilde{\mu} + \tilde{m}_1(x^1) + \tilde{m}_{-1}(X_i^{(-1)})]\}$$
$$G'[\tilde{\mu} + \tilde{m}_1(x^1) + \tilde{m}_{-1}(X_i^{(-1)})](X_i^1 - x^1)^{\ j}K\left(\frac{x^1 - X_i^1}{h}\right)$$

for $j = 0,\ 1$ and

$$S''_{nj1}(x^1,\ \tilde{m}) = 2\sum_{i=1}^{n} G'[\tilde{\mu} + \tilde{m}_1(x^1) + \tilde{m}_{-1}(X_i^{(-1)})]^2(X_i^1 - x^1)^j K\left(\frac{x^1 - X_i^1}{h}\right)$$
$$-2\sum_{i=1}^{n}\{Y_i - G[\tilde{\mu} + \tilde{m}_1(x^1) + \tilde{m}_{-1}(X_i^{(-1)})]\}$$
$$G''[\tilde{\mu} + \tilde{m}_1(x^1) + \tilde{m}_{-1}(X_i^{(-1)})](X_i^1 - x^1)^j K\left(\frac{x^1 - X_i^1}{h}\right)$$

for $j = 0,\ 1,\ 2$. The second-stage estimator of $m_1(x^1)$ is

$$\hat{m}_{1,\,LL}(x^1) = \tilde{m}_1(x^1) - \frac{S''_{n21}(x^1,\ \tilde{m})S'_{n01}(x^1,\ \tilde{m}) - S''_{n11}(x^1,\ \tilde{m})S'_{n11}(x^1,\ \tilde{m})}{S''_{n01}(x^1,\ \tilde{m})S''_{n21}(x^1,\ \tilde{m}) - S''_{n11}(x^1,\ \tilde{m})^2}. \qquad (3.22)$$

The second-stage estimators of $m_2(x^2),\ \ldots,\ m_d(x^d)$ are obtained similarly. The estimator (3.22) can be understood intuitively as follows. If $\tilde{\mu}$ and $\tilde{m}_{-1}$ were the true values of μ and m_{-1}, the local-linear estimator of $m_1(x^1)$ would minimize

$$S_{n1}(x^1,\ b_0,\ b_1) = \sum_{i=1}^{n}\{Y_i - G[\tilde{\mu} + b_0 + b_1(X_i^1 - x^1) + \tilde{m}_{-1}(X_i^{(-1)})]\}^2 K\left(\frac{x^1 - X_i^1}{h}\right). \qquad (3.23)$$

Moreover, $S'_{nj1}(x^1,\ \tilde{m}) = \partial S_{n1}(x^1,\ b_0,\ b_1)/\partial b_j$ $(j = 0,\ 1)$ evaluated at $b_0 = \tilde{m}_1(x^1)$ and $b_1 = 0$. $S''_{nj1}(x^1,\ \tilde{m})$ gives the second derivatives of $S_{n1}(x^1,\ b_0,\ b_1)$ evaluated at the same point. The estimator (3.22) is the result of taking one Newton step from the starting values $b_0 = \tilde{m}_1(x^1)$, $b_1 = 0$ toward the minimum of the right-hand side of (3.23).

To obtain the asymptotic distribution of the local-linear second-stage estimator, define

$$S'_{nj1}(x^1, m) = -2\sum_{i=1}^{n}\{Y_i - G[\mu + m_1(x^1) + m_{-1}(\tilde{X}_i)]\}$$
$$G'[\mu + m_1(x^1) + m_{-1}(\tilde{X}_i)](X_i^1 - x^1)^{\ j} K\left(\frac{x^1 - X_i^1}{h}\right)$$

for $j = 0, 1$,

$$D_1(x^1) = 2\int G'[\mu + m_1(x^1) + m_{-1}(\tilde{x})]^2[\partial f_X(x^1, \tilde{x})/\partial x^1]d\tilde{x},$$

$$g_{LL}(x^1, \tilde{x}) = G''[\mu + m_1(x^1) + m_{-1}(\tilde{x})]m_1'(x^1) + G'[\mu + m_1(x^1) + m_{-1}(\tilde{x})]m_1''(x^1),$$

and

$$\beta_{1,\ LL}(x^1) = 2C_h^2 A_K D_0(x^1)^{-1}\int g_{LL}(x^1, \tilde{x})G'[\mu + m_1(x^1) + m_{-1}(\tilde{x})]f_X(x^1, \tilde{x})d\tilde{x}.$$

The next theorem gives the asymptotic properties of the second-stage estimator.

Theorem 3.8: *Let assumptions ADD1–ADD7 and ADD3∗ hold. Then*

(a) $\hat{m}_{1,\ LL}(x^1) - m_1(x^1) = [nhD_0(x^1)]^{-1}\{-S'_{n01}(x^1, m) + [D_1(x^1)/D_0(x^1)] S'_{n11}(x^1, m)\} + o_p(n^{-2/5})$ *uniformly over* $|x^1| \leq 1 - h$ *and* $\hat{m}_{1,\ LL}(x^1) - m_1(x^1) = O_p[(\log n)^{1/2}n^{-2/5}]$ *uniformly over* $|x^1| \leq 1$.

(b) $n^{2/5}[\hat{m}_{1,\ LL}(x^1) - m_1(x^1)] \xrightarrow{d} N[\beta_{1,\ LL}(x^1),\ V_1(x^1)]$.

(c) If $j \neq 1$, *then* $n^{2/5}[\hat{m}_{1,\ LL}(x^1) - m_1(x^1)]$ *and* $n^{2/5}[\hat{m}_{j,\ LL}(x^j) - m_j(x^j)]$ *are asymptotically independently normally distributed.*■

Part (a) of Theorem 3.8 provides an asymptotic representation of $\hat{m}_{1,\ K}(x^1)$ that is identical to the representation that would be obtained from solving (3.23) with the true additive components m_{-1} in place of the estimates $\tilde{m}_{-1}$. Therefore, part (a) implies that the second-stage estimator is oracle efficient. Parts (b) and (c) of Theorem 3.8 show that $\hat{m}_{1,\ K}$ is $n^{-2/5}$-consistent and asymptotically normal. The rate of convergence does not depend on d, so there is no curse of dimensionality.

3.2.2 Bandwidth Selection

This section describes a data-based method for selecting the bandwidth h that is used in the second estimation stage with either an identity or nonidentity link function. The presentation here assumes a general link function G. The result for an identity link function is obtained by replacing G with the identity function. The method simultaneously estimates the bandwidths for estimating all the functions m_j ($j = 1, \ldots, d$). In general, the bandwidth can be different for different m_js. Accordingly, denote the bandwidth for estimating m_j by h_j. Assume that $h_j = C_{hj} n^{-1/5}$ for some finite constant $C_{hj} > 0$.

The method described here selects the C_{hj}s to minimize an estimate of the average-squared estimation error (ASE), which is

$$ASE(\bar{h}) = n^{-1} \sum_{i=1}^{n} \{G[\tilde{\mu} + \hat{m}(X_i)] - G[\mu + m(X_i)]\}^2,$$

where $\bar{h} = (C_{h1} n^{-1/5}, \ldots, C_{hd} n^{-1/5})$. Specifically, the method selects the C_{hj}s to

$$\begin{aligned} \underset{C_{h1}, \ldots, C_{hd}}{\text{minimize}} : PLS(\bar{h}) &= n^{-1} \sum_{i=1}^{n} \{Y_i - G[\tilde{\mu} + \hat{m}(X_i)]\}^2 \\ &+ 2K(0) n^{-1} \sum_{i=1}^{n} \{G'[\tilde{\mu} + \hat{m}(X_i)]^2 \hat{V}(X_i)\} \sum_{j=1}^{d} [n^{4/5} C_{hj} \hat{D}_j(X_i^j)]^{-1}, \end{aligned} \tag{3.24}$$

where the C_{hj}s are restricted to a compact, positive interval that excludes 0,

$$\hat{D}_j(x^j) = \frac{1}{nh_j} \sum_{i=1}^{n} K_{h_j}(X_i^j - x^j) G'[\tilde{\mu} + \hat{m}(X_i)]^2,$$

and

$$\begin{aligned} \hat{V}(x) = &\left[\sum_{i=1}^{n} K\left(\frac{X_i^1 - x^1}{h_1}\right) \cdots K\left(\frac{X_i^d - x^d}{h_d}\right) \right]^{-1} \\ &\times \sum_{i=1}^{n} K\left(\frac{X_i^1 - x^1}{h_1}\right) \cdots K\left(\frac{X_i^d - x^d}{h_d}\right) \{Y_i - G[\tilde{\mu} + \hat{m}(X_i)]\}^2. \end{aligned}$$

The bandwidths used for $\hat{V}$ may be different from those used for $\hat{m}$ because $\hat{V}$ is a nonparametric estimator of a function with a d-dimensional argument.

We now present Horowitz's and Mammen's (2004) heuristic argument that (3.24) estimates the bandwidths that minimize $ASE(\bar{h})$. Specifically, the difference

$$n^{-1} \sum_{i=1}^{n} U_i^2 + ASE(\bar{h}) - PLS(\bar{h})$$

is asymptotically negligible. For this purpose, note that

$$n^{-1}\sum_{i=1}^{n} U_i^2 + ASE(\bar{h}) - PLS(\bar{h}) = 2n^{-1}\sum_{i=1}^{n}\{G[\tilde{\mu}+\hat{m}(X_i)] - G[\mu+m(X_i)]\}U_i$$
$$- 2K(0)n^{-1}\sum_{i=1}^{n} G'[\mu+m(X_i)]^2\hat{V}(X_i)$$
$$\sum_{j=1}^{d}[n^{4/5}C_{hj}\hat{D}_j(X_i^j)]^{-1}.$$

Now approximate $G[\tilde{\mu}+\hat{m}(X_i)] - G[\mu+m(X_i)]$ by a linear expansion in $\hat{m}-m$ and replace $\hat{m}-m$ with the stochastic approximation of Theorem 3.8(a). Thus, $G[\tilde{\mu}+\hat{m}(X_i)] - G[\mu+m(X_i)]$ is approximated by a linear form in U_i. Dropping higher-order terms leads to an approximation of

$$\frac{2}{n}\sum_{i=1}^{n}\{G[\tilde{\mu}+\hat{m}(X_i)] - G[\mu+m(X_i)]\}U_i$$

that is a U statistic in U_i. The off-diagonal terms of the U statistic can be shown to be of higher order and, therefore, asymptotically negligible. Thus, we get

$$\frac{2}{n}\sum_{i=1}^{n}\{G[\tilde{\mu}+\hat{m}(X_i)] - G[\mu+m(X_i)]\}U_i \approx \frac{2}{n}\sum_{i=1}^{n} G'[\mu+m(X_i)]^2 Var(U_i|X_i)$$
$$\times \sum_{j=1}^{d}[n^{4/5}C_{hj}D_{0j}(X_i^j)]h^{-1}K(0),$$

where

$$D_{0j}(x^j) = 2E\{G'[\mu+m(X_i)]^2|X_i^j = x^j\}f_{X^j}(x^j)$$

and f_{X^j} is the probability density function of X^j. Now by standard kernel smoothing arguments, $D_{0j}(x^j) \approx \hat{D}_j(x^j)$. In addition, it is clear that $\hat{V}(X_i) \approx V(U_i|X_i)$, which establishes the desired result.

3.3 Estimation with an Unknown Link Function

This section discusses estimation of model (3.1) when the link function, G, is unknown. As was explained in the introduction to this chapter, model (3.1) with an unknown link function provides a flexible class of models that nests semiparametric single-index and nonparametric additive models.

The main problem is to estimate the additive components $m_1, \ldots, m_d$. Given estimates $\hat{m}_1, \ldots, \hat{m}_d$, G can be estimated by carrying out a nonparametric mean regression of Y on $\hat{m}_1(X^1)+\ldots+\hat{m}_d(X^d)$. Horowitz (2001a) proposed an estimator of the additive components, but this estimator has a curse of dimensionality and does not achieve the optimal one-dimensional nonparametric rate of convergence (e.g., $n^{-2/5}$ for additive components that are twice differentiable). This section describes a penalized least-squares (PLS) estimator that was developed by Horowitz and Mammen (2007). The PLS estimator does not have a curse of dimensionality and achieves the optimal one-dimensional nonparametric rate of convergence.

Before presenting the estimator, it is necessary to specify normalizations that ensure identification of G and $m_1, \ldots, m_d$. Observe that (3.1) remains unchanged if each m_j is replaced by m_j+a_j for any constants a_j and $G(v)$ is replaced by $G^*(v) = G(v - a_1 - \cdots - a_d)$. Similarly, (3.1) is unchanged if each m_j is replaced by cm_j for any $c \neq 0$ and $G(v)$ is replaced by $G^*(v) = G(v/c)$. Therefore, location and scale normalizations are needed to make identification possible. Horowitz and Mammen (2007) use the normalizations $\mu = 0$,

$$\int m_j(v)dv = 0; \quad j = 1, \ldots, d, \tag{3.25}$$

and

$$\sum_{j=1}^{d} \int m_j^2(v)dv = 1. \tag{3.26}$$

Relation (3.25) is the location normalization. It prevents replacing m_j by $m_j + a_j$ for some nonzero constant a_j. Relation (3.26) is the scale normalization. It prevents replacing each m_j with cm_j for some constant $c \neq 1$.

Identification also requires at least two additive components to be nonconstant. To see why, suppose that all additive components except m_1 are constant. Then (3.1) becomes

$$E(Y|X = x) = G[m_1(x^1) + a], \tag{3.27}$$

where a is a constant. It is clear that (3.27) is satisfied by many different choices of G and m_1, so (3.27) does not identify G and m_1.

The PLS estimator of Horowitz and Mammen (2007) chooses the estimators of G and the additive components to solve

$$\underset{\breve{G},\, \breve{m}_1,\, \ldots,\, \breve{m}_d}{\text{minimize:}} \quad \frac{1}{n}\sum_{i=1}^{n} \{Y_i - \breve{G}[\breve{m}_1(X_i^1) + \cdots + \breve{m}_d(X_i^d)]\}^2 + \lambda_n^2 J(\breve{G}, \breve{m}_1, \ldots, \breve{m}_d),$$
$$\text{subject to: (3.25),(3.26)} \tag{3.28}$$

where $\{\lambda_n\}$ is a sequence of constants and J is a penalty term that penalizes roughness of the estimated functions. If G and the m_js are k times differentiable, the penalty term is

$$J(\breve{G}, \breve{m}_1, \ldots, \breve{m}_d) = J_1^{\nu_1}(\breve{G}, \breve{m}_1, \ldots, \breve{m}_d) + J_2^{\nu_2}(\breve{G}, \breve{m}_1, \ldots, \breve{m}_d),$$

where ν_1 and ν_2 are constants satisfying $\nu_2 \geq \nu_1 > 0$,

$$J_1(\breve{G}, \breve{m}_1, \ldots, \breve{m}_d) = T_k(\breve{G}) \left\{ \sum_{j=1}^{d} [T_1^2(\breve{m}_j) + T_k^2(\breve{m}_j)] \right\}^{(2k-1)/4},$$

$$J_2(\breve{G}, \breve{m}_1, \ldots, \breve{m}_d) = T_1(\breve{G}) \left\{ \sum_{j=1}^{d} [T_1^2(\breve{m}_j) + T_k^2(\breve{m}_j)] \right\}^{1/4},$$

and

$$T_\ell^2(f) = \int f^{(\ell)}(v)^2 dv$$

for $0 \leq \ell \leq k$ and any function f whose ℓ th derivative is square integrable. The PLS estimator can be computed by approximating $\breve{G}$ and the $\breve{m}_j$ s by B-splines and minimizing (3.28) over the coefficients of the spline approximation. Powell (1981) explains B-splines and their properties. Section A.2.3 of the Appendix describes B-splines briefly. The computation can be carried out by a backfitting algorithm that alternates between two steps. In one step, $\breve{G}$ is held fixed and the objective function is minimized over the spline coefficients of the $\breve{m}_j$s. This is an equality-constrained mathematical programming problem that can be solved by the method of Lagrangian multipliers. In the second step, the $\breve{m}_j$s are held fixed, and the objective function is optimized over the coefficients of $\breve{G}$. This is an unconstrained quadratic programming problem that can be solved analytically.

We present the properties of the PLS estimator under the following assumptions, which are those of Horowitz and Mammen (2007).

PLS1: The data $\{Y_i, X_i: i = 1, \ldots, n\}$ are an independent random sample from some distribution. The covariates, $X^1, \ldots, X^d$, take values in a compact subset of $\mathbb{R}^d$ that, without loss of generality, may be taken to be $[0, 1]^d$. Moreover, the probability density function of the covariates is bounded away from 0 and ∞ on $[0, 1]^d$.

PLS2: The functions G and $m_1, \ldots, m_d$ have $k \geq 1$ derivatives that satisfy

$$\int_0^1 G^{(k)}(v)^2 dv < \infty, \quad \int_0^1 m_j^{(k)}(v)^2 dv < \infty; \quad (j = 1, \ldots, d).$$

$G'(v)$ is bounded away from 0 for $v \in \{m_1(x^1) + \cdots + m_d(x^d)\colon 0 \leq x^1, \ldots, x^d \leq 1\}$. Moreover, the m_js are nonconstant for at least two values of j ($1 \leq j \leq d$). The m_js satisfy (3.25) and (3.26).

PLS3: For each $i = 1, \ldots, n$, define $U_i = Y_i - G[m_1(X_i^1) + \cdots + m_d(X_i^d)]$. Then $E(U_i|X_i^1, \ldots, X_i^d) = 0$. Moreover there are finite constants $t_U > 0$ and $c_U > 0$ such that

$$\sup_{1 \leq i \leq n} E[\exp(t|U_i|)|X_i^1, \ldots, X_i^d)] < c_U$$

almost surely for $|t| < t_U$.

PLS4: The penalty parameter satisfies $\lambda_n^{-1} = O_p(n^{k/(2k+1)})$ and $\lambda_n = O_p(n^{-k/(2k+1)})$.

Assumption PLS1 specifies the sampling process that generates the data. Assumption PLS2 gives smoothness and identifying conditions. Assumption PLS3 requires the tails of the distribution of U to be thin, and assumption PLS4 specifies the behavior of the penalty parameter. This assumption allows the possibility that the penalty parameter is random.

Horowitz and Mammen (2007) prove the following theorem, which states asymptotic properties of the PLS estimator.

Theorem 3.9: *Denote the PLS estimator by $\hat{G}, \hat{m}_1, \ldots, \hat{m}_d$. Let assumptions PLS1–PLS4 hold. Then*

$$\int_0^1 [\hat{m}_j(v) - m_j(v)]^2 dv = O_p(n^{-2k/(2k+1)})$$

for each $j = 1, \ldots, d$ and

$$\int \left\{ \hat{G}\left[\sum_{j=1}^{d} m_j(x^j)\right] - G\left[\sum_{j=1}^{d} m_j(x^j)\right]\right\}^2 dx^1 \cdots dx^d = O_p(n^{-2k/(2k+1)}).\blacksquare$$

The theorem states that the integrated squared errors of the PLS estimates of the link function and additive components converge in probability to 0 at the fastest possible rate under the assumptions. There is no curse of dimensionality.

The available results do not provide an asymptotic distribution for the PLS estimator. Therefore, it is not yet possible to carry out statistical inference with this estimator. Similarly, methods for choosing the tuning parameters in applications are not yet available. The PLS estimator does demonstrate, however, that an a nonparametric additive model with an unknown link function can be estimated with no curse of dimensionality and optimal one-dimensional rates of convergence.

3.4 Estimation of a Conditional Quantile Function

This section is concerned with estimation of the unknown functions m_j in the model

$$Y = \mu + m_1(x^1) + \cdots + m_d(x^d) + U_\alpha, \tag{3.29}$$

where U_α is an unobserved random variable whose α-quantile conditional on $X = x$ is zero for almost every x. Model (3.29) is equivalent to (3.1b) with an identity link function. The extension to the case of a nonidentity link function is discussed later in this section.

Existing estimation methods for (3.29) include series estimation (Doksum and Koo 2000) and backfitting (Fan and Gijbels 1996), but the rates of convergence and other asymptotic distributional properties of these estimators are unknown. De Gooijer and Zerom (2003) proposed a marginal integration estimator that is asymptotically normally distributed, but it begins with a d-dimensional nonparametric quantile regression and, therefore, suffers from a curse of dimensionality. This section describes a two-stage estimator that was developed by Horowitz and Lee (2005). The estimator is similar in concept to the method of Horowitz and Mammen (2004) that is described in Section 3.1.3. Like the estimator of Section 3.1.3, the quantile estimator is asymptotically normal, oracle efficient, and has no curse of dimensionality.

Horowitz and Lee (2005) assume that the support of X is $[-1, \ 1]^d$ and use the location normalization

$$\int_{-1}^{1} m_j(v)dv = 0.$$

Define the function $\rho_\alpha(u) = |u| + (2\alpha - 1)u$ for $0 < \alpha < 1$. As in Section 3.1.3, the first stage in estimating a conditional quantile function is estimating the coefficients of a series approximation to $\mu + m(x)$. As in estimation of a conditional mean function, this is done by solving an optimization problem, but the objective function is different in conditional quantile estimation. Specifically let $\hat{\theta}_{n\kappa}$ be a solution to

$$\underset{\theta}{\text{minimize}}: S_{n\kappa}(\theta) = n^{-1}\sum_{i=1}^{n} \rho_\alpha[Y_i - \Psi_\kappa(X_i)'\theta],$$

where Ψ_κ is defined as in (3.17). The first-stage series estimator of $\mu + m(x)$ is

$$\tilde{\mu} + \tilde{m}(x) = \Psi_\kappa(x)'\hat{\theta}_{n\kappa},$$

where $\tilde{\mu}$ is the first component of $\hat{\theta}_{n\kappa}$.

To describe the second-stage estimator of (say) m_1, assume that m_1 is twice continuously differentiable on $[-1, \ 1]$. The second stage then consists of local-linear estimation. Specifically, using the notation of Section 3.1.3, the estimator of $m_1(x^1)$ is defined as $\hat{m}_1(x^1) = \hat{b}_0$, where $\hat{b}_n = (\hat{b}_0,\ \hat{b}_1)$ minimizes

$$S_n(b) = (nh)^{-1}\sum_{i=1}^{n}\rho_\alpha[Y_i - \tilde{\mu} - b_0 - b_1(X_i^1 - x^1) - \tilde{m}_{-1}(X_i^{(-1)})]K_h(X_i^1 - x^1).$$

Because quantiles of monotone transformations of Y are equal to monotone transformations of quantiles of Y, it is straightforward to extend the estimator of Horowitz and Lee to a model of the form

$$G(Y) = \mu + m_1(x^1) + \cdots + m_d(x^d) + U_\alpha,$$

where G is a known, strictly increasing function and the α-quantile of U_α conditional on $X = x$ is zero. Estimation of the m_j s can be carried out by replacing Y with $G(Y)$ in the two-stage procedure. The α-quantile of Y conditional on $X = x$ is estimated by $G^{-1}[\tilde{\mu} + \hat{m}_1(x^1) + \cdots + \hat{m}_d(x^d)]$.

Horowitz and Lee (2005) make the following assumptions to obtain the asymptotic properties of the two-stage estimator.

QA1: The data, $\{Y_i,\ X_i\colon i = 1,\ \ldots,\ n\}$ are iid, and the α-quantile of Y conditional on $X = x$ is $\mu + m(x)$ for almost every x.

QA2: The support of X is $\mathcal{X} = [-1,\ 1]^d$. The distribution of X is absolutely continuous with respect to Lebesgue measure. The probability density function of X, denoted by $f_X(x)$, is bounded, bounded away from 0, twice differentiable in the interior of $\mathcal{X}$, and has continuous one-sided second derivatives at the boundary of $\mathcal{X}$.

QA3: Let $F(u|x)$ denote the distribution function of U_α conditional on $X = x$. Then $F(0|x) = \alpha$ for almost every $x \in \mathcal{X}$, and $F(\cdot|x)$ has a probability density function $f(\cdot|x)$. There is a constant $L_f < \infty$ such that $|f(u_1|x) - f(u_2|x)| \le L_f|u_1 - u_2|$ for all u_1 and u_2 in a neighborhood of 0 and all $x \in \mathcal{X}$. There are constants $c_f > 0$ and $C_f < \infty$ such that $c_f \le f(u|x) \le C_f$ for all u in a neighborhood of 0 and all $x \in \mathcal{X}$.

QA4: For each $j = 1,\ \ldots,\ d$, m_j is twice continuously differentiable in the interior of $[-1,\ 1]$ and has continuous, one-sided second derivatives at the boundaries of $[-1,\ 1]$.

QA5: Define $\Phi_\kappa = E[f(0|X)\Psi_\kappa(X)\Psi_\kappa(X)']$. The smallest eigenvalue of Φ_κ is bounded away from 0 for all κ, and the largest eigenvalue is bounded for all κ.

QA6: The basis functions satisfy (3.15) and (3.16). Moreover, $\zeta_\kappa = O(\kappa^{1/2})$ and $\sup_{x\in\mathcal{X}}|\mu + m(x) - \Psi_\kappa(x)'\theta_{\kappa 0}| = O(\kappa^{-2})$.

QA7. (i) $\kappa = C_\kappa n^\nu$ for some constant C_κ satisfying $0 < C_\kappa < \infty$ and some ν such that $1/5 < \nu < 7/30$. (ii) The bandwidth $h = C_h n^{-1/5}$ for some finite, positive constant C_h.

QA8: The kernel function K is a bounded, continuous probability density function on $[-1,\ 1]$ and is symmetrical about 0.

Now define

$$\bar{\Psi}_\kappa(\tilde{x}) = [1, \underbrace{0, \ldots, 0}_{\kappa}, \psi_1(x^2), \ldots, \psi_\kappa(x^2), \ldots, \psi_1(x^d), \ldots, \psi_\kappa(x^d)]',$$

where $\tilde{x} = (x^2, \ldots, x^d)$.

QA9: The largest eigenvalue of $E[\bar{\Psi}_\kappa(X^{(-1)})\bar{\Psi}_\kappa(X^{(-1)})'|X^1 = x^1]$ is bounded for all κ and each component of $E[\bar{\Psi}_\kappa(X^{(-1)})\bar{\Psi}_\kappa(X^{(-1)})'|X^1 = x^1]$ is twice continuously differentiable with respect to x^1.

These assumptions are similar to those of the two-step estimator of a conditional mean function that is described in Section 3.1.3.

For $j = 0, 1, 2$ define $\rho_j = \int_{-1}^{1} v^j K(v)dv$. Let S_K be the 2×2 matrix whose (i, j) component is ρ_{i+j-2}. Also, define $e_1 = (1, 0)'$. Set $K_*(u) = e_1' S_K^{-1}(1, u)'K(u)$. Let f_{X^1} denote the probability density function of X^1, and let $f_1(u|x^1)$ denote the probability density function of U_α conditional on $X^1 = x^1$. Finally, define

$$\beta_1(x^1) = 0.5C_h^2 \left[\int_{-1}^{1} v^2 K_*(v)dv\right] m_1''(x^1)$$

and

$$V_1(x^1) = \left[\int_{-1}^{1} K_*(v)^2 dv\right] C_h^{-1}\alpha(1-\alpha)/[f_{X^1}(x^1)f_1(0|x^1)^2].$$

The main result of Horowitz and Lee (2005) is given by the following theorem.

Theorem 3.10: *Let assumptions QA1–QA9 hold. Then as $n \to \infty$ and for any x^1 satisfying $|x^1| \le 1 - h$, the following results hold:*

(a) $|\hat{m}_1(x^1) - m_1(x^1)| = O_p(n^{-2/5})$.

(b) $n^{2/5}[\hat{m}_1(x^1) - m_1(x^1)] \xrightarrow{d} N[\beta_1(x^1), V_1(x^1)]$.

(c) If $j \ne 1$, then $n^{2/5}[\hat{m}_1(x^1) - m_1(x^1)]$ and $n^{2/5}[\hat{m}_j(x^j) - m_1(x^j)]$ are asymptotically independently normally distributed for any x^j satisfying $|x^j| \le 1 - h$.

■

This theorem implies that the second-stage estimator achieves the optimal rate of convergence for a nonparametric estimator of a twice-differentiable function. Only two derivatives are needed regardless of *d*, so there is no curse of dimensionality. Moreover, the second-stage estimator is oracle efficient. That is, it has the same asymptotic distribution as it would have if $m_2, \ldots, m_d$ were known.

3.5 An Empirical Example

This section illustrates the application of the estimator of Horowitz and Mammen (2004) by using it to estimate an earnings function. The specification of the model is

$$\log W = m_{EXP}(EXP) + m_{EDUC}(EDUC) + U,$$

where W is an individual's wage; EXP and $EDUC$, respectively, are the number of years of work experience and education that the individual has had; and U is an unobserved random variable satisfying $E(U|EXP,\ EDUC) = 0$. The functions m_{EXP} and m_{EDUC} are unknown and are estimated by the Horowitz–Mammen procedure. The data are taken from the 1993 Current Population Survey and consist

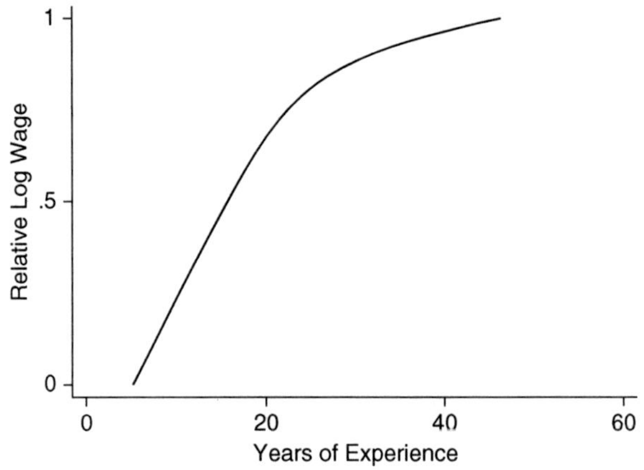

Fig. 3.1a Nonparametric estimate of m_{EXP}

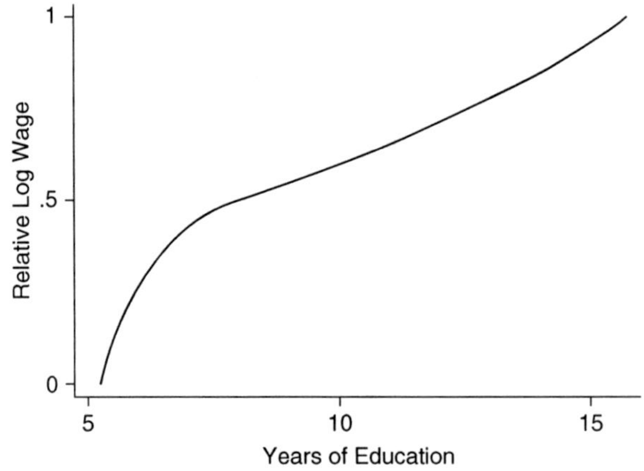

Fig. 3.1b Nonparametric estimate of m_{EDUC}

of observations on 3123 individuals. The estimation results are shown in Fig. 3.1. The estimates of m_{EXP} (Fig. 3.1a) and m_{EDUC} (Fig. 3.1b) are nonlinear and differently shaped. They are not well approximated by simple parametric functions such as quadratic functions. A lengthy specification search might be needed to find a parametric model that produces the shapes shown in Fig. 3.1. This illustrates the usefulness of nonparametric estimation methods.

3.6 The Partially Linear Model

We now consider estimation of the partially linear model (3.2a) from data $\{Y_i, X_i, Z_i : i = 1, \ldots, n\}$ consisting of a random sample from the distribution of (Y, X, Z). The discussion here is based mainly on Robinson (1988). Härdle et al. (2000) provide a more detailed discussion and many additional references. The discussion here concentrates on $n^{-1/2}$-consistent estimation of the finite-dimensional parameter β. Given an $n^{-1/2}$-consistent estimator $\hat{b}$, g can be estimated by carrying out the nonparametric regression of $y - X'\hat{b}$ on Z. This can be done using kernel, local-linear, or series estimation. Arguments like those made in Section 2.4 then show that the resulting estimator has the same asymptotic distribution that it would have if β were known. That is, the estimator obtained by the nonparametric regression of $y - X'\hat{b}$ on Z and the estimator obtained from the regression of $y - X'\beta$ on Z have the same asymptotic distribution.

3.6.1 *Identification*

This section gives conditions for identification of β in (3.2a). Define

$$U = Y - X'\beta - g(Z).$$

Then (3.2a) is equivalent to

$$Y = X'\beta + g(Z) + U; E(U|X, Z) = 0. \tag{3.30}$$

Now (3.30) implies that

$$E(Y|Z) = E(X|Z)'\beta + g(Z). \tag{3.31}$$

Subtracting (3.31) from (3.30) gives

$$Y - E(Y|Z) = [X - E(X|Z)]'\beta + U; E(U|X, Z) = 0. \tag{3.32}$$

Define $\tilde{Y} = Y - E(Y|Z)$ and $\tilde{X} = X - E(X|Z)$. Then application of the theory of ordinary least-squares estimation of linear models to (3.32) shows that β is identified by the relation

$$\beta = [E(\tilde{X}\tilde{X}')]^{-1}E(\tilde{X}\tilde{Y})$$

provided that the matrix $E(\tilde{X}\tilde{X}')$ is nonsingular. This is equivalent to requiring $E(\tilde{X}\tilde{X}') > 0$ or

$$\Sigma_X \equiv E[X - E(X|Z)][X - E(X|Z)]' > 0, \tag{3.33}$$

where the inequality signifies that the matrix on the left-hand side is positive definite. For the remainder of this section, inequality (3.33) is assumed to hold in order to identify β.

Inequality (3.33) implies that X cannot be determined perfectly by Z. If X is determined by Z, then $X = E(X|Z)$ and (3.33) does not hold. Thus, for example, X cannot be a component of a vector-valued Z. In addition, (3.33) precludes an intercept (constant) component of X. This is because any intercept component can be absorbed in g. In particular, the model

$$Y = \beta_0 + X'\beta + g(Z) + U,$$

where β_0 is a constant, is indistinguishable from

$$Y = X'\beta + \breve{g}(Z) + U,$$

where $\breve{g}(Z) = \beta_0 + g(Z)$.

3.6.2 Estimation of β

If $E(Y|Z)$ and $E(X|Z)$ were known, then β could be estimated by applying ordinary least squares to (3.32). The resulting estimator would be

$$\tilde{b} = \left(\sum_{i=1}^{n} \tilde{X}_i\tilde{X}_i'\right)^{-1} \sum_{i=1}^{n} \tilde{X}_i\tilde{Y}_i, \tag{3.34}$$

where $\tilde{X}_i = X_i - E(X|Z = Z_i)$ and $\tilde{Y}_i = Y_i - E(Y|Z = Z_i)$. A feasible estimator can be obtained from (3.34) by replacing $E(X|Z = Z_i)$ and $E(Y|Z = Z_i)$ with nonparametric estimators. Specifically, set $q = \dim(Z)$,

$$\hat{f}(z) = \frac{1}{nh_n^q} \sum_{i=1}^{n} K\left(\frac{z - Z_i}{h_n}\right),$$

$$\hat{E}(Y|Z = z) = \frac{1}{nh_n^q \hat{f}(z)} \sum_{i=1}^{n} Y_i K\left(\frac{z - Z_i}{h_n}\right),$$

and

$$\hat{E}(X|Z = z) = \frac{1}{nh_n^q \hat{f}(z)} \sum_{i=1}^{n} X_i K\left(\frac{z - Z_i}{h_n}\right),$$

where K is a kernel function of a q-dimensional argument. Define $\hat{Y}_i = Y_i - \hat{E}(Y|Z = Z_i)$, $\hat{X}_i = X_i - \hat{E}(X|Z = Z_i)$, and $J_i = I[\hat{f}(Z_i) > c_n]$, where I is the indicator function and $\{c_n\}$ is a sequence of strictly positive constants that converges to 0 as $n \to \infty$. The estimator of β is obtained by the ordinary least-squares regression of $\hat{Y}_i$ on $\hat{X}_i$ but using only observations i for which $\hat{f}(Z_i) > c_n$. This trimming of the data prevents $\hat{f}(z)$ in the denominators of $\hat{E}(Y|Z = z)$ and $\hat{E}(X|Z = z)$ from being too close to 0. The resulting estimator of β is

$$\hat{b} = \left(\sum_{i=1}^{n} J_i \hat{X}_i \hat{X}_i'\right)^{-1} \sum_{i=1}^{n} J_i \hat{X}_i \hat{Y}_i. \tag{3.35}$$

Under assumptions that are given below, $n^{1/2}(\hat{b} - \beta)$ is asymptotically normally distributed with mean 0 and covariance matrix $\sigma^2 \Sigma_X^{-1}$, where $\sigma^2 = Var(U)$.

Robinson (1988) provides general but rather complicated assumptions under which the foregoing result holds. Here, we state a simplified and, therefore, less general version of Robinson's (1988) assumptions. The assumptions are

PL1: $\{Y_i, X_i, Z_i: i = 1, \ldots, n\}$ is a simple random sample of (Y, X, Z).
PL2: Model (3.2a) holds.
PL3: U is independent of (X, Z) and $E(U^2) = \sigma^2 < \infty$.
PL4: $E\|X\|^4 < \infty$.
PL5: Z has a probability density function, f. The functions f, $E(X|Z = z)$, and g are $m \geq 1$ times continuously differentiable on the support of Z. The mth derivatives are uniformly bounded on the support of Z.
PL6: Inequality (3.33) holds.
PL7: The tuning parameters satisfy $nh_n^{2q} c_n^4 \to \infty$, $nh_n^{4m} c_n^{-4} \to 0$, $h_n^m c_n^{-2} \to 0$, and $c_n \to 0$ as $n \to \infty$.
PL8: The kernel function K has the form

$$K(v) = \prod_{j=1}^{q} \kappa(v^j),$$

where v^j is the jth component of the q-vector v, κ is a bounded function with support $[-1, 1]$, and

$$\int_{-1}^{1} v^j \kappa(v) dv = \begin{cases} 1 \text{ if } j = 0 \\ 0 \text{ if } 1 \leq j \leq 2m-1 \end{cases}.$$

Assumption PL3 requires U to be homoskedastic. Relaxation of this assumption to allow heteroskedasticity is discussed below. Assumption PL5 is a smoothness condition. A necessary condition for PL7 is that $m > d/2$, so increasing smoothness is needed as d increases. Thus, the least-squares estimator of β has a form of the curse of dimensionality. PL8 requires K to be a higher-order kernel if $d > 3$.

The following theorem, which is a simplified version of a theorem of Robinson (1988), establishes the asymptotic distributional properties of b.

Theorem 3.11: *Let PL1–PL8 hold. Then* $n^{1/2}(\hat{b} - \beta) \xrightarrow{d} N(0, \sigma^2 \Sigma_X^{-1})$.■

The covariance matrix can be estimated consistently by replacing σ^2 with the usual estimator

$$\hat{\sigma}^2 = \frac{1}{n} \sum_{i=1}^{n} J_i (\hat{Y}_i - \hat{X}_i' \hat{b}_n)^2$$

and replacing Σ_X with the estimator

$$\hat{\Sigma}_X = \frac{1}{n} \sum_{i-1}^{n} J_i \hat{X}_i \hat{X}_i'.$$

If U is heteroskedastic with $Var(U|X = x,\ Z = z) = \sigma^2(x,\ z)$, then the covariance matrix of the asymptotic distribution of $n^{1/2}(\hat{b} - \beta)$ is

$$\Sigma_X^{-1} E\{\sigma^2(X,\ Z)[X - E(X|Z)][X - E(X|Z)]'\} \Sigma_X^{-1}.$$

This can be estimated consistently by $\hat{\Sigma}_X^{-1} \hat{\Omega} \Sigma_X^{-1}$, where

$$\hat{\Omega} = \frac{1}{n} \sum_{i=1}^{n} J_i \hat{U}_i^2 \hat{X}_i \hat{X}_i'$$

and $\hat{U}_i = \hat{Y}_i - \hat{X}_i' \hat{b}$.

If U is homoskedastic, then $\hat{b}$ is asymptotically efficient. Specifically, $\hat{b}$ achieves the asymptotic efficiency bound of Chamberlain (1987). If U is heteroskedastic, then $\hat{b}$ is not asymptotically efficient, but an asymptotically efficient estimator of β can be obtained by suitable versions of weighted least squares. We now provide an informal discussion of asymptotically efficient estimation when U is heteroskedastic. Ai and Chen (2003) provide a formal discussion of asymptotically efficient estimation of heteroskedastic partially linear models using the method of sieves.

The asymptotic efficiency bound with heteroskedasticity is given by Ai and Chen (2003). If $Var(U|X,\ Z)$ depends only on Z, then the bound is

$$E\{\sigma^{-2}(Z)[X - E(X|Z)][X - E(X|Z)]'\},$$

where $\sigma^2(Z) = Var(U|Z)$ and $\sigma^{-2}(Z) = 1/\sigma^2(Z)$. An asymptotically efficient estimator of β can be obtained by applying weighted least squares to (3.31) with weights $\hat{\sigma}^{-2}(Z_i) = 1/\hat{\sigma}^2(Z_i)$, where $\hat{\sigma}^2(z)$ is a nonparametric estimator of $Var(U|Z = z)$. The resulting estimator of β is

$$\hat{b}_W = \left(\sum_{i=1}^{n} J_i\hat{\sigma}^{-2}(Z_i)\hat{X}_i\hat{X}_i'\right)^{-1} \sum_{i=1}^{n} J_i\hat{\sigma}^{-2}(Z_i)\hat{X}_i\hat{Y}_i.$$

The estimator $\hat{\sigma}^2(z)$ can be obtained from a nonparametric regression of $\hat{U}_i^2$ on Z_i, where $\hat{U}_i = \hat{Y}_i - \hat{X}_i'\hat{b}$ and $\hat{b}$ is the estimator of (3.35).

The situation is more complicated if $Var(U|X,\ Z)$ depends on X or X and Z. To analyze this case, define $\sigma^2(x,\ z) = Var(U|X = x,\ Z = z)$, $\sigma^{-2}(x,z) = 1/\sigma^2(x,\ z)$,

$$\begin{aligned}
\omega_X(z) &= [E\sigma^{-2}(X,\ Z)|Z = z]^{-1}E[\sigma^{-2}(X,\ Z)X|Z = z],\\
\omega_Y(z) &= [E\sigma^{-2}(X,\ Z)|Z = z]^{-1}E[\sigma^{-2}(X,\ Z)Y|Z = z],\\
\bar{X} &= X - \omega_X(Z),\\
\bar{X}_i &= X_i - \omega_X(Z_i),\\
\bar{Y} &= Y - \omega_Y(Z),
\end{aligned}$$

and

$$\bar{Y}_i = Y_i - \omega_Y(Z_i).$$

Equation (3.30) implies that

$$\sigma^{-2}(X,\ Z)Y = \sigma^{-2}(X,\ Z)X'\beta + \sigma^{-2}(X,\ Z)g(Z) + \sigma^{-2}(X,\ Z)U.$$

Therefore,

$$E[\sigma^{-2}(X,\ Z)Y|Z] = E[\sigma^{-2}(X,\ Z)X'|Z]\beta + [E\sigma^{-2}(X,\ Z)|Z]g(Z)$$

and

$$[E\sigma^{-2}(X,\ Z)|Z]^{-1}E[\sigma^{-2}(X,\ Z)Y|Z] = [E\sigma^{-2}(X,\ Z)|Z]^{-1}E[\sigma^{-2}(X,\ Z)X'|Z]\beta + g(Z). \tag{3.36}$$

Subtracting (3.36) from (3.30) yields

$$\bar{Y} = \bar{X}'\beta + U$$

and, therefore,

$$\bar{Y}_i = \bar{X}_i' \beta + U_i; \quad i = 1, \; \ldots, \; n. \tag{3.37}$$

An asymptotically efficient estimator of β can be obtained by applying weighted least squares to (3.37). The weights are $\hat{\sigma}^{-2}(X_i, \; Z_i)$, where $\hat{\sigma}^2(x, \; z)$ is a consistent estimator of $Var(U|X = x, \; Z = z)$. This estimator can be obtained from a nonparametric regression of $\hat{U}_i^2$ on $(X_i, \; Z_i)$, where $\hat{U}_i = \hat{Y}_i - \hat{X}_i' \hat{b}$ and $\hat{b}$ is the estimator of (3.35). The weighted least-squares estimator of β is

$$\bar{b}_W = \left(\sum_{i=1}^{n} J_i \hat{\sigma}^{-2}(X_i, \; Z_i) \bar{X}_i \bar{X}_i' \right)^{-1} \sum_{i=1}^{n} J_i \hat{\sigma}^{-2}(X_i, \; Z_i) \bar{X}_i \bar{Y}_i .$$

3.6.3 Partially Linear Models of Conditional Quantiles

Estimating β in the partially linear conditional quantile function (3.2b) is harder than estimating β in the partially linear conditional mean function (3.2a). The differencing procedure that eliminates g from (3.2a) and yields (3.31) reduces estimation of β to estimation of the slope coefficients in a parametric linear model. The differencing procedure works because the mean of a sum of random variables is the sum of the individual means. The quantile of the sum of random variables is not the sum of the individual quantiles. Consequently, differencing cannot be used to eliminate g from (3.2b), and estimation of β in partially linear quantile regression model cannot be reduced to estimation of a parametric quantile regression model.

To see how this problem can be overcome write (3.2b) in the form

$$Y = X' \beta + g(Z) + U,$$

where

$$P(U \leq 0 | X = x, \; Z = z) = \alpha$$

for all $(x, \; z)$ and some α satisfying $0 < \alpha < 1$. Lee (2003) shows that β is identified if the probability density of U conditional on $X = x$ and $Z = z$ is strictly positive at 0 for all $(x, \; z)$ and $Var(X|Z = z)$ is nonsingular for every z. Lee (2003) then uses a version of local polynomial quantile regression to estimate β and g at each value of Z in the data. This yields n estimators of β, one for each data point. These estimators are not $n^{-1/2}$-consistent, but Lee (2003) shows that $n^{-1/2}$-consistency can be achieved by averaging them in a suitable way. Let $\bar{b}$ denote the estimator obtained by averaging. Lee (2003) gives conditions under which $n^{1/2}(\bar{b} - \beta)$ is asymptotically normally distributed with a mean of 0. Moreover, a suitably weighted average estimator is asymptotically efficient if U is homoskedastic or independent of X conditional on Z. Lee (2003) also shows how to achieve asymptotic efficiency by taking an additional estimation step if the conditional distribution of U depends on both X and Z.

Chen et al. (2003) proposed an estimator that is based on the observation that under (3.2b)

$$EX\{\alpha - I[Y - X'\beta - g(Z) \leq 0]\} = 0. \tag{3.38}$$

If g were known, β could be estimated by applying the generalized method of moments to (3.38). The resulting estimator would be

$$\tilde{b} = \arg\min_b \left[\frac{1}{n} \sum_{i=1}^{n} X_i\{\alpha - I[Y_i - X_i'b - g(Z_i) \leq 0]\} \right]^2 .$$

As in Ichimura's (1993) estimator for a single-index model, Chen, Linton, and Van Keilegom propose replacing g with a nonparametric estimator. Specifically, observe that $g(z)$ is the α-quantile of $Y - X'\beta$ conditional on $Z = z$. Accordingly, for each b in a compact parameter set B that contains β, let $\hat{g}(z, b)$ be a nonparametric estimator of the α-quantile of $Y - X'b$ conditional on $Z = z$. Nonparametric quantile estimation is discussed in the Appendix. Now estimate β by

$$\hat{b} = \arg\min_b \left[\frac{1}{n} \sum_{i=1}^{n} X_i\{\alpha - I[Y_i - X_i'b - \hat{g}(Z_i, b) \leq 0]\} \right]^2 .$$

Chen et al. (2003) give conditions under which $n^{1/2}(\hat{b} - \beta)$ is asymptotically normally distributed with a mean of 0. They also show that the bootstrap can be used to estimate the asymptotic distribution.

3.6.4 Empirical Applications

Sometimes a semiparametric model suggests a parametric form that provides a parsimonious description of the data. Schmalensee and Stoker (1999) estimated a partially linear mean-regression model of gasoline demand in the United States using data from the 1991 Residential Transportation Energy Consumption Survey. The model is

$$\log Y = \sum_{j=1}^{20} \beta_j X^j + g(Z^1, Z^2) + U,$$

where Z^1 denotes the logarithm of a household's annual income in thousands of dollars; Z^2 denotes the logarithm of the age of the head of the household in years; the X^js are discrete variables describing such things as the number of drivers in the household, household size and composition, and the region of the country in which the household is located; and $E(U|X^1, \ldots, X^{20}, Z^1, Z^2) = 0$. Figures 3.2a and b show the estimate of g. Figure 3.2a plots $\hat{g}$ as a function of z^1 (logarithm

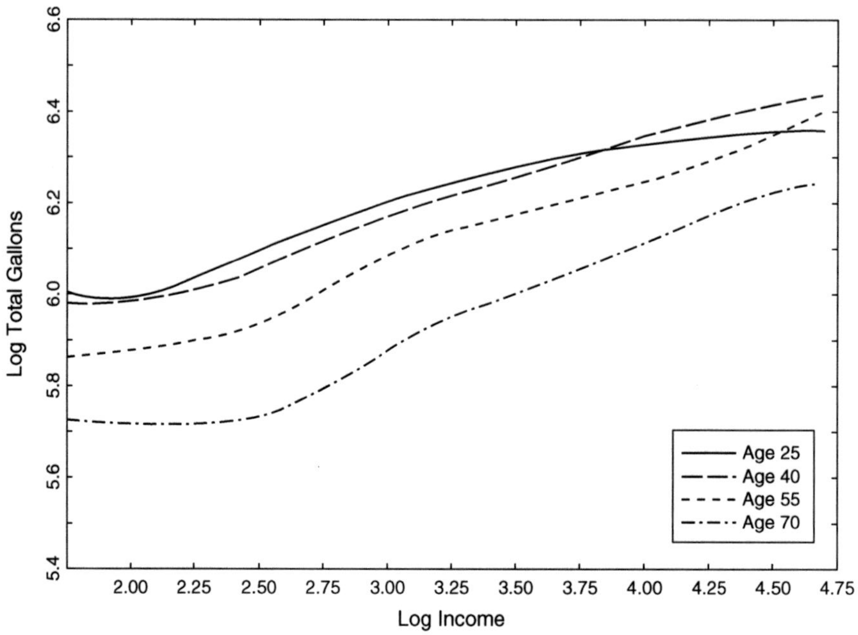

Fig. 3.2a Plot of $\hat{g}(Z^1, Z^2)$ as a function of Z^1 (log income) for various values of Z^2 (age of head of household). Source: Schmalensee and Stoker (1999)

of household income) for various values of z^2 (logarithm of the age of the head of the household). Figure 3.2b plots $\hat{g}$ as a function of z^2 at various values of z^1. The figures suggest that g may be adequately described as the sum of piecewise linear functions of z^1 and z^2. This led Schmalensee and Stoker to estimate the model

$$\log Y = \beta_0 + \sum_{j=1}^{21} \beta_j X^j + \gamma_1 (Z^1 - \log 12) I(Z^1 \geq \log 12) + \gamma_2 (Z^2 - \log 50) I(Z^2 \geq \log 50) + U,$$

where β_0, γ_1, and γ_2 are constants and all of the βs and γs are estimated by ordinary least squares. Diagnostic testing led Schmalensee and Stoker to conclude that the piecewise linear specification provides an adequate representation of g.

It is important to understand that this does not justify using the parametric model to carry out inference about the β_js or the effects of $Z^{(1)}$ and $Z^{(2)}$ on the conditional mean function. The parametric model has been fit to the semiparametric model and would not have been retained if it had not fit adequately. The parametric model is simply a parsimonious representation of the semiparametric model. It would be incorrect to use the parametric model for inference as if it had been known to be correct a priori.

There are also examples in which simple parametric models do not adequately summarize nonparametric estimates. Engle et al. (1986) estimated a model of the

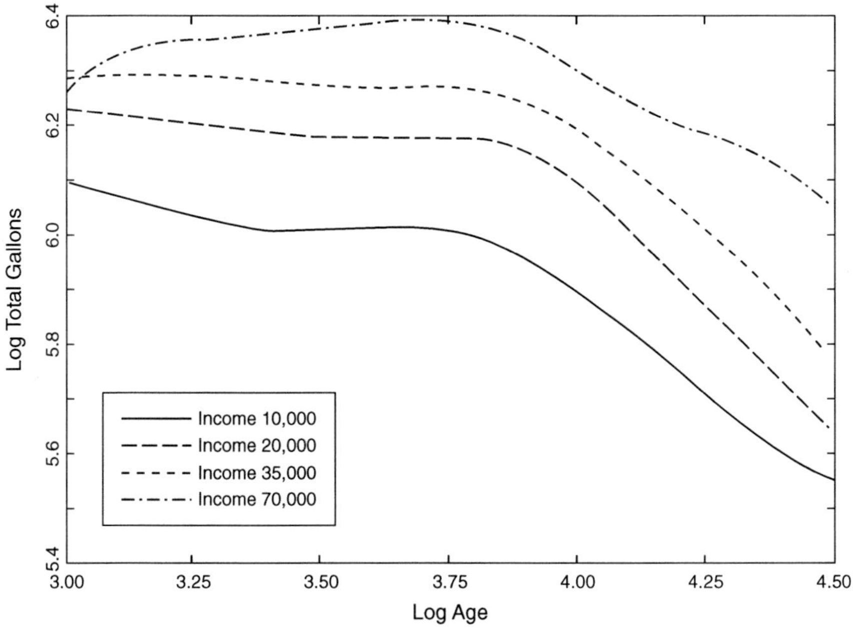

Fig. 3.2b Plot of $\hat{g}(Z^1, Z^2)$ as a function of Z^2 (age of head of household) for various values of Z^1 (log income). Source: Schmalensee and Stoker (1999)

demand for electricity in several US cities. In their model, Z denotes the temperature, so g describes the effect of temperature on electricity demand. The X variables were household income, the price of electricity, and dummy variables indicating the month of the year. In most cities, the estimates showed that g is a decreasing function of temperature up to approximately 65ºF and an increasing function of temperature thereafter. However, piecewise linear parametric models with one piece decreasing linearly up 65ºF and the other piece increasing linearly thereafter did not capture this behavior of g satisfactorily.

Chapter 4
Binary-Response Models

This chapter is concerned with estimating the binary-response model

$$Y = \begin{cases} 1 \text{ if } Y^* > 0 \\ 0 \text{ otherwise} \end{cases}, \tag{4.1a}$$

where

$$Y^* = X'\beta + U, \tag{4.1b}$$

Y is the observed dependent variable, X is a $d \times 1$ vector of observed explanatory variables, β is a $d \times 1$ vector of constant parameters, Y^* is an unobserved, latent dependent variable, and U is an unobserved random variable. The inferential problem is to use observations of (Y, X) to estimate β and, to the extent possible, the probability that $Y = 1$ conditional on X.

If the distribution of U belongs to a known, finite-dimensional parametric family, β and any parameters of the distribution of U can be estimated by maximum likelihood. As was demonstrated in Section 2.8, however, the results of maximum-likelihood estimation can be highly misleading if the distribution of U is misspecified. If the distribution of U does not belong to a known finite-dimensional family but is known to be independent of X or to depend on X only through the index $X'\beta$, then (4.1) is a semiparametric single-index model. The parameters β can be estimated using the methods of Chapter 2. As was discussed in Chapter 2, semiparametric single-index models have wide applicability. They do not, however, permit a form of heteroskedasticity of U called *random coefficients* that is often important in applications. This chapter presents a semiparametric binary-response model that accommodates many different kinds of heteroskedasticity, including random coefficients.

4.1 Random-Coefficients Models

To understand what a random-coefficients model is and why such models can be important in applications, suppose that (4.1) is a model of an individual's choice

J.L. Horowitz, *Semiparametric and Nonparametric Methods in Econometrics*,
Springer Series in Statistics, DOI 10.1007/978-0-387-92870-8_4,

between two alternatives, say traveling to work by automobile and traveling to work by bus. Automobile is chosen if $Y = 1$, and bus is chosen otherwise. Suppose that X represents differences between attributes of automobile and bus travel that are relevant to choice. For example, one component of X might be the difference between the costs of travel to work by automobile and bus, another component might be the difference between travel times by automobile and bus, etc. The parameter β characterizes an individual's preferences or tastes regarding the attributes in X. It is entirely possible that different individuals have different tastes for reasons that cannot be explained by X or other variables that are observed by an analyst. Then, from the point of view of the analyst, the parameters β of model (4.1) vary randomly among individuals, thereby making (4.1) a random-coefficients model. Hausman and Wise (1978), Fischer and Nagin (1981), and Horowitz (1993a) present empirical models of travel choices in which the coefficients are random.

The formal structure of a random-coefficients, binary-response model is

$$Y = \begin{cases} 1 \text{ if } Y^* > 0 \\ 0 \text{ otherwise} \end{cases}, \tag{4.2a}$$

where

$$Y^* = X'(\beta + \nu) + V \tag{4.2b}$$

$$= X'\beta + (X'\nu + V) \tag{4.2c}$$

$$= X'\beta + U, \tag{4.2d}$$

and $U = X'\nu + V$. In (4.2b), the coefficient of X is $\beta + \nu$, where β is a constant vector and ν is a random vector. The constant β is assumed to be the mean or median of the distribution of the coefficient of X. The random vector ν is unobserved and accounts for deviations of the coefficient of X from its population mean or median. Equations (4.2a) and (4.2d) show that the random-coefficients model has the form of the general binary-response model (4.1) but with a heteroskedastic random component U.

The problem of estimating β without assuming that the distributions of ν and V belong to known parametric families will now be addressed. The methods that will be developed permit a wide variety of different forms of heteroskedasticity of U, not just random coefficients.

4.2 Identification

The first task is to find conditions under which β is identified. That is, it is necessary to determine when β is uniquely determined by the population distribution of (Y, X).

To begin, observe that $P(Y = 1|X = x)$ is unchanged if both sides of (4.1b) are multiplied by a positive constant. Therefore, β can only be identified up to scale, and a scale normalization is needed. In this chapter, as in Chapter 2, scale normalization will be achieved by setting $|\beta_1| = 1$, where β_1 is the first component of β. For reasons that will be explained below, it will be assumed that the first component of X is a continuously distributed random variable.

It can also be seen from (4.1) that $P(Y = 1|X = x)$ is unchanged if a constant (positive or negative) is added to both sides of (4.1b). Therefore, a location normalization is needed. The most familiar location normalization sets the mean of U conditional on $X = x$ equal to zero: $E(U|X = x) = 0$. Under this location normalization, β in a random-coefficients model is the mean of the coefficient of X. If Y^* were observable, so that (4.1b) were a linear model, then the assumptions that $E(U|X = x) = 0$ and that there is no exact linear relation among the components of X would be sufficient to identify β. It turns out, however, that in a binary-response model, where Y^* is not observable, the location normalization $E(U|X = x) = 0$ is not sufficient to identify β even if the components of X are not linearly related. This nonidentification result was first obtained by Manski (1985, 1988). The following example, which is given in Horowitz (1993b), illustrates the problem.

Example 4.1: A Binary-Response Model with Mean Independence Suppose that $P(Y = 1|X = x)$ is given by a binary logit model

$$P(Y = 1|X = x) = \frac{1}{1 + \exp(-x'\beta)}.$$

This model can be obtained from (4.1) by assuming that U has the standard logistic distribution. The CDF of the standard logistic distribution is

$$F_L(u) = \frac{1}{1 + \exp(-u)}.$$

It is easy to show that $E(U) = 0$ if U has this CDF.

Now let $b \neq \beta$ be any parameter value that satisfies the scale normalization. It is shown below that for each X in the support of X, there is a random variable V_x with CDF $F_{V|x}$ such that $E(V_x|X = x) = 0$ and

$$F_{V|x}(x'b) = \frac{1}{1 + \exp(-x'\beta)}. \tag{4.3}$$

Therefore $P(Y = 1|X = x)$ can be obtained from a binary logit model with parameter β and from the model consisting of (4.1a) and

$$Y^* = X'b + V_X,$$

where $E(V_x|X = x) = 0$. This implies that β is not identified because identical choice probabilities are obtained with parameter value β and parameter value $b \neq \beta$.

To see how the random variable V_x can be constructed, let x be given. Consider the random variable W whose CDF conditional on $X = x$ is

$$F_W(w|x) = \frac{1}{1 + \exp[-w + x'(b - \beta)]}.$$

Then

$$F_W(x'b|x) = \frac{1}{1 + \exp(-x'\beta)}$$

and $E(W|X = x) = x'(b - \beta) \equiv \delta_x$. Suppose that $\delta_x > 0$. Then construct $F_{V|x}$ from the distribution of W by taking part of the probability mass of W that is to the left of $x'b$ and moving it enough further to the left to make the resulting distribution have mean 0 conditional on $X = x$. If $\delta_x < 0$, construct $F_{V|x}$ by moving probability mass rightward from the part of the distribution of W that is to the right of $x'b$. Since no probability mass crosses the point $W = x'b$ in these movements, the resulting distribution satisfies (4.3) with $E(V_x|X = x) = 0$ as required. ■

Example 4.1 shows that the mean-independence assumption $E(U|X = x) = 0$ does not restrict the distribution of U sufficiently to identify β. Identification is possible if mean independence is replaced with the stronger assumption that U is statistically independent of X. However, statistical independence of U and X precludes heteroskedasticity and, therefore, is too strong an assumption for the models of interest in this chapter. A location normalization condition that permits heteroskedasticity and identifies β is *median independence* or median$(U|X = x) = 0$. More generally, it suffices to assume that any quantile of the distribution of U is independent of X, but only median independence will be discussed here. The following theorem gives conditions that are sufficient for identification of β.

Theorem 4.1 *(Identification under median independence): Let median $(U|X = x) = 0$ for all X in the support of X. Let $|\beta_1| = 1$. Then β is identified if*

(a) The support of the distribution of X is not contained in any proper linear subspace of $\mathbb{R}^d$.
(b) For almost every $\tilde{x} = (x^2, \ldots, x^d)$ the distribution of X_1 conditional on $\tilde{X} = \tilde{x}$ has an everywhere positive density. ■

Theorem 4.1 is a slightly modified version of an identification result that was originally obtained by Manski (1985). Manski did not impose the scale normalization $|\beta_1| = 1$. Instead, he showed that β is identified up to scale under conditions (a) and (b) of Theorem 4.1.

Condition (a) implies that there is no exact linear relation among the components of X. To understand the role of condition (b) and why median $(U|X = x) = 0$ permits identification, let $\tilde{\beta}$ and $\tilde{b}$, respectively, denote the vectors consisting of all components of β and b but the first. Observe that $P(Y = 1|X=x) = P(U > -x'\beta|X = x) = 1 - P(U \leq -x'\beta|X = x)$. Therefore,

$$\begin{aligned} P(Y = 1|X = x) &\geq 0.5 \text{ if } x'\beta \geq 0 \\ &< 0.5 \text{ if } x'\beta < 0. \end{aligned}$$

Let $b \neq \beta$ be a parameter value that satisfies the scale normalization. Let $S_1(b)$ and $S_2(b)$ be the following sets:

$$S_1(b) = \{x : x'\beta < 0 \leq x'b\}, \tag{4.4}$$

$$S_2(b) = \{x : x'b < 0 \leq x'\beta\}. \tag{4.5}$$

If $P[S_1(b)] > 0$, then b is observationally distinguishable from β because there is a subset of the support of X that occurs with nonzero probability and on which $P(Y = 1|X = x) < 0.5$ with parameter value β but $P(Y = 1|X = x) \geq 0.5$ with parameter value b. Similarly, if $P[S_2(b)] > 0$, then b is observationally distinguishable from β because there is a subset of the support of X that occurs with nonzero probability and on which $P(Y = 1|X = x) \geq 0.5$ with parameter value β but $P(Y = 1|X = x) < 0.5$ with parameter value b. Therefore, β is identified if

$$P[S_1(b) \cup S_2(b)] > 0, \tag{4.6}$$

for all $b \neq \beta$. Indeed, Manski (1988) has shown that (4.6) is necessary as well as sufficient for identification of β relative to b. The necessity of (4.6) will be used in Sections 4.2.1 and 4.2.2, which deal with identification when the support of X is bounded or discrete.

Let X^1 and x^1, respectively, denote the first components of X and x. Because the first components of b and β equal 1, for any $b \neq \beta$,

$$S_1(b) = \{x: -\tilde{x}'\tilde{b} \leq x^1 < -\tilde{x}\tilde{\beta}\}$$

and

$$S_2(b) = \{x: -\tilde{x}'\tilde{\beta} \leq x^1 < -\tilde{x}'\tilde{b}\}.$$

If the distribution of X^1 has everywhere positive density conditional on $\tilde{X} = \tilde{x}$, then $S_1(b)$ has positive probability whenever $-\tilde{x}'\tilde{b} < -\tilde{x}'\tilde{\beta}$ and $S_2(b)$ has positive probability whenever $-\tilde{x}'\tilde{\beta} < -\tilde{x}'\tilde{b}$. Therefore, β is identified if

$$P(\tilde{X}'\tilde{b} = \tilde{X}'\tilde{\beta}) < 1. \tag{4.7}$$

Inequality (4.7) holds whenever condition (a) of Theorem 4.1 holds, thereby establishing identification of β under the assumptions of this theorem.

Condition (b) of Theorem 4.1 implies that X has at least one continuously distributed component, X^1, and that this component has unbounded support. It is worth considering whether identification is possible if these conditions fail to hold. In the next section, it is shown that unbounded support of X^1 is not necessary for identification of β. Continuity is necessary except in special cases.

4.2.1 Identification Analysis When X Has Bounded Support

In this section it is assumed that X has bounded support but that the distribution of X^1 conditional on $\tilde{X}$ has a density. Condition (b) of Theorem 4.1 is violated because the density of X^1 conditional on $\tilde{X}$ is not everywhere positive.

Let S_X denote the bounded support of X. It can be seen from (4.4) to (4.6) that β is not identified if there is a $\delta > 0$ such that $|x'\beta| \geq \delta$ for all $x \in S_X$. If $|x'\beta| \geq \delta$ for all $x \in S_X$, then $x'b$ has the same sign as $x'\beta$ for all $x \in S_X$ and any b that is sufficiently close to β. Therefore, $S_1(b)$ and $S_2(b)$ are empty sets for all such bs, and (4.6) does not hold for them. Since (4.6) is necessary for identification of β relative to b, β is not identified if $|x'\beta| \geq \delta$ for all $x \in S_X$. This result was first obtained by Manski (1985).

Identification is possible, however, if the support of $X'\beta$ conditional on $\tilde{X}$ includes an interval containing $X'\beta = 0$ for sufficiently many values of $\tilde{X}$. The following corollary to Theorem 4.1 gives conditions sufficient for identification of β when X has bounded support.

Corollary 4.1 (Identification of β when X has bounded support): Let X have bounded support. Let median $(U|X = x) = 0$ for all x in the support of X. Let the first component of β equal 1. Then β is identified if for some $\delta > 0$, there are an interval $I_\delta = [-\delta, \delta]$ and a set $N_\delta \in \mathbb{R}^{d-1}$ such that

(a) N_δ is not contained in any proper linear subspace of $\mathbb{R}^{d-1}$.
(b) $P(\tilde{X} \in N_\delta)$.
(c) For almost every $\tilde{x} \in N_\delta$, the distribution of $X'\beta$ conditional on $\tilde{X} = \tilde{x}$ has a probability density that is everywhere positive on I_δ. ■

Conditions (a–c) of Corollary 4.1 imply that for each $\tilde{x}$ in a sufficiently rich set, there is an interval of the real line with the property that $P(Y = 1|X^1 = x^1, \tilde{X} = \tilde{x}) > 0.5$ for some values of x^1 in this interval and $P(Y = 1|X^1 = x^1, \tilde{X} = \tilde{x}) \leq 0.5$ for others. If $P(Y = 1|X = x)$ is a continuous function of the components of x corresponding to continuous components of X, this implication can be tested, at least in principle, by estimating the nonparametric mean regression of Y on X.

To understand why conditions (a–c) of Corollary 4.1 are sufficient to identify β, observe that the sets $S_1(b)$ and $S_2(b)$ defined in (4.4) and (4.5) can be written in the form

$$S_1(b) = \{x: -\tilde{x}'(\tilde{b} - \tilde{\beta}) \leq x'\beta < 0\}$$

and

$$S_2(b) = \{x: 0 \leq x'\beta < -\tilde{x}'(\tilde{b} - \tilde{\beta})\}.$$

Condition (c) of Corollary (4.1) implies that at least one of these sets has nonzero probability if $x \in N_\delta$ and $\tilde{x}'(\tilde{b} - \tilde{\beta}) \neq 0$. Conditions (a) and (b) imply that $P[\tilde{X}'(\tilde{b} - \tilde{\beta}) \neq 0] > 0$ if $b \neq \beta$. Therefore, condition (4.6) holds, and β is identified.

If $|x'\beta| \geq \delta$ for some $\delta > 0$ and all $x \in S_X$, then β is not identified but it may be possible to bound individual components of β. Manski (1988) has given the following conditions under which the signs of components of β are identified.

Theorem 4.2 (Manski 1988): *Let X^* be the vector of all components of X except the mth ($m \neq 1$). Let S_x^* denote the support of X^*. For any $b \in \mathbb{R}^d$, define*

$$S_b = \{x^* \in S_X^* : P(X'b < 0|X^* = x^*) > 0 \text{ or } P(X'b > 0|X^* = x^*) > 0\}.$$

If $\beta_m \neq 0$, then the sign of β_m is identified if $P(X^* \in S_\beta) > 0$. If $\beta_m = 0$, then β_m is identified if $P(X^* \in S_b) > 0$ for all $b \in \mathbb{R}^d$ such that $b_m \neq 0$. ■

To obtain further results on bounding β, suppose that $P(Y = 1|X = x)$ is a continuous function of the components of x that correspond to continuous components of X. Under this continuity assumption, $P(Y = 1|X = x)$ is identified by the nonparametric mean regression of Y on X. Therefore, bounds (possibly infinite) on β_m ($m \neq 1$) can be obtained by solving the problems

$$\begin{aligned}
&\text{maximize (minimize): } b_m \\
&\text{subject to: } x'\beta \leq 0 \text{ if } P(Y = 1|X = x) < 0.5 \\
&\qquad\qquad\quad x'\beta \geq 0 \text{ if } P(Y = 1|X = x) \leq 0.5 \\
&\text{for all } x \in S_X.
\end{aligned} \tag{4.8}$$

Problem (4.8) finds the largest and smallest values of b_m that allow the signs of $x'b$ and $x'\beta$ to be the same for every $x \in S_X$. The sign of $x'\beta$ is identified because it is determined by whether the identified quantity $P(Y = 1|X = x)$ does or does not exceed 0.5.

The linear programming problem (4.8) has infinitely many constraints, so solving it in practice can be difficult. A version of (4.8) that can be solved with standard linear programming techniques can be obtained by considering only the constraints for which x takes values in a finite subset of S_x, possibly the values contained in the available data. The resulting bounds are looser than the ones obtained by solving the infinitely constrained problem but are arbitrarily close to the bounds obtained from the infinitely constrained (4.8) if the chosen subset is sufficiently dense.

Example 4.3 in Section 4.2.2 illustrates the use of (4.8).

4.2.2 *Identification When X Is Discrete*

In this section, it is assumed that the support of X, S_X, consists of finitely many discrete points. Suppose, first, that $|x'\beta| > 0$ for all $x \in S_X$. Then arguments identical to those made at the beginning of Section 4.2.1 show that there are points b for which (4.6) does not hold. Therefore, β is not identified.

The situation is more complicated if $x'\beta = 0$ for one or more points $x \in S_X$. To analyze this case, define $S_0 = \{x \in S_X : x'\beta = 0\}$. Let N_0 be the number of points in S_0. Because S_X is finite, $|x'\beta| \geq \delta$ for all $x \in S_X - S_0$ and some $\delta > 0$. Choose M so that $\|x\| \leq M$ for all $x \in S_X$, and choose ε such that $0 < \varepsilon < \delta/M$. Then $x'\beta$ and $x'b$ have the same sign if $x \in S_X - S_0$ and $\|b - \beta\| \leq \varepsilon$. Therefore, if $\|b - \beta\| \leq \varepsilon$, $S_1(b)$, is empty and

$$S_2(b) = \{x \in S_0 : x'b < 0\}. \tag{4.9}$$

Because (4.6) is necessary for identification of β relative to b, β is not identified if there is any b such that $\|b - \beta\| \leq \varepsilon$ and $S_2(b)$ in (4.9) is empty.

It is not difficult to show that such b's always exist if $N_0 \leq d - 1$, where $d = \dim(X)$. Let $\breve{x}$ be the $d \times N_0$ matrix that is obtained by placing the elements of S_0 side by side. Let e be a $N_0 \times 1$ vector of ones. Let $c > 0$ be a scalar. Consider the equation

$$\breve{x}'b^* = c. \tag{4.10}$$

Because $\breve{x}'\beta = 0$, (4.10) is equivalent to

$$\breve{x}'(b^* - \beta) = c. \tag{4.11}$$

Scale normalization equates the first components of b^* and β, so (4.11) is N_0 linear equations with $k-1$ unknown quantities. Let $(b^* - \beta)$ be a solution. If $\|b^* - \beta\| \leq \varepsilon$, set $b = b^*$. Then $\breve{x}'b > 0$, $S_2(b)$ is empty, and β is not identified relative to this b. If $\|b^* - \beta\| = \lambda > \varepsilon$, set $b = (1, \tilde{b}')'$, where

$$\tilde{b} = \tilde{\beta} + \frac{\varepsilon}{\lambda}(\tilde{b}^* - \tilde{\beta})$$

and $\tilde{b}^*$ denotes components 2 through d of b^*. Then $\|b - \beta\| = \varepsilon$ and

$$\begin{aligned}\breve{x}'b &= \breve{x}'\beta + \frac{\varepsilon}{\lambda}\breve{x}'(b^* - \beta)\\ &= \frac{\varepsilon}{\lambda}c\\ &> 0.\end{aligned}$$

It follows that $S_2(b)$ is empty, and β is not identified relative to this b. Therefore, if $N_0 \leq d - 1$, there are always points b for which $S_2(b)$ is empty. It follows that β is not identified if $N_0 \leq d - 1$.

If $N_0 \geq d$, β may or may not be identified, depending on the configuration of points in S_0. This is illustrated by the following example.

Example 4.2: Identification of β When X Is Discrete Let $d = 2$. Let $S_0 = \{(1, -1)', (-1, 1)'\}$ and $\beta = (1, 1)'$. Then

$$\breve{x}'b = \begin{pmatrix} 1 & -1 \\ -1 & 1 \end{pmatrix} \begin{pmatrix} 1 \\ \tilde{b} \end{pmatrix}$$
$$= \begin{pmatrix} 1 - \tilde{b} \\ -1 + \tilde{b} \end{pmatrix}$$

for any b. Therefore, $\breve{x}'b$ always has a negative element when $b \neq \beta$, and β is identified.

Now let $S_0 = \{(1{,}1)', (2{,}2)'\}$ and $\beta = (1, -1')$. Then

$$\breve{x}'b = \begin{pmatrix} 1 & 1 \\ 2 & 2 \end{pmatrix} \begin{pmatrix} 1 \\ \tilde{b} \end{pmatrix}$$
$$= \begin{pmatrix} 1 + \tilde{b} \\ 2 + 2\tilde{b} \end{pmatrix}.$$

Given any $\varepsilon > 0$, let $b = (1, -1 + \varepsilon/2')$. Then

$$\breve{x}'b = \begin{pmatrix} \varepsilon/2 \\ \varepsilon \end{pmatrix}.$$

It follows that $S_2(b)$ is empty and β is not identified. ■

The discussion in this section shows that β is identified only in special cases when X is discrete. However, β can be bounded even if it is not identified by solving the linear programming problem (4.8). This procedure is illustrated in the following example.

Example 4.3: Bounding β When It Is Not Identified Let $d = 2$ and $\beta = (1,-0.5)'$. Suppose that $P(Y = 1|X = x)$ and the points of support of X are as shown in Table 4.1. Then β is not identified because X has finite support and $P(X'\beta = 0) = 0$. The first component of β is known by scale normalization, so only β_2 needs to be bounded. Problem (4.8) is, therefore,

$$\begin{aligned} &\text{maximize (minimize): } b_2 \\ &\text{subject to: } b_2 \leq 0 \\ &\qquad 0.6 + 0.5b_2 \geq 0 \\ &\qquad 1 + b_2 \geq 0. \end{aligned}$$

It is clear that the solutions are $-1 \leq b_2 \leq 0$. Thus, although b_2 is not identified, it can be bounded from both above and below. ■

Table 4.1 An unidentified binary-response model

(x^1, x^2)	$P(Y = 1\|X = x)$	$x^1 + b_2x^2$
(1, 0)	0.8	1
(0, 1)	0.3	b_2
(0.6, 0.5)	0.6	$0.6+0.5b_2$
(1, 1)	0.7	$1 + b_2$

4.3 Estimation

We now turn to the problem of estimating β in the binary-response model (4.1) with the location normalization median $(U|X = x) = 0$. It is assumed throughout the remainder of this chapter that β is identified and that the distribution of X^1 conditional on $\tilde{X}$ has a density. When it is necessary to specify the conditions insuring identification of β, it will be assumed for convenience that conditions (a) and (b) of Theorem 4.1 are satisfied. However, all results also hold under the conditions of Corollary 4.1.

Although the main task of this section is developing estimators of β, it is also important to consider estimating $P(Y = 1|X = x)$. This problem is addressed in Section 4.3.1. It turns out that little information about $P(Y = 1|X = x)$ can be obtained without making assumptions that are considerably stronger than the ones needed to estimate β. Estimators of β are developed in Sections 4.3.2 and 4.3.3.

4.3.1 Estimating P(Y = 1|X = x)

The assumptions needed to identify and, as will be seen in Section 4.3.2, estimate β do not require $P(Y = 1|X = x)$ to be a continuous function of the continuous components of x. As a result, $P(Y = 1|X = x)$ is not identified over most of the support of X, and estimation of $P(Y = 1|X = x)$ under these assumptions is not possible. The only information about $P(Y = 1|X = x)$ that can be obtained is that implied by knowledge of $x'\beta$, which is identified and estimable. This information is

$$P(Y = 1|X = x) \begin{array}{l} \geq 0.5 \text{ if } x'\beta \geq 0 \\ = 0.5 \text{ if } x'\beta = 0 \\ < 0.5 \text{ if } x'\beta < 0 \end{array} \tag{4.12}$$

Thus, the numerical value of $P(Y = 1|X = x)$ is known if $x'\beta = 0$. Otherwise, only bounds on $P\,(Y = 1|X = x)$ can be obtained.

Now let b_n be a consistent estimator of β. Let x be fixed, and consider the problem of finding an empirical analog of (4.12). Observe that if $x'\beta > 0$, then $P(x'b_n > 0) \to 1$ as $n \to \infty$. Conversely, if $x'\beta < 0$, then $P(x'b_n < 0) \to 1$ as $n \to \infty$. On the other hand, if $x'\beta = 0$, then $x'b_n$ can be either positive or negative, regardless of the size of n. Therefore, the following estimated bounds on $P(Y = 1|X = x)$ hold with probability approaching 1 as $n \to \infty$.

$$P_n(Y = 1|X = x) \begin{array}{l} \geq 0.5 \text{ if } x'b_n \geq 0 \\ \leq 0.5 \text{ if } x'b_n \leq 0 \end{array} \tag{4.13}$$

If it is assumed that $P(Y = 1|X = x)$ is a continuous function of $x'\beta$ in a neighborhood of $x'\beta = 0$, then the bounds (4.13) can be sharpened to

$$P_n(Y = 1|X = x) \begin{array}{l} \geq 0.5 \text{ if } x'b_n > 0 \\ = 0.5 \text{ if } x'b_n = 0 \\ \leq 0.5 \text{ if } x'b_n < 0 \end{array} \tag{4.14}$$

Finally, suppose it is assumed that $P(Y = 1|X = x)$ is a continuous function of the components of x that correspond to continuous components of X. Then $P(Y = 1|X = x)$ can be estimated as the nonparametric mean regression of Y on X. The continuity assumption required by this approach is reasonable in many applications but is stronger than necessary to identify or estimate β.

4.3.2 Estimating β: The Maximum-Score Estimator

The maximum-score estimator was proposed by Manski (1975, 1985) as a method for estimating β consistently in the binary-response model (4.1) when median $(U|X = x) = 0$. This estimator is the binary-response analog of the least-absolute-deviations (LAD) estimator of a linear median-regression model. In a linear median-regression model, the dependent variable Y is related to explanatory variables X by

$$Y = X'\beta + U,$$

where median $(U|X = x) = 0$. It follows that median $(Y|X = x) = x'\beta$. Moreover, β minimizes the quantity

$$S_{lin}(b) = E|Y - X'b| \tag{4.15}$$

whenever the expectation exists. The LAD estimator of β minimizes the sample analog of $E|Y - X'b|$ that is obtained by replacing the expectation with a sample average. Thus, the LAD estimator solves the problem

$$\text{minimize: } \frac{1}{n}\sum_{i=1}^{n} |Y_i - X_i'b|,$$

where $\{Y_i, X_i : i = 1, \ldots, n\}$ is a random sample of (Y, X).

To motivate the maximum-score estimator, observe that by the definition of the median,

$$\text{median } (Y|X = x) = \inf\{y : P(Y \geq y|X = x) \geq 0.5\}. \tag{4.16}$$

Combining (4.12) and (4.16) yields

$$\text{median } (Y|X = x) = I(x'\beta \geq 0).$$

Therefore the binary-response version of (4.15) is

$$S_{bin}(b) = E|Y - I(X'b \geq 0)|. \tag{4.17}$$

Some easy algebra shows that

$$S_{bin}(b) = E[Y - (2Y - 1)I(X'b \geq 0)]. \tag{4.18}$$

Therefore

$$S_{bin}(b) - S_{bin}(\beta) = E\{(2Y - 1)[I(X'\beta \geq 0) - I(X'b \geq 0)]\},$$

and

$$S_{bin}(b) - S_{bin}(\beta) = E\{[2P(Y = 1|X) - 1][I(X'\beta \geq 0) - I(x'b \geq 0)]\}. \tag{4.19}$$

The right-hand side of (4.19) is zero if $b = \beta$ and nonnegative otherwise. Therefore, $b = \beta$ minimizes $S_{bin}(b)$. Indeed, by using arguments similar to those made following the statement of Theorem 4.1, it can be shown that β is the unique minimizer of $S_{bin}(b)$ under the assumptions of that theorem. Thus, we have

Theorem 4.3 *Let median* $(U|X = x) = 0$ *for all* x *in the support of* X. *Let* $|\beta_1| = 1$. *Then* β *is the unique minimizer of* $E[S_{bin}(b)]$ *if*

(a) *The support of the distribution of* X *is not contained in any proper linear subspace of* $\mathbb{R}^d$.
(b) *For almost every* $\tilde{x} = (x^2, \ldots, x^d)$ *the distribution of* X^1 *conditional on* $\tilde{X} = \tilde{x}$ *has an everywhere positive density.* ■

This result is proved formally in Manski (1985).

The sample analog of $S_{bin}(b)$ is obtained by replacing the expectation with a sample average. This yields

$$\tilde{S}_n(b) = \frac{1}{n}\sum_{i=1}^{n} Y_i - \frac{1}{n}\sum_{i=1}^{n}(2Y_i - 1)I(X_i'b \geq 0). \tag{4.20}$$

The maximum-score estimator of β minimizes $\tilde{S}_n(b)$. Observe, however, that the first term on the right-hand side of (4.20) does not depend on b and, therefore, does not affect the minimization of $\tilde{S}_n(b)$. Therefore, taking account of the minus sign that precedes the second term, it suffices to solve

$$\underset{|b_1|=1,b}{\text{maximize}}: S_{ms}(b) \equiv \frac{1}{n}\sum_{i=1}^{n}(2Y_i - 1)I(X_i'b \geq 0). \tag{4.21}$$

Any solution to (4.21) is a maximum-score estimator of β. Florios and Skouras (2008) give an algorithm for computing the maximum-score estimator.

Equations (4.17) and (4.18) show that the maximum-score estimator is the binary-response analog of the LAD estimator of the coefficient vector of a linear median-regression model. Another interpretation of the maximum-score estimator can be obtained by observing that solving (4.21) is equivalent to solving

$$\underset{|b_1|=1,b}{\text{maximize}}: S_{ms}^*(b) \equiv \frac{1}{n}\sum_{i=1}^{n}(2Y_i - 1)[2I(X_i'b \geq 0) - 1]. \tag{4.22}$$

The summand in (4.22) equals 1 if $Y_i = 1$ and $X_i'b \geq 0$ or if $Y_i = 0$ and $X_i b < 0$. The summand equals –1 otherwise. Suppose one predicts that $Y_i = 1$ if $X_i'b \geq 0$ and $Y_i = 0$ otherwise. Assign a score value of 1 if the predicted and observed values of Y_i are the same and –1 if they are not. Then $S_{ms}^*(b)$ is the sum of the scores, and the maximum-score estimator maximizes the total score or total number of correct predictions.

Manski (1985) has proved that the maximum-score estimator is strongly consistent for β. This result is stated formally in Theorem 4.4:

Theorem 4.4 *Let median* $(U|X = x) = 0$ *for all* x *in the support of* X *. Let the first component of* β *equal* 1*. Assume that there is a known, compact set* B *that contains* β*. Let* b_n *solve*

$$\underset{|b_1|=1,b\in B}{\text{maximize}}: S_{ms}^*(b) \equiv \frac{1}{n}\sum_{i=1}^{n}(2Y_i - 1)[2I(X_i'b \geq 0) - 1] \tag{4.23}$$

or, equivalently,

$$\underset{|b_1|=1,b\in B}{\text{maximize}}: S_{ms}(b) \equiv \frac{1}{n}\sum_{i=1}^{n}(2Y_i - 1)I(X_i'b \geq 0). \tag{4.24}$$

Then $b_n \to \beta$ *almost surely as* $n \to \infty$ *if*

(a) $\{Y_i, X_i : i = 1, \ldots, n\}$ *is a random sample from the distribution of* (Y, X)*.*
(b) The support of the distribution of X *is not contained in any proper linear subspace of* $\mathbb{R}^d$*.*
(c) For almost every $\tilde{x} = (x^2, \ldots, x^d)$*, the distribution of* X^1 *conditional on* $\tilde{X} = \tilde{x}$ *has an everywhere positive density.* ■

Cavanagh (1987) and Kim and Pollard (1990) have derived the rate of convergence and asymptotic distribution of the maximum-score estimator. This is a difficult task because $S_{ms}(b)$ and $S_{ms}^*(b)$ are discontinuous functions of b. Therefore, the standard Taylor-series methods of asymptotic distribution theory cannot be applied to the maximum-score estimator. Cavanagh (1987) and Kim and Pollard (1990) show that the maximum-score estimator converges in probability at the rate $n^{-1/3}$. The limiting distribution of $n^{1/3}(b_n - \beta)$ is that of the point that maximizes a multidimensional Brownian motion with quadratic drift. This distribution is too complex for use in carrying out statistical inference in applications.

Manski and Thompson (1986) proposed using the bootstrap to estimate the distribution of the maximum-score estimator and to carry out statistical inference. However, Abrevaya and Huang (2005) have shown that the bootstrap does not consistently estimate the asymptotic distribution of the maximum-score estimator. The asymptotic distribution can be estimated consistently by nonreplacement subsampling (Politis and Romano 1994; Politis et al. 1999). In this procedure, subsamples of size $m < n$ are drawn by sampling the data randomly without replacement. The maximum-score estimator b_m is computed from each subsample. The asymptotic distribution of $n^{1/3}(b_n - \beta)$ is estimated by the empirical distribution of $m^{1/3}(b_m - b_n)$ that is induced by the subsampling procedure. Delgado et al. (2001) provide further details and Monte Carlo evidence on the performance of the procedure. Subsampling can be used to obtain a confidence interval for β or test a hypothesis about β. It should not be used to obtain standard errors. This is because the maximum-score estimator is not normally distributed, even asymptotically. Therefore, there is no simple relation between standard errors and the distribution of the estimator, and standard errors cannot be used to construct a confidence interval or hypothesis test.

The rate of convergence of the maximum-score estimator, $n^{-1/3}$, is much slower than the $n^{-1/2}$ rate of parametric and single-index estimators. The slow rate of convergence of the maximum-score estimator is sometimes interpreted as implying that this estimator is not as useful as parametric or single-index estimators. This interpretation is incorrect. The maximum-score estimator makes assumptions about the distribution of (Y, X) that are different from the assumptions made by parametric and single-index estimators. Most importantly for influencing the rate of convergence, the maximum-score estimator permits U to have arbitrary heteroskedasticity of unknown form subject to the centering restriction $\text{median}(U|X = x) = 0$. In contrast, single-index models permit only limited forms of heteroskedasticity, and parametric models require the form of any heteroskedasticity to be known up to finitely many parameters. As will be discussed in Section 4.3.3, the maximum-score estimator converges at the fastest rate possible under its assumptions. Thus, its slow rate of convergence is not a defect but a reflection of the difficulty in carrying out estimation under its assumptions, especially its assumptions about heteroskedasticity.

4.3.3 Estimating β: The Smoothed Maximum-Score Estimator

The maximum-score estimator has a complicated limiting distribution that is difficult to derive because the maximum-score objective function is discontinuous. Horowitz (1992) proposed smoothing the discontinuities in $S_{ms}^*(b)$ to achieve a differentiable function. He showed that under assumptions that are slightly stronger than those of Theorem 4.4, the resulting smoothed maximum-score estimator has a limiting normal distribution and a rate of convergence that is at least $n^{-2/5}$ and can be arbitrarily close to $n^{-1/2}$ under certain smoothness assumptions. This section describes the smoothed maximum-score estimator.

The smoothed maximum-score estimator can be obtained from either $S_{ms}(b)$ or $S^*_{ms}(b)$, and its properties are the same regardless of which is used. Only $S_{ms}(b)$ will be considered in this discussion. $S_{ms}(b)$ is a discontinuous function of b because each term in the sum on the right-hand side of (4.24) contains the factor $I(X_i'b \geq 0)$, which is a step function. The smoothed maximum-score estimator is obtained by replacing this indicator function with a function that is twice differentiable. To do this, let K be a function satisfying $|K(v)| < M$ for all v and some $M < \infty$, $\lim_{v\to-\infty} K(v) = 0$, and $\lim_{v\to\infty} K(v) = 1$. K can be thought of as the integral of a kernel function for nonparametric density estimation. K is not a kernel function itself. Let $\{h_n\}$ be a sequence of positive numbers (bandwidths) that converges to 0 as $n \to \infty$. The smoothed maximum-score estimator of β solves

$$\underset{|b_1|=1, b\in B}{\text{maximize}}: S_{sms}(b) \equiv \frac{1}{n}\sum_{i=1}^{n}(2Y_i - 1)K\left(\frac{X_i'b}{h_n}\right). \tag{4.25}$$

Horowitz (1992) showed that the smoothed maximum-score estimator is consistent for β under the conditions of Theorem 4.4. The intuition for this result is as follows. It is not difficult to prove that $|S_{ms}(b) - S_{sms}(b)| \to 0$ with probability 1 as $n \to \infty$ uniformly over $b \in B$ (see Horowitz 1992, Lemma 4). The reason for this is that as $h_n \to 0$,

$$K\left(\frac{X_i'b}{h_n}\right) \to 1 \text{ if } X_i'b > 0$$
$$\to 0 \text{ if } X_i'b < 0$$

for each $i = 1, \ldots, n$. Therefore,

$$K\left(\frac{X_i'b}{h_n}\right) \to I(X_i'b \geq 0)$$

if $X_i'b \neq 0$. $K(X_i'b/h_n)$ may not converge to $I(X_i'b \geq 0)$ if $X_i'b = 0$, but $P(X_i'b = 0) = 0$. Therefore, with probability 1, $S_{sms}(b)$ and $S_{ms}(b)$ can be made arbitrarily close to one another for all $b \in B$ by making n sufficiently large. Indeed, it can be shown that this result holds uniformly over $b \in B$. Therefore, the values of b that maximize $S_{sms}(b)$ and $S_{ms}(b)$ can also be made arbitrarily close to one another.

The rate of convergence and asymptotic distribution of the smoothed maximum-score estimator can be obtained by using Taylor-series methods like those used to obtain the asymptotic distributions of parametric estimators (see, e.g., Amemiya 1985, Newey and McFadden 1994). To do this, define $d = \dim(\beta)$, and let β_j denote the j'th component of β. Let $\tilde{\beta}$ be the $(d-1) \times 1$ vector consisting of components 2 through d of β. Similarly, let b_n denote any solution to (4.25), and let $\tilde{b}_n$ denote components 2 through d of b_n. Observe that because β_1, the first component of β, can have only two values, every consistent estimator b_{n1} of β_1 satisfies $\lim_{n\to\infty} P(b_{n1} = \beta_1) = 1$ and converges in probability faster than n^{-r} for any $r > 0$.

This is not true of the remaining components of β, which can take on a continuum of values. Therefore, it is necessary to derive only the asymptotic distribution of $\tilde{b}_n$.

To do this, let β be an interior point of the parameter set B. Since b_n is consistent for β, b_n is an interior point of B with probability approaching 1 as $n \to \infty$. Therefore, with probability approaching 1, b_n satisfies the first-order condition

$$\frac{\partial S_{sms}(b_n)}{\partial \tilde{b}} = 0. \tag{4.26}$$

A Taylor-series expansion of the left-hand side of (4.26) about $b_n = \beta$ gives

$$\frac{\partial S_{sms}(\beta)}{\partial \tilde{b}} + \frac{\partial^2 S_{sms}(b_n^*)}{\partial \tilde{b} \partial \tilde{b}'}(\tilde{b}_n - \tilde{\beta}) = 0, \tag{4.27}$$

where b_n^* is between $\tilde{b}_n$ and $\tilde{\beta}$. Now suppose that there is a nonsingular matrix Q such that

$$\operatorname*{plim}_{n\to\infty} \frac{\partial^2 S_{sms}(b_n^*)}{\partial \tilde{b} \partial \tilde{b}'} = Q. \tag{4.28}$$

Suppose, also, that as $n \to \infty$,

$$n^r \frac{\partial S_{sms}(\beta)}{\partial \tilde{b}} \xrightarrow{d} W \tag{4.29}$$

for some $r > 0$ and some random variable W. Then (4.27) can be written in the form

$$W + Qn^r(\tilde{b}_n - \tilde{\beta}) = o_p(1)$$

and

$$n^r(\tilde{b}_n - \tilde{\beta}) = -Q^{-1}W + o_p(1).$$

Thus, $n^r(\tilde{b}_n - \tilde{\beta})$ is asymptotically distributed as $-Q^{-1}W$. It turns out that W is normally distributed, as is discussed below. The value of r and, therefore, the rate of convergence of the smoothed maximum-score estimator depend on certain smoothness properties of $P(Y = 1|X = x)$ and the probability distribution of $X'\beta$ conditional on $\tilde{X}$. Under regularity conditions that are given below, the rate of convergence is at least $n^{-2/5}$ and can be arbitrarily close (though not equal) to $n^{-1/2}$ if $P(Y = 1|X = x)$ and the conditional distribution of $X'\beta$ are sufficiently smooth.

Additional notation is needed to formalize these ideas and make them precise. Define $Z = X'\beta$ and observe that since $|\beta_1| = 1$, there is a one-to-one relation between $(Z, \tilde{X})$ and X for any fixed β. Assume that the distribution of Z conditional on $\tilde{X} = \tilde{x}$ has a probability density $p(z|\tilde{x})$ that is strictly positive for almost every $\tilde{x}$. For each positive integer j, define

$$p^{(j)}(z|\tilde{x}) = \frac{\partial^j p(z|\tilde{x})}{\partial z^j}$$

whenever the derivative exists, and define $p^{(0)}(z|\tilde{x}) = p(z|\tilde{x})$. Let P denote the CDF of $\tilde{X}$, and let $F(\cdot|z, \tilde{x})$ denote the CDF of U conditional on $Z = z$ and $\tilde{X} = \tilde{x}$. For each positive integer j, define

$$F^{(j)}(-z|z, \tilde{x}) = \frac{\partial^j F(-z|z, \tilde{x})}{\partial z^j}$$

whenever the derivative exists. For example,

$$F^{(1)}(-z|z, \tilde{x}) = -\left[\frac{\partial F(u|z,\tilde{x})}{\partial u} - \frac{\partial F(u|z,\tilde{x})}{\partial z}\right]_{u=-z}.$$

Let K' and K'', respectively, denote the first and second derivatives of K. Let s be a positive integer that is defined according to criteria that are stated below. Define the scalar constants α_A and α_D by

$$\alpha_A = \int_{-\infty}^{\infty} v^s K'(v) dv$$

and

$$\alpha_D = \int_{-\infty}^{\infty} K'(v)^2 dv.$$

whenever these quantities exist. Define the $(d-1) \times 1$ vector A and the $(d-1) \times (d-1)$ matrices D and Q by

$$A = -2\alpha_A \sum_{j=1}^{s} \frac{1}{j!(s-j)!} E[F^{(j)}(0|0, \tilde{X}) p^{(s-j)}(0|\tilde{X})\tilde{X}],$$

$$D = \alpha_D E[\tilde{X}\tilde{X}' p(0|\tilde{X})],$$

and

$$Q = 2E[\tilde{X}\tilde{X}' F^{(1)}(0|0, \tilde{X}) p(0|\tilde{X})]$$

whenever these quantities exist.

The asymptotic distribution of the smoothed maximum-score estimator is derived under the following assumptions:

SMS1: $\{Y_i, X_i: i = 1, \ldots, n\}$ is a random sample of (Y, X), where $Y = I(X'\beta + U \geq 0)$, $X \in \mathbb{R}^d (d \geq 1)$, U is a random scalar, and $\beta \in \mathbb{R}^d$ is a constant.

SMS2: (a) The support of the distribution of X is not contained in any proper linear subspace of $\mathbb{R}^d$. (b) $0 < P(Y = 1|X = x) < 1$ for almost every

x. (c) $|\beta_1| = 1$, and for almost every $\tilde{x} = (x^2, \ldots, x^d)$, the distribution of X^1 conditional on $\tilde{X} = \tilde{x}$ has an everywhere positive probability density.

SMS3: Median$(U|X = x) = 0$ for almost every x.

SMS4: $\tilde{\beta} = (\beta_2, \ldots, \beta_d)'$ is an interior point of a compact set $\tilde{B} \in \mathbb{R}^{d-1}$.

SMS5: The components of $\tilde{X}$ are bounded.

SMS6: As $n \to \infty$, $h_n \to 0$ and $(\log n)/(nh_n^4) \to 0$.

SMS7: (a) K is twice differentiable everywhere, $|K'|$ and $|K''|$ are uniformly bounded, and each of the following integrals is finite:

$$\int_{-\infty}^{\infty} K'(v)dv, \int_{-\infty}^{\infty} K''(v)dv, \int_{-\infty}^{\infty} |v^2 K''(v)|dv.$$

(b) For some integer $s \geq 2$ and each integer j $(1 \leq j \leq s)$

$$\int_{-\infty}^{\infty} v^j K'(v)dv = \begin{cases} 0 \text{ if } j < s \\ \text{finite if } j = s \end{cases}. \tag{4.30}$$

(c) For each integer j between 0 and s, any $\eta > 0$, and any positive sequence $\{h_n\}$ converging to 0

$$\lim_{n\to\infty} h_n^{j-2} \int_{|h_n v| > \eta} |v^j K'(v)|dv = 0$$

and

$$\lim_{n\to\infty} h_n^{-1} \int_{|h_n v| > \eta} |K''(v)|dv = 0.$$

SMS8: For each integer j such that $1 \leq j \leq s-1$, all z in a neighborhood of 0, almost every $\tilde{x}$, and some $M < \infty$, $p^{(j)}(z|\tilde{x})$ exists and is a continuous function of z satisfying $|p^{(j)}(z|\tilde{x})| < M$ for all z and almost every $\tilde{x}$.

SMS9: For each integer j such that $1 \leq j \leq s$, all z in a neighborhood of 0, almost every $\tilde{x}$, and some $M < \infty$, $F^{(j)}(-z|z, \tilde{x})$ exists and is a continuous function of z satisfying $|F^{(j)}(-z|z, \tilde{x})| < M$.

SMS9 is satisfied if $[\partial^{j+k} F(u|z, \tilde{x})/\partial u^j \partial z^k]_{u=-z}$ is bounded and continuous in a neighborhood of $z = 0$ for almost every $\tilde{x}$ whenever $j + k \leq s$.

SMS10: The matrix Q is negative definite.

The reasons for making these assumptions will now be explained. Assumptions SMS1–SMS3 except for SMS2(b) and the compactness part of SMS4 are the requirements for consistency of both the smoothed and the unsmoothed maximum-score estimators. SMS2(b) rules out certain degenerate cases in which β can be learned perfectly from a finite sample (Manski 1985). The assumption that $\tilde{\beta}$ is an interior point of the parameter set ensures that the first-order condition $\partial S_{sms}(b_n)/\partial \tilde{b} = 0$ is satisfied with probability approaching 1 as $n \to \infty$. A similar assumption is made for the same reason in parametric maximum-likelihood estimation. SMS5 and SMS7–SMS9 ensure the existence of A, D, and Q as well as the convergence of certain sequences that arise in the proof of asymptotic normality. SMS5 strengthens an assumption of Horowitz (1992). De Jong and Woutersen (2007) pointed out the need for a stronger assumption, though not necessarily one as strong as SMS5. Examples of functions satisfying SMS7 are given by Müller (1984).

Assumptions SMS6–SMS9 are analogous to assumptions made in kernel density estimation. In kernel density estimation, a kernel K' that satisfies (4.30) is an s'th-order kernel. With an s'th-order kernel and a bandwidth parameter h_n satisfying $nh_n \to \infty$, the bias of the density estimator is $O(h_n^s)$, and the variance is $O[(nh_n)^{-1}]$ if the density being estimated is s times differentiable. Moreover, with an s'th-order kernel, the fastest achievable rate of convergence of the density estimator is $n^{-s/(2s+1)}$, so use of a higher-order kernel speeds convergence if the required derivatives of the density exist. Analogous results hold in smoothed maximum-score estimation. If assumptions SMS1–SMS10 are satisfied, the bias of the smoothed maximum-score estimator is $O(h_n^s)$, the variance is $O[(nh_n)^{-1}]$, and the fastest achievable rate of convergence is $n^{-s/(2s+1)}$. Thus, faster convergence can be achieved by using a higher-order K' if the necessary derivatives of F and p exist.

The matrix Q is analogous to the Hessian form of the information matrix in parametric quasi-maximum-likelihood estimation (White 1982), and SMS10 is analogous to the familiar assumption that the Hessian information matrix is nonsingular.

The main results concerning the asymptotic distribution of the smoothed maximum-score estimator are given by the following theorem.

Theorem 4.5: *Let SMS1–SMS10 hold for some* $s \geq 2$, *and let* $\{b_n\}$ *be a sequence of solutions to problem (4.25). Then*

(a) If $nh_n^{2s+1} \to \infty$ *as* $n \to \infty$, $h_n^{-2}(\tilde{b}_n - \tilde{\beta}) \xrightarrow{p} -Q^{-1}A$.
(b) If nh_n^{2s+1} *has a finite limit* λ *as* $n \to \infty$, *then*

$$(nh_n)^{1/2}(\tilde{b}_n - \tilde{\beta}) \xrightarrow{d} N(-\lambda^{1/2}Q^{-1}A, Q^{-1}DQ^{-1}).$$

(c) Let $h_n = (\lambda/n)^{1/(2s+1)}$ *with* $0 < \lambda < \infty$. *Let* Ω *be any nonstochastic, positive-semidefinite matrix such that* $A'Q^{-1}\Omega Q^{-1}A \neq 0$. *Let* E_A *denote the expectation with respect to the asymptotic distribution of* $(nh_n)^{1/2}(\tilde{b}_n - \tilde{\beta})$, *and* $MSE = E_A(\tilde{b}_n - \tilde{\beta})'\Omega(\tilde{b}_n - \tilde{\beta})$. *MSE is minimized by setting* $\lambda = \lambda^*$, *where*

$$\lambda^* = \frac{trace(Q^{-1}\Omega Q^{-1}D)}{2sA'Q^{-1}\Omega Q^{-1}A}, \tag{4.31}$$

in which case

$$n^{s/(2s+1)}(\tilde{b}_n - \tilde{\beta}) \xrightarrow{d} N[-(\lambda^*)^{s/(2s+1)}Q^{-1}A, (\lambda^*)^{-1/(2s+1)}Q^{-1}DQ^{-1}]. \blacksquare$$

Theorem 4.5 implies that the fastest possible rate of convergence in probability of $\tilde{b}_n$ is $n^{-s/(2s+1)}$. A sufficient condition for this to occur is $h_n = (\lambda/n)^{1/(2s+1)}$ with $0 < \lambda < \infty$. The asymptotically optimal value of λ in the sense of minimizing *MSE* is λ^*. Horowitz (1993c) shows that $n^{-s/(2s+1)}$ is the fastest achievable rate of convergence of any estimator of $\tilde{\beta}$ under SMS1–SMS5 and SMS8–SMS10. Thus, no estimator can converge faster than the smoothed maximum-score estimator under these assumptions. The fastest rate of convergence if $s < 2$ is $n^{-1/3}$. Moreover, $n^{1/3}(\tilde{b}_n - \tilde{\beta})$ has a complicated, nonnormal limiting distribution if $s < 2$. Thus, in terms of the rate of convergence and simplicity of the asymptotic distribution, the smoothed maximum-score estimator has no advantage over the unsmoothed one unless $F(-z|z,\tilde{x})$ and $p(z|\tilde{x})$ have sufficiently many derivatives.

Theorem 4.5 also implies that the mean of the asymptotic distribution of $n^{s/(2s+1)}(\tilde{b}_n - \tilde{\beta})$ is not 0 when $h_n \propto n^{-1/(2s+1)}$. In other words, $n^{s/(2s+1)}(\tilde{b}_n - \tilde{\beta})$ is asymptotically biased when h_n is chosen so that $\tilde{b}_n$ has its fastest possible rate of convergence. Asymptotic bias also arises in kernel nonparametric density estimation and nonparametric mean regression. One way to remove the asymptotic bias is by using a bandwidth h_n that converges more rapidly than $n^{-1/(2s+1)}$. This is called *undersmoothing*. Theorem 4.5(b) shows that $\lambda = 0$ with undersmoothing, so there is no asymptotic bias.

Undersmoothing as a method of bias reduction has the disadvantage that it slows the rate of convergence of $\tilde{b}_n$ to $\tilde{\beta}$. This problem can be avoided by forming an estimate of the bias and subtracting the estimate from $\tilde{b}_n$. A method for doing this is described below.

To make the results of Theorem 4.5 useful in applications, it is necessary to be able to estimate A, D, and Q consistently. Theorem 4.6 shows how this can be done. For any $b \in B$, define

$$D_n = \frac{1}{nh_n}\sum_{i=1}^{n}\tilde{X}_i\tilde{X}_i' K'\left(\frac{X_i'b_n}{h_n}\right)^2$$

and

$$Q_n = \frac{\partial^2 S_{sms}(b_n)}{\partial\tilde{b}\partial\tilde{b}'}.$$

Theorem 4.6: *Let b_n be a consistent smoothed maximum-score estimator based on the bandwidth $h_n \propto n^{-\kappa}$, where $\kappa \geq 1/(2s+1)$. Then $D_n \to^p D$ and $Q_n \to^p Q$ as $n \to \infty$. Let $\{h_n^*\}$ be a sequence of positive numbers satisfying $h_n^* \propto n^{-\delta/(2s+1)}$, where $0 < \delta < 1$. Define*

$$A_n = \frac{1}{n(h_n^*)^{s+1}}\sum_{i=1}^{n}(2Y_i - 1)\tilde{X}_i K'\left(\frac{X_i'b_n}{h_n^*}\right).$$

If $h_n \propto n^{-1/(2s+1)}$, then $A_n \xrightarrow{p} A$ as $n \to \infty$. ■

Theorem 4.6 implies that the covariance matrix of the asymptotic distribution of $(nh_n)^{1/2}(\tilde{b}_n - \tilde{\beta})$, $Q^{-1}DQ^{-1}$, is estimated consistently by

$$V_n = Q_n^{-1}D_nQ_n^{-1}. \tag{4.32}$$

This result will be used below to form tests of hypotheses about $\tilde{\beta}$.

Theorem 4.6 also provides a way to remove the asymptotic bias of $\tilde{b}_n$ without slowing its rate of convergence. Recall that if $h_n \propto n^{-1/(2s+1)}$, then the asymptotic bias of $(nh_n)^{1/2}(\tilde{b}_n - \tilde{\beta})$ is $-\lambda^{s/(2s+1)}Q^{-1}A$. By Theorem 4.6, this bias is estimated consistently by $-\lambda^{s/(2s+1)}Q_n^{-1}A_n$. Therefore, an asymptotically unbiased estimator of $\tilde{\beta}$ is

$$\hat{b}_n = \tilde{b}_n + \left(\frac{\lambda}{n}\right)^{s/(2s+1)} Q_n^{-1}A_n.$$

The asymptotic normality of $(nh_n)^{1/2}(\tilde{b}_n - \tilde{\beta})$ makes it possible to form asymptotic t and χ^2 statistics for testing hypotheses about $\tilde{\beta}$. Consider, first, a t test of a hypothesis about a component of $\tilde{\beta}$. Let $\tilde{b}_{nj}$, $\hat{b}_{nj}$, and $\tilde{\beta}_j$, respectively, denote the j'th components of $\tilde{b}_n$, $\hat{b}_n$, and $\tilde{\beta}$. Let V_{nj} denote the (j,j) component of the matrix V_n defined in (4.32). The t statistic for testing the hypothesis $H_0 : \tilde{\beta}_j = \tilde{\beta}_{j0}$ is

$$t = \frac{(nh_n)^{1/2}(\hat{b}_{nj} - \tilde{\beta}_j)}{V_{nj}^{1/2}}$$

if $h_n \propto n^{-1/(2s+1)}$ and

$$t = \frac{(nh_n)^{1/2}(\tilde{b}_{nj} - \tilde{\beta}_j)}{V_{nj}^{1/2}}$$

with undersmoothing. In either case, t is asymptotically distributed as $N(0,1)$ if H_0 is true. Therefore, H_0 can be rejected or accepted by comparing t with the relevant quantile of the standard normal distribution.

Now let R be an $r \times (d-1)$ matrix with $r \le d-1$, and let c be an $r \times 1$ vector of constants. Consider a test of the hypothesis $H_0 : R\tilde{\beta} = c$. Assume that the matrix $RQ^{-1}DQ^{-1}R'$ is nonsingular. Suppose that $h_n \propto n^{-1/(2s+1)}$. Then under H_0, the statistic

$$\chi^2 = (nh_n)(R\hat{b}_n - c)'(RV_nR')^{-1}(R\hat{b}_n - c)$$

is asymptotically chi-square distributed with r degrees of freedom. If undersmoothing is used so that $h_n \propto n^{-\kappa}$ with $\kappa > 1/(2s+1)$, then the statistic

$$\chi^2 = (nh_n)(R\tilde{b}_n - c)'(RV_nR')^{-1}(R\tilde{b}_n - c)$$

is asymptotically chi-square distributed with r degrees of freedom. In either case, H_0 can be accepted or rejected by comparing χ^2 with the appropriate quantile of the chi-square distribution with r degrees of freedom.

The asymptotic distributions of t and χ^2 are only approximations to the exact, finite-sample distributions of these statistics. The approximation errors can be made arbitrarily small by making n sufficiently large. With the sample sizes encountered in applications, however, the approximation errors can be large. As a result, the true and nominal probabilities of rejecting a correct null hypothesis can be very different when the critical value is obtained from the asymptotic distribution of the test statistic. For example, a symmetrical t test rejects a true null hypothesis with nominal probability α if $|t|$ exceeds the $1 - \alpha/2$ quantile of the standard normal distribution. However, the true rejection probability may be much larger than α if, as often happens in finite samples, the asymptotic distribution of t (the standard normal distribution) is not a good approximation to its exact distribution. Horowitz (1992) provides Monte Carlo evidence showing that the true rejection probability can exceed the nominal probability by a factor of three or more with samples of practical size.

This problem can be greatly reduced through the use of the bootstrap. The bootstrap estimates the distribution of a statistic by treating the estimation data as if they were the population. The bootstrap distribution of a statistic is the distribution induced by sampling the estimation data randomly with replacement. The α-level bootstrap critical value of a symmetrical t test is the $1 - \alpha$ quantile of the bootstrap distribution of $|t|$. The α-level bootstrap critical value of a test based on χ^2 is the $1 - \alpha$ quantile of the bootstrap distribution of χ^2. Similar procedures can be used to obtain bootstrap critical values for one-tailed and equal-tailed t tests.

Under certain conditions (see, e.g., Beran 1988; Hall 1986, 1992), the bootstrap provides a better finite-sample approximation to the distribution of a statistic than does asymptotic distribution theory. When this happens, the use of bootstrap critical values instead of asymptotic ones reduces the differences between the true and nominal probabilities that a t or χ^2 test rejects a true null hypothesis. The use of bootstrap critical values also reduces the differences between the true and nominal coverage probabilities of confidence intervals. To achieve these results, the statistic in question must be *asymptotically pivotal*, meaning that its asymptotic distribution does not depend on unknown population parameters. Horowitz (1997, 2001b) reviews the theory of the bootstrap and provides numerical examples of its use in econometrics.

The t and χ^2 statistics for testing hypotheses using smoothed maximum-score estimates are asymptotically pivotal. However, they do not satisfy the standard regularity conditions under which the bootstrap provides asymptotic refinements (that is, improvements in the approximation to the finite-sample distribution of a statistic). Nonetheless, it is possible to prove that the bootstrap provides asymptotic refinements for t and χ^2 tests based on the smoothed maximum-score estimator. See Horowitz (2002). The main problem is that the standard theory of the bootstrap assumes that the statistic in question can be approximated by a function of sample moments whose probability distribution has an Edgeworth expansion. However, because the t and χ^2statistics based on the smoothed maximum-score estimator depend on the bandwidth parameter h_n that decreases to 0 as $n \to \infty$, they cannot be approximated by functions of sample moments. Horowitz (2002) shows how to modify the standard theory of Edgeworth expansions to deal with this problem.

The bootstrap distributions of t and χ^2 cannot be calculated analytically, but they can be estimated with arbitrary accuracy by Monte Carlo simulation. To specify the Monte Carlo procedure, let the bootstrap sample be denoted by $\{Y_i^*, X_i^* : i = 1, \ldots, n\}$. This sample is obtained by sampling the estimation data randomly with replacement. Define the bootstrap analog of $S_{sms}(b)$ by

$$S_{sms}^*(b) = \frac{1}{n}\sum_{i=1}^{n}(2Y_i^* - 1)K\left(\frac{X_i'^* b}{h_n}\right).$$

Let $(b_{n1}^*, \tilde{b}_n^*)$ be a solution to (4.25) with S_{sms} replaced by S_{sms}^*. Define bootstrap analogs of Q_n and D_n by

$$D_n^* = \frac{1}{nh_n}\sum_{i=1}^{n}\tilde{X}_i^*\tilde{X}_i'^* K'\left(\frac{X_i'^* b_n^*}{h_n}\right)^2$$

and

$$Q_n^* = \frac{\partial^2 S_{sms}^*(b_n^*)}{\partial\tilde{b}\partial\tilde{b}'}$$

Let V_{nj}^* be the (j,j) component of the matrix $Q_n^{*-1}D_n^*Q_n^{*-1}$.

The Monte Carlo procedure for estimating the bootstrap critical value of the symmetrical t test is as follows. The procedures for estimating bootstrap critical values of one-tailed and equal-tailed t tests and the χ^2 test are similar:

1. Generate a bootstrap sample $\{Y_i^*, X_i^* : i = 1, \ldots, n\}$ by sampling the estimation data randomly with replacement.
2. Using the bootstrap sample, compute the bootstrap t statistic for testing the bootstrap hypothesis H_0^*: $\tilde{\beta}_j = \tilde{b}_{nj}$, where b_n solves (4.25). The bootstrap t statistic is

$$t^* = \frac{(nh_n)^{1/2}(\tilde{b}_{nj}^* - \tilde{b}_{nj})}{(V_{nj}^*)^{1/2}},$$

where $\tilde{b}_{nj}^*$ is the j'th component of $\tilde{b}_n^*$.
3. Estimate the bootstrap distribution of $|t^*|$ by the empirical distribution that is obtained by repeating Steps 1 and 2 many times. The bootstrap critical value of the symmetrical t test is estimated by the $1 - \alpha$ quantile of this empirical distribution.

The theory of the bootstrap requires h_n to be chosen so as to undersmooth. Thus, it is not necessary to use $\hat{b}_n$ to carry out bootstrap-based testing. Horowitz (2002) shows that when critical values based on the bootstrap are used for a symmetrical t or χ^2 test, the difference between the true and nominal probabilities of rejecting a true null hypothesis (the error in the rejection probability) has size $o[(nh_n)^{-1}]$. By contrast, the error in the rejection probability exceeds $O[(nh_n)^{-1}]$ if asymptotic critical values are used. Therefore, the error in the rejection probability converges to 0 as $n \to \infty$ more rapidly with bootstrap critical values than with asymptotic ones. Accordingly, the error in the rejection probability is smaller with bootstrap critical values than with asymptotic ones if n is sufficiently large. Similar results are available for one-tailed and equal-tailed t tests, although the order of the asymptotic refinement for these is not the same as it is for symmetrical tests. Horowitz (2002) presents Monte Carlo evidence indicating that with samples of practical size, the bootstrap essentially eliminates errors in the rejection probabilities of symmetrical t tests. Thus, it is better in applications to use the bootstrap to obtain critical values for a test based on the smoothed maximum-score estimator than to use the asymptotic distribution of the test statistic.

A final problem in practical implementation of the smoothed maximum-score estimator or tests based on it is bandwidth selection. The bandwidth that minimizes the asymptotic mean-square error of $\tilde{b}_n$ is $h_{n,opt} = (\lambda^*/n)^{1/(2s+1)}$, where λ^* is given by (4.31). The value of λ^* can be estimated by replacing unknown quantities on the right-hand side of (4.31) by estimates based on a preliminary bandwidth. This is called the *plug-in* method of bandwidth selection. To implement the plug-in method, choose a preliminary bandwidth $h_{n1} \propto n^{-1/(2s+1)}$ and any $h_{n1}^* \propto n^{-\delta/(2s+1)}$ for $0 < \delta < 1$. Compute the smoothed maximum-score estimate b_n based on h_{n1}, and use b_n and h_{n1}^* to compute A_n, D_n, and Q_n. Then estimate λ^* by λ_n, where λ_n is obtained from (4.31) by replacing A,D, and Q with A_n, D_n, and Q_n.

This method of bandwidth selection is analogous to the plug-in method of kernel density estimation. As in density estimation, it has the disadvantage of not being fully automatic; the estimated optimal bandwidth depends on the bandwidth used to obtain the initial estimate of β and on δ. Jones et al. (1996) discuss ways to reduce the dependence on the initial bandwidth in the case of density estimation. There has been no research on whether similar methods can be developed for smoothed maximum-score estimation.

The bootstrap method for obtaining improved finite-sample critical values for t and χ^2 tests of hypotheses about β requires a bandwidth that undersmooths. That is, it requires h_n to converge faster than $n^{-1/(2s+1)}$. Existing theory provides no guidance on how such a bandwidth should be chosen in applications. However, Monte Carlo evidence presented by Horowitz (2002) indicates that the empirical levels of tests with bootstrap critical values are not sensitive to the value of h_n over the range $0.5h_{n,opt}$ to $h_{n,opt}$. These results suggest that, as a practical rule-of-thumb method for selecting the bandwidth for bootstrap calculations, one can use the plug-in method to estimate $h_{n,opt}$ and then implement the bootstrap with a bandwidth that is between the estimated $h_{n,opt}$ and half the estimate.

4.4 Extensions of the Maximum-Score and Smoothed Maximum-Score Estimators

This section shows how the maximum-score and smoothed maximum-score estimators can be extended for use with choice-based samples, panel data, and ordered-response models.

4.4.1 Choice-Based Samples

The discussion in the preceding sections assumes that the estimation data are a random sample from the distribution of (Y, X). A choice-based sample is not random in this way. Instead, it is stratified on the dependent variable Y. The fraction of observations with $Y = 1$ is selected by design, and X is sampled randomly conditional on Y. For example, suppose the modes that are available for travel between two cities are airplane and automobile. Then a data set for analyzing the mode choices of travelers between these cities might be obtained by interviewing randomly selected air travelers at the airport and randomly selected automobile travelers at the roadside. Choice-based sampling can be much more efficient than random sampling. For example, suppose that one percent of the population makes the choice of interest in a given time period. Then data acquisition by randomly sampling the population would require contacting 100 persons on average to obtain one useful observation. By contrast, all contacts made in a choice-based sample are potentially useful.

Except in special cases, estimators that work with random samples are inconsistent when the sample is choice based. Parametric estimation with choice-based samples has been investigated by Cosslett (1981), Imbens (1992), Hsieh et al. (1985), Manski and Lerman (1977), and Manski and McFadden (1981). This section discusses semiparametric estimation with choice-based samples under the assumption that the distribution of U is unknown. It is assumed that the population values of the aggregate shares, $\pi_1 \equiv P(Y = 1)$ and $\pi_0 \equiv 1 - \pi_1$, are known. It is not unusual in applications for aggregate shares to be known quite accurately. For example, in the United States, aggregate shares for certain types of travel choices are available from the US Census. However, census data do not include information on all of the variables needed to develop a useful choice model.

Manski (1986) has given conditions under which β can be estimated consistently from a choice-based sample by maximizing the modified maximum-score objective function

$$S_{n,CB}(b) = \frac{\pi_1}{n_1} \sum_{i=1}^{n} Y_i(X_i'b \geq 0) - \frac{\pi_0}{n_0} \sum_{i=1}^{n} (1 - Y_i)I(X_i'b \geq 0) \tag{4.33}$$

subject to scale normalization, where n_j $(j = 0, 1)$ is the number of observations for which $Y_j = j$ and $n = n_0 + n_1$. Note that n_0 and n_1 are chosen by the designer of the choice-based sample and are not random. The modified maximum-score estimator solves

$$\underset{|b_1|=1,\, b\in B}{\text{maximize}} : S_{n,CB}(b). \tag{4.34}$$

The solution to (4.34) is consistent for β under conditions that are stated in the following theorem, which is a modified version of Theorem 4.4.

Theorem 4.7: *Let median* $(U|X = x) = 0$ *for all* x *in the support of* X. *Let* $|\beta_1| = 1$. *Assume that* B *is a compact subset of* $\mathbb{R}^d$. *Let* b_n *solve problem (4.34). Then* $b_n \to \beta$ *almost surely as* $n_1, n_2 \to \infty$ *if*

(a) For each $j = 0$ *or* 1, $\{X_i : i = 1, \ldots, n\}$ *is a random sample from the distribution of* X *conditional on* $Y = j$.
(b) The support of the distribution of X *is not contained in any proper linear subspace of* $\mathbb{R}^d$.
(c) For almost every $\tilde{x} = (x^2, \ldots, x^d)$, *the distribution of* X^1 *conditional on* $\tilde{X} = \tilde{x}$ *has an everywhere positive density.*■

Conditions (b) and (c) of Theorem 4.7 are identical to conditions in Theorem 4.4. Condition (a) of Theorem 4.7 specifies a choice-based sampling process instead of the random sampling process that is used in Theorem 4.4.

To understand why solving (4.34) yields a consistent estimator of β, define $q_1 = n_1/n$ and $q_0 = n_0/n$, respectively, to be the fractions of the sample for which $Y = 1$ and $Y = 0$. To minimize the complexity of the discussion, suppose that X has a probability density function f. Similar but notationally more complex arguments apply if X has one or more discrete components. Let $f(\cdot|Y = j)$ be the probability density of X conditional on $Y = j (j = 0,1)$. Observe that by the algebra of conditional probabilities

$$\begin{aligned} E[I(X'b \geq 0)|Y = 1] &= \int I(X'b \geq 0) f(x|Y = 1)dx \\ &= \int I(X'b \geq 0) \frac{P(Y = 1|X = x)f(x)}{q_1} dx \\ &= \frac{1}{q_1} \int I(X'b \geq 0)P(Y = 1|X = x)f(x)dx. \end{aligned}$$

Similarly

$$E[I(X'b \geq 0)|Y = 0] = \frac{1}{q_0} \int I(X'b \geq 0)P(Y = 0|X = x)f(x)dx.$$

Therefore, the population version of (4.33) is

$$\begin{aligned} E[S_{n,CB}(b)] &= \int I(X'b \geq 0)[P(Y = 1|X = x) - P(Y = 0|X = x)]f(x)dx \\ &= E[2P(Y = 1|X) - 1]I(X'b \geq 0) \\ &= E[Y - S_{bin}(b)], \end{aligned}$$

where S_{bin} is as defined in (4.18). It was shown in Section 4.3.2 that β minimizes $E[S_{bin}(b)]$ and, therefore, maximizes $E[Y - S_{bin}(b)]$. It follows that β maximizes the population version of $S_{n,CB}(b)$. Arguments like those used to prove Theorem 4.4 now show that the solution to (4.34) is consistent for β under choice-based sampling. Manski (1986) provides the technical details.

$S_{n,CB}(b)$, like $S_{ms}(b)$, is discontinuous and can be smoothed by replacing the indicator function with an integral of a kernel function. The resulting smoothed maximum-score estimator for choice-based samples maximizes the objective function

$$S_{sms,CB} = \frac{\pi_1}{n_1}\sum_{i=1}^{n} Y_i K\left(\frac{X_i'b}{h_n}\right) - \frac{\pi_0}{n_0}\sum_{i=1}^{n}(1-Y_i)K\left(\frac{X_i'b}{h_n}\right), \tag{4.35}$$

where K and h_n are defined as in (4.25). Define s as in Theorem 4.5. Define $Z = X'\beta$, and let $p(\cdot\,|\tilde{x}, Y = j)$ denote the probability density function of Z conditional on $\tilde{X} = \tilde{x}$ and $Y = j\,(j = 0, 1)$. Set

$$p^{(s)}(z|\tilde{X} = \tilde{x}, Y = j) = \frac{\partial^s p(z|\tilde{X} = \tilde{x}, Y = j)}{\partial z^s}.$$

Suppose that there is a finite λ such that $(nh_n)^{2s+1} \to \lambda$ as $n \to \infty$. By using Taylor-series methods like those used to prove Theorem 4.5, it can be shown that under suitable assumptions, the centered, normalized, smoothed maximum-score estimator for choice-based samples is asymptotically normally distributed. To state the result formally, define

$$A_C = \frac{\alpha_A}{s!}\{\pi_1 E[\tilde{X}p^{(s)}(0|\tilde{X}, Y = 1)|Y = 1] - \pi_0 E[\tilde{X}p^{(s)}(0|\tilde{X}, Y = 0)|Y = 0]\},$$

$$D_C = \frac{\alpha_D}{2}\left(\frac{\pi_1}{q_1} + \frac{\pi_0}{q_0}\right) E[\tilde{X}\tilde{X}'p(0|\tilde{X})],$$

and

$$Q_C = -\pi_1 E[\tilde{X}\tilde{X}'p^{(1)}(0|\tilde{X}, Y = 1)|Y = 1] + \pi_0 E[\tilde{X}\tilde{X}'p^{(1)}(0|\tilde{X}, Y = 0)|Y = 0].$$

Make the following assumptions.

CB1: For each $j = 0$ or 1, $\{X_i : i = 1, \ldots, n_j\}$ is a random sample from the distribution of X conditional on $Y = j$.

CB2: (a) The support of the distribution of X is not contained in any proper linear subspace of $\mathbb{R}^d$. (b) $|\beta_1| = 1$, and the distribution of X^1 conditional on $\tilde{X} = \tilde{x}$ has an everywhere positive density for almost every $\tilde{x}$.

CB3: Median$(U|X = x) = 0$ for almost every x.

CB4: $\tilde{\beta}$ is an interior point of a compact subset $\tilde{B}$ of $\mathbb{R}^{d-1}$.

CB5: The components of $\tilde{X}$ are bounded.

CB6: (a) K is twice differentiable everywhere, $|K'|$ and $|K''|$ are uniformly bounded, and each of the following integrals is finite:

$$\int_{-\infty}^{\infty} K'(v)^4 dv, \int_{-\infty}^{\infty} K''(v)^2 dv, \int_{-\infty}^{\infty} |v^2 K''(v)| dv.$$

(b) For some integer $s \geq 2$ and each integer j $(1 \leq j \leq s)$

$$\int_{-\infty}^{\infty} v^j K'(v) dv = \begin{cases} 0 \text{ if } j < s \\ \text{finite if } j = s \end{cases}.$$

(c) For each integer j between 0 and s, any $\eta > 0$, and any positive sequence $\{h_n\}$ converging to 0

$$\lim_{n\to\infty} h_n^{j-2} \int_{|h_n v|>\eta} |v^j K'(v)| dv = 0$$

and

$$\lim_{n\to\infty} h_n^{-1} \int_{|h_n v|>\eta} |K''(v)| dv = 0.$$

CB7: For each integer j such that $1 \leq j \leq s$, all z in a neighborhood of 0, almost every $\tilde{x}$, and some $M < \infty$, $p^{(j)}(z|\tilde{x}, Y = m)$ $(m = 0,1)$ exists and is a continuous function of z satisfying $|p^{(j)}(z|\tilde{x}, Y = m)| < M$ for all z and almost every $\tilde{x}$.

CB8: The matrix Q_C is negative definite.

Asymptotic normality of the smoothed maximum-score estimator for choice-based samples is given by the following theorem.

Theorem 4.8: *Let assumptions CB1–CB8 hold for some $s \geq 2$ and let $\{b_n\}$ be a sequence of solutions to problem (4.35). Assume that $nh_n^{2s+1} = \lambda$ for some finite $\lambda > 0$. Then*

$$(nh_n)^{1/2}(\tilde{b}_n - \tilde{\beta}) \xrightarrow{d} N(-\lambda^{1/2} Q_C A_C, Q_C^{-1} D_C Q_C^{-1}). \blacksquare \tag{4.36}$$

A_C, D_C, and Q_C can be estimated by using methods like those described in Section 4.3.3. Let $h_n^* \propto n^{-\sigma/(2s+1)}$ for some δ satisfying $0 < \delta < 1$. Then A_C is estimated consistently by

$$A_{nC} = \left(\frac{1}{h_n^*}\right)^s \left[\frac{\pi_1}{n_1} \sum_{i=1}^{n} Y_i \frac{\tilde{X}_i}{h_n^*} K'\left(\frac{X_i' b_n}{h_n^*}\right) - \frac{\pi_0}{n_0} \sum_{i=1}^{n} (1 - Y_i) \frac{X_i}{h_n^*} K'\left(\frac{X_i' b_n}{h_n^*}\right)\right].$$

D_C and Q_C are estimated consistently by

$$D_{nC} = \left(\frac{\pi_1}{q_1} + \frac{\pi_0}{q_0}\right)\left[\frac{\pi_1}{n_1 h_n}\sum_{i=1}^{n} Y_i \tilde{X}_i \tilde{X}_i' K'\left(\frac{X_i' b_n}{h_n}\right) + \frac{\pi_0}{n_0 h_n}\sum_{i=1}^{n}(1 - Y_i)\tilde{X}_i \tilde{X}_i' K'\left(\frac{X_i' b_n}{h_n}\right)\right]$$

and

$$Q_{nC} = \frac{\partial^2 S_{sms,CB}(b_n)}{\partial \tilde{b} \partial \tilde{b}'}.$$

The formula for D_{nC} corrects (6.35) of Horowitz (1993b), which omits the factor $(\pi_1/q_1 + \pi_0/q_0)$.

As in smoothed maximum-score estimation with random samples, an asymptotically unbiased smoothed maximum-score estimator of β for choice-based samples is given by

$$\hat{b}_n = \tilde{b}_n + \left(\frac{\lambda}{n}\right)^{s/(2s+1)} Q_{nC}^{-1} A_{nC}.$$

The asymptotically optimal value of λ is given by (4.31) but with A, D, and Q replaced with A_C, D_C, and Q_C.

Tests of hypotheses about β can be carried out by replacing A_n, D_n, and Q_n with A_{nC}, D_{nC}, and Q_{nC} in the formulae for the random-sample t and χ^2 statistics. Bootstrap versions of the test statistics can be obtained by sampling the estimation data conditional on Y. That is, one draws n_1 observations randomly with replacement from the subset of the estimation data for which $Y = 1$, and one draws n_0 observations randomly with replacement from the subset of the estimation data for which $Y = 0$.

In a choice-based sample, the analyst chooses n_1 and n_0 or, equivalently, q_1 and q_0. It is useful, therefore, to ask how this can be done so as to minimize the asymptotic mean-square error or variance of the resulting estimator. This question can be answered for the smoothed maximum-score estimator, whose asymptotic variance is known. To find the answer, observe that the right-hand side of (4.36) depends on q_1 and q_0 only through the factor $(\pi_1/q_1 + \pi_0/q_0)$ that multiplies D_C. Therefore, the asymptotic mean-square estimation errors and asymptotic variances of all components $\tilde{b}_n$ are minimized by choosing q_1 and q_0 to minimize $(\pi_1/q_1 + \pi_0/q_0)$. The result is $q_0 = \pi_0^{1/2}/(\pi_0^{1/2} + \pi_1^{1/2})$, $q_1 = \pi_1^{1/2}/(\pi_0^{1/2} + \pi_1^{1/2})$.

4.4.2 Panel Data

Panel data consist of observations on individuals at each of several discrete points in time. Thus, there are two or more observations of each individual. The observations of the same individual at different times may be correlated, even if individuals are sampled independently. For example, there may be unobserved attributes of individuals that affect choice and remain constant over time. This section shows how to carry out maximum-score and smoothed maximum-score estimation of the following binary-response model for panel data:

$$Y_{it} = \begin{cases} 1 \text{ if } Y_{it}^* > 0 \\ 0 \text{ otherwise} \end{cases}, \tag{4.37a}$$

where

$$Y_{it}^* = X_{it}'\beta + U_i + \varepsilon_{it}. \tag{4.37b}$$

In this model, Y_{it} is the dependent variable corresponding to individual i at time t ($i = 1, \ldots, n$; $t = 1, \ldots, T$), X_{it} is a vector of explanatory variables corresponding to individual i at time t, β is a conformable vector of constant parameters, U_i is an unobserved random variable that is constant over time, and ε_{it} is an unobserved random variable that varies across both individuals and time. The random variable U_i represents unobserved, time-invariant attributes of individual i, whereas the random variable ε_{it} represents unobserved variables influencing choice that vary across both individuals and time. It is typical in panel data to have observations of many individuals but at only a few points in time. Accordingly, asymptotics will be carried out by assuming that $n \to \infty$ but that T is fixed.

Heckman (1981a, b) discusses estimation of β in parametric models. Manski (1987) has shown how the maximum-score method can be used to estimate β without assuming that the distributions of U and ε belong to known, finite-dimensional parametric families. Indeed, the maximum-score method places no restrictions on the distribution of U and permits arbitrary serial dependence among the random variables $\{\varepsilon_{it} : t = 1, \ldots, T\}$ for each i.

The estimator is most easily explained by assuming that $T = 2$. The generalization to larger values of T is straightforward. Assume that for any i, ε_{i1} and ε_{i2} have identical distributions conditional on $(X_{it}, U_i; t = 1, 2)$. Define $W_i = X_{i2} - X_{i1}$ and $\eta_i = \varepsilon_{12} - \varepsilon_{i1}$. Then it follows from (4.37b) that

$$Y_{i2}^* - Y_{i1}^* = W_i'\beta + \eta_i. \tag{4.38a}$$

Moreover, median $(\eta_i | W_i = w) = 0$ because ε_{i1} and ε_{i2} have the same distributions conditional on (X_{i1}, X_{i2}). Now define

$$\tilde{Y}_i = \begin{cases} 1 \text{ if } Y_{i2}^* - Y_{i1}^* > 0 \\ 0 \text{ otherwise} \end{cases}. \tag{4.38b}$$

By comparing (4.38) with (4.1), it can be seen that β in the panel-data model could be estimated by the maximum-score method if $\tilde{Y}_i$ were observable. But $Y_{i2} - Y_{i1} = 2\tilde{Y} - 1$ whenever $Y_{i2} \neq Y_{i1}$, so $\tilde{Y}_i$ is observable if $Y_{i2} \neq Y_{i1}$. Consider, therefore, the estimator of β that is obtained by solving the problem

$$\underset{|b_1|=1,\, b\in B}{\text{maximize}}: S_{ms,pan}(b) = \frac{1}{n}\sum_{i=1}^{n}(Y_{i2} - Y_{i1})I(W_i'b \geq 0). \tag{4.39}$$

The resulting estimator b_n is the maximum-score estimator of β based on observations for which $Y_{i2} \neq Y_{i1}$. Therefore, arguments similar to those leading to Theorem 4.4 can be used to obtain conditions under which b_n is consistent for β . The result is given in the following theorem, which is proved in Manski (1987). Define $d = \dim(W_i)$ for each $i = 1, \ldots, n$.

Theorem 4.9: *Let model (4.37) hold. Let B be a compact subset of* $\mathbb{R}^d$. *Let* $|\beta_1| = 1$. *Let* b_n *solve problem (4.39). Then* $b_n \to \beta$ *almost surely as* $n \to \infty$ *if the following conditions hold:*

(a) For each i, the random variables ε_{i1} *and* ε_{i2} *are identically distributed conditional on* (X_{i1}, X_{i2}, U_i). *The support of the common distribution is* $(-\infty, \infty)$ *for all* (X_{i1}, X_{i2}, U_i).
(b) The support of the distribution of W_i $(i = 1, \ldots, n)$ *is not contained in any proper linear subspace of* $\mathbb{R}^d$.
(c) For almost every $\tilde{w} = (w^2, \ldots, w^d)$, *the distribution of* W^1 *conditional on* $(W^2, \ldots, W^d) = \tilde{w}$ *has an everywhere positive density.*
(d) The random vector $\{Y_{it}, X_{it} : t = 1,2\}$ *has the same distribution for each* $i = 1, \ldots, n$. *The data consist of an independent random sample from this distribution.* ■

The second sentence of condition (a) in Theorem 4.9 ensures that the event $Y_{i2} \neq Y_{i1}$ has nonzero probability. The other conditions are similar to the conditions of Theorem 4.4 and are needed for reasons explained in Section 4.3.2.

Observe that Theorem 4.9 places no restrictions on the distribution of U_i. In particular, U_i may be correlated with X_{i1} and X_{i2}. In this respect, the maximum-score estimator for panel data is analogous to the so-called fixed-effects estimator for a linear, mean-regression model for panel data. As in the fixed-effects model, a component of β is identified only if the corresponding component of $X_{i2} - X_{i1} \neq 0$ with nonzero probability. Thus, any intercept component of β is not identified. Similarly, components of β corresponding to explanatory variables that are constant over time within individuals are not identified. As in the linear model, the effects of explanatory variables that are constant over time cannot be separated from the effects of the individual effect U_i under the assumptions of Theorem 4.9.

To extend the maximum-score estimator to panels with $T > 2$, define $W_{itr} = X_{it} - X_{ir}$ $(t, r = 2, \ldots, T)$. Then β can be estimated consistently by solving

$$\underset{|b_1|=1,\, b\in B}{\text{maximize}}: \frac{1}{n}\sum_{i=1}^{n}\sum_{t=2}^{T}\sum_{r<t}(Y_{it} - Y_{ir})I(W_{itr}'b \geq 0).$$

See Charlier et al. (1995).

The panel-data maximum-score estimator, like the forms of the maximum-score estimator that are discussed in Sections 4.3.3 and 4.4.1, has a discontinuous objective function that can be smoothed. The smoothed estimator solves

$$\underset{|b_1|=1,\, b\in B}{\text{maximize}}: S_{sms,PD}(b) = \frac{1}{n}\sum_{i=1}^{n}\sum_{t=2}^{T}\sum_{r<t}(Y_{it} - Y_{ir})K\left(\frac{W'_{itr}b}{h_n}\right), \tag{4.40}$$

where K is the integral of a kernel function and $\{h_n\}$ is a sequence of bandwidths. To analyze this estimator, let $\tilde{\beta}$ denote the vector consisting of all components of β except the first. Let $\tilde{b}_n$ denote the resulting estimator of $\tilde{\beta}$. Charlier (1994) and Charlier et al. (1995) use Taylor-series methods like those used to prove Theorem 4.5 to show that $\tilde{b}_n$ is asymptotically normally distributed after centering and normalization. To state the result, define W^1_{itr} to be the first component of W_{itr} and $\tilde{W}_{itr}$ to be the vector consisting of all components of W_{itr} except the first. Let $s \geq 2$ be an integer. Also define $Z_{tr} = W'_{\cdot tr}\beta$,

$$A_{PD} = -2\alpha_A \sum_{t=2}^{T}\sum_{r<t}\sum_{j=1}^{s}\frac{1}{j!(s-j)!}E[F^{(j)}(0|0,\tilde{W}_{\cdot tr},Y_t \neq Y_r)$$
$$\times\, p^{(s-j)}(0|\tilde{W}_{\cdot tr},Y_t \neq Y_r)|Y_t \neq Y_r]P(Y_t \neq Y_r),$$

$$D_{PD} = \alpha_D \sum_{t=2}^{T}\sum_{r<t}E[\tilde{W}_{\cdot tr}\tilde{W}\prime_{\cdot tr}p(0|\tilde{W}_{\cdot tr},Y_t \neq Y_r)|Y_t \neq Y_r]P(Y_t \neq Y_r),$$

and

$$Q_{PD} = 2\sum_{t=2}^{T}\sum_{r<t}E[\tilde{W}_{\cdot tr}\tilde{W}\prime_{\cdot tr}F^{(1)}(0|0,\tilde{W}_{\cdot tr},Y_t \neq Y_r)$$
$$p(0|\tilde{W}_{\cdot tr},Y_t \neq Y_r)|Y_t \neq Y_r]P(Y_t \neq Y_r).$$

Make the following assumptions:

PD1: For each i, the random variables ε_{it} $(t=1,\ldots,T)$ are identically distributed conditional on $(X_{i1},\ldots,X_{iT},U_i)$. The support of the common distribution is $(-\infty,\infty)$ for all $(X_{i1},\ldots,X_{iT},U_i)$.

PD2: For all $t = 1,\ldots,T$ and $r = 1,\ldots,t-1$ the support of W_{itr} $(i = 1,\ldots,n)$ is not contained in any proper linear subspace of $\mathbb{R}^d$.

PD3: For all $t = 1,\ldots,T$ and $r = 1,\ldots,t-1$and almost every $\tilde{w}_{tr}$, the distribution of W^1_{itr}conditional on $\tilde{W}_{itr} = \tilde{w}_{tr}$ has everywhere positive density.

PD4: The random vector $\{Y_{it},X_{it}: t = 1,\ldots,T\}$ has the same distribution for each $i = 1,\ldots,n$. The data consist of an independent random sample from this distribution.

PD5: $\tilde{\beta} = (\beta_2,\ldots,\beta_d)'$is an interior point of a compact subset $\tilde{B}$ of $\mathbb{R}^{d-1}$.

PD6: The components of $\tilde{W}$ are bounded.

PD7: (a) K is twice differentiable everywhere, $|K'|$ and $|K''|$ are uniformly bounded, and each of the following integrals is finite:

$$\int_{-\infty}^{\infty} K'(v)^4 dv, \int_{-\infty}^{\infty} K''(v)^2 dv, \int_{-\infty}^{\infty} |v^2 K''(v)| dv.$$

(b) For some integer $s \geq 2$ and each integer j $(1 \leq j \leq s)$

$$\int_{-\infty}^{\infty} v^j K'(v) dv = \begin{cases} 0 \text{ if } j < s \\ \text{finite if } j = s \end{cases}.$$

(c) For each integer j between 0 and s, any $\eta > 0$, and any positive sequence $\{h_n\}$ converging to 0

$$\lim_{n\to\infty} h_n^{j-2} \int_{|h_n v|>\eta} |v^j K'(v)| dv = 0$$

and

$$\lim_{n\to\infty} h_n^{-1} \int_{|h_n v|>\eta} |K''(v)| dv = 0.$$

PD8: For each integer j such that $1 \leq j \leq s-1$, all z in a neighborhood of 0, almost every $\tilde{w}_{ts}$, $y_t \neq y_s$, and some $M < \infty$, $p^{(j)}(z_{tr}|\tilde{W}_{\cdot tr} = w_{tr}, y_t \neq y_r)$ exists and is a continuous function of z_{tr} satisfying $|p^{(j)}(z_{tr}|\tilde{W}_{\cdot tr} = w_{tr}, y_t \neq y_r)| < M$for all z_{tr}. In addition

$$|p(z_{tr}, z_{km}|\tilde{W}_{\cdot tr} = w_{tr}, \tilde{W}_{\cdot km} = w_{km}, y_t \neq y_r, y_k \neq y_m)| < M$$

for all (z_{tr}, z_{tm}) and almost every $(\tilde{w}_{tr}, \tilde{w}_{tm})$, $y_t \neq y_r$, and $y_k \neq y_m$.

PD9: For each integer j such that $1 \leq j \leq s$, all z in a neighborhood of 0, almost every $\tilde{w}_{tr}$, $y_t \neq y_r$, and some $M < \infty$, $F^{(j)}(-z_{tr}|z_{tr}, \tilde{w}_{tr}, y_t \neq y_r)$ exists and is a continuous function of z_{tr} satisfying $|F^{(j)}(-z_{tr}|z_{tr}, \tilde{w}_{tr}, y_t \neq y_r)| < M$.

PD10: The matrix Q_{PD} is negative definite.

These assumptions are analogous to the ones made in Theorem 4.5. The following theorem is proved in Charlier (1994).

Theorem 4.10: *Let model (4.37) and assumptions PD1–PD10 hold for some $s \geq 2$. Assume that $nh_n^{2s+1} = \lambda$ for some finite $\lambda > 0$. Let b_n solve problem (4.40). Then $b_n \to \beta$ almost surely as $n \to \infty$, and*

$$(nh_n)^{1/2}(\tilde{b}_n - \tilde{\beta}) \xrightarrow{d} N(-\lambda^{1/2} Q_{PD}^{-1} A_{PD}, Q_{PD}^{-1} D_{PD} Q_{PD}^{-1}).$$

Let Ω be a nonstochastic, positive-semidefinite matrix such that $A'_{PD} Q_{PD}^{-1} \Omega Q_{PD}^{-1} A_{PD} \neq 0$. Let E_A denote the expectation with respect to the asymptotic distribution of $(nh_n)^{1/2}(\tilde{b}_n - \tilde{\beta})$ and let $MSE = E_A(\tilde{b}_n - \tilde{\beta})'\Omega(\tilde{b}_n - \tilde{\beta})$. MSE is minimized by setting $\lambda = \lambda^*$, where

$$\lambda^* = \frac{trace\,(Q_{PD}^{-1}\Omega Q_{PD}^{-1}D_{PD})}{2sA'_{PD}Q_{PD}^{-1}\Omega Q_{PD}^{-1}A_{PD}}.\blacksquare$$

The quantities A_{PD}, D_{PD}, and Q_{PD} can be estimated consistently as follows. Define

$$a_{its}(b,h) = \frac{\tilde{W}_{its}}{h_n}K'\left(\frac{W'_{its}b}{h}\right)(Y_{it} - Y_{is}).$$

Let $\{h_n^*\}$ be a sequence of positive numbers satisfying $h_n^* \propto n^{-\delta/(2s+1)}$, where $0 < \delta < 1$. Then A_{PD}, D_{PD}, and Q_{PD}, respectively, are estimated consistently by

$$A_{n,PD} = \frac{1}{n(h^*{}_n)^{s+1}}\sum_{i=1}^{n}\sum_{t=2}^{T}\sum_{s<t}\tilde{W}_{its}K'\left(\frac{W'_{its}b_n}{h^*{}_n}\right)(Y_{it} - Y_{is}),$$

$$D_{n,PD} = \frac{h_n}{n}\sum_{i=1}^{n}\sum_{t=2}^{T}\sum_{s<t}a_{its}(b_n,h_n)a_{its}(b_n,h_n)',$$

and

$$Q_{n,PD} = \frac{\partial^2 S_{sms,PD}(b_n)}{\partial\tilde{b}\partial\tilde{b}'}.$$

As in smoothed maximum-score estimation based on cross-sectional data, an asymptotically unbiased smoothed maximum-score estimator of β for panel data is given by

$$\hat{b}_n = \tilde{b}_n + \left(\frac{\lambda}{n}\right)^{s/(2s+1)} Q_{n,PD}^{-1}A_{n,PD}.$$

The asymptotically optimal value of λ is given by (4.31) but with A, D, and Q replaced with A_{PD}, D_{PD}, and Q_{PD}. Tests of hypotheses about β can be carried out by replacing A_n, D_n, and Q_n with $A_{n,PD}$, $D_{n,PD}$, and $Q_{n,PD}$ in the formulae for the random-sample t and χ^2 statistics.

4.4.3 Ordered-Response Models

An ordered-response model is a modification of the binary-response model in which the dependent variable Y takes more than two discrete values. The most frequently used form of this model is

$$Y = I(\alpha_{m-1} < Y^* \leq \alpha_m);\ m = 1, \ldots, M, \tag{4.41a}$$

where

$$Y^* = X'\beta + U, \tag{4.41b}$$

α_m $(m = 0, \cdots, M)$ are constants, $-\infty = \alpha_0 < \alpha_1 < \cdots < \alpha_{M-1} < \alpha_M = \infty$, Y is the dependent variable, X is a vector of explanatory variables, β is a conformable vector of constant parameters, and Y^* and U are unobserved random variables. The constants α_m may be known or unknown to the analyst.

Assume for the moment that the α_m are known. Consider the problem of estimating β from a random sample of (Y, X). If the distribution of U is known up to a finite-dimensional parameter, then β can be estimated by maximum likelihood. See, for example, Davidson and MacKinnon (1993). Kooreman and Melenberg (1989) and Lee (1992) have developed versions of the maximum-score estimator that permit estimation of β without assuming that the distribution of Y belongs to a known, finite-dimensional parametric family.

To describe the semiparametric estimator, assume that median $(U|X = x) = 0$ for almost every x. Define the random variable W by

$$W = \sum_{m=0}^{M-1} I(Y^* > \alpha_m).$$

Note that W is observed by virtue of (4.41a). In addition, median $(U|X = x) = 0$ implies that median $(Y^*|X = x) = x'\beta$. Therefore, it follows from (4.41a) that

$$\text{median } (W|X = x) = \sum_{m=0}^{M-1} I(x'\beta > \alpha_m). \tag{4.42}$$

Let the data, $\{Y_i, X_i : i = 1, \ldots, n\}$ be a random sample of (Y, X). Consider, the modified maximum-score estimator of β that is obtained by solving the problem

$$\underset{b \in B}{\text{maximize}} : S_{n,OR}(b) \equiv \frac{1}{n} \sum_{i=1}^{n} \left| W_i - \sum_{m=0}^{M-1} I(X_i'b > \alpha_m) \right|, \tag{4.43}$$

where B is the parameter set. Let b_n be the resulting estimator. Observe that because of (4.42), b_n amounts to a median-regression estimator of β. Consistency of this estimator is established in the following theorem, which is proved in Kooreman and Melenberg (1989).

Theorem 4.11: *Let model (4.41) hold with median $(U|X = x) = 0$ for all x in the support of X. Assume that B is a compact subset of $\mathbb{R}^d$. Let b_n solve problem (4.43). Then $b_n \to \beta$ almost surely as $n \to \infty$ if*

(a) $\{Y_i,\ X_i : i = 1, \ldots, n\}$ is a random sample from the distribution of (Y,X).
(b) The support of the distribution of X is not contained in any proper linear subspace of $\mathbb{R}^d$.
(c) The first component of β is nonzero. For almost every $\tilde{x} = (x^2, \ldots, x^d)$ the distribution of X^1 conditional on $\tilde{X} = \tilde{x}$ has an everywhere positive density.
(d) The bounds $\{m = 0, \ldots, M\}$ are known constants, and $M > 2$. ■

These assumptions are similar to those of Theorem 4.4. The main difference is that the ordered-response model does not require a scale normalization for β. This is because levels of Y^* are observable in the ordered-response model. In contrast, only the sign of Y^* is observable in the binary-response model.

Lee (1992) showed that the maximum-score estimator for an ordered-response model can be extended to the case of unknown α_ms by normalizing the absolute value of the first component of β to be 1, normalizing $\alpha_1 = 0$, and minimizing the right-hand side of (4.42) with respect to α_m $(m = 1, \ldots, M - 1)$ as well as β. Melenberg and van Soest (1996) have derived a smoothed version of the ordered-response maximum-score estimator with unknown α_ms. This estimator is obtained by replacing the indicator function $I(X_i'b > \alpha_m)$ on the right-hand side of (4.42) with the smooth function $K[(X_i'b - a_m)/h_n]$, where $\{h_n\}$ is a sequence of bandwidths. Define $W_{im} = I(Y_i^* > a_m)$. Then the smoothed estimator solves

$$\underset{b \in B, a_1 = 0, a_2, \ldots, a_m}{\text{maximize}} : S_{n,SOR}(b,\ a) \equiv \frac{1}{n} \sum_{i=1}^{n} \sum_{m=1}^{M} (2W_{im} - 1) K\left(\frac{X_i'b - a_m}{h_n} \right).$$

Melenberg and van Soest provide informal arguments showing that the centered, normalized, smoothed maximum-score estimator of $\tilde{\beta}$ and the α_m's for ordered-response models is asymptotically normally distributed under regularity conditions similar to those of Theorem 4.5.

To state the result of Melenberg and van Soest, define $Z_m = X'\beta - \alpha_m$. Assume that $\alpha_1 = 0$ to achieve location normalization, and let $\tilde{\alpha}$ be the vector $(\alpha_2, \ldots, \alpha_{M-1})'$. Let $\tilde{a}_n$ be the smoothed maximum-score estimator of $\tilde{\alpha}$. Let $\tilde{X}$ denote the vector consisting of all components of X except the first, and let $p_m(\cdot\,|\tilde{x})$ denote the probability density function of Z_m conditional on $\tilde{X} = \tilde{x}$. Let $F(\cdot\,|z,\tilde{x})$ denote the CDF of U conditional on $Z = z$ and $\tilde{X} = \tilde{x}$. Define $\tilde{X}_m = (\tilde{X}, -d_m')'$, where $d_m = 0$ if $m = 1$, $d_m = (0, \ldots, 1, 0, \ldots, 0)'$ if $2 \le m \le M - 1$, and 1 is the $(m-1)$'th component of the vector. Then define the matrix A_{OR} by

$$A_{OR} = \sum_{m=1}^{M-1} A_m,$$

where

$$A_m = -2\alpha_A \sum_{j=1}^{s} \left\{ \frac{1}{j!(s-j)!} E\left[F^{(j)}(0|0,\ \tilde{X}) p_m^{(s-j)}(0|\tilde{X}) \tilde{X}_m \right] \right\},$$

and $s \ge 2$ is an integer. Also define

$$D_{OR} = \sum_{m=1}^{M-1} D_m + \sum_{m=1}^{M-1} \sum_{k \ne m} D_{mk},$$

where for $m, k = 1, \ldots, M - 1$

$$D_m = \alpha_D E[\tilde{X}\tilde{X}' p_m(0|\tilde{X})],$$
$$D_{mk} = \alpha_D E\{[P_{mk}(1|0,\ \tilde{X}) - P_{mk}(0|0,\ \tilde{X})]\tilde{X}_k \tilde{X}_m' p_m(0|\tilde{X}) p_k(0|\tilde{X})\},$$
$$P_{mk}(1|0,\tilde{x}) = P(Y_{im} = Y_{ik}|Z_m = 0, Z_s = 0, \tilde{x}),$$

and

$$P_{mk}(-1|0,\tilde{x}) = P(Y_{im} \neq Y_{ik}|Z_m = 0, Z_s = 0, \tilde{x}).$$

Finally, define

$$Q_{OR} = \sum_{m=1}^{M-1} Q_m,$$

where

$$Q_m = 2E[\tilde{X}_m \tilde{X}_m' F^{(1)}(0|0,\tilde{X}) p_m(0|\tilde{X})].$$

Melenberg and van Soest (1996) provide informal arguments showing that if $nh_n^{2s+1} \to \lambda$ for some $s \geq 2$, then under regularity conditions similar to those of Theorem 4.5, the ordered-response smoothed maximum-score estimator satisfies

$$(nh_n)^{1/2}[(\tilde{b}_n',\tilde{a}_n')' - (\tilde{\beta}',\tilde{\alpha}')'] \overset{d}{\to} N(-\lambda^{1/2} Q_{OR}^{-1} A_{OR}, Q_{OR}^{-1} D_{OR} Q_{OR}^{-1}).$$

A_{OR}, D_{OR}, and Q_{OR} can be estimated consistently by replacing the derivatives of the summand of S_{sms} with the derivatives of the summand of $S_{n,SOR}$ in the formulae for A_n, D_n, and Q_n in smoothed maximum-score estimation of a binary-response model.

4.5 Other Estimators for Heteroskedastic Binary-Response Models

The maximum-score and smoothed maximum-score estimators are consistent and, in the case of the smoothed maximum-score estimator, asymptotically normal under weak assumptions. But these assumptions do not permit identification of $P(Y=1|X=x)$, and the estimator of β has a rate of convergence that is slower than $n^{-1/2}$. Estimation of $P(Y = 1|X = x)$ and $n^{-1/2}$-consistency are possible under stronger assumptions. Lewbel (2000) considered estimation of β in the model $Y = I(Z + X'\beta + U > 0)$ where Z is an observed scalar covariate, X is a possibly vector-valued observed covariate, and U is an unobserved random variable that has mean 0 and is uncorrelated with X. Lewbel (2000) allows U to have heteroskedasticity of unknown form but requires U to be independent of Z conditional on X. Thus, Z is a "special regressor" in Lewbel's formulation. In the case of a random-coefficients model, the independence assumption implies that the coefficient of Z is known to be nonstochastic. This happens, for example, in applications where the values of Z are chosen through an experimental design that makes Z independent of (X, U). Lewbel presents an estimator of β that is $n^{-1/2}$-consistent and asymptotically normal under his independence assumption and other regularity conditions. Lewbel also describes an extension to ordered-response models.

Chen and Khan (2003) considered estimation of β in an ordered-response model consisting of (4.41a) and

$$Y^* = X'\beta + \sigma(X)U,$$

where σ is an unknown function and U is an unobserved random variable that is independent of X and has mean 0. This form of heteroskedasticity precludes random coefficients but is used frequently in statistics. Chen and Khan (2003) develop an estimator of β for this model and show that it is $n^{-1/2}$-consistent and asymptotically normal if the number of response categories is at least 3. They prove that $n^{-1/2}$-consistency is not possible if there are only two response categories (binary response).

4.6 An Empirical Example

This section presents an empirical example that illustrates the use of the smoothed maximum-score estimator for a binary-response model. The example is taken from Horowitz (1993a) and consists of estimating a model of the choice between automobile and transit for the trip to work. The data consist of 842 observations of work trips that were sampled randomly from the Washington, D.C., area transportation study. The dependent variable is 1 if automobile was used for the trip and 0 if transit was used. The independent variables are an intercept (*INT*), the number of cars owned by the traveler's household (*CARS*), transit out-of-vehicle travel time minus automobile out-of-vehicle travel time (*DOVTT*), transit in-vehicle travel time minus automobile in-vehicle travel time (*DIVTT*), and transit fare minus automobile travel cost (*DCOST*). *DOVTT* and *DIVTT* are in units of minutes, and *DCOST* is in units of dollars. Scale normalization is achieved by setting $\beta_{DCOST} = 1$.

The model is specified as in (4.1). The coefficients were estimated by parametric maximum likelihood using a binary probit model and the smoothed maximum-score estimator. In smoothed maximum-score estimation, K was the standard normal distribution function. The smoothed maximum-score estimates are bias corrected.

The estimation results are shown in Table 4.2. The quantities in parentheses are the half-widths of nominal 90% confidence intervals. For the binary probit model, these were obtained using standard asymptotic distribution theory. For the smoothed maximum-score estimator, the confidence intervals were obtained using the bootstrap method described in Section 4.3.3. The resulting $1 - \alpha$ confidence interval for the j th component of $\tilde{\beta}$is

$$\tilde{b}_{nj} - z^*_{\alpha/2} V_{nj}^{1/2} \leq \tilde{\beta}_j \leq \tilde{b}_{nj} + z^*_{\alpha/2} V_{nj}^{1/2},$$

Table 4.2 Estimated parameters of a work-trip mode-choice model

Estimator	INT	CARS	DOVTT	DIVTT
Probit	−0.628	1.280	0.034	0.006
	(0.382)	(0.422)	(0.024)	(0.006)
Smooth. max. score	−1.576	2.242	0.027	0.014
	(0.766)	(0.749)	(0.031)	(0.009)

Source: Horowitz (1993a). The coefficient of *DCOST* is 1 by scale normalization.

where $z^*_{\alpha/2}$ is the$1 - \alpha/2$ quantile of the distribution of the bootstrap t statistic, t^*. Half-widths of confidence intervals, rather than standard errors, are used to indicate estimation precision. This is because the bootstrap provides a higher-order approximation to the distribution of the smoothed maximum-score estimator, and the higher-order approximation is nonnormal.

The estimates of the components of β obtained by the two estimation methods differ by up to a factor of 2.5, depending on the component. Thus, the different methods yield very different results. The smoothed maximum-score estimates indicate much greater sensitivity of choice to *CARS* and *DIVTT* relative to *DCOST* than do the probit estimates. The half-widths of the confidence intervals for nonintercept coefficients are largest for the smoothed maximum-score estimates and narrowest for the probit estimates. This is consistent with the relative rates of convergence of the two estimators, which are $n^{-2/5}$ for the smoothed maximum-score estimator and $n^{-1/2}$ for the probit model.

The coefficient of *CARS* is statistically significantly different from 0 at the 0.10 level according to both estimation methods. That is, the 90% confidence intervals for β_{CARS} do not contain 0. However, the smoothed maximum-score estimates yield inferences about β_{DOVTT} and β_{DIVTT} that are different from those obtained from the probit model. The smoothed maximum-score method gives a smaller point estimate of β_{DOVTT} and a larger point estimate of β_{DIVTT} than does the probit model. In addition, β_{DOVTT} is not significantly different from 0 at the 0.10 level and β_{DIVTT} is significantly different from 0 according to the smoothed maximum-score estimates, whereas the opposite is the case according to the probit estimates. The nonsignificance of the smoothed maximum-score estimate of β_{DOVTT} does not necessarily indicate that the true value of β_{DOVTT} is close to 0 because the smoothed maximum-score estimate is relatively imprecise. However, the probit model is nested in the model assumed by the smoothed maximum-score estimator. Therefore, the differences between the probit and smoothed maximum-score estimates suggest that the probit model is misspecified and that its estimates are misleading.

In fact the probit model is rejected by a variety of specification tests. These include likelihood-ratio, Wald, and Lagrangian multiplier tests against a random-coefficients probit model. Thus the differences between the probit and smoothed maximum-score estimates reflect genuine features of the data-generation process, not just random sampling errors.

Chapter 5
Statistical Inverse Problems

This chapter is concerned with estimation of a function g that is the solution to an integral equation called a Fredholm equation of the first kind. The equation is named after the Swedish mathematician Erik Ivar Fredholm and has the form

$$m(w) = \int k(x,\ w)g(x)dx, \tag{5.1}$$

where m and k are functions that are either known or easily estimated. Deconvolution and nonparametric instrumental-variables (IV) estimation are two important classes of estimation problems in which the function being estimated is the solution to an equation with the form of (5.1). Nonparametric density estimation is another example (Härdle and Linton 1994).

In deconvolution, one wants to estimate the probability density function of a continuously distributed random variable U, but U is not observed. Instead, one observes the random variable $W = U + \varepsilon$, where ε is a random variable that is independent of U. Such estimation problems are called deconvolution problems because the distribution of the observed random variable W is the convolution of the distributions of U and ε. Specifically, let f_W, f_ε, and f_U denote the probability density functions of W, ε, and U, respectively. Then

$$f_W(w) = \int f_\varepsilon(w - x)f_U(x)dx. \tag{5.2}$$

Equation (5.2) has the form (5.1) with $m(w) = f_W(w)$, $k(x,\ w) = f_\varepsilon(w - x)$, and $g(x) = f_U(x)$. Deconvolution problems arise, among other places, in models of measurement error. For example, suppose W is the measured value of a variable, U is the true value, and ε is the measurement error. If error-free measurement is not possible, then estimating the distribution of the true variable U is a problem in deconvolution. Section 5.1 shows how to solve this problem.

Deconvolution problems also arise in mean-regression models for panel data. For example, consider the model

$$Y_{jt} = X_{jt}\beta + U_j + \varepsilon_{jt};\ j = 1,\ \ldots,\ n;\ \ t = 1,\ \ldots, T. \tag{5.3}$$

J.L. Horowitz, *Semiparametric and Nonparametric Methods in Econometrics*, Springer Series in Statistics, DOI 10.1007/978-0-387-92870-8_5,

In this model, Y_{jt} is the observed value of the dependent variable Y for individual j at time t, X_{jt} is the observed value of a (possibly vector-valued) explanatory variable X for individual j at time t, and β is a vector of constant parameters. U_j is the value of an unobserved random variable U that varies across individuals but is constant over time, and ε_{jt} is the value of an unobserved random variable ε that varies across both individuals and time. Suppose one wants to estimate the probability distribution of Y_{js} at time $s > T$ conditional on observations of Y_{jt} at times $t \leq T$ and observations or forecasts of X_{jt} for $s > T$. For example, Y_{js} may be the income of individual j at time s, and one may want to estimate the probability that individual j's future income exceeds a specified value conditional on observations of this individual's past income and the values of the covariates. To solve this problem, it is necessary to estimate the distributions of U and ε, which is a deconvolution problem. Section 5.2 shows how to carry out deconvolution for the panel-data model (5.3).

In nonparametric IV estimation, the problem is to estimate the function g in the model

$$Y = g(X) + U;\ E(U|W = w) = 0 \tag{5.4}$$

for every w in support of the random variable W except, possibly, w values in a set whose probability is zero. In (5.4), Y is the dependent variable, and X is an explanatory variable that may be endogenous. That is, we do not assume that $E(U|X) = 0$. The random variable W is an instrument for X. If g were known to be a linear function, say $g(x) = \beta_0 + \beta_1 x$, then β_0 and β_1 could be estimated using IV methods that are described in introductory econometrics textbooks and widely used in applied econometrics. Here, we assume that the functional form of g is unknown. Let $f_{X|W}$ denote the probability density function of X conditional on W. Then (5.4) implies that

$$E(Y|W = w) = \int f_{X|W}(x,\ w)g(x)dx.$$

Multiplying both sides of this equation by the probability density function of W yields an equivalent equation that is more convenient for estimating g. This is

$$E(Y|W = w)f_W(w) = \int f_{XW}(x,\ w)g(x)dx, \tag{5.5}$$

where f_{XW} is the probability density function of $(X,\ W)$ and f_W is the marginal density of W. Equation (5.5) has the form of (5.1) with $m(w) = E(Y|W = w)f_W(w)$ and $k(x,\ w) = f_{XW}(x,\ w)$. Nonparametric IV estimation is discussed in Sections 5.3 and 5.4.

Equation (5.2) has a relatively simple analytic solution, whereas (5.5) does not, except in special cases. This makes deconvolution problems easier to analyze than problems in nonparametric IV estimation. Accordingly, deconvolution is discussed first (Sections 5.1 and 5.2) followed by nonparametric IV estimation.

5.1 Deconvolution in a Model of Measurement Error

This section is concerned with estimating the probability density function of the random variable U in the model

$$W = U + \varepsilon. \tag{5.6}$$

The data, $\{W_j: j = 1, \ldots, n\}$, are a random sample of observations of W. The symbol j is used to index observations in this discussion because i is used later to denote the imaginary number $\sqrt{-1}$. It is assumed that ε is independent of U and that ε has a known probability density function f_ε. In an application, knowledge of f_ε might be obtained from a validation data set. A validation data set contains observations of both U and W, thereby permitting estimation of the probability distribution of ε. Typically, the validation data set is much smaller than the full estimation data set that contains observations of W but not U. Therefore, the validation data set is not a substitute for the full estimation data set.

The procedure described here for estimating the distribution of U has two main steps. The first is to express the density of U as a functional of the distributions of W and ε. Equation (5.2) does this, but it is not as convenient for estimation of the density of U as is another equivalent relation that is described in the next paragraph. The second step of the estimation procedure is to replace the unknown distribution of W with a suitable sample analog.

To take the first estimation step, define ψ_W, ψ_U, and ψ_ε, respectively, to be the characteristic functions of the distributions of W, U, and ε. That is, $\psi_W(t) = Ee^{itW}$, where $i = \sqrt{-1}$. ψ_U and ψ_ε are defined similarly. Rao (1973) and Stuart and Ord (1987) discuss characteristic functions and their properties. Assume that $\psi_\varepsilon(\tau) \neq 0$ for all finite, real τ. Then for any finite, real τ, $\psi_W(\tau) = \psi_U(\tau)\psi_\varepsilon(\tau)$ (because U and ε are assumed to be independent), and $\psi_U(\tau) = \psi_W(\tau)/\psi_\varepsilon(\tau)$. It follows from the inversion formula for characteristic functions that

$$f_U(u) = \frac{1}{2\pi}\int_{-\infty}^{\infty} e^{-i\tau u}\frac{\psi_W(\tau)}{\psi_\varepsilon(\tau)}d\tau. \tag{5.7}$$

Equation (5.7) provides the desired expression for f_U in terms of the distributions of W and ε. This completes the first estimation step.

The only unknown quantity on the right-hand side of (5.7) is ψ_W. Therefore, the second estimation step consists of replacing ψ_W with a suitable sample analog. One possibility is the empirical characteristic function of W. This is

$$\psi_{nW}(\tau) = \frac{1}{n}\sum_{j=1}^{n} \exp\ (i\tau W_j).$$

One could now consider replacing ψ_W with ψ_{nW} in (5.7). In general, however, the resulting integral does not exist. This is because (5.7) assumes that the distribution of W has a density so that $\psi_W(t)/\psi_\varepsilon(\tau) \to 0$ as $\tau \to \infty$. But the empirical distribution of W is discrete and has no density. Consequently, $\psi_{nW}(\tau)/\psi_\varepsilon(\tau)$ need not converge to 0 as $\tau \to \infty$. This problem can be solved by modifying or "regularizing" (5.7) so as to ensure existence of the integral when ψ_W is replaced by ψ_{nW}. Recall that (5.7) is a version of the integral equation (5.1). Regularization (that is, modification of the original estimation problem to ensure that it has a solution) is always needed in estimation based on (5.1) to ensure existence of a solution to (5.1) when m and, possibly, k are replaced by sample analogs. The "amount" of regularization decreases as $n \to \infty$ to achieve consistency of the estimator of f_U in (5.7) or g in (5.1). In deconvolution, regularization can be carried out by convoluting the empirical distribution of W with the distribution of a continuously distributed random variable that becomes degenerate (a point mass at zero) as $n \to \infty$. This amounts to kernel smoothing of the empirical distribution of W. Other ways of carrying out regularization are needed for nonparametric IV. These are discussed in Section 5.3.

To carry out the smoothing, let ψ_ζ be a bounded characteristic function whose support is $[-1, 1]$. Let ζ be the random variable that has this characteristic function, and let $\{\nu_n\}$ be a sequence of positive constants that converges to 0 as $n \to \infty$. The idea of the smoothing procedure is to use the inversion formula for characteristic functions to estimate the density of the random variable $W + \nu_n\varepsilon$. The resulting smoothed (or regularized) estimator of $f_U(u)$ is

$$f_{nU}(u) = \frac{1}{2\pi}\int_{-\infty}^{\infty} e^{-i\tau u}\frac{\psi_{nW}(\tau)\psi_\zeta(\nu_n\tau)}{\psi_\varepsilon(\tau)}d\tau. \tag{5.8}$$

The integral in (5.8) exists because the integrand is 0 if $|\tau| > 1/\nu_n$. If ν_n does not converge to 0 too rapidly as $n \to \infty$, then $f_{nU}(u)$ is consistent for $f_U(u)$. This is analogous to the situation in kernel nonparametric density estimation, where consistency is achieved if the bandwidth converges to 0 at a rate that is not too fast.

The CDF of U, F_U, can be estimated by integrating f_{nU}. The estimator is

$$F_{nU}(u) = \int_{-M_n}^{u} f_{nU}(u)du,$$

where $M_n \to \infty$ as $n \to \infty$.

5.1.1 Rate of Convergence of the Density Estimator

The asymptotic properties of f_{nU} have been investigated by Carroll and Hall (1988), Fan (1991a,b), and Stefanski and Carroll (1990, 1991), among others. The main results concern the rate of convergence of f_{nU} to f_U, which is often very slow. Slow convergence is unavoidable in deconvolution problems and is not an indication that f_{nU} in (5.8) is unsatisfactory. This section states the formal results on the rates of convergence of deconvolution estimators. Section 5.1.2 provides a heuristic explanation of these results.

To state the results, make the following assumptions.

DC1: f_U has m bounded derivatives for some $m > 0$.
DC2: $\psi_\varepsilon(\tau) \neq 0$ for all finite, real τ.
DC3: ψ_ζ is real-valued, has support $[-1, 1]$, is symmetrical about 0, and has $m+2$ bounded, integrable derivatives.
DC4: $\psi_\zeta(\tau) = 1 + O(\tau^m)$ as $\tau \to 0$.

Assumption DC1 is a smoothness condition. Assumption DC2 ensures that the denominator of the integrand in (5.7) is nonzero. Assumptions DC3 and DC4 can always be satisfied by making a suitable choice of ψ_ζ.

The following theorems on the rate of convergence of f_{nU} are proved in Fan (1991a). Fan (1991a) also investigates the rates of convergence of estimators of derivatives of f_U, but estimation of derivatives will not be discussed here.

Theorem 5.1: *Let assumptions DC1–DC4 hold. Also assume that*

$$|\psi_\varepsilon(\tau)||\tau|^{-\beta_0} \exp\ (|\tau|^{\beta_1}/\gamma) \geq d_0 \tag{5.9}$$

as $|\tau| \to \infty$ for positive constants β_0, β_1, γ, and d_0. Let $\nu_n = (4/\gamma)^{1/\beta_1}(\log n)^{-1/\beta_1}$. Then for any u,

$$E[f_{nU}(u) - f_u(u)]^2 = O[(\log n)^{-2m/\beta_1}]$$

as $n \to \infty$. Moreover, if

$$|\psi_\varepsilon(\tau)||\tau|^{-\beta_2} \exp\ (|\tau|^{\beta_1}/\gamma) \leq d_1 \tag{5.10}$$

as $|\tau| \to \infty$ for positive constants β_2 and d_2 and if

$$P(|\varepsilon - x| \leq |x|^{\alpha_0}) = O[|x|^{-(a-\alpha_0)}] \tag{5.11}$$

as $|x| \to \infty$ for some α_0 satisfying $0 < \alpha_0 < 1$ and $a > 1 + \alpha_0$, then no estimator of $f_U(u)$ can converge faster than $(\log n)^{-m/\beta_1}$ in the sense that for every estimator $f_{nU}(u)$

$$E[f_{nU}(u) - f_U(u)]^2 > d(\log n)^{-2m/\beta_1}$$

for some $d > 0$. ■

The technical condition (5.11) holds if $f_\varepsilon(x) = O(|x|^{-a})$ as $|x| \to \infty$ for some $a > 1$. Thus, (5.11) is a restriction on the thickness of the tails of f_ε.

Theorem 5.2: *Let assumptions DC1–DC4 hold. Also assume that*

$$|\psi_\varepsilon(\tau)||\tau|^{\beta} \geq d_0 \tag{5.12}$$

as $|\tau| \to \infty$ *for positive constants* β *and* d_0. *Let* $\nu_n = dn^{-(1/2)[(m+\beta)+1]}$ *for some* $d > 0$. *Then for any* u,

$$E[f_{nU}(u) - f_U(u)]^2 = O\{n^{-2m/[2(m+\beta)+1]}\}$$

as $n \to \infty$. *Moreover, if* ψ_ε^j *denotes the jth derivative of* ψ_ε *and*

$$|\psi_\varepsilon^j(\tau)\tau^{-(\beta+j)}| \leq d_j; j = 0,\ 1,\ 2$$

as $\tau \to \infty$ *for positive constants* d_j $(j = 0,\ 1,\ 2)$, *then no estimator of* $f_U(u)$ *can converge faster than* $n^{-m/[2(m+\beta)+1]}$ *in the sense that for every estimator* $f_{nU}(u)$

$$E[f_{nU}(u) - f_U(u)]^2 > dn^{-2m/[2(m+\beta)+1]}$$

for some $d > 0$. ■

Similar results can be obtained regarding the rate of uniform convergence of f_{nU} and the rate of convergence of the integrated mean-square error of f_{nU}. In particular, under the assumptions of Theorem 5.1, $\sup_u |f_{nU}(u) - f_U(u)|$ converges in probability to 0 at the rate given by the theorem. Fan (1991a) also shows that F_{nU} is a consistent estimator of F_U if $M_n = O(n^{1/3})$ as $n \to \infty$. Moreover, under the assumptions of Theorem 5.1, $F_{nU}(u)$ converges to $F_U(u)$ at the same rate at which $f_{nU}(u)$ converges to $f_U(u)$. Hall and Lahiri (2008) give conditions under which faster rates of convergence of F_{nU} are possible. Butucea and Tsybakov (2008) assume that ψ_U and ψ_ε both have exponentially decreasing tails and give conditions under which f_{nU} has a faster than logarithmic rate of convergence. Butucea (2004) considers the case in which ψ_U has exponentially decreasing tails and ψ_ε has geometric tails.

Theorems 5.1 and 5.2 imply that f_{nU} converges to f_U at the fastest possible rate, but that rate can be excruciatingly slow. Under the assumptions of Theorem 5.1, the fastest possible rate of convergence of f_{nU} is a power of $(\log n)^{-1}$. By contrast, parametric estimators usually converge at the rate $n^{-1/2}$. Nonparametric mean-regression estimators converge at the rate $n^{-2s/(2s+d)}$, where d is the dimension of the explanatory variable and s is the number of times that the conditional mean function and the density of the explanatory variables are differentiable. As will be discussed further in Section 5.3, slow convergence is related to properties of the function k in (5.1) and can also arise in nonparametric IV estimation.

Theorems 5.1 and 5.2 also imply that the rate of convergence of f_{nU} is controlled mainly by the thickness of the tails of the characteristic function of ε. Conditions (5.9) and (5.10) of Theorem 5.1 are satisfied by distributions whose characteristic functions have tails that decrease exponentially fast. These include the normal, Cauchy, and Type 1 extreme value distributions. The fastest possible rate of convergence of f_{nU} is logarithmic when ε has one of these distributions. Theorem 5.2 shows that faster rates of convergence of f_{nU} are possible when the tails of the characteristic function of ε decrease only geometrically fast (e.g., a negative power of its argument), as is assumed in condition (5.12). The Laplace and symmetrical gamma distributions have this property.

5.1.2 Why Deconvolution Estimators Converge Slowly

This section provides a heuristic explanation of why the tail of ψ_ε has such a strong influence on the rate of convergence of f_{nU} and why the rate of convergence can be very slow. To begin, write $f_{nU} - f_U$ in the form

$$f_{nU}(u) - f_U(u) = I_{n1}(u) + I_{n2}(u),$$

where

$$I_{n1}(u) = \frac{1}{2\pi}\int_{-\infty}^{\infty} e^{-i\tau u}\frac{[\psi_{nW}(\tau) - \psi_W(\tau)]\psi_\zeta(\nu_n\tau)}{\psi_\varepsilon(\tau)}d\tau$$

and

$$\begin{aligned} I_{n2}(u) &= \frac{1}{2\pi}\int_{-\infty}^{\infty} e^{-i\tau u}\frac{\psi_W(\tau)\psi_\zeta(\nu_n\tau) - \psi_W(\tau)}{\psi_\varepsilon(\tau)}d\tau \\ &= \frac{1}{2\pi}\int_{-\infty}^{\infty} e^{-i\tau u}\psi_U(\tau)[\psi_\zeta(\nu_n\tau) - 1]d\tau \\ &= \frac{1}{2\pi}\int_{-\infty}^{\infty} e^{-i\tau u}\psi_U(\tau)\psi_\zeta(\nu_n\tau)d\tau - f_U(u). \end{aligned}$$

$I_{n1}(u)$ is a random variable that captures the effects of random sampling error in estimating ψ_W. $I_{n2}(u)$ is a nonstochastic bias arising from the smoothing of the empirical distribution of W. It is analogous to the bias caused by smoothing in non-parametric density estimation and mean regression.

Now, $\psi_{nW}(\tau) - \psi_W(\tau) = O_p(n^{-1/2})$. Moreover, as $\nu_n \to 0$, the denominator of the integral on the right-hand side of $I_{n1}(u)$ will be smallest when $|\tau| = 1/\nu_n$. Therefore, the integral can be expected to converge as $n \to \infty$ only if

$$\frac{1}{n^{1/2}\psi_\varepsilon(1/|\nu_n|)} \to 0 \tag{5.13}$$

as $n \to \infty$. Note that (5.13) is only a necessary condition for convergence of the integral. It is not sufficient in general because the relation $\psi_{nW}(\tau) - \psi_W(\tau) = O_p(n^{-1/2})$ does not hold uniformly over τ. The exact rate of convergence of $I_{n1}(u)$ can be obtained by calculating its variance and applying Chebyshev's inequality. This more elaborate calculation is not needed, however, for the heuristic argument that is made here.

Now consider $I_{n2}(u)$. Observe that $\psi_U(\tau)\psi_\zeta(\nu_n\tau)$ is the characteristic function evaluated at τ of the random variable $U + \nu_n\zeta$. Therefore,

$$I_{n2}(u) = \int f_U(u - \nu_n z) f_\zeta(z) dz - f_U(u), \quad (5.14)$$

where f_ζ is the probability density function of ζ. By assumption DC3, ψ_ζ is real, which implies that f_ζ is symmetrical about 0 and $E(\zeta) = 0$. Therefore, a Taylor-series expansion of the integrand of (5.14) gives

$$I_{n2}(u) = \frac{1}{2}\nu_n^2 f_U''(u)\sigma_\zeta^2 + o(\nu_n^2), \quad (5.15)$$

where σ_ζ^2 denotes the variance of ζ.

Suppose that ε is normally distributed with mean 0. Then $\psi_\varepsilon(\tau) \propto \exp(-a\tau^2)$ for some constant $a > 0$. Moreover, (5.13) implies that $n^{-1/2}\exp(a/\nu_n^2) \to 0$ or $a/\nu_n^2 - (1/2)\log n \to -\infty$ as $n \to \infty$. This relation can hold only if ν_n converges to 0 no faster than $(\log n)^{-1/2}$. But $I_{n2}(u) = O(\nu_n^2)$, so $I_{n2}(u)$ converges to 0 most rapidly when the rate of convergence of ν_n is the fastest possible. Therefore, the fastest possible rate of convergence of $I_{n2}(u)$ is $(\log n)^{-1}$. Since $f_{nU}(u)$ can converge to $f_U(u)$ no faster than $I_{n2}(u)$, the fastest possible rate of convergence of $f_{nU}(u)$ is $(\log n)^{-1}$.

This heuristic result can be compared with the conclusions of Theorem 5.1. In the notation of that theorem, $\beta_1 = 1$. If it is assumed that the unknown f_U belongs to a class of twice-differentiable densities ($m = 2$), then the fastest possible rate of convergence of $f_{nU}(u)$ according to Theorem 5.1 is $(\log n)^{-1}$, and this occurs when $\nu_n \propto (\log n)^{-1/2}$. Thus, the heuristic analysis of the previous paragraph is consistent with the conclusions of the theorem.

Now suppose that the tails of ψ_ε converge to 0 at a geometric rate so that $\psi_\varepsilon(\tau) \propto |\tau|^{-\beta}$ for some $\beta > 0$. Then (5.13) implies that $n^{-1/2}\nu_n^{-\beta} \to 0$ as $n \to \infty$, which permits a geometric rate of convergence of ν_n and, therefore, of $f_{nU}(u)$. This result is consistent with the conclusions of Theorem 5.2.

The rate of convergence $n^{-2m/[2(m+\beta)+1]}$ that is given by Theorem 5.2 is obtained by equating the rates of convergence of the variance and squared bias of $f_{nU}(U)$. An argument that is more precise than the heuristic one made here shows that $Var[I_{n1}(u)] = O[n^{-1}\nu_n^{-(2\beta+1)}]$ when $m = 2$. This is larger than the left-hand side of (5.13), which is not surprising because, as has already been explained, (5.13) is only necessary for convergence of $I_{n2}(u)$ to 0, not sufficient. Setting $O[n^{-1}\nu_n^{-(2\beta+1)}] = (\nu_n^4)$ yields $\nu_n = O[n^{-1/(2\beta+5)}]$. With this rate of convergence of ν_n, $Var[I_{n1}(u)]$ and $I_{n2}(u)^2$ are both $O[n^{-4/(2\beta+5)}]$, which is the rate given by Theorem 5.2 for $m = 2$.

When $m > 2$, convergence of $f_{nU}(u)$ can be accelerated by replacing ψ_ζ with the Fourier transform of a higher-order kernel. This causes f_ζ on the right-hand side of (5.15) to be replaced by the higher-order kernel. Taylor-series arguments similar to those made in nonparametric density estimation then show that $I_{n2}(u) = O(\nu_n^m)$. As in nonparametric density estimation, existence of higher-order derivatives and use of a higher-order kernel accelerates convergence of $f_{nU}(u)$ by accelerating the rate of convergence of the bias for any given bandwidth sequence.

5.1.3 Asymptotic Normality of the Density Estimator

Asymptotic normality of the standardized form of $f_n(u)$ can be proved by showing that it satisfies the conditions of a triangular-array central limit theorem. See Serfling (1980) for a discussion of triangular-array central limit theorems. Fan (1991b) has proved that if $\nu_n = o\{n^{-1/[2(m+\beta)+1]}\}$, then under the assumptions of Theorem 5.2,

$$\frac{f_{nU}(u) - f_U(u)}{\{Var[f_{nU}(u)]\}^{1/2}} \xrightarrow{d} N(0,\ 1). \tag{5.16}$$

Obtaining asymptotic normality when the tails of ψ_ε decrease exponentially fast requires strengthening the conditions of Theorem 5.1. The required conditions are stated in the following theorem.

Theorem 5.3: *Let assumptions DC1–DC4 hold. Also assume that*

(a) There are positive constants β_0, β_1, γ, d_0, and d_1 such that $d_1 \geq |\psi_\varepsilon(\tau)|$ $|\tau|^{-\beta_0} \exp\ (|\tau|^{\beta_1}/\gamma) \geq d_0$.
(b) As $|\tau| \to \infty$, either $\mathrm{Re}[\psi_\varepsilon(\tau)] = o\{\mathrm{Im}[\psi_\varepsilon(\tau)]\}$ or $\mathrm{Im}[\psi_\varepsilon(\tau)] = o\{\mathrm{Re}[\psi_\varepsilon(\tau)]\}$.
(c) $\psi_\zeta(\tau)$ has $m+2$ continuous derivatives. Moreover, $\psi_\zeta(\tau) > d_3(1-\tau)^{m+3}$ for $\tau \in [1-\delta,\ 1)$ and some $d_3 > 0$ and $\delta > 0$.

Let $\nu_n \propto (\log n)^{-1/\beta_1}$. Then (5.16) holds. ■

To use (5.16) for inference, it is necessary to have an estimator of $Var[f_{nU}(u)]$. To this end, for any real w, define

$$g_n(w) = \frac{1}{2\pi} \int e^{-i\tau w} \frac{\psi_\zeta(\tau)}{\psi_\varepsilon(\tau/\nu_n)} d\tau$$

and

$$Z_{nj} = \frac{1}{\nu_n} g_n\left(\frac{u - W_j}{\nu_n}\right).$$

Fan (1991b) shows that $Var[n^{1/2} f_{nU}(u)]$ is estimated consistently by

$$s_n^2 = \frac{1}{n} \sum_{j=1}^{n} Z_{nj}^2 \tag{5.17}$$

in the sense that $s_n^2/Var[n^{1/2} f_{nU}(u)] \xrightarrow{p} 1$. Let s_n be the positive square root of s_n^2. Then (5.16) and (5.17) may be combined to give

$$\frac{n^{1/2}[f_{nU}(u) - f_U(u)]}{s_n} \xrightarrow{d} N(0,\ 1). \tag{5.18}$$

Equation (5.18) can be used in the usual way to form confidence intervals for and test hypotheses about $f_U(u)$. For example, an asymptotic 100(1 − α)% confidence interval for $f_U(u)$ is

$$f_{nU}(u) - z_{\alpha/2}n^{-1/2}s_n \leq f_U(u) \leq f_{nU}(u) + z_{\alpha/2}n^{-1/2}s_n. \qquad (5.19)$$

Because of the slow rates of convergence of deconvolution density estimators, the true coverage probability of the confidence interval (5.19) may be very different from the nominal coverage probability of $(1 - \alpha)$ unless n is very large. Therefore, (5.19) must be used with caution.

5.1.4 A Monte Carlo Experiment

Because the rate of convergence of f_{nU} under the assumptions of Theorem 5.1 is very slow, it useful to investigate whether f_{nU} can provide useful information about f_U under these assumptions and with samples of the sizes likely to be encountered in applications. Such an investigation can be carried out through Monte Carlo experimentation. This section reports the results of one such experiment.

Data for the experiment were generated by simulation from model (5.6). The sample size is $n = 1000$. The distributions of U and ε are both $N(0,\ 1)$, so Theorem 5.1 applies. If it is assumed that $m = 2$, then the fastest possible rate of convergence in probability of f_{nU} is $(\log n)^{-1}$. The smoothing function ψ_ζ is the fourfold convolution of the uniform density with itself. This is the characteristic function of the density $c[(\sin x)/x]^4$, where c is a normalization constant. The smoothing parameter ν_n was chosen by Monte Carlo to approximately minimize the integrated mean-square error of f_{nU}. Of course, this method is not available in applications. It is possible, however, to construct a resampling method that is available in applications and that mimics the Monte Carlo procedure. The method consists of generating samples of size $m < n$ by sampling the estimation data randomly *without* replacement. Each data set created this way is a random sample from the true population distribution of W. By treating f_{nU} based on a preliminary value of ν_n as if it were the true f_U, one can find the value of ν_m that minimizes the integrated mean-square error of f_{mU} as an estimator of f_{nU}. The resulting ν_m can be rescaled to apply to a sample of size n by setting $\nu_n = [r(m)/r(n)]\nu_m$, where $r(n)$ is the rate of convergence of ν_n given by Theorem 5.1 or 5.2.

There were 100 Monte Carlo replications in the experiment. Each replication consisted of computing $f_{nU}(u)$ at 25 different values of u. The Monte Carlo estimates of f_{nU} are summarized in Fig. 5.1. The left-hand panel of the figure shows the true f_U (dashed line) and the average of 100 estimates f_{nU} (solid line). The right-hand panel shows the true f_U (dashed line) and 10 individual realizations of f_{nU} (solid lines). It can be seen that although the estimates are flatter than the true f_U, their shapes are qualitatively similar to the shape of the true f_U on average and, in most cases, individually. Thus, at least for the distributions used in this experiment, f_{nU} is a useful estimator of f_U despite its slow rate of convergence.

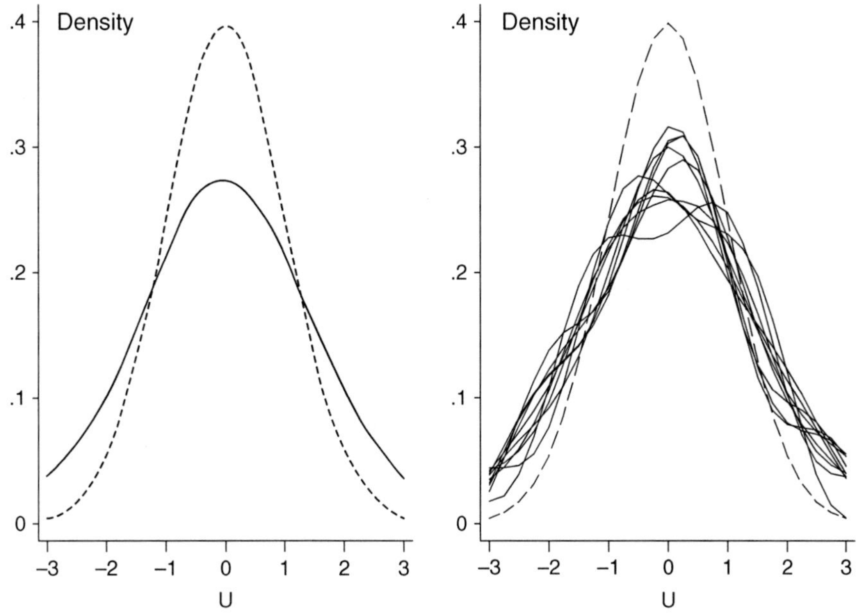

Fig. 5.1 Results of Monte Carlo experiment with deconvolution

5.2 Models for Panel Data

This section is concerned with estimating the probability density functions f_U and f_ε of the random variables U and ε in model (5.3). Although f_U and f_ε by themselves are rarely of interest in applications, knowledge of these densities is needed to compute certain quantities that are of interest, such as transition probabilities and first-passage times.

To illustrate, consider first-passage times. The first-passage time for individual j in model (5.3) is the smallest t for which Y_{jt} exceeds a specified threshold, say y^*. Suppose one is interested in the first-passage time conditional on the initial value of Y for individual j, Y_{j1}, and the values of covariates X_{jt}. For example, if Y_{jt} is earnings of individual j in year t, the first-passage time conditional on Y_{j1} and the covariates might be the earliest year in which an individual whose earnings are currently low according to some criterion becomes a high earner. X might represent characteristics of the individual such as age, education, and experience in the labor force.

Given an integer $\theta > T$, let $P(\theta | y_1, y^* x)$ denote the probability that the first-passage time for threshold y^* and individual j exceeds θ conditional on $Y_{j1} = y_1$ and $X_{jt} = x_t$ $(t = 1, \ldots, \theta)$. Then

$$P(\theta | y_1, y^*, x) = P(Y_{j2} \le y^*, \ldots, Y_{j\theta} \le y^* | Y_{j1} = y_1, X_{j1} = x_1, \ldots, X_{j\theta} = x_\theta).$$

To obtain a formula for $P(\theta|y_1, y^*, x)$, let f_W denote the probability density function of the random variable $W = U + \varepsilon$, and let F_ε denote the CDF of ε. If U is independent of ε and X and if ε_{jt} is independently and identically distributed for all j and t, then some algebra shows that

$$P(\theta|y_1, y^*, x) = \frac{1}{f_W(y_1 - \beta' x_1)} \int_{-\infty}^{\infty} f_\varepsilon(y_1 - \beta' x_1) \left[\prod_{k=2}^{\theta} F_\varepsilon(y^* - \beta' x_k - u) \right] f_U(u) du. \tag{5.20}$$

It can be seen from (5.20) that $P(\theta|y_1, y^*, x)$ depends on both f_U and f_ε. Thus, estimation of these densities is needed to estimate the probability distribution of first-passage times.

In this discussion, the data used to estimate f_U and f_ε are assumed to consist of T observations on each of n randomly sampled individuals. Thus, the data have the form $\{Y_{jt}, X_{jt} : j = 1, \ldots, n;\ t = 1, \ldots, T\}$. Typically in panel data, the number of sampled individuals is large but the number of observations per individual is not. Thus, asymptotic results will be developed under the assumption that $n \to \infty$ while T stays fixed. It will be assumed that U is independent of ε and X. It will also be assumed that the distribution of ε_{jt} is symmetrical about 0 for each j and t and that ε_{jt} is independently and identically distributed for all j and t. Horowitz and Markatou (1996) and Horowitz (1998) show how to relax the assumption that ε_{jt} is symmetrically, independently, and identically distributed.

5.2.1 *Estimating* f_U *and* f_ε

This section explains how to estimate f_U and f_ε nonparametrically. The asymptotic properties of the estimators are discussed in Section 5.2.2.

To begin, let b_n be a $n^{-1/2}$-consistent estimator of β in (5.3), possibly one of the least-squares estimators described by Hsiao (1986), among others. Let W_{njt} ($j = 1, \ldots, n;\ t = 1, \ldots, T$) denote the residuals from the estimate of (5.3). That is

$$W_{njt} = Y_{jt} - b_n' X_{jt}. \tag{5.21}$$

In addition, let η_{njt} ($j = 1, \ldots, n;\ t = 2, \ldots, T$) denote the residuals from the estimate of the differenced model for $Y_{jt} - Y_{j1}$. That is

$$\eta_{njt} = (Y_{jt} - Y_{j1}) - b_n'(X_{jt} - X_{j1}). \tag{5.22}$$

Observe that as $n \to \infty$ while T remains fixed, W_{njt} converges in distribution to $W = U + \varepsilon$ and η_{njt} converges in distribution to the random variable η that is distributed as the difference between two independent realizations of ε. Thus, the estimation data $\{Y_{jt}, X_{jt}\}$ provide estimates of random variables that are distributed as W and η. The data do not provide estimates of U and ε. However, the distribution of W is the convolution of the distributions of U and ε, whereas the distribution of

η is the convolution of the distribution of ε with itself. Thus, estimation of f_U and f_ε are problems in deconvolution.

The deconvolution problems involved in estimating f_U and f_ε are different from the one discussed in Section 5.1. Section 5.1 considered a problem in which the distribution of the observed random variable W is the convolution of U and another random variable whose distribution is known. In (5.3), however, the distribution of W is the convolution of the distribution of U with the distribution of a random variable ε whose distribution is unknown. The distribution of the observed random variable η is the convolution of the unknown distribution of ε with itself. Despite these differences, the approach to solving the deconvolution problems presented by (5.3) is similar to the approach used in Section 5.1, and the resulting estimators have the same slow rates of convergence.

To obtain estimators of f_U and f_ε, let ψ_W and ψ_η, respectively, denote the characteristic functions of W and η. Let ψ_U and ψ_ε denote the characteristic functions of U and ε. Then for any real τ

$$\psi_W(\tau) = \psi_U(\tau)\psi_\varepsilon(\tau)$$

and

$$\psi_\eta(\tau) = |\psi_\varepsilon(\tau)|^2.$$

Because f_ε is assumed to be symmetrical about 0, ψ_ε is real-valued. Also assume, as in Section 5.1, that $\psi_\varepsilon(\tau) \neq 0$ for all finite τ. This implies that $\psi_\varepsilon(\tau) > 0$ for all finite τ because ψ_ε is a continuous function and $\psi_\varepsilon(0) = 1$. Therefore,

$$\psi_\varepsilon(\tau) = \psi_\eta(\tau)^{1/2}$$

and

$$\psi_U(\tau) = \frac{\psi_W(\tau)}{\psi_\eta(\tau)^{1/2}},$$

where both square roots are positive. It follows from the inversion formula for characteristic functions that for any real z,

$$f_\varepsilon(z) = \frac{1}{2\pi}\int_{-\infty}^{\infty} e^{-i\tau z}\psi_\eta(\tau)^{1/2}d\tau \tag{5.23}$$

and

$$f_U(u) = \frac{1}{2\pi}\int_{-\infty}^{\infty} e^{-i\tau u}\frac{\psi_W(\tau)}{\psi_\eta(\tau)^{1/2}}d\tau. \tag{5.24}$$

The unknown characteristic functions ψ_W and ψ_η can be estimated by

$$\psi_{nW}(\tau) = \frac{1}{nT}\sum_{j=1}^{n}\sum_{t=1}^{T}\exp\ (i\tau W_{njt})$$

for ψ_W and

$$\psi_{n\eta}(\tau) = \frac{1}{n(T-1)}\sum_{j=1}^{n}\sum_{t=2}^{T}\exp\ (i\tau \eta_{njt})$$

for ψ_η. As in Section 5.1, however, f_ε and f_U cannot be estimated by simply substituting ψ_W and ψ_η with ψ_{nW} and $\psi_{n\eta}$ in (5.23) and (5.24), respectively, because the resulting integrals do not exist in general. Also as in Section 5.1, this problem can be solved by a regularization procedure that is the Fourier-transform analog of kernel smoothing. To this end, let ζ be a random variable whose characteristic function ψ_ζ has support $[-1, 1]$ and satisfies other conditions that are stated below. Let $\{\nu_{n\varepsilon}\}$ and $\{\nu_{nU}\}$ be sequences of positive bandwidths that converge to 0 as $n \to \infty$. The smoothed estimators of f_ε and f_U are

$$f_{n\varepsilon}(z) = \frac{1}{2\pi}\int_{-\infty}^{\infty} e^{-i\tau z}|\psi_{n\eta}(\tau)|^{1/2}\psi_\zeta(\nu_{n\varepsilon}\tau)d\tau \tag{5.25}$$

and

$$f_{nU}(u) = \frac{1}{2\pi}\int_{-\infty}^{\infty} e^{-i\tau u}\frac{\psi_{nW}(\tau)\psi_\zeta(\nu_{nU}\tau)}{|\psi_{n\eta}(\tau)|^{1/2}}d\tau. \tag{5.26}$$

5.2.2 Large Sample Properties of $\mathbf{f_{n\varepsilon}}$ *and* $\mathbf{f_{nU}}$

The consistency and rates of convergence of $f_{n\varepsilon}$ and f_{nU} have been investigated by Horowitz and Markatou (1996). The results are summarized in this section. It is also shown that the centered, normalized estimators are asymptotically normally distributed.

Make the following assumptions.

P1: The distributions of ε and U are continuous and f_ε is symmetrical about 0. Moreover, f_ε and f_U are everywhere twice continuously differentiable with uniformly bounded derivatives, and $\psi_\varepsilon(\tau) > 0$ for all finite τ.

P2: The distribution of X has bounded support.

P3: The estimator b_n satisfies $n^{1/2}(b_n - \beta) = O_p(1)$.

P4: Define $A_{n\varepsilon} = (\log n)/[n^{1/2}\psi_\varepsilon(1/\nu_{n\varepsilon})^2]$ and $B_{n\varepsilon} = 1/[n^{1/2}\nu_{n\varepsilon}\psi_\varepsilon(1/\nu_{n\varepsilon})^2]$. Define A_{nU} and B_{nU} by replacing $\nu_{n\varepsilon}$ with ν_{nU} and $\psi_{n\varepsilon}$ with ψ_{nU} in $A_{n\varepsilon}$ and $B_{n\varepsilon}$. As $n \to \infty$, $\nu_{n\varepsilon} \to 0$, $\nu_{nU} \to 0$, $B_{n\varepsilon}/\nu_{n\varepsilon} \to 0$, $B_{nU}/\nu_{nU} \to 0$, $A_{n\varepsilon}/\nu_{n\varepsilon} = O(1)$, and $A_{nU}/\nu_{nU} = O(1)$.

Assumption P1 ensures, among other things, that f_ε and f_U are identified. Examples of distributions with strictly positive characteristic functions are the normal, Cauchy, and scale mixtures of these. Symmetry is not required for identification, however, as is explained in Horowitz and Markatou (1996) and Horowitz (1998). Assumption P2 is made to avoid technical complications that arise when X has unbounded support. This assumption can always be satisfied by dropping observations with very large values of X. Assumption P3 insures that random sampling errors in the estimator of β are asymptotically negligible. All commonly used estimators of β satisfy this assumption. Finally, assumption P4 restricts the rates at which $\nu_{n\varepsilon}$ and ν_{nU} converge to 0.

The following theorem establishes uniform consistency of $f_{n\varepsilon}$ and f_{nU}.

Theorem 5.4: *Let ψ_ζ be a bounded, real characteristic function with support $[-1,\ 1]$. If ψ_ζ is twice differentiable in a neighborhood of 0 and assumptions P1–P4 hold, then as $n \to \infty$*

$$\sup_z |f_{n\varepsilon}(z) - f_\varepsilon(z)| = O_p(\nu_{n\varepsilon}^2) + O_p(B_{n\varepsilon}/\nu_{n\varepsilon}) + o_p(A_{n\varepsilon}/\nu_{n\varepsilon})$$

and

$$\sup_u |f_{nU}(u) - f_U(u)| = O_p(\nu_{nU}^2) + O_p(B_{nU}/\nu_{nU}) + o_p(A_{nU}/\nu_{nU}). \blacksquare$$

The proof of this theorem is given in Horowitz and Markatou (1996). The theorem can be explained heuristically by using arguments similar to those used to explain Theorems 5.1 and 5.2. Consider f_{nU}. Define $\psi_{n\varepsilon} = |\psi_{n\eta}|^{1/2}$. The only difference between (5.7) and (5.26) is that the denominator of the integrand of (5.26) is an estimator of ψ_ε instead of the true ψ_ε. Therefore, to obtain the conclusion of Theorem (5.4) for f_{nU}, it suffices to show that if assumptions P1–P4 hold, then an asymptotically negligible error is made by replacing $\psi_{n\varepsilon}$ with ψ_ε in (5.26). By using an extension of the delta method, it can be shown that

$$|\psi_{n\varepsilon}(\tau) - \psi_\varepsilon(\tau)| = \psi_\varepsilon(\tau)\left[\frac{\psi_{n\eta}(\tau) - \psi_\eta(\tau)}{\psi_\eta(\tau)}\right][(1/2) + o_p(1)] \tag{5.27}$$

and

$$\sup_{|\tau|\le 1/\nu_{nU}} |\psi_{n\eta}(\tau) - \psi_\eta(\tau)| = o_p\left(\frac{\log n}{n^{1/2}}\right) + O_p\left(\frac{1}{n^{1/2}\nu_{nU}}\right). \tag{5.28}$$

See Horowitz and Markatou (1996) for details. Substituting (5.28) into (5.27) yields

$$\sup_{|\tau|\le 1/\nu_{nU}} |\psi_{n\varepsilon}(\tau) - \psi_\varepsilon(\tau)| = o_p(A_{nU}) + O_p(B_{nU})$$

and

$$\sup_{|\tau|\leq 1/\nu_{nU}} \left| \frac{\psi_{n\varepsilon}(\tau)}{\psi_\varepsilon(\tau)} - 1 \right| = o_p(A_{nU}) + O_p(B_{nU}). \tag{5.29}$$

A further application of the delta method to the right-hand side of (5.26) shows that

$$\frac{1}{2\pi}\int_{-\infty}^{\infty} e^{-i\tau u}\frac{\psi_{nW}(\tau)\psi_\zeta(\nu_{nU}\tau)}{\psi_{n\varepsilon}(\tau)}d\tau = \frac{1}{2\pi}\int_{-\infty}^{\infty} e^{-i\tau u}\frac{\psi_{nW}(\tau)\psi_\zeta(\nu_{nU}\tau)}{\psi_\varepsilon(\tau)}d\tau + R_{nU}, \tag{5.30}$$

where $R_{nU} = O_p(A_{nU})$ is an asymptotically negligible remainder term. Therefore, it suffices to investigate the convergence of the first term on the right-hand side of (5.30). This term, however, is the same as the right-hand side of (5.7), so the arguments used with (5.7) also apply to (5.26).

The rate of convergence of $f_{n\varepsilon}$ can be obtained by writing (5.25) in the form

$$f_{n\varepsilon}(z) = \frac{1}{2\pi}\int_{-\infty}^{\infty} e^{-i\tau z}\frac{\psi_{n\eta}(\tau)\psi_\zeta(\nu_{n\varepsilon}\tau)}{\psi_{n\varepsilon}(\tau)}d\tau. \tag{5.31}$$

The arguments leading to (5.29) show that (5.29) continues to hold if ν_{nU} is replaced by $\nu_{n\varepsilon}$ and A_{nU} and B_{nU} are replaced by $A_{n\varepsilon}$ and $B_{n\varepsilon}$. By applying this modified form of (5.29) to the right-hand side of (5.31), it can be shown that

$$\frac{1}{2\pi}\int_{-\infty}^{\infty} e^{-i\tau z}\frac{\psi_{n\eta}(\tau)\psi_\zeta(\nu_{n\varepsilon}\tau)}{\psi_{n\varepsilon}(\tau)}d\tau = \frac{1}{2\pi}\int_{-\infty}^{\infty} e^{-i\tau z}\frac{\psi_{n\eta}(\tau)\psi_\zeta(\nu_{n\varepsilon}\tau)}{\psi_\varepsilon(\tau)}d\tau + R_{n\varepsilon}, \tag{5.32}$$

where $R_{n\varepsilon} = O_p(A_{n\varepsilon})$ is an asymptotically negligible remainder term. Therefore, the asymptotic properties of $f_{n\varepsilon}$ are the same as those of the first term on the right-hand side of (5.32). This term is the same as the right-hand side of (5.7) except with $\psi_{n\eta}$ in place of ψ_{nW}. Therefore, the arguments used with (5.7) can also be used to analyze $f_{n\varepsilon}$.

As in the deconvolution problem of Section 5.1, the rates of convergence of $f_{n\varepsilon}$ and f_{nU} are controlled by the rates at which the bandwidths $\nu_{n\varepsilon}$ and ν_{nU} converge to 0. These, in turn, are controlled by the thickness of the tails of ψ_ε, as can be seen from assumption P4. Faster rates of convergence are possible when the tails are thick than when they are thin. Horowitz and Markatou (1996) investigate in detail the case of $\varepsilon \sim N(0, \sigma^2)$. They show that when f_ε and f_U are assumed to be twice differentiable, the fastest possible rate of convergence of an estimator of either density is $(\log n)^{-1}$. Under the assumptions of Theorem 5.4, this rate is achieved by $f_{n\varepsilon}$ and f_{nU} in (5.24) and (5.25).

Equations (5.30) and (5.32) can also be used to show that the standardized versions of $f_{n\varepsilon}$ and f_{nU} are asymptotically normally distributed. Let $g_{nU}(u)$ and $g_{n\varepsilon}(z)$, respectively, denote the first terms on the right-hand sides of (5.30) and (5.32). When f_{nU} and $f_{n\varepsilon}$ have their fastest rates of convergence, their rates of convergence and variances are $O(\nu_{nU}^2)$ and $O(\nu_{n\varepsilon}^2)$. Denote these rates by $\rho_U(n)$ and $\rho_\varepsilon(n)$. Then

$$\rho_\varepsilon(n)^{-1}[f_{n\varepsilon}(z) - f_\varepsilon(z)] = \rho_\varepsilon(n)^{-1}[g_{n\varepsilon}(z) - f_\varepsilon(z)] + \rho_\varepsilon(n)^{-1}R_{n\varepsilon}$$

and

$$\rho_U(n)^{-1}[f_{nU}(u) - f_U(u)] = \rho_U(n)^{-1}[g_{nU}(u) - f_U(u)] + \rho_U(n)^{-1}R_{nU}.$$

Therefore, $\rho_{n\varepsilon}(n)^{-1}[f_{n\varepsilon}(z) - f_\varepsilon(z)]$ is asymptotically equivalent to $\rho_{n\varepsilon}(n)^{-1}$ $[g_{n\varepsilon}(z) - f_\varepsilon(z)]$ and the asymptotic normality results of Section 5.1.3 can be applied to $f_{n\varepsilon}(z)$ if $\rho_\varepsilon(n)^{-1}R_{n\varepsilon} = o_p(1)$ as $n \to \infty$. Similarly, the asymptotic normality results of Section 5.1.3 apply to $f_{nU}(u)$ if $\rho_U(n)^{-1}R_{nU} = o_p(1)$. When $f_{n\varepsilon}$ and f_{nU} have their fastest possible rates of convergence, $\rho_\varepsilon(n) = O(\nu_{n\varepsilon}^2)$ and $\rho_U(n) = O(\nu_{nU}^2)$. In addition $R_{n\varepsilon} = O_p(A_{n\varepsilon})$ and $R_{nU} = O_p(A_{nU})$. Therefore, if $\nu_{n\varepsilon}$ and ν_{nU} are chosen to optimize the rates of convergence of $f_{n\varepsilon}$ and f_{nU}, the asymptotic normality results of Section 5.1.3 apply to $f_{n\varepsilon}(z)$ and $f_{nU}(u)$ provided that assumption P4 is strengthened to require $A_{n\varepsilon}/\nu_{n\varepsilon}^2 \to 0$ and $A_{nU}/\nu_{nU}^2 \to 0$ as $n \to \infty$.

5.2.3 Estimating First-Passage Times

This section shows how to estimate $P(\theta|y_1, y^*, x)$, the probability distribution of first-passage times conditional on the covariates and the initial value of Y when Y_{it} follows model (5.3). An application of the estimator is presented in Section 5.4.

Equation (5.20) provides a formula for $P(\theta|y_1, y^*, x)$. The right-hand side of (5.20) can be estimated consistently by replacing β with b_n, f_ε with $f_{n\varepsilon}$, f_U with f_{nU}, f_W with a kernel estimator of the density of the residuals W_{njt}, and F_ε with a consistent estimator. One way to obtain an estimator of F_ε is by integrating $f_{n\varepsilon}$. The resulting estimator is

$$F_{n\varepsilon}(z) = \int_{-M_n}^{z} f_{n\varepsilon}(\xi)d\xi,$$

where $M_n \to \infty$ at a suitable rate as $n \to \infty$. This estimator has the practical disadvantage of requiring selection of the tuning parameter M_n.

The need to choose the additional tuning parameter M_n can be avoided by taking advantage of the symmetry of the distribution of ε. Symmetry implies that $F_\varepsilon(z) = 1 - F_\varepsilon(-z)$. Therefore, $F_\varepsilon(z) = 0.5 + 0.5[F_\varepsilon(z) - F_\varepsilon(-z)]$. But

$$0.5 + 0.5[F_\varepsilon(z) - F_\varepsilon(-z)] = 0.5 + 0.5\int_{-z}^{z} f_\varepsilon(\xi)d\xi. \tag{5.33}$$

In addition,

$$f_\varepsilon(z) = \frac{1}{2\pi}\int_{-\infty}^{\infty} e^{-iz\tau}\psi_\varepsilon(\tau)d\tau. \tag{5.34}$$

Therefore, substituting (5.34) into (5.33) yields

$$F_\varepsilon(z) = 0.5 + \frac{1}{\pi}\int_{-\infty}^{\infty}\frac{\sin z\tau}{\tau}\psi_\varepsilon(\tau)d\tau. \tag{5.35}$$

But $(\sin z\tau)/\tau$ is an even function, and symmetry of f_ε implies that ψ_ε also is even. Therefore, (5.35) can be written in the form

$$F_\varepsilon(z) = 0.5 + \frac{2}{\pi}\int_{0}^{\infty}\frac{\sin z\tau}{\tau}\psi_\varepsilon(\tau)d\tau. \tag{5.36}$$

Equation (5.36) forms the basis of the estimator of F_ε that is proposed here. Using arguments similar to those applicable to Theorem 5.4, it may be shown that $F_\varepsilon(z)$ is estimated consistently by

$$F_{n\varepsilon}(z) = 0.5 + \frac{2}{\pi}\int_{0}^{\infty}\frac{\sin z\tau}{\tau}|\psi_{n\eta}(\tau)|^{1/2}\psi_\zeta(\nu_{n\varepsilon}\tau)d\tau. \tag{5.37}$$

The estimator of the right-hand side of (5.20) is completed by replacing F_ε with $F_{n\varepsilon}$ from (5.37). The result is that $P(\theta|y_1,\ y^*,\ x)$ is estimated consistently by

$$\begin{aligned} P_n(\theta|y_1,\ y^*,\ \theta) = & \frac{1}{f_{nW}(y_1 - b_n'x_1)}\int_{-m_n}^{m_n} f_{n\varepsilon}(y_1 - b_n'x_1) \\ & \left[\prod_{k=2}^{\theta} F_{n\varepsilon}(y^* - b_n'x_k - u)\right] f_{nU}(u)du, \end{aligned} \tag{5.38}$$

where f_{nW} is a kernel estimator of the density of W_{njt} and $\{m_n\}$ is a sequence of positive constants that satisfy $m_n \to \infty$,

$$\sup_z \ m_n|f_{n\varepsilon}(z) - f_\varepsilon(z)| \xrightarrow{p} 0,$$

and

$$\sup_u \ m_n|f_{nU}(u) - f_U(u)| \xrightarrow{p} 0$$

as $n \to \infty$.

5.2.4 Bias Reduction

As was discussed in Section 5.2.1, $f_{n\varepsilon}$ and f_{nU} are asymptotically equivalent to the density estimator (5.7). Therefore, it follows from (5.15) that $f_{n\varepsilon}$ and f_{nU} have biases of sizes $O(\nu_{n\varepsilon}^2)$ and $O(\nu_{nU}^2)$, respectively. The results of Monte Carlo experiments reported by Horowitz and Markatou (1996) and summarized in Section 5.2.5 show that this bias can have a large effect on the accuracy of $P_n(\theta|y_1,\ y^*,\ x)$ as an estimator of $P(\theta|y_1,\ y^*,\ x)$. This section describes corrections for $f_{n\varepsilon}$ and f_{nU} that remove parts of these biases. The Monte Carlo experiments reported in Section 5.2.5 show that the accuracy of $P_n(\theta|y_1,\ y^*,\ x)$ is greatly increased when the corrected density estimators are used. The arguments leading to the corrections for $f_{n\varepsilon}$ and f_{nU} are identical, so only $f_{n\varepsilon}$ is discussed here.

To derive the correction for $f_{n\varepsilon}$ write $f_{n\varepsilon}(z) - f_\varepsilon(z)$ in the form

$$f_{n\varepsilon}(z) - f_\varepsilon(z) = \Delta_{n1}(z) + \Delta_{n2}(z),$$

where

$$\Delta_{n1}(z) = \frac{1}{2\pi}\int_{-\infty}^{\infty} e^{-i\tau z}[|\psi_{n\eta}(\tau)|^{1/2} - \psi_\varepsilon(\tau)]\psi_\zeta(\nu_{n\varepsilon}\tau)d\tau$$

and

$$\Delta_{n2}(z) = \frac{1}{2\pi}\int_{-\infty}^{\infty} e^{-i\tau z}[\psi_\zeta(\nu_{n\varepsilon}\tau) - 1]\psi_\varepsilon(\tau)d\tau.$$

The quantity $\Delta_{n2}(z)$ is nonstochastic. In a finite sample, neither $E\Delta_{n1}(z)$ nor $\Delta_{n2}(z)$ is zero in general, so $f_{n\varepsilon}(z)$ is biased. Of course, the biases vanish as $n \to \infty$, as is needed for consistency of $f_{n\varepsilon}(z)$. $E\Delta_{n1}(z)$ is the component of bias caused by estimating ψ_ε, and $\Delta_{n2}(z)$ is the component of bias caused by smoothing the empirical distribution of η. The correction described in this section removes the second component of bias through $O(\nu_{n\varepsilon}^2)$.

The correction is obtained by proceeding in a manner similar to that used to derive (5.15). The quantity $\psi_\zeta(\nu_{n\varepsilon}\tau)\psi_\varepsilon(\tau)$ is the characteristic function of the random variable $\varepsilon + \nu_{n\varepsilon}\zeta$. Therefore, $\Delta_{n2}(z)$ is the difference between the probability densities of $\varepsilon + \nu_{n\varepsilon}\zeta$ and ε. Let f_ζ denote the probability density function of ζ. Then

$$\Delta_{n2}(z) = \int_{-\infty}^{\infty} f_\varepsilon(z - \nu_{n\varepsilon}\tau)f_\zeta(\tau)d\tau - f_\varepsilon(z).$$

A Taylor-series expansion of $f_\varepsilon(z - \nu_{n\varepsilon}\tau)$ about $\nu_{n\varepsilon} = 0$ yields

$$\Delta_{n2}(z) = (1/2)\nu_{n\varepsilon}^2 f_\varepsilon''(z)\sigma_\zeta^2 + o(\nu_{n\varepsilon}^2), \tag{5.39}$$

where σ_ζ^2 is the variance of ζ. The first term on the right-hand side of (5.39) is the smoothing bias in $f_{n\varepsilon}(z)$ through $O(\nu_{n\varepsilon}^2)$.

Note that σ_ζ^2 is known because ψ_ζ and, therefore, f_ζ is chosen by the analyst. Let $f_{n\varepsilon}''(z)$ be a consistent estimator of $f_\varepsilon''(z)$. Then the $O(\nu_{n\varepsilon}^2)$ smoothing bias in $f_{n\varepsilon}(z)$ can be removed by estimating $f_\varepsilon(z)$ with

$$\hat{f}_{n\varepsilon}(z) = f_{n\varepsilon}(z) - (1/2)\nu_{n\varepsilon}^2 f_{n\varepsilon}''(z)\sigma_\zeta^2.$$

A consistent estimator of $f_\varepsilon''(z)$ can be obtained by differentiating $f_{n\varepsilon}(z)$. As is normal in kernel estimation, however, estimating the derivative requires using a bandwidth that converges more slowly than the bandwidth that is used for estimating $f_\varepsilon(z)$ itself. The formal result is stated in the following theorem, which is proved in Horowitz and Markatou (1996).

Theorem 5.5: *Let assumptions P1–P4 hold. Assume that f''_ε is Lipschitz continuous. That is $|f''_\varepsilon(z+\delta) - f_\varepsilon(z)| \leq c\delta$ for any z, all sufficiently small $\delta > 0$, and some finite $c > 0$. Let $\{\gamma_{n\varepsilon}\}$ be a positive sequence satisfying $\gamma_{n\varepsilon} \to 0$, $B_{n\varepsilon}/\gamma^2_{n\varepsilon} \to 0$, and $A_{n\varepsilon}/\gamma_{n\varepsilon} = O(1)$as $n \to \infty$. Define*

$$f''_{n\varepsilon}(z) = -\frac{1}{2\pi}\int_{-\infty}^{\infty} e^{-iz\tau}\tau^2|\psi_{n\eta}(\tau)|^{1/2}\psi_\zeta(\gamma_{n\varepsilon}\tau)d\tau.$$

Then

$$\operatorname*{plim}_{n\to\infty}\sup_z |f''_{n\varepsilon}(z) - f''_\varepsilon(z)| = 0. \qquad \blacksquare$$

The procedure for removing smoothing bias from f_{nU} is similar. The resulting estimator is

$$\hat{f}_{nU}(u) = f_{nU}(u) - (1/2)\nu^2_{nU} f''_{nU}(u)\sigma^2_\zeta,$$

where $f''_{nU}(u)$ is the following consistent estimator of $f''_U(u)$:

$$f''_{nU}(u) = -\frac{1}{2\pi}\int_{-\infty}^{\infty} e^{-iu\tau}\tau^2\psi_{nW}(\tau)\psi_\zeta(\gamma_{nU}\tau)d\tau$$

and $\{\gamma_{nU}\}$ is a positive sequence that converges to zero sufficiently slowly. The following modified version of Theorem 5.5 applies to $f''_{nU}(u)$.

Theorem 5.5′: *Let assumptions P1–P4 hold. Assume that f''_U is Lipschitz continuous. That is $|f''_U(u+\delta) - f_U(u)| \leq c\delta$ for any u, all sufficiently small $\delta > 0$, and some finite $c > 0$. Let $\{\gamma_{nU}\}$ be a positive sequence satisfying $\gamma_{nU} \to 0$, $B_{nU}/\gamma^2_{nU} \to 0$, and $A_{nU}/\gamma_{nU} = O(1)$ as $n \to \infty$. Then*

$$\operatorname*{plim}_{n\to\infty}\sup_u |f''_{nU}(u) - f''_U(u)| = 0. \qquad \blacksquare$$

5.2.5 Monte Carlo Experiments

Horowitz and Markatou (1996) carried out a Monte Carlo investigation of the ability of $P_n(\theta|y_1, y^*, x)$ to provide useful information about $P(\theta|y_1, y^*, x)$ with samples of moderate size. Data for the experiments were generated by simulation from the model

$$Y_{jt} = U_j + \varepsilon_{jt}; j = 1, \ldots, 1000; \; t = 1, 2.$$

Thus, the simulated data correspond to a panel of length $T = 2$ composed of $n = 1000$ individuals. There were no covariates in the experiments. The distribution of U was $N(0,\ 1)$. The distribution of ε was $N(0,\ 1)$ in one experiment. In the other, ε was sampled from $N(0,\ 1)$ with probability 0.9 and from $N(0,\ 16)$ with probability 0.1. This mixture distribution has tails that are thicker than the tails of the normal distribution. In both sets of experiments, the fastest possible rate of convergence in probability of estimators of f_ε and f_U is $(\log n)^{-1}$, so the experiments address situations in which the estimators converge slowly.

As in the experiments reported in Section 5.1.3, the smoothing function ψ_ζ was the fourfold convolution of the uniform density with itself. The density f_W was estimated using a kernel estimator with the standard normal density function as the kernel. In estimating $P(\theta|y_1,\ y^*)$, $y_1 = -1$, $y^* = 1$, and $\theta = 3, 5, 7, 9, 11$. The bandwidths were set at values such that $\psi_{n\varepsilon}(\nu_{n\varepsilon}^{-1})$ and $\psi_{nU}(\nu_{nU}^{-1})$ were both approximately zero. There were 100 Monte Carlo replications per experiment.

The results are shown in Table 5.1. Columns 3–5 present the true values of $P(\theta|y_1 = -1,\ y^* = 1)$, the means of the Monte Carlo estimates of $P(\theta|y_1 = -1,\ y^* = 1)$ that were obtained using $f_{n\varepsilon}$ and f_{nU} without bias correction, and the means of the Monte Carlo estimates that were obtained using the bias-corrected forms of $f_{n\varepsilon}$ and f_{nU}. The estimates of $P(\theta|y_1 = -1,\ y^* = 1)$ that were obtained without using bias correction for $f_{n\varepsilon}$ and f_{nU} are biased downward by 12–20%, depending on the distribution of ε and the value of θ. Using the bias-corrected density estimates, however, reduces the downward bias of $P_n(\theta|y_1 = -1,\ y^* = 1)$ to 1–13%. Thus, the bias correction removes 35% to virtually all of the bias of $P_n(\theta|y_1 = -1,\ y^* = 1)$, depending on the distribution of ε and the value of θ. This illustrates the usefulness of the bias-correction procedure.

Table 5.1 Results of Monte Carlo experiments with estimator $P(\theta\ |y_1, y*)$

Distr. of ε	θ	True prob.	With bias corr.	Without bias corr.	Assuming normal ε
Normal	3	0.89	0.88	0.78	
	5	0.81	0.77	0.69	
	7	0.74	0.69	0.62	
	9	0.69	0.62	0.56	
	11	0.64	0.57	0.51	
Mixture	3	0.86	0.83	0.74	0.76
	5	0.76	0.71	0.73	0.60
	7	0.67	0.61	0.55	0.49
	9	0.60	0.54	0.49	0.41
	11	0.55	0.48	0.44	0.35

Source: Horowitz and Markatou (1996)

The last column of Table 5.1 shows the means of the estimates of $P(\theta|y_1 = -1,\ y^* = 1)$ that were obtained by assuming that ε is normally distributed when, in fact, it has the mixture distribution $N(0,\ 1)$ with probability 0.9 and $N(0,\ 16)$ with probability 0.1. This is an important comparison because normality is often assumed in applications. It can be seen that the erroneous assumption of normality produces estimates that are biased downward by 12–16%, whereas the downward bias is only 1–13% when the bias-corrected nonparametric density estimators are used. Although not shown in the table, the Monte Carlo results also reveal that use of the nonparametric density estimators reduces the mean-square error of the estimator of $P(\theta|y_1 = -1,\ y^* = 1)$ as well as the bias.

There is a simple intuitive explanation for the severe downward bias of the parametric estimator of $P(\theta|y_1 = -1,\ y^* = 1)$. The mixture distribution used in the experiment has less probability in its tails than does a normal distribution with the same variance. Therefore, the normal distribution has a higher probability of a transition from one tail to another than does the mixture distribution. Since $P(\theta|y_1 = -1,\ y^* = 1)$ is the probability that a transition between the tails does not occur, the probabilities obtained from the normal distribution are too low. In summary, the Monte Carlo evidence indicates that the nonparametric estimation procedure with bias correction can yield estimates of first-passage probabilities that are considerably more accurate than the ones obtained from a misspecified parametric model.

5.3 Nonparametric Instrumental-Variables Estimation

We now consider nonparametric estimation of the function g in (5.4). Assume that X and W are scalar random variables. We wish to estimate g from a random sample of observations of $(Y,\ X,\ W)$. Denote the data by $\{Y_i,\ X_i,\ W_i\colon i = 1,\ \ldots,\ n\}$.

Equation (5.4) does not have an analytic solution analogous to (5.7) for deconvolution. This makes estimation of g in (5.4) more complicated mathematically than deconvolution. The mathematical methods used to study (5.4) come from the field of functional analysis. This section formulates the estimation problem in functional analytic terms, presents the relevant results from functional analysis, and explores some of their implications for estimation of g. The results from functional analysis are stated informally. Rigorous treatments are available in textbooks such as Liusternik and Sobolev (1961). The use of the methods of this section with deconvolution can be difficult because in deconvolution, the operator analogous to T in (5.44) below does not necessarily have a discrete set of eigenvalues. However, these methods are not needed for deconvolution because the deconvolution problem has an analytic solution.

To begin, assume that the support of $(X,\ W)$ is contained in $[0,\ 1]^2$. This assumption entails no loss of generality because it can always be satisfied by, if necessary, carrying out a monotone increasing transformation of $(X,\ W)$. For example, define $\tilde{X} = \Phi(X)$ and $\tilde{W} = \Phi(W)$. Then the support of $(\tilde{X},\ \tilde{W})$ is contained in $[0,\ 1]^2$, regardless of the support of $(X,\ W)$. Recall that model (5.4) is equivalent to (5.5). Under the assumption that the support of $(X,\ W)$ is contained in $[0,\ 1]^2$, (5.5) becomes

$$E(Y|W = w)f_W(w) = \int_0^1 f_{XW}(x,\ w)g(x)dx. \tag{5.40}$$

Now multiply both sides of (5.40) by $f_{XW}(z, w)$ ($z \in [0, 1]$) and integrate with respect to w to obtain

$$r(z) = \int_0^1 \tau(x, z)g(x)dx, \tag{5.41}$$

where

$$r(z) = \int_0^1 E(Y|W = w)f_{XW}(z, w)f_W(w)dw \tag{5.42}$$

and

$$\tau(x, z) = \int_0^1 f_{XW}(x, w)f_{XW}(z, w)dw. \tag{5.43}$$

Under the assumptions that are made later in this section, (5.41) is equivalent to (5.4). Therefore, it suffices to estimate g in (5.41).

Assume that g is contained in the function space $L_2[0, 1]$. This is the space of functions h that map $[0, 1]$ to the real numbers and satisfy

$$\int_0^1 h(x)^2 dx < \infty.$$

$L_2[0, 1]$ belongs to a class of function spaces called Hilbert spaces. Hilbert spaces are defined formally in Section A.2.3 of the Appendix. For any two functions $h_1, h_2 \in L_2[0, 1]$, define the inner product $\langle h_1, h_2 \rangle$ by

$$\langle h_1, h_2 \rangle = \int_0^1 h_1(x)h_2(x)dx.$$

Define the norm, $\|h\|$, of any $h \in L_2[0, 1]$ by $\|h\| = \langle h, h \rangle^{1/2}$. Thus

$$\|h\|^2 = \int_0^1 h(x)^2 dx < \infty.$$

Now observe that r is in $L_2[0, 1]$ if f_{XW} is bounded. Therefore, (5.41) can be written in the form

$$r = Tg, \tag{5.44}$$

where T is an operator (that is a mapping from one set of functions to another) that is defined by

$$(Th)(z) = \int_0^1 \tau(x, z)h(x)dx$$

for any $h \in L_2[0, 1]$. It may be convenient to think of (5.44) as the infinite-dimensional analog of a matrix equation in which r and g play the role of vectors and T plays the role of the matrix. Observe that T is positive semidefinite. That is,

$$\langle h, Th \rangle = \int_0^1 \left[\int_0^1 f_{XW}(x, w)h(x)dx \right]^2 dw \geq 0 \tag{5.45}$$

for any $h \in [0, 1]$.

Now call the number λ and the function $\phi \in L_2[0, 1]$ an eigenvalue and eigenfunction of T if $T\phi = \lambda\phi$. It is proved in functional analysis that if f_{XW} is bounded, then T has a set of eigenvalues and eigenfunctions $\{\lambda_j, \phi_j: j = 1, 2, \ldots\}$ satisfying $T\phi_j = \lambda_j\phi_j$, $\|\phi_j\| = 1$ for each $j = 1, 2, \ldots$, and $\langle \phi_j, \phi_k \rangle = 0$ if $j \neq k$. Because T is positive semidefinite, $\lambda_j = \langle \phi_j, T\phi_j \rangle \geq 0$. Moreover, any function $h \in L_2[0, 1]$ has the series representation

$$h(x) = \sum_{j=1}^{\infty} \langle h, \phi_j \rangle \phi_j(x).$$

In addition,

$$\|h\|^2 = \sum_{j=1}^{\infty} \langle h, \phi_j \rangle^2. \tag{5.46}$$

The function τ defined in (5.43) has the representation

$$\tau(x, z) = \sum_{j=1}^{\infty} \lambda_j \phi_j(x)\phi_j(z).$$

Moreover,

$$Th = \sum_{j=1}^{\infty} \lambda_j \langle h, \phi_j \rangle \phi_j,$$

and

$$\|Th\|^2 = \sum_{j=1}^{\infty} \lambda_j^2 \langle h, \phi_j \rangle^2$$

for any $h \in L_2[0, 1]$.

If some eigenvalues of T are zero, then T is said to be singular. Otherwise, T is nonsingular. When T is singular, there are nonzero functions $h \in L_2[0, 1]$ such that $Th = 0$. To see why, let $\{b_j: j = 1, 2, \ldots\}$ be a sequence of numbers such that $b_j = 0$ if $\lambda_j > 0$, $b_j \neq 0$ for at least one j for which $\lambda_j = 0$, and

$$\sum_{j:\ \lambda_j=0} b_j^2 < \infty.$$

Then the function

$$h = \sum_{j=1}^{\infty} b_j \phi_j$$

is in $L_2[0,\ 1]$, $h \neq 0$, and $Th = 0$. Equation (5.44) does not have a unique solution when T is singular. This is because if $Tg = r$, then $T(g + h) = r$ for any h such that $Th = 0$.

Nonsingularity of T is a necessary condition for identification of g in model (5.4). To see why, suppose that g is identified. That is, there is only one function that satisfies (5.4). Also, suppose that T is singular. Then $Th = 0$ and $\langle h,Th\rangle = 0$ for some nonzero $h \in L_2[0,\ 1]$. But

$$\langle h,Th\rangle = \int_0^1 \left[\int_0^1 f_{XW}(x,\ w)h(x)dx\right]^2 dw,$$

so singularity of T implies that

$$\int_0^1 f_{XW}(x,\ w)h(x)dx = 0 \tag{5.47}$$

for every w except, possibly, for a set of w values whose probability is zero. Adding (5.47) to (5.40) gives

$$E(Y|W = w)f_W(w) = \int_0^1 f_{XW}(x,\ w)[g(x) + h(x)]dx \tag{5.48}$$

for some nonzero $h \in L_2[0,\ 1]$. But the solution to (5.40) is unique if g is identified. Therefore, there is no nonzero h satisfying (5.48), which contradicts the assumption that T is singular. It follows that non-singularity of T is necessary for identification of g. Accordingly, T is assumed to be non-singular for the remainder of this chapter.

If T is non-singular, then $\lambda_j > 0$ for all $j = 1,\ 2,\ \ldots$, and T has an inverse, T^{-1}. Moreover, if $h \in L_2[0,\ 1]$, then

$$T^{-1}h = \sum_{j=1}^{\infty} \frac{\langle h,\ \phi_j\rangle}{\lambda_j} \phi_j$$

provided that

$$\sum_{j=1}^{\infty} \frac{\langle h,\ \phi_j\rangle^2}{\lambda_j^2} < \infty.$$

Otherwise, $T^{-1}h$ does not exist. It follows that the solution to (5.44) is

$$g = T^{-1}r = \sum_{j=1}^{\infty} \frac{\langle r, \phi_j \rangle}{\lambda_j} \phi_j. \tag{5.49}$$

In addition, it follows from a result in functional analysis called Picard's theorem (see, e.g., Kress 1999, Theorem 15.18) that (5.49) is the unique solution to (5.40). Therefore, (5.49) constitutes a mapping from the probability distribution of (Y, X, W) to g. In other words, (5.49) identifies g in model (5.4).

Equations (5.44) and (5.49) suggest a simple way to estimate g: replace the unknown quantities on the right-hand side of (5.44) or (5.49) with consistent estimators. For example, suppose that f_{XW} and, therefore, T are known. Then r is the only unknown quantity on the right-hand side of (5.44) and (5.49), so one can consider estimating g by

$$\hat{g} = T^{-1}\hat{r} = \sum_{j=1}^{\infty} \frac{\langle \hat{r}, \phi_j \rangle}{\lambda_j} \phi_j, \tag{5.50}$$

where $\hat{r}$ is a consistent estimator of r. Unfortunately, the estimator $\hat{g}$ obtained this way is not consistent for g. This is because zero is a limit point of the sequence of eigenvalues of the operator T whenever f_{XW} is square integrable on $[0, 1]^2$. As a consequence, T^{-1} is discontinuous, and $T^{-1}\hat{r}$ may not converge to $T^{-1}r$ even if $\hat{r}$ converges to r. This is called the ill-posed inverse problem. As is explained below, the ill-posed inverse problem causes $T^{-1}\hat{r}$ to be an inconsistent estimator of g. The ill-posed inverse problem is also present in deconvolution and is the reason why regularization of (5.7) is needed to estimate f_U.

An operator A on $L_2[0, 1]$ is continuous if, as $n \to \infty$, $\|Ah_n\| \to 0$ for any sequence of functions $\{h_n\}$ in $L_2[0, 1]$ such that $\|h_n\| \to 0$. To see why T^{-1} is discontinuous, let $\{h_n\}$ be sequence in $L_2[0, 1]$. Define $h_{nj} = \langle h_n, \phi_j \rangle$. Then it follows from (5.46) that

$$\|h_n\|^2 = \sum_{j=1}^{\infty} h_{nj}^2. \tag{5.51}$$

Moreover,

$$T^{-1}h_n = \sum_{j=1}^{\infty} \frac{h_{nj}}{\lambda_j} \phi_j,$$

so a further application of (5.46) gives

$$\left\|T^{-1}h_n\right\|^2 = \sum_{j=1}^{\infty} \frac{h_{nj}^2}{\lambda_j^2}. \tag{5.52}$$

Because $\lambda_j \to 0$, it is possible to choose the h_{nj}s so that the right-hand side of (5.51) converges to zero as $n \to \infty$ but the right-hand side of (5.52) does not. Therefore, T^{-1} is discontinuous.

To see how convergence of λ_j to zero (or, equivalently, the discontinuity of T^{-1} and the ill-posed inverse problem) affects estimation of g, assume, as before, that f_{XW} is known. Then $r(z)$ is estimated consistently by

$$\hat{r}(z) = n^{-1} \sum_{i=1}^{n} Y_i f_{XW}(z, \ W_i). \tag{5.53}$$

Define

$$\hat{r}_j = \langle \hat{r}, \ \phi_j \rangle = n^{-1} \sum_{i=1}^{n} Y_i \int_0^1 \phi_j(z) f_{XW}(z, \ W_i)dz. \tag{5.54}$$

Then (5.50) gives

$$\hat{g} = \sum_{j=1}^{\infty} \frac{\hat{r}_j}{\lambda_j}\phi_j.$$

In addition,

$$g = \sum_{j=1}^{\infty} \frac{r_j}{\lambda_j}\phi_j, \tag{5.55}$$

where $r_j = \langle r, \ \phi_j \rangle$. Therefore,

$$\hat{g} - g = \sum_{j=1}^{\infty} \frac{\hat{r}_j - r_j}{\lambda_j}\phi_j,$$

$$\|\hat{g} - g\|^2 = \sum_{j=1}^{\infty} \frac{(\hat{r}_j - r_j)^2}{\lambda_j^2},$$

and

$$E\|\hat{g} - g\|^2 = \sum_{j=1}^{\infty} \frac{E(\hat{r}_j - r_j)^2}{\lambda_j^2}.$$

But $E\hat{r}_j = r_j$, so $E(\hat{r}_j - r_j)^2 = Var(\hat{r}_j)$ and

$$E\left\|\hat{g} - g\right\|^2 = \sum_{j=1}^{\infty} \frac{Var(\hat{r}_j)}{\lambda_j^2}.$$

Equation (5.54) shows that $\hat{r}_j$ is a sample average, so $Var(\hat{r}_j) = \sigma_j^2/n$, where

$$\sigma_j^2 = Var\left[Y \int_0^1 \phi_j(z) f_{XW}(z, W)dz\right]. \tag{5.56}$$

Therefore,

$$E\left\|\hat{g} - g\right\|^2 = n^{-1} \sum_{j=1}^{\infty} \frac{\sigma_j^2}{\lambda_j^2}. \tag{5.57}$$

Because $\lambda_j \to 0$ as $j \to \infty$, σ_j^2/λ_j^2 does not converge to 0 as $j \to \infty$, except in special cases, and may diverge to ∞. Therefore, except in special cases, the infinite series on the right-hand side of (5.57) diverges for every n. As a consequence, $E\left\|\hat{g} - g\right\|^2 = \infty$ for each n, and $\hat{g}$ is not a consistent estimator of g.

The following example further illustrates the consequences of the ill-posed inverse problem (discontinuity of T^{-1}) for estimation of g.

Example 5.1: The Ill-Posed Inverse Problem

This example provides a numerical illustration of the effects of the ill-posed inverse problem on estimation of g. Let model (5.4) hold with $g(x) = x$. Let

$$f_{XW}(x, w) = \sum_{j,\ k=1}^{\infty} \lambda_j^{1/2} \phi_j(x)\phi_j(w), \quad 0 \le x,\ w \le 1,$$

where $\phi_1(x) = 1$, $\phi_j(x) = \sqrt{2}\cos[(j-1)\pi x]$ $(j \ge 2)$, $\lambda_1 = 1$, and $\lambda_j = 0.2/(j-1)^4$ $(j \ge 2)$. Figure 5.2 shows a graph of f_{XW}. The marginal distributions of X and W are $U[0,\ 1]$. The function g has the series representation

$$g(x) = 0.5 + \sum_{j=2}^{\infty} \sqrt{2}[(j-1)\pi]^{-2} \cos[(j-1)\pi x],$$

so $r_j/\lambda_j = 0.5$ if $j = 1$ and $[(j-1)\pi]^{-2}$ if $j \ge 2$. In addition,

$$E[g(X)|W = w] = 0.5 + \sum_{j=1}^{\infty} \frac{\sqrt{0.4}}{\pi^2 (j-1)^4} \cos[(j-1)\pi w].$$

Therefore, the reduced form model for Y is

$$\begin{aligned} Y &= E[g(X)|W] + V \\ &= 0.5 + \sum_{j=1}^{\infty} \frac{\sqrt{0.4}}{\pi^2 (j-1)^4} \cos[(j-1)\pi W] + V, \end{aligned}$$

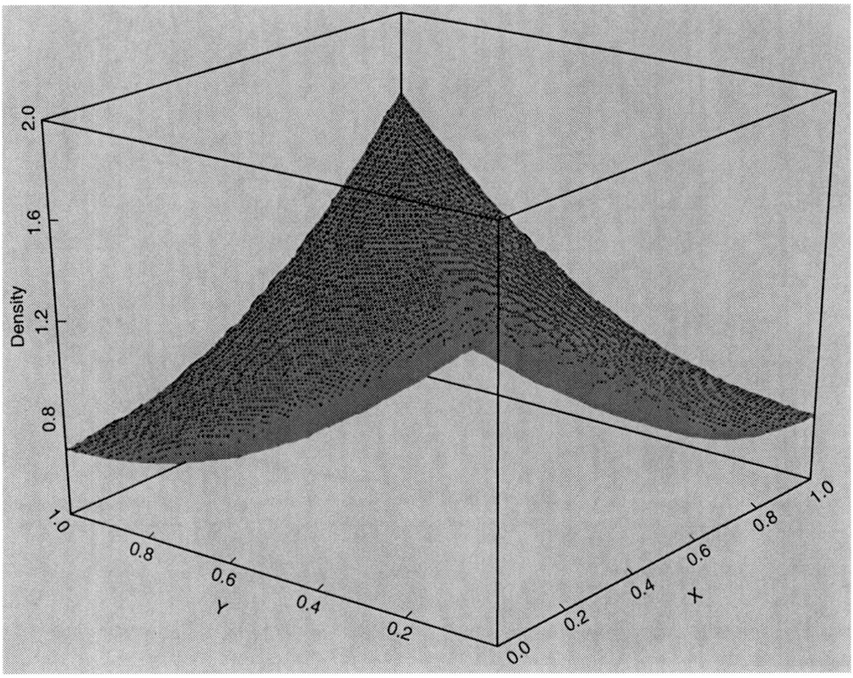

Fig. 5.2 $f_{XW}(x,\ w)$ for Example 5.1

where $V = g(X) - E[g(X)|W] + U$. Assume that $V \sim N(0,\ 0.01)$ and is independent of W.

We have

$$\int_0^1 \phi_j(z) f_{XW}(z,\ w)dz = \lambda_j^{1/2}\phi_j(w),$$

so (5.54) gives

$$\hat{r}_j = \begin{cases} n^{-1}\sum_{i=1}^{n} Y_i & \text{if } j = 1 \\ \dfrac{\sqrt{0.4}}{n}\sum_{i=1}^{n} Y_i(j-1)^{-2}\cos[(j-1)\pi W_i] & \text{if } j \geq 2 \end{cases}$$

and

$$\frac{\hat{r}_j}{\lambda_j} = \begin{cases} n^{-1}\sum_{i=1}^{n} Y_i & \text{if } j = 1 \\ \dfrac{\sqrt{10}}{n}\sum_{i=1}^{n} Y_i(j-1)^{2}\cos[(j-1)\pi W_i] & \text{if } j \geq 2 \end{cases}.$$

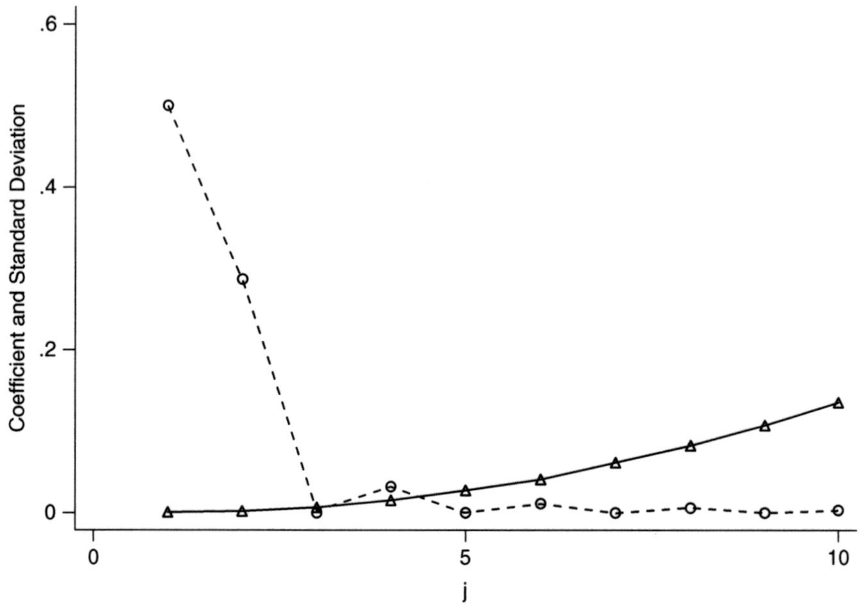

Fig. 5.3 Absolute values of coefficients (*dashed line*) and standard errors of estimates (*solid line*) in Example 5.1

Under the assumption that $V \sim N(0,\ 0.01)$, $\hat{r}_j/\lambda_j$ is asymptotically equivalent to the maximum-likelihood estimator of r_j/λ_j and, therefore, asymptotically efficient. The variance of $\hat{r}_j/\lambda_j$ is analytically complicated but easy to compute. Figure 5.3 shows a graph of r_j/λ_j and the standard deviation of $\hat{r}_j/\lambda_j$ as functions of j for $n = 1000$. The figure shows that r_j/λ_j is estimated with useful precision only through $j = 4$. The standard deviation of $\hat{r}_j/\lambda_j$ is much larger than r_j/λ_j when $j > 4$. Recall from (5.55) that r_j/λ_j is the coefficient of ϕ_j in the series expansion of g. Therefore, as a consequence of the ill-posed inverse problem, only low-order coefficients of this expansion can be estimated with useful precision. Section 5.3.1 describes methods for dealing with this problem. ■

5.3.1 Regularization Methods

The inconsistency of the estimator (5.50) can be overcome by modifying the operator T to make it continuous. The modification is called *regularization*. This section describes two regularization methods. One is named after the Russian mathematician A.N. Tikhonov and is called Tikhonov regularization. The other is regularization by truncating the series representation of g. To minimize the complexity of the discussion, it is assumed in this section that f_{XW} and, therefore, T are known. Section 5.4 presents the extensions of Tikhonov regularization and series truncation to the more realistic setting in which f_{XW} and T are unknown.

5.3.1.1 Tikhonov Regularization

Tikhonov regularization consists of replacing T with $T + a_n I$, where I is the identity operator and $\{a_n\}$ is a sequence of strictly positive constants that converges to zero as $n \to \infty$. The eigenvalues of $T + a_n I$ are $\{\lambda_j + a_n\colon\ j = 1,\ 2,\ \ldots\}$, where the λ_js are the eigenvalues of T. Therefore, the eigenvalues of $T + a_n I$ exceed a_n. The eigenvalues of $(T + a_n I)^{-1}$ are $\{(\lambda_j + a_n)^{-1}\colon\ j = 1,\ 2,\ \ldots\}$. These are bounded from above by a_n^{-1}, so $(T+a_n I)^{-1}$ is a continuous operator for each n. The Tikhonov regularized estimator of g is

$$\hat{g} = (T + a_n I)^{-1}\hat{r}. \tag{5.58}$$

If a_n had the fixed value $a_0 > 0$ instead of converging to zero, then $(T + a_0 I)^{-1}\hat{r}$ would be a consistent estimator of $(T + a_0 I)^{-1} r$. However, the function of interest is $g = T^{-1} r$, not $(T + a_0 I)^{-1} r$. Therefore, a_n must converge to zero to ensure that $\hat{g}$ converges to g.

We now investigate the rate of convergence of $\hat{g}$ in (5.58) to g. To do this, write $\hat{g} - g$ in the form

$$\hat{g} - g = (T + a_n I)^{-1}(\hat{r} - r) + [(T + a_n I)^{-1} - T^{-1}]r, \tag{5.59}$$

where $\hat{r}$ is as in (5.53). The first term on the right-hand side of (5.59) has mean zero, and the second term is nonstochastic. Therefore,

$$E(\hat{g} - g)^2 = E[(T + a_n I)^{-1}(\hat{r} - r)]^2 + \{[(T + a_n I)^{-1} - T^{-1}]r\}^2$$

and

$$E\left\|\hat{g} - g\right\|^2 = E\left\|(T + a_n I)^{-1}(\hat{r} - r)\right\|^2 + \left\|[(T + a_n I)^{-1} - T^{-1}]r\right\|^2. \tag{5.60}$$

The first term on the right-hand side of (5.60) is the integral of the variance of $\hat{g} - g$, and the second term is the integral of the square of the bias that is caused by regularization. Arguments like those used to obtain (5.57) show that

$$E\left\|(T + a_n I)^{-1}(\hat{r} - r)\right\|^2 = n^{-1}\sum_{j=1}^{\infty}\frac{\sigma_j^2}{(\lambda_j + a_n)^2}, \tag{5.61}$$

where σ_j^2 is as defined in (5.56). In addition,

$$\begin{aligned}\left\|[(T + a_n I)^{-1} - T^{-1}]r\right\|^2 &= \sum_{j=1}^{\infty}\left(\frac{1}{\lambda_j + a_n} - \frac{1}{\lambda_j}\right)^2 r_j^2 \\ &= a_n^2\sum_{j=1}^{\infty}\frac{r_j^2}{\lambda_j^2(\lambda_j + a_n)^2},\end{aligned} \tag{5.62}$$

where, as before, $r_j = \langle r, \phi_j \rangle$. It can be seen from (5.61) and (5.62) that rapid convergence of a_n to zero increases the integrated variance of $\hat{g}$ but decreases the integrated squared bias. The optimal rate of convergence of a_n equates the rates of convergence of the integrated variance and integrated squared bias.

The rate of convergence of the integrated variance (right-hand side of (5.61)) depends on the behavior of σ_j^2. It follows from (5.56) that

$$\sigma_j^2 \le E\left[Y \int_0^1 \phi_j(z) f_{XW}(z, W)dz\right]^2.$$

Suppose that $E(Y^2|W = w) \le C_Y$ for all $w \in [0, 1]$ and some finite constant C_Y. Then

$$\sigma_j^2 \le C_Y E\left[\int_0^1 \phi_j(z) f_{XW}(z, W)dz\right]^2.$$

Also assume that $f_W(w) \le C_W$ for all w and some finite constant C_W. Then

$$\begin{aligned} E\left[\int_0^1 \phi_j(z) f_{XW}(z, W)dz\right]^2 &= \int_0^1 \left[\int_0^1 \phi_j(z) f_{XW}(z, w)dz\right]^2 f_W(w)dw \\ &\le C_W \int_0^1 \left[\int_0^1 \phi_j(z) f_{XW}(z, w)dz\right]^2 dw. \end{aligned}$$

But

$$\begin{aligned} \int_0^1 \left[\int_0^1 \phi_j(z) f_{XW}(z, w)dz\right]^2 dw &= \langle \phi_j, T\phi_j \rangle \\ &= \lambda_j \end{aligned}$$

by (5.45). Therefore, $\sigma_j^2 \le C_Y C_W \lambda_j$, and

$$E\left\|(T + a_n I)^{-1}(\hat{r} - r)\right\|^2 \le n^{-1} C_Y C_W \sum_{j=1}^{\infty} \frac{\lambda_j}{(\lambda_j + a_n)^2}. \tag{5.63}$$

Now let $J > 0$ be a finite integer. Observe that

$$\sum_{j=1}^{J} \frac{\lambda_j}{(\lambda_j + a_n)^2} \le \sum_{j=1}^{J} \frac{1}{\lambda_j}$$

and

$$\sum_{j=J+1}^{\infty} \frac{\lambda_j}{(\lambda_j + a_n)^2} \le \frac{1}{a_n^2} \sum_{j=J+1}^{\infty} \lambda_j.$$

Therefore,

$$\sum_{j=1}^{\infty} \frac{\lambda_j}{(\lambda_j + a_n)^2} \le \sum_{j=1}^{J} \lambda_j^{-1} + \frac{1}{a_n^2} \sum_{j=J+1}^{\infty} \lambda_j. \tag{5.64}$$

Similarly, (5.62) gives

$$\begin{aligned} \left\| [(T + a_n I)^{-1} - T^{-1}]r \right\|^2 &\le a_n^2 \sum_{j=1}^{J} \frac{r_j^2}{\lambda_j^4} + \sum_{j=J+1}^{\infty} \frac{r_j^2}{\lambda_j^2} \\ &= a_n^2 \sum_{j=1}^{J} \frac{b_j^2}{\lambda_j^2} + \sum_{j=J+1}^{\infty} b_j^2, \end{aligned} \tag{5.65a}$$

where $b_j = r_j/\lambda_j$. To proceed further, it is necessary to specify the rates at which λ_j and b_j converge to zero. The constants b_j are the coefficients of the series expansion of g in terms of the eigenfunctions of T. Therefore, rate of convergence of b_j controls the error made by truncating the series. Assume that $\lambda_j \ge C^{-1} j^{-\alpha}$ and $|b_j| \le C j^{-\beta}$ for some $\alpha > 1$, $\beta > 1/2$, and $C < \infty$. Also assume that $\alpha > \beta - 1/2$. Then

$$\sum_{j=1}^{J} \lambda_j^{-1} \le C_1 J^{\alpha+1}$$

and

$$\frac{1}{a_n^2} \sum_{j=J+1}^{\infty} \lambda_j \le C_2 \frac{J^{-\alpha+1}}{a_n^2}$$

for finite constants C_1 and C_2. Therefore,

$$\sum_{j=1}^{\infty} \frac{\lambda_j}{(\lambda_j + a_n)^2} \le C_1 J^{\alpha+1} + C_2 \frac{J^{-\alpha+1}}{a_n^2}. \tag{5.65b}$$

The quantity on the right-hand side of (5.65b) is minimized by setting $J \propto a_n^{-1/\alpha}$. With this J,

$$\sum_{j=1}^{\infty} \frac{\lambda_j}{(\lambda_j + a_n)^2} = O[a_n^{-(\alpha+1)/\alpha}]$$

and

$$E\left\|(T+a_nI)^{-1}(\hat{r}-r)\right\|^2 = O[n^{-1}a_n^{-(\alpha+1)/\alpha}]. \tag{5.66}$$

Similarly,

$$a_n^2\sum_{j=1}^{J}\frac{b_j^2}{\lambda_j^2} \le C_3a_n^2\ J^{2\alpha-2\beta+1}$$

and

$$\sum_{j=J+1}^{\infty} b_j^2 \le C_4J^{-2\beta+1}$$

for finite constants C_3 and C_4. Therefore,

$$\left\|[(T+a_nI)^{-1}-T^{-1}]r\right\|^2 \le C_3a_n^2\ J^{2\alpha-2\beta+1} + C_4J^{-2\beta+1}.$$

The right-hand side of this inequality is minimized by setting $J \propto a_n^{-1/\alpha}$, which yields

$$\left\|[(T+a_nI)^{-1}-T^{-1}]r\right\|^2 \le O[a_n^{(2\beta-1)/\alpha}]. \tag{5.67}$$

Combining (5.60), (5.66), and (5.67) gives

$$E\left\|\hat{g}-g\right\|^2 = O[n^{-1}a_n^{-(\alpha+1)/\alpha} + a_n^{(2\beta-1)/\alpha}].$$

The rate of convergence of the right-hand side of this equality is fastest when $a_n \propto n^{-\alpha/(2\beta+\alpha)}$, which yields

$$E\left\|\hat{g}-g\right\|^2 = O[n^{-(2\beta-1)/(2\beta+\alpha)}].$$

If $\alpha < \beta - 1/2$, then the series $\sum_{j=1}^{\infty} b_j^2/\lambda_j^2$ converges. Therefore,

$$\left\|[(T+a_nI)^{-1}-T^{-1}]r\right\|^2 \propto a_n^2.$$

Equation (5.66) continues to hold, so

$$E\left\|\hat{g}-g\right\|^2 = O[n^{-1}a_n^{-(\alpha+1)/\alpha} + a_n^2].$$

The rate on the right-hand side of this equation is fastest when $a_n \propto n^{-\alpha/(3\alpha+1)}$, which gives

$$E\left\|\hat{g}-g\right\|^2 = O[n^{-2\alpha/(3\alpha+1)}].$$

The rate $n^{-2\alpha/(3\alpha+1)}$ is slower than $n^{-(2\beta-1)/(2\beta+\alpha)}$ when $\alpha < \beta - 1/2$.

The following proposition summarizes the results obtained so far for estimation of g with Tikhonov regularization. Let the notation $a_n \asymp b_n$ mean that a_n/b_n is bounded away from 0 and ∞ as $n \to \infty$.

Proposition 5.1: *Assume that*

TR1: The data $\{Y_i, X_i, W_i: i = 1, \ldots, n\}$ *are a simple random sample of* (Y, X, W), *where the support of* (X, W) *is contained in* $[0, 1]^2$ *and* $E[Y - g(X)|W = w] = 0$.

TR2: The distribution of (X, W) *has a density,* f_{XW}, *and* $E(Y^2) < \infty$.

TR3: (i) There are finite constants $\beta > 1/2$, $\alpha > 1$, *and* $C > 0$ *such that* $\lambda_j \geq C^{-1}j^{-\alpha}$ *and* $|b_j| \leq Cj^{-\beta}$. *(ii)* $\alpha > \beta - 1/2$.

TR4: The regularization parameter a_n *satisfies* $a_n \asymp n^{-\alpha/(2\beta+\alpha)}$.

Then $E\left\|\hat{g} - g\right\|^2 = O[n^{-(2\beta-1)/(2\beta+\alpha)}]$.

Now assume that TR1–TR3(i) hold. In addition, instead of TR3(ii) and TR4, let $\alpha < \beta - 1/2$ *and* $a_n \asymp n^{-\alpha/(3\alpha+1)}$. *Then* $E\left\|\hat{g} - g\right\|^2 = O[n^{-2\alpha/(3\alpha+1)}]$. ■

It turns out that $n^{-(2\beta-1)/(2\beta+\alpha)}$ is the fastest possible rate of convergence of the integrated mean-square error of an estimator of g under TR1–TR3 (Hall and Horowitz 2005). Specifically, let $\mathcal{G}$ denote the class of distributions of (Y, X, W) that satisfy TR1–TR3 for fixed values of α, β, and C. Let P denote any member of this class, and let E_P denote the expectation relative to $P \in \mathcal{G}$. Let $\tilde{g}$ denote an arbitrary estimator of g. Then

$$\liminf_{n\to\infty} \inf_{\tilde{g}} \sup_{P\in\mathcal{G}} n^{(2\beta-1)/(2\beta+\alpha)} E_P \|\tilde{g} - g\|^2 > 0. \tag{5.68}$$

This result states that no estimator of g can have a rate of convergence faster than $n^{-(2\beta-1)/(2\beta+\alpha)}$ uniformly over distributions of (Y, X, W) that satisfy the regularity conditions. Observe that increasing β accelerates the convergence of $\hat{g}$ whereas increasing α makes convergence slower. This is because fewer terms in the series expansion (5.49) are needed to obtain a good approximation to g when β is large than when it is small, whereas increasing α increases the severity of the ill-posed inverse problem.

5.3.1.2 Regularization by Series Truncation

This approach to regularization consists of truncating the series expansion of (5.50) after J terms to obtain

$$\hat{g} = \sum_{j=1}^{J} \frac{\hat{r}_j}{\lambda_j}\phi_j. \tag{5.69}$$

Combining (5.69) with (5.55) gives

$$\hat{g} - g = \sum_{j=1}^{J} \frac{\hat{r}_j - r_j}{\lambda_j} \phi_j - \sum_{j=J+1}^{\infty} b_j \phi_j,$$

where $b_j = r_j/\lambda_j$ as before. Therefore

$$E\left\|\hat{g} - g\right\|^2 = n^{-1} \sum_{j=1}^{J} \frac{\sigma_j^2}{\lambda_j^2} + \sum_{j=J+1}^{\infty} b_j^2. \tag{5.70}$$

Assume that TR2 holds, $\lambda_j \geq C_\lambda j^{-\alpha}$, and $|b_j| \leq C_b j^{-\beta}$. Then $\sigma_j^2 \leq C_Y C_W \lambda_j$,

$$n^{-1} \sum_{j=1}^{J} \frac{\sigma_j^2}{\lambda_j^2} = O(n^{-1} J^{\alpha+1}),$$

and

$$\sum_{j=J+1}^{\infty} b_j^2 = O(J^{-2\beta+1}).$$

Therefore, (5.70) gives

$$E\left\|\hat{g} - g\right\|^2 = O(n^{-1} J^{\alpha+1} + J^{-2\beta+1}).$$

The rate of convergence of the right-hand side of this expression is fastest when $J \propto n^{1/(2\beta+\alpha)}$, in which case

$$E\left\|\hat{g} - g\right\|^2 = O[n^{-(2\beta-1)/(2\beta+\alpha)}].$$

Thus, we obtain

Proposition 5.2: *Assume that*

ST1: The data $\{Y_i, X_i, W_i : i = 1, \ldots, n\}$ are a simple random sample of (Y, X, W), where the support of (X, W) is contained in $[0, 1]^2$ and $E[Y - g(X)|W = w] = 0$.
ST2: The distribution of (X, W) has a density, f_{XW}, and $E(Y^2) < \infty$.
ST3: There are finite constants $\beta > 1/2$, $\alpha > 1/2$, and $C > 0$ such that $\lambda_j \geq C^{-1} j^{-\alpha}$ and $|b_j| \leq C j^{-\beta}$.
ST4: The truncation point J satisfies $J \asymp n^{1/(2\beta+\alpha)}$.

Then $E\left\|\hat{g} - g\right\|^2 = O[n^{-(2\beta-1)/(2\beta+\alpha)}]$. ■

The rate of convergence of $E\left\|\hat{g}-g\right\|^2$ with regularization through series truncation is the same as it is with Tikhonov regularization. However, series truncation does not require $\alpha > \beta - 1/2$ to achieve this rate and, therefore, is less restrictive than Tikhonov regularization.

5.4 Nonparametric Instrumental-Variables Estimation When *T* Is Unknown

In empirical economics, f_{XW} and T are rarely if ever known. This section considers estimation of g in (5.4) when f_{XW} and, therefore, T are unknown.

5.4.1 Estimation by Tikhonov Regularization When T *Is Unknown*

When f_{XW} and T are unknown, estimation by Tikhonov regularization can be carried out by replacing f_{XW} in (5.53) and T in (5.58) with consistent estimators. It is convenient to use Nadaraya–Watson kernel estimators. To this end, define

$$\hat{f}_{XW}(x,\ w) = \frac{1}{nh_n}\sum_{i=1}^{n} K\left(\frac{x - X_i}{h_n}\right) K\left(\frac{w - W_i}{h_n}\right)$$

and

$$\hat{f}_{XW}^{(-i)}(x,\ w) = \frac{1}{(n-1)h_n}\sum_{\substack{j=1 \\ j\neq i}}^{n} K\left(\frac{x - X_j}{h_n}\right) K\left(\frac{w - W_j}{h_n}\right),$$

where h_n is the bandwidth. Set

$$\hat{r}(z) = n^{-1}\sum_{i=1}^{n} Y_i\, \hat{f}_{XW}^{(-i)}(z,\ W_i). \tag{5.71}$$

The leave-one-out estimator $\hat{f}_{XW}^{(-i)}$ is used in $\hat{r}$ to avoid biases that arise if the estimator of f_{XW} is not statistically independent of its argument. Now define

$$\hat{t}(x,\ z) = \int_0^1 \hat{f}_{XW}(x,\ w)\hat{f}_{XW}(z,\ w)dz.$$

Let $\hat{T}$ be the operator defined by

$$(\hat{T}h)(z) = \int_0^1 \hat{t}(x,\ z)h(x)dx$$

for any function $h \in L_2[0,\ 1]$. $\hat{T}$ is the required estimator of T. The resulting estimator of g is

$$\hat{g} = (\hat{T} + a_n)^{-1}\hat{r}, \tag{5.72}$$

where $\hat{r}$ is given by (5.71).

The derivation of the rate of convergence of $\hat{g}$ to g is much more complicated when T is estimated than when it is known. The details are provided by Hall and Horowitz (2005). Only their result is stated here. Darolles et al. (2006) describe an alternative approach to Tikhonov regularization with kernel density estimators. Define

$$A_1 = \max\left(\frac{2\alpha + 2\beta - 1}{2\beta - \alpha}, \frac{5}{2}\frac{2\alpha + 2\beta - 1}{4\beta - \alpha + 1},\ 2\right).$$

Let $r \geq A_1$ be an integer. Define

$$A_2 = \frac{1}{2r}\frac{2\alpha + 2\beta - 1}{2\beta + \alpha}$$

and

$$A_3 = \min\left[\frac{1}{2}\frac{2\beta - \alpha}{2\beta + \alpha}, \frac{4\beta - \alpha + 1}{5(2\beta + \alpha)}\right].$$

Let r be sufficiently large that $A_2 \leq A_3$, and let $\gamma \in [A_2, A_3]$ be a constant. Note that f_{XW} has the series representation

$$f_{XW}(x,\ w) = \sum_{j=1}^{\infty}\sum_{k=1}^{\infty} d_{jk}\phi_j(x)\phi_k(w),$$

where

$$d_{jk} = \int_0^1\int_0^1 f_{XW}(x,\ w)\phi_j(x)\phi_j(w)dxdw.$$

Make the following assumptions.

HH1: (i) The data $\{Y_i,\ X_i,\ W_i: i = 1,\ \ldots,\ n\}$ are a simple random sample of $(Y,\ X,\ W)$. (ii) The support of $(X,\ W)$ is contained in $[0,\ 1]^2$. (iii) $E[Y - g(X)|W = w] = 0$ for all w except, possibly, a set of w values whose probability is 0.

HH2: (i) The distribution of $(X,\ W)$ has a density, f_{XW}, with r derivatives that are bounded in absolute value by a constant C. (ii) The functions $E(Y^2|W = w)$ and $E(Y^2|X = x,\ W = w)$ are bounded uniformly by C.

HH3: The constants α and β satisfy $\alpha > 1$, $\beta > 1/2$, and $\beta - 1/2 < \alpha \leq 2\beta$. Moreover, $|b_j| \leq Cj^{-\beta}, j^{-\alpha} \geq C^{-1}\lambda_j$, and $\sum_{k=1}^{\infty} |d_{jk}| \leq Cj^{-\alpha/2}$ for all $j \geq 1$ and some finite constant $C > 0$.

HH4: The parameters a_n and h_n satisfy $a_n \asymp n^{-\alpha/(2\beta+\alpha)}$ and $h_n \asymp n^{-\gamma}$ as $n \to \infty$.

HH5: The kernel function K is supported on $[-1, 1]$, bounded, and satisfies

$$\int_{-1}^{1} v^j K(v)dv \begin{cases} 1 \text{ if } j = 0 \\ 0 \text{ if } 1 \leq j \leq r-1 \end{cases} .$$

These assumptions are similar to but stronger than assumptions TR1–TR4 in Section 5.3. Most importantly, f_{XW} must be sufficiently smooth (assumption HH2(i)) and there is an upper bound on α (assumption HH3). The stronger assumptions ensure that the effects of random sampling errors and the bias of $\hat{T}$ converge to zero rapidly enough to achieve the rate of convergence $n^{-(2\beta-1)/(2\beta-\alpha)}$, which is the fastest possible rate in the sense of (5.68). Assumption HH2(i) requires f_{XW} to approach 0 smoothly at the boundaries of its support. However, discontinuities at the boundary (as occur, for example, if f_{XW} is bounded away from zero) can be accommodated by replacing the kernel K with a boundary kernel. Gasser et al. (1985) and Hall and Horowitz (2005) describe these kernels. Methods for choosing a_n and h_n in applications are not yet available. A method for computing $\hat{g}(z)$ is described at the end of this section.

Let $\mathcal{J}$ denote the class of probability distributions of (Y, X, W) that satisfy assumptions HH1–HH3 with fixed values of α, β, and C. Let P be any member of this class. Hall and Horowitz (2005) prove the following theorem.

Theorem 5.6: *Let assumptions HH1–HH5 hold. Let $\hat{g}$ be as in (5.72). Then*

$$\sup_{P \in \mathcal{J}} E_P \left\| \hat{g} - g \right\|^2 = O[n^{-(2\beta-1)/(2\beta+\alpha)}]. \qquad \blacksquare$$

The rate of convergence in Theorem 5.6 is the fastest possible in the minimax sense of (5.68).

The estimator (5.72) is consistent, but does not necessarily achieve the optimal rate of convergence $n^{-(2\beta-1)/(2\beta+\alpha)}$, under assumptions that are much weaker than HH1–HH5. Specifically, if $E(Y^2) < \infty$ and f_{XW} is continuous, it is possible to choose a_n and h_n so that $E\left\| \hat{g} - g \right\|^2 \to 0$ as $n \to \infty$.

Hall and Horowitz (2005) also show how to extend the approach of (5.72) to the multivariate model

$$Y = g(X, Z) + U; \quad E(U|Z = z, W = w) = 0, \tag{5.73}$$

where Y and U are scalars, X and W are p-dimensional random variables that are supported on $[0, 1]^p$ for some $p \geq 2$, and Z is a q-dimensional random variable that is supported on $[0, 1]^q$ for some $q \geq 0$, where $q = 0$ means that the right-hand side of (5.73) is $g(X) + U$ with $E(U|W = w) = 0$. In (5.73), X is a p-dimensional endogenous explanatory variable and Z is a q-dimensional exogenous explanatory variable. W is an instrument for X.

Horowitz (2007) shows that $\hat{g} - g$ is asymptotically normal under assumptions that are somewhat stronger than HH1–HH5. To see how asymptotic normality is obtained, define $U_i = Y_i - g(X_i)$,

$$S_{n1}(z) = n^{-1} \sum_{i=1}^{n} U_i (\hat{T} + a_n)^{-1} \hat{f}_{XW}^{(-i)}(z,\ W_i),$$

and

$$S_{n2}(z) = n^{-1} \sum_{i=1}^{n} g(X_i)(\hat{T} + a_n)^{-1} \hat{f}_{XW}^{(-i)}(z,\ W_i).$$

Then

$$\hat{g}(z) = S_{n1}(z) + S_{n2}(z). \tag{5.74}$$

Observe that $ES_{n1}(z) = 0$ but $ES_{n2}(z) - g(z) \neq 0$ in finite samples except, possibly, in special cases. Therefore, $S_{n2}(z)$ is a source of bias in $\hat{g}(z)$. However, this bias is asymptotically negligible under conditions that are given below.

We now outline the argument leading to the asymptotic normality result. Write

$$\begin{aligned} S_{n1}(z) &= n^{-1} \sum_{i=1}^{n} U_i (T + a_n)^{-1} f_{XW}(z,\ W_i) \\ &\quad + n^{-1} \sum_{i=1}^{n} U_i [(\hat{T} + a_n)^{-1} \hat{f}_{XW}^{(-i)}(z,\ W_i) - (T + a_n)^{-1} f_{XW}(z,\ W_i)] \\ &\equiv S_{n11}(z) + S_{n12}(z). \end{aligned}$$

Define

$$V_n(z) = n^{-1} Var[U(T + a_n)^{-1} f_{XW}(z,\ W)].$$

It follows from a triangular-array version of the Lindeberg–Levy central limit theorem that

$$S_{n11}(z) \xrightarrow{d} N(0,\ 1)$$

as $n \to \infty$. Therefore,

$$[\hat{g}(z) - g(z)]/\sqrt{V_n(z)} \xrightarrow{d} N(0,\ 1) \tag{5.75}$$

if

$$[S_{n12}(z) + S_{n2}(z) - g(z)]/\sqrt{V_n(z)} = o_p(1). \tag{5.76}$$

We can ensure that (5.76) holds by requiring a_n to converge to zero at a rate that is faster than the asymptotically optimal rate of assumption HH4 and restricting the bandwidth h_n to a range that is narrower than that in HH4. The faster than optimal convergence of a_n results in an estimator of g whose rate of convergence is slower than optimal. As often happens in nonparametric estimation, slower than optimal convergence is the price of a normal limiting distribution that is centered at zero. It is also necessary for g to be sufficiently smooth.

To state the result formally, let ρ be a constant satisfying $1 < \rho < (2\beta + \alpha)/(\alpha + 1)$. Define

$$A_2' = \max\left[\frac{1}{2r-1}\frac{2\rho\alpha}{2\beta+\alpha}, \frac{1}{4r-1}\frac{\rho(\alpha-1)}{2\beta+\alpha}, \frac{1}{2r}\frac{(\rho+1)\alpha+2\beta-\rho}{2\beta+\alpha}\right]$$

and

$$A_3' = \min\left[\frac{1}{2}\frac{2\beta+\alpha(\rho+1)-\rho}{2\beta+\alpha}, \frac{1}{5}\frac{4\beta-(3\rho-2)\alpha+1}{2\beta+\alpha}\right].$$

Make the following new assumptions.

HH2′: The distribution of (X, W) has a density f_{XW} that is r times differentiable with respect to any combination of its arguments. The derivatives are bounded in absolute value by C. In addition, g is r times differentiable on $[0, 1]$ with derivatives at 0 and 1 defined as one sided. The derivatives of g are bounded in absolute value by C. Moreover, $E(Y^2|W = w) \le C$, $E(Y^2|X = x, W = w) \le C$, and $E(U^2|W = w) \ge C_U$ for all $w, x \in [0, 1]$ and some finite constant $C_U > 0$.

HH3′: The constants α and β satisfy $\alpha > 1$, $\beta > 1/2$, and $\beta - 1/2 < \alpha < 2\beta$. Moreover, $b_j \le Cj^{-\beta}$ and $\sum_{k=1}^{\infty} |d_{jk}| \le Cj^{-\alpha/2}$ for all $j \ge 1$. In addition, there are finite, strictly positive constants, $C_{\lambda 1}$ and $C_{\lambda 2}$, such that $C_{\lambda 1} j^{-\alpha} \le \lambda_j \le C_{\lambda 2} j^{-\alpha}$ for all $j \ge 1$.

HH4′: The tuning parameters a_n and h_n satisfy $a_n \asymp n^{-\rho\alpha/(2\beta+\alpha)}$ and $h_n \asymp n^{-\gamma}$, where $\gamma \in [A_2', A_3']$.

HH6: $E_W[(T + a_n I)^{-1} f_{XW}(z, W)]^2 \asymp E_W \left\|(T + a_n I)^{-1} f_{XW}(\cdot, W)\right\|^2$ and $E_W \left\|(T + a_n I)^{-1} f_{XW}(\cdot, W)\right\|^2 \asymp \int_0^1 \left\|(T + a_n I)^{-1} f_{XW}(\cdot, w)\right\|^2 dw$.

Assumption HH2′ strengthens HH2 by requiring differentiability of g and $E(U^2|W) \ge C_U$. HH3′ specifies the rate of convergence of the eigenvalues λ_j. This assumption and HH6 make it possible to obtain the precise rate of convergence of $V_n(z)$, whereas HH3 yields only a bound on this rate. A bound is not sufficient to ensure that (5.76) holds. HH4′ requires a_n to converge at a rate that is faster than the asymptotically optimal one. This and the assumption about h_n make the bias of $\hat{g}$ asymptotically negligible. The first part of HH6 implies that

$$V_n(z) \asymp \int_0^1 V_n(\zeta) d\zeta.$$

This rules out a form of superconvergence in which $\hat{g}(z) - g(z)$ converges to 0 more rapidly than $\|\hat{g} - g\|$. This can happen, for example, if $\phi_j(z) = 0$ for too many values of j. Such superconvergence can cause $S_{n11}(z)$ to converge to 0 more rapidly than $S_{n12}(z) + S_{n2}(z) - g(z)$, in which case (5.75) does not hold. The second part of HH6 restricts f_{XW} so as to prevent a form of superconvergence that occurs if the distribution of W is concentrated on points w for which $\phi_j(w)$ is close to 0 for too many values of j.

The formal asymptotic normality result is given by the following theorem, which is proved in Horowitz (2007).

Theorem 5.7: *Let HH1, HH2′, HH3′, HH4′, HH5, and HH6 hold. Then (5.75) holds except, possibly, on a set of z values whose probability is zero.* ■

Result (5.75) continues to hold if $V_n(z)$ is replaced with the consistent estimator

$$\hat{V}(z) = n^{-2} \sum_{i=1}^{n} \hat{U}_i^2 \{[(\hat{T} + a_n)^{-1} f_{XW}^{(-i)}](z, W_i)\}^2, \tag{5.77}$$

where $\hat{U}_i = Y_i - \hat{g}(X_i)$. This yields the studentized statistic $[\hat{g}(z) - g(z)]/\sqrt{\hat{V}(z)}$. Under the assumptions of Theorem 5.7,

$$[\hat{g}(z) - g(z)]/\sqrt{\hat{V}(z)} \xrightarrow{d} N(0, 1)$$

except, possibly, on a set of z values whose probability is zero.

This result can be used to form an asymptotic confidence interval for $g(z)$. Let $z_{\tau/2}$ denote the $1 - \tau/2$ quantile of the standard normal distribution. Then a symmetrical, asymptotic $1 - \tau$ confidence interval for $g(z)$ is

$$\hat{g}(z) - z_{\tau/2}\sqrt{\hat{V}(z)} \le g(z) \le \hat{g}(z) + z_{\tau/2}\sqrt{\hat{V}(z)}. \tag{5.78}$$

In addition, (5.78) can be modified to accommodate the possibility that z is in a set of probability zero to which the asymptotic normality result does not apply. To do this, let $z \in (0, 1)$. For some small $\varepsilon > 0$ such that $0 < z - \varepsilon < z < z + \varepsilon < 1$, let z_0 be sampled from the $U[z - \varepsilon, z + \varepsilon]$ distribution. Then (5.78) with z replaced by z_0 is a $1 - \tau$ confidence interval for $g(z_0)$ because z_0 has zero probability of being in an exceptional set of Theorem 5.7. Moreover, assumption HH2′ implies that $|g(z) - g(z_0)| \le C\varepsilon$. Therefore,

$$g(z_0) - C\varepsilon - z_{\tau/2}\sqrt{\hat{V}(z_0)} \le g(z) \le g(z_0) + C\varepsilon + z_{\tau/2}\sqrt{\hat{V}(z_0)}$$

is a confidence interval for $g(z)$ whose asymptotic coverage probability is at least $1 - \tau$ for any $z \in (0, 1)$ and converges to $1 - \tau$ as $\varepsilon \to 0$. C is not known in applications, but this does not matter because ε and, therefore, $C\varepsilon$ can be chosen to be arbitrarily small.

Horowitz (2007) found through Monte Carlo simulations that the coverage probability of the confidence interval (5.78) is closest to $1-\tau$ when the bootstrap, rather than quantiles of the normal distribution, is used to obtain the critical values. The bootstrap procedure is as follows:

Step 1: Draw a bootstrap sample $\{Y_i^*,\ X_i^*,\ W_i^*: i=1,\ \ldots,\ n\}$ by sampling the data $\{Y_i,\ X_i,\ W_i\}$ randomly with replacement. Compute bootstrap versions of $\hat{g}(z)$ and $\hat{V}(z)$ by substituting the bootstrap sample into the formulae for $\hat{g}(z)$ and $\hat{V}(z)$. Let $\hat{g}^*(z)$ and $V^*(z)$ denote the bootstrap versions of $\hat{g}(z)$ and $\hat{V}(z)$.

Step 2: By repeating Step 1 many times, obtain the bootstrap empirical distribution of $[\hat{g}^*(z)-\hat{g}(z)]/\sqrt{V^*(z)}$. The $1-\tau$ bootstrap critical value, $z_{\tau/2}^*$, is the $1-\tau/2$ quantile of this distribution. The asymptotic $1-\tau$ confidence interval for $g(z)$ based on the bootstrap critical value is

$$\hat{g}(z)-z_{\tau/2}^*\sqrt{\hat{V}(z)} \le g(z) \le \hat{g}(z)+z_{\tau/2}^*\sqrt{\hat{V}(z)}.$$

5.4.1.1 Computation of $\hat{g}$

The computation of $\hat{g}$ can be converted to a finite-dimensional matrix operation by replacing the kernel estimators of f_{XW} by a series expansions that are equivalent up to arbitrarily small truncation errors. With basis functions $\{\psi_j\}$, such as trigonometric functions, the series approximations are

$$\hat{f}_{XW}^{(-i)}(x,\ w)=\sum_{j=1}^{J}\sum_{k=1}^{J}\hat{d}_{jk}^{(-i)}\psi_j(x)\psi_k(w)$$

and

$$\hat{f}_{XW}(x,\ w)=\sum_{j=1}^{J}\sum_{k=1}^{J}\hat{d}_{jk}\psi_j(x)\psi_k(w),$$

where J is the point at which the series is truncated for computational purposes,

$$\hat{d}_{jk}=\frac{1}{nh_n^2}\sum_{\ell=1}^{n}\int_{[0,\ 1]^2}K\left(\frac{x-X_\ell}{h_n}\right)K\left(\frac{w-W_\ell}{h_n}\right)\psi_j(x)\psi_k(w)dxdw,$$

and

$$\hat{d}_{jk}^{(-i)}=\frac{1}{(n-1)h_n^2}\sum_{\substack{\ell=1\\ \ell\neq i}}^{n}\int_{[0,\ 1]^2}K\left(\frac{x-X_\ell}{h_n}\right)K\left(\frac{w-W_\ell}{h_n}\right)\psi_j(x)\psi_k(w)dxdw.$$

The series approximation to $\hat{t}(x, z)$ is

$$\hat{t}(x, z) = \sum_{j=1}^{J} \sum_{k=1}^{J} \hat{c}_{jk} \psi_j(x) \psi_k(w),$$

where

$$\hat{c}_{jk} = \sum_{\ell=1}^{J} \hat{d}_{j\ell} \hat{d}_{k\ell}.$$

K is a known function, so it is always possible to choose J large enough to make the series approximations as accurate as one likes. Let $\hat{D}^{(-i)}$ and $\hat{C}$ be the $J \times J$ matrices whose (j, k) elements are $\hat{d}_{jk}^{(-i)}$ and $\hat{c}_{jk}$, respectively. Let $\Psi(z, w)$ be the $J \times J$ matrix whose (j, k) element is $\psi_j(z)\psi_k(w)$. Then with the series approximations to the kernel estimators,

$$\hat{g}(z) = n^{-1} \sum_{i=1}^{n} Y_i (\hat{C} + a_n)^{-1} \hat{D}^{(-i)} \Psi(z, W_i).$$

The right-hand side of this equation can be computed using only finite-dimensional matrix operations.

5.4.2 Estimation by Series Truncation When T *Is Unknown*

When T is unknown, its eigenvalues and eigenfunctions, $\{\lambda_j, \phi_j: j = 1, 2, \ldots, J\}$, are also unknown, so (5.69) cannot be implemented. One way of solving this problem is to estimate T consistently, as is done in Tikhonov regularization, and then replace $\{\lambda_j, \phi_j\}$ in (5.69) with the eigenvalues and eigenfunctions of the estimated operator. However, Hall and Horowitz (2007) show that consistent estimation of eigenfunctions requires assumptions about the spacing of eigenvalues that may be undesirable in applications. The need for these assumptions can be avoided by using a series estimation method whose basis consists of known functions instead of the unknown eigenfunctions of T. We now describe this estimation method.

Let $\{\psi_j: j = 1, 2, \ldots\}$ be a basis for $L_2[0, 1]$. That is, for each function $h \in L_2[0, 1]$, there are coefficients $\{\gamma_j: j = 1, 2, \ldots\}$ such that

$$\lim_{J\to\infty} \left\| h - \sum_{j=1}^{J} \gamma_j \psi_j \right\| = 0. \tag{5.79}$$

Write

$$h = \sum_{j=1}^{\infty} \gamma_j \psi_j$$

when (5.79) holds. Examples of bases are given in Section A.2.3 of the Appendix.

Using the basis $\{\psi_j\}$, the series representation of g is

$$g = \sum_{j=1}^{\infty} \beta_j \psi_j,$$

where $\{\beta_j\colon\ j = 1,\ 2,\ \ldots\}$ are constant coefficients. If $\{\psi_j\}$ is an orthonormal basis, meaning that $\langle \psi_j,\ \psi_k \rangle = 1$ if $j = k$ and 0 otherwise, then $\beta_j = \langle g,\ \psi_j \rangle$. Otherwise, the β_js solve the problem

$$\underset{b_1,\ b_2,\ \ldots}{\text{minimize:}} \left\| g - \sum_{j=1}^{\infty} b_j \psi_j \right\|^2 .$$

The truncated series approximation to g is

$$g = \sum_{j=1}^{J} \beta_j \psi_j$$

for some finite J. We now discuss how to estimate the coefficients $\{\beta_j\}$. The discussion is based on Blundell et al. (2007). Newey and Powell (2003) describe an alternative approach to series estimation of g.

For any $h \in L_2[0,\ 1]$, define $\rho(w,\ h) = E[Y - h(X)|W = w]$. Model (5.4) implies that $\rho(w,\ g) = 0$ for all $w \in [0,\ 1]$ except, possibly, a set of w values whose probability is zero. In addition, if g is identified, then

$$E[\rho(W,\ h)]^2 = 0 \tag{5.80}$$

only if $h = g$. Therefore, g minimizes the left-hand side of (5.80). If the distribution of $(Y,\ X,\ W)$ were known, the β_js and, therefore, g could be found by solving the problem

$$\underset{b_1,\ b_2,\ \ldots}{\text{minimize}} : E\left[\rho\left(W,\ \sum_{j=1}^{\infty} b_j \psi_j \right) \right]^2 . \tag{5.81}$$

When the distribution of $(Y,\ X,\ W)$ is unknown, we can solve an empirical analog of (5.81).

To construct the empirical analog, observe that $\rho(w,\ h)$ can be estimated by carrying out the nonparametric regression of $Y - h(X)$ on W. Suppose this is done by using a series estimator. Nonparametric series estimation is discussed in Section A.3.2 of the Appendix. In general, the basis functions and length of the series used to approximate ρ can be different from those used to approximate g. Here, however, we use the same basis functions and series length for both purposes.

For any $h \in L_2[0, 1]$, $\rho(w, h)$ is estimated by

$$\hat{\rho}(w, h) = \sum_{k=1}^{J} \hat{\alpha}_k(h)\psi_k(w),$$

where the coefficients $\hat{\alpha}_k(h)$ solve

$$\underset{a_1, \ldots, a_J}{\text{minimize:}} \sum_{i=1}^{n} \left[Y_i - h(X_i) - \sum_{k=1}^{J} a_k \psi_k(W_i) \right]^2.$$

The solution to this least-squares estimation problem is

$$\hat{\alpha}(h) = (\Psi'\Psi)^{-}\Psi' R(h),$$

where $\hat{\alpha}(h)$ is the $J \times 1$ vector whose jth component is $\hat{\alpha}_j(h)$, Ψ is the $n \times J$ matrix whose (i, j) component is $\psi_j(W_i)$, $R(h)$ is the $n \times 1$ vector whose i'th component is $Y_i - h(X_i)$, and $(\Psi'\Psi)^{-}$ is the Moore–Penrose generalized inverse of $\Psi'\Psi$. The sample analog of $E[\rho(W, h)]^2$ is the sample average of $\hat{\rho}(w, h)^2$. This is

$$n^{-1} \sum_{i=1}^{n} \hat{\rho}(W_i, h)^2.$$

The coefficients of the series approximation of h are estimated by minimizing this sample average. Thus, the estimated coefficients $\hat{\beta}_1, \ldots, \hat{\beta}_J$ solve

$$\underset{b_1, b_2, \ldots, b_J \in \mathcal{B}_J}{\text{minimize}} : n^{-1} \sum_{i=1}^{n} \hat{\rho}\left(W_i, \sum_{j=1}^{J} b_j \psi_j \right)^2, \tag{5.82}$$

where $\mathcal{B}_J$ is a parameter set that is described below. The estimator of g is

$$\hat{g} = \sum_{j=1}^{J} \hat{\beta}_j \psi_j. \tag{5.83}$$

We now investigate the statistical properties of $\hat{g}$. To see the issues that are involved with a minimum of complexity, assume for now that $\{\psi_j\}$ is an orthonormal basis. Observe that the moment condition $E[Y - h(X)|W = w] = 0$ is equivalent to the operator equation

$$m = Ag, \tag{5.84}$$

where $m(w) = E(Y|W = w)$,

$$(Ah)(w) = \int_0^1 h(x) f_{X|W}(x|W = w)dx$$

for any $h \in L_2[0,\ 1]$, and $f_{X|W}$ is the density of X conditional on W. The functions m and $f_{X|W}$ have series representations

$$m(w) = \sum_{j=1}^{\infty} m_j \psi_j(w)$$

and

$$f_{X|W}(x|W = w) = \sum_{j=1}^{\infty} \sum_{k=1}^{\infty} q_{jk} \psi_j(x) \psi_k(w),$$

where

$$m_j = \int_0^1 m(w) \psi_j(w) dw$$

and

$$q_{jk} = \int_0^1 \int_0^1 f_{X|W}(x|W = w) \psi_j(x) \psi_k(w) dx dw.$$

Therefore, (5.84) is equivalent to

$$\sum_{k=1}^{\infty} m_k \psi_k(w) = \sum_{j=1}^{\infty} \sum_{k=1}^{\infty} \beta_j q_{jk} \psi_k(w),$$

and to the system of linear equations

$$m_k = \sum_{j=1}^{\infty} \beta_j q_{jk}; \quad k = 1,\ 2,\ \ldots.$$

Regularization by series truncation keeps only the first J terms in the series expansions of m and g. Thus, series truncation yields the system of equations

$$m_k = \sum_{k=1}^{J} b_j q_{jk}; \quad k = 1,\ \ldots,\ J. \tag{5.85}$$

The estimator (5.83) is obtained by replacing the m_ks and q_{jk}s with estimators. The estimators of the m_ks are the slope coefficients obtained from the nonparametric series regression of Y on W. The resulting estimator of m_k is the kth component of the $J \times 1$ vector

$$\hat{m} = (\Psi' \Psi)^{-} \Psi' Y.$$

The estimators of the q_{jk}s are the coefficients obtained from the nonparametric series regressions of $\psi_j(X)$ $(j = 1,\ \ldots,\ J)$ on W. The resulting estimator of q_{jk} is the $(j,\ k)$

element of the $J \times J$ matrix

$$\hat{Q} = (\Psi'\Psi)^{-}\Psi'\Psi_X,$$

where $Y = (Y_1, \ldots, Y_n)'$ and Ψ_X is the $n \times J$ matrix whose (i, j) element is $\psi_j(X_i)$. The β_ks are estimated by solving the problem

$$\underset{b_1, b_2, \ldots, b_J \in \mathcal{B}_J}{\text{minimize}} : \sum_{k=1}^{J} \left(\hat{m}_k - \sum_{k=1}^{J} b_j \hat{q}_{jk} \right)^2. \tag{5.86}$$

Let $\tilde{m}$ and b denote the $J \times 1$ vectors whose jth elements are m_j and b_j, respectively. Let Q denote the $J \times J$ matrix whose elements are q_{jk} $(j, k = 1, \ldots, J)$. The solution to (5.85) is $b = Q^{-1}\tilde{m}$. If the constraint $b_1, \ldots, b_j \in \mathcal{B}$ is not binding, then the solution to (5.86) is the $J \times 1$ vector

$$\hat{\beta} = \hat{Q}^{-1}\hat{m}.$$

The corresponding series estimator of g is given by (5.83).

The factors that control the rate of convergence of the series estimator $\hat{g}$ in (5.83) to g can now be seen. One factor is the rate of convergence to zero of the errors made by truncating the series expansions of g and m. If these errors converge slowly, then $\hat{g}$ will converge to g slowly. Second, the rate convergence of $\hat{g}$ depends on the rate at which the smallest singular value of Q converges to zero as $J \to \infty$. The singular values of Q are the square roots of the eigenvalues of $Q'Q$. If the smallest singular value converges to zero rapidly, then small changes in m can produce large changes in $Q^{-1}m$. Similarly, random sampling errors in $\hat{m}$ and $\hat{Q}$ can produce large changes in $\hat{Q}^{-1}\hat{m}$, thereby causing the variance of $\hat{b}$ to be large and the rate of convergence of $\hat{g}$ to be slow. The dependence of the rate of convergence of $\hat{g}$ on the singular values of Q is a reflection of the ill-posed inverse problem.

The errors made by truncating the series expansions of g and m are related to the smoothness of these functions. Let h have r continuous derivatives that are bounded by a constant, $C_1 < \infty$. Then for a wide variety of bases $\{\psi_j\}$ including trigonometric functions, orthogonal polynomials, and splines (see the Appendix), there are a constant $C_2 < \infty$ that does not depend on h and coefficients $\{\gamma_j\}$ for which

$$\sup_{x \in [0, 1]} \left| h(x) - \sum_{j=1}^{J} \gamma_j \psi_j(x) \right| = C_2 J^{-r}. \tag{5.87}$$

It follows that the error made by truncating the series to approximations g and m can be controlled by requiring these functions to have r derivatives for some $r > 0$ so that (5.87) holds with $h = g$ and $h = m$. It is useful for the series estimators of these functions to have the same smoothness properties. This can be accomplished by defining the set $\mathcal{B}$ in (5.82) and (5.86) by

$$\mathcal{B}_J = \left\{ b_1, \ldots, b_J \colon \sup_{x\in[0,\ 1]} \left| \frac{d^k}{dx^k} \sum_{j=1}^{J} b_j \psi_j(x) \right| \le C_1; k = 0, \ldots, r \right\},$$

where $d^k h/dx^k = h$ if $k = 0$. If $b_1, \ldots, b_J \in \mathcal{B}_J$, then $h = \sum_{j=1}^{J} b_j \psi_j$ is in the function space

$$\mathcal{H}_J = \left\{ h = \sum_{j=1}^{J} b_j \psi_j \colon \sup_{x\in[0,\ 1]} |d^k h(x)/dx^k| \le C_1,\ k = 0, \ldots, r \right\}.$$

The sequence $\{\mathcal{H}_J\colon\ J = 1, 2, \ldots\}$ of expanding sets of functions is called a sieve. Estimators consisting of members of these sets are called sieve estimators of g. Using the sieve space $\mathcal{H}_J$, (5.82) and (5.83) can be combined to yield

$$\hat{g} = \arg\min_{h\in\mathcal{H}_J}\ n^{-1} \sum_{i=1}^{n} \hat{\rho}\,(W_i,\ h)^2. \tag{5.88}$$

To state the condition that controls the rate of convergence of the eigenvalues of Q, define

$$\tau_J = \sup_{h\in\mathcal{H}_J,\ h\neq 0} \sqrt{\frac{E[h(X)]^2}{E_W\{E_X[h(X)|W]\}^2}}.$$

The required condition is $\tau_J \asymp J^s$ (Blundell et al. 2007). There is no simple intuitive interpretation of this condition.

Now make the following assumptions.

SE1: (i) The data $\{Y_i, X_i, W_i\colon i = 1, \ldots, n\}$ are a simple random sample of (Y, X, W). (ii) The support of (X, W) is contained in $[0, 1]^2$. (iii) $E[Y - g(X)|W = w] = 0$ for all w except, possibly, a set of w values whose probability is 0. (iv) The operator A defined in (5.84) is nonsingular.

SE2: (i) The distribution of (X, W) has a bounded density. (ii) The probability density of W satisfies $f_W(w) \ge C_f$ for some constant $C_f > 0$ and all $w \in [0, 1]$. (iii) $E(Y^2|W = w)$ is bounded uniformly by C. (iv) $\tau_J \asymp J^s$ for some $s > 0$.

SE3: The function g has $r \ge 1$ continuous derivatives that are bounded in absolute value by C everywhere on $[0, 1]$.

SE4: (i) The basis functions $\{\psi_j\}$ satisfy (5.87). (ii) The eigenvalues of $E(\Psi'\Psi)$ are bounded away from zero, where Ψ is the $n \times J$ matrix whose (i, j) component is $\psi_j(W_i)$. (iii) The truncation parameter, J, satisfies $J \propto n^{1/(2r+2s+1)}$.

Assumption SE1 specifies the model and the sampling process that generates the data. SE2(i) controls the rate of convergence of the singular values of the series approximation to the operator A. SE2(ii) is needed because $\hat{\rho}$ is an estimator of a conditional mean function. SE2(ii) ensures that $\hat{\rho}$ converges to ρ near the boundaries of the support of W. SE3 and SE4(i) control the rates of convergence of the series approximations used to obtain $\hat{g}$. SE4(ii) is analogous to assuming that the information matrix in maximum-likelihood estimation is nonsingular.

The following theorem gives the rate of convergence of $\hat{g}$ in (5.88). It is a simplified version of the results of Theorems 2 and 3 of Blundell et al. (2007).

Theorem 5.8: *Let SE1–SE4 hold. Let $\hat{g}$ be the estimator (5.88). Then*

$$\|\hat{g} - g\|^2 = O_p[n^{-2r/(2r+2s+1)}]. \qquad \blacksquare$$

Chen and Reiss (2007) show that this rate is the fastest possible under assumptions SE1–SE4. Specifically, let $\mathcal{P}$ denote the class of distributions of (Y, X, W) that satisfy SE1–SE3 with fixed values of C, C_f, r, and s. Let $\tilde{g}$ denote any estimator of g. Then for any $\varepsilon > 0$,

$$\liminf_{n\to\infty} \inf_{\tilde{g}} \sup_{P\in\mathcal{G}} P[n^{2r/(2r+2s+1)} \|\tilde{g} - g\|^2 > \varepsilon] > 0.$$

5.4.2.1 *Computation of $\hat{g}$*

Problems (5.82) and (5.88) are quadratic programming problems that can be solved using algorithms that are implemented in many software packages. In large samples, the constraint $h \in \mathcal{H}_J$ is not binding, and g can be estimated by solving (5.82) or (5.88) without imposing the constraint $b_1, \ldots, b_J \in \mathcal{B}$ or $h \in \mathcal{H}_J$. The unconstrained problem has the analytic solution

$$\hat{g} = \tilde{\psi}'_X[\Psi'_X\Psi(\Psi'\Psi)^-\Psi'\Psi_X]^-\Psi'_X\Psi(\Psi'\Psi)^-\Psi'Y,$$

where $\tilde{\psi}_X = [\psi_1(x), \ldots, \psi_J(x)]'$. In smaller samples, it is possible to replace (5.82) and (5.88) with a suitable unconstrained optimization problem that also has an analytic solution. Blundell et al. (2007) obtained good numerical results by replacing (5.82) with the unconstrained penalized optimization problem

$$\underset{b_1,\, b_2,\, \ldots,\, b_J}{\text{minimize}} : \sum_{i=1}^{n} \hat{\rho}\left(W_i, \sum_{j=1}^{J} b_j\psi_j\right)^2 + \lambda_n b'\Phi b, \tag{5.89}$$

where $\{\lambda_n\}$ is a sequence of positive constants that converges to zero as $n \to \infty$ and Φ is a $J \times J$ positive-definite matrix. Problem (5.89) has the analytic solution

$$\hat{g} = \tilde{\psi}_X[\Psi'_X\Psi(\Psi'\Psi)^-\Psi'\Psi_X + \lambda_n\Phi]^-\Psi'_X\Psi(\Psi'\Psi)^-\Psi'Y.$$

Blundell et al. (2007) set

$$\Phi = \Phi_1 + \Phi_2,$$

where $\Phi_1 = \Psi'\Psi/n$,

$$\Phi_2 = \int_0^1 \psi^{(r)}(w)\psi^{(r)}(w)'dy,$$

and $\psi^{(r)}$ is the $J \times 1$ vector whose jth component is $d^r\psi_j/dw$. Limited Monte Carlo experimentation suggests that good results can also be obtained with $\Phi = \Phi_1$ or by setting Φ equal to the $J \times J$ identity matrix, but more experience is needed before this conclusion can be drawn with confidence.

The choice of the basis functions $\{\psi_j\}$ is an important practical concern in series estimation. Because the ill-posed inverse problem prevents accurate estimation of high-order coefficients of the series approximation to g, it is desirable to choose a basis that provides a good low-order approximation. Formal methods for doing this are not yet available. Similarly, methods for choosing J and λ in applications are not yet available.

5.5 Other Approaches to Nonparametric Instrumental-Variables Estimation

This section outlines two additional approaches to nonparametric IV estimation. One is a quantile version of nonparametric IV. The other approach is based on an assumption about the conditional mean of U that is different from the assumption $E(U|W = w) = 0$ that is used in Sections 5.3 and 5.4.

5.5.1 Nonparametric Quantile IV

In nonparametric quantile IV estimation

$$Y = g(X) + U; \quad P(U \leq 0|W = w) = \alpha \tag{5.90}$$

for some α satisfying $0 < \alpha < 1$ and every w in the support of W except, possibly, w values in a set whose probability is zero. In this model, the α-quantile of U conditional on W is zero. The conditional mean of U is not specified and need not exist.

To outline the issues involved in estimation of g in this model, assume as before that the support of (X, W) is contained in $[0, 1]^2$. Let $F_{Y|XW}$ denote the cumulative distribution function of Y conditional on (X, W), f_{XW} denote the probability density function of (X, W), and f_W denote the probability density function of W. Define $F_{YXW} = F_{Y|XW} f_{XW}$. Then (5.90) is equivalent to

$$P[Y - g(X) \leq 0 | W = w] = \alpha.$$

which implies that

$$\int_0^1 F_{YXW}[g(x), x, w] dx = \alpha f_W(w). \tag{5.91}$$

Equation (5.91) shows that g in (5.90) is the solution to a nonlinear integral equation. In contrast, g in (5.4) is the solution to the linear integral equation (5.40). Chernozhukov and Hansen (2005, Theorem 4) give conditions under which (5.91) uniquely identifies g.

The nonlinearity of (5.91) makes estimation of g in (5.90) much more complicated than estimation of g in (5.4). As in (5.4), estimation of g presents an ill-posed inverse problem, so g cannot be estimated consistently by simply replacing F_{YXW} and f_W in (5.91) with consistent estimators. It is necessary to regularize the ill-posed problem. Horowitz and Lee (2007) proposed using a version of Tikhonov regularization with kernel estimators of F_{YXW} and f_W to estimate g. Horowitz and Lee (2007) give conditions under which their estimator is consistent for g in the L_2 norm, and they derive its rate of convergence in probability. Chen and Pouzo (2008) propose a sieve estimator. They give conditions for its consistency and derive its rate of convergence in probability.

5.5.2 Control Functions

Another version of the nonparametric IV problem is given by the model

$$Y = g(X) + U, E(U|V = v, W = w) = E(U|V = v), \tag{5.92}$$

where $V = X - E(X|W)$. This model is nonnested with (5.4) because it does not require $E(U|W = w) = 0$, and $E(U|W = w) = 0$ does not imply that $E(U|V = v, W = w) = E(U|V = v)$.

In model (5.92), conditioning on (X, W) is equivalent to conditioning on (V, W), so

$$E(Y|X, W) = g(X) + E(U|X, W)$$

is equivalent to

$$\begin{aligned} E(Y|X, W) &= g(X) + E(U|V, W) \\ &= g(X) + E(U|V). \end{aligned}$$

Define $h(v) = E(U|V = v)$. Then we can write

$$E(Y|X,V) = g(X) + h(V). \tag{5.93}$$

The unknown function h is called a control function because it "controls" for the influence of X on U. If V were observable, then (5.93) would be a nonparametric additive model, and g and h could be estimated using the methods of Chapter 3. Although V is not observed, it can be estimated by replacing $E(X|W)$ by a nonparametric estimator such as a kernel or series estimator. Let $\hat{E}(X|W)$ denote the estimator. Then V is estimated by $\hat{V} = X - \hat{E}(X|W)$, and g and h can be estimated by replacing V with $\hat{V}$ in (5.93). Newey et al. (1999) give conditions under which this procedure results in a consistent estimator of g, and they derive the estimator's rate of convergence in probability.

5.6 An Empirical Example

Blundell et al. (2007) used data from the British Family Expenditure Survey to estimate Engel curves for a variety of goods. An Engel curve relates expenditures on a

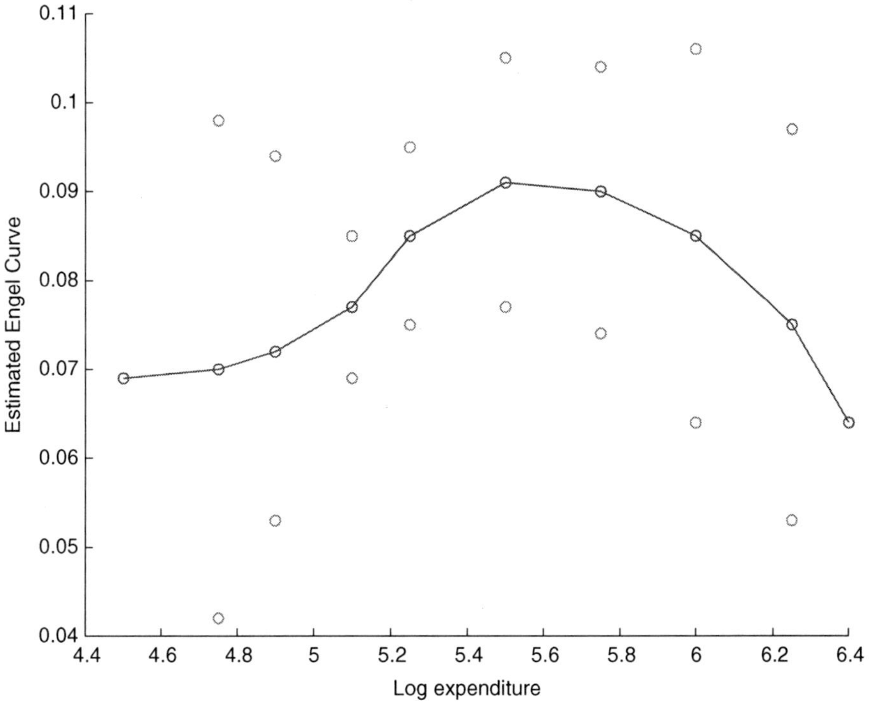

Fig. 5.4 Nonparametric estimate of Engel curve for food consumed out of the home. Source: Blundell et al. (2007)

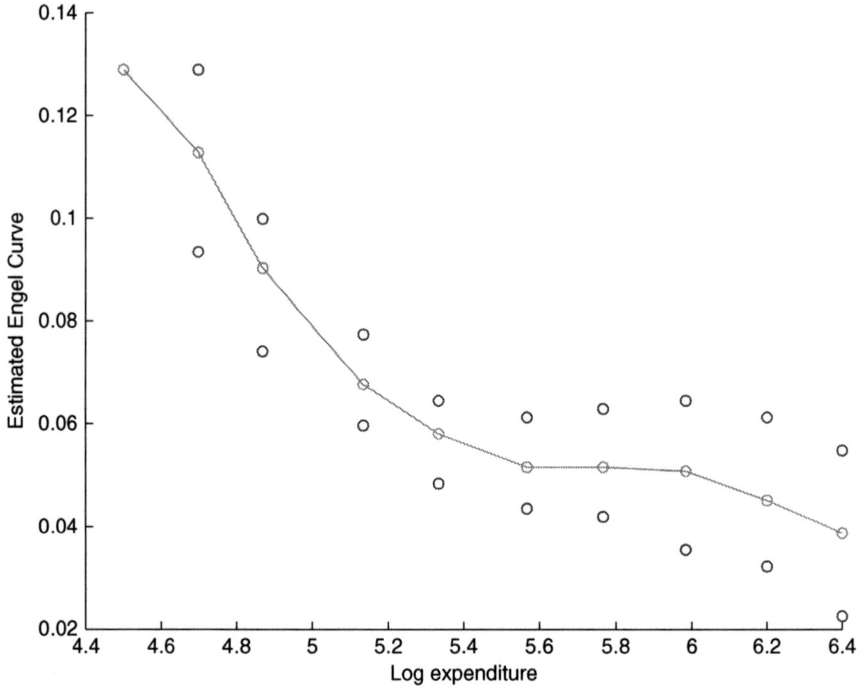

Fig. 5.5 Nonparametric estimate of Engel curve for fuel.
Source: Blundell et al. (2007)

specific good or class of goods to a household's total expenditures. The model that Blundell, Chen, and Kristensen estimated is (5.4), where Y is a household's expenditure share on the good in question (that is, expenditures on the good divided by total expenditures), X is the logarithm of the household's total expenditures, and W is the logarithm of the household's gross earnings. The estimation method was series truncation with a cubic B-spline basis. The sample included 628 households without children. Figures 5.4 and 5.5 show the estimated Engel curves for food consumed out of the home (Fig. 5.4) and fuel (Fig. 5.5) for such households. In each figure, the solid line is the estimated Engel curve, and the dotted lines are pointwise 95% confidence limits that were obtained by a bootstrap procedure. Both Engel curves are nonlinear with shapes that are different from those produced by simple parametric models such as linear or quadratic models. Thus, the estimation results illustrate the ability of nonparametric methods to reveal aspects of data that would be hard to detect using conventional parametric models.

Chapter 6
Transformation Models

This chapter is concerned with estimating models of the form

$$T(Y) = X'\beta + U, \tag{6.1}$$

where T is a strictly increasing function, Y is an observed dependent variable, X is an observed random vector, β is a vector of constant parameters that is conformable with X, and U is an unobserved random variable that is independent of X. T is assumed to be strictly increasing to ensure that (6.1) uniquely determines Y as a function of X and U. In applied econometrics, models of the form (6.1) are used frequently for the analysis of duration data and estimation of hedonic price functions. Familiar versions of (6.1) include the proportional hazards model, the accelerated failure time model, and the Box–Cox (1964) regression model.

Let F denote the CDF of U. The statistical problem addressed in this chapter is estimating β, T, and F when T and F are not both known. If T and F are known or known up to finite-dimensional parameters, then β and any parameters of T and F can be estimated by the method of maximum likelihood. In this chapter, it is assumed that at least one of the functions T and F does not belong to a known, finite-dimensional parametric family. Three cases are discussed. In Section 6.1, T is parametric (that is, known up to a finite-dimensional parameter) but F is not. In Section 6.2, F is parametric but T is not, and in Section 6.3, T and F are both nonparametric. Section 6.4 discusses the problem of predicting Y conditional on X from estimates of β, T, and F. Section 6.5 presents an empirical illustration of some of the methods that are discussed in Sections 6.1–6.4.

This chapter does not discuss estimation of (6.1) when Y is censored. Censoring occurs when one observes not Y but $\min(Y, C)$, where C is a variable that may be either fixed or random. Censoring often arises in the analysis of duration data, which is one of the main applications of transformation models. If Y is the duration of an event, censoring occurs if data acquisition terminates before all the events under observation have terminated. Most of the estimators described in this chapter can be adapted for use with censored data. Methods for doing this are given in references cited in Sections 6.1–6.3.

J.L. Horowitz, *Semiparametric and Nonparametric Methods in Econometrics*, Springer Series in Statistics, DOI 10.1007/978-0-387-92870-8_6,

It is assumed in this chapter that $E[T(Y)|X = x]$ is a linear function of x. Linton et al. (1997) and Linton et al. (2008) present estimators for versions of (6.1) in which T is parametric but $E[T(Y)|X = x]$ contains nonparametric components. An example of this is $E[T(Y)|X = x] = m_1(x^1) + \cdots + m_d(x^d)$, where x^j is the j th component of the d-vector x and $m_1, \ldots, m_d$ are unknown functions.

6.1 Estimation with Parametric *T* and Nonparametric *F*

In this section it is assumed that T is known up to a finite-dimensional parameter, α. In this case, (6.1) has the form

$$T(Y, \alpha) = X'\beta + U, \tag{6.2}$$

where T is a known function and U is independent of X. It can be assumed without loss of generality that $E(U) = 0$, and this will be done except as otherwise noted. The discussion in this section begins by presenting some important forms of T. Then methods for estimating α, β, and F are discussed.

One well-known form of T is the Box–Cox (1964) transformation:

$$T(Y, a) = \begin{cases} \dfrac{y^a - 1}{a} \text{ if } a \neq 0 \\ \log y \text{ if } a = 0 \end{cases}. \tag{6.3}$$

This transformation is widely used but has the disadvantage of requiring Y in (6.2) to be nonnegative unless a is a nonzero integer. Moreover, $T(y, a)$ is bounded from below (above) if $a > 0$ ($a < 0$) unless a is an odd integer or 0. Therefore, the Box–Cox transformation cannot be applied to models in which the dependent variable can be negative or the distribution of U has unbounded support (e.g., U is normally distributed).

Bickel and Doksum (1981) proposed overcoming this problem by assuming that $a > 0$ and replacing (6.3) with

$$T(y, a) = \frac{|y|^a \ \text{sgn}(y) - 1}{a}. \tag{6.4}$$

MacKinnon and Magee (1990) pointed out that (6.4) also can have disadvantages in applications. In particular, $T(y, a)$ does not have a finite limit as $a \to 0$ if $y < 0$ and $T(y, a)$ is very steep near $y = 0$ if a is small.

MacKinnon and Magee (1990) proposed the family of transformations

$$T(y, a) = \frac{H(ay)}{a},$$

where H is an increasing function that satisfies $H(0) = 0$, $H'(0) = 1$, and $H''(0) \neq 0$. Of course, this family also has certain undesirable properties. It does not nest $\log\ y$

if $y > 0$, and it does not permit transformations that are skew-symmetric about 0. Other forms of T have been proposed by Johnson (1949) and John and Draper (1980). Every parametric family of transformations, however, has characteristics that make it unsuitable for certain applications. This is one of the motivations for using models in which T is nonparametric. Such models are discussed in Sections 6.2 and 6.3.

Regardless of the form of T, the inferential problem in (6.2) is to estimate α, β, and F from observations of (Y, X). Denote the estimation data by $\{Y_i, X_i : i = 1, \ldots, n\}$ and assume that they are a random sample from the joint distribution of (Y, X). Let a_n and b_n denote the estimators of α and β, respectively.

Given consistent estimators of α and β, estimation of F is straightforward. Suppose that a_n and b_n are $n^{-1/2}$-consistent. Suppose, also, that F is differentiable and that T is a differentiable function of both of its arguments. Then, it is not difficult to show that F is estimated $n^{-1/2}$-consistently by the empirical distribution function of the residuals $T(Y_i, a_n) - X_i'b_n$ $(i = 1, \ldots, n)$.

Now consider the problem of estimating α and β. One estimation method that may seem attractive is nonlinear least squares. That is, a_n and b_n solve

$$\underset{a,\ b}{\text{minimize}}: S_n(a, b) = \frac{1}{n}\sum_{i=1}^{n}[T(Y_i, a) - X_i'b]^2.$$

However, the resulting estimators are inconsistent for α and β. To see why, observe that the first-order conditions for minimizing S_n are

$$\frac{\partial S_n(a, b)}{\partial a} = \frac{2}{n}\sum_{i=1}^{n}\frac{\partial T(Y_i, a)}{\partial a}\left[T(Y_i, a) - X_i'b\right] = 0 \tag{6.5}$$

and

$$\frac{\partial S_n(a, b)}{\partial b} = -\frac{2}{n}\sum_{i=1}^{n}X_i\left[T(Y_i, a) - X_i'b\right] = 0. \tag{6.6}$$

Suppose that T and $\partial T(y, a)/\partial a$ are continuous functions of a. Suppose, also, that a_n and b_n converge almost surely to α and β. Then it follows from the uniform strong law of large numbers (Jennrich 1969) that

$$\frac{\partial S_n(a_n, b_n)}{\partial a} \to E\frac{\partial S_n(\alpha, \beta)}{\partial a}$$

and

$$\frac{\partial S_n(a_n, b_n)}{\partial b} \to E\frac{\partial S_n(\alpha, \beta)}{\partial b}$$

almost surely as $n \to \infty$. Therefore

$$E\frac{\partial S_n(\alpha,\ \beta)}{\partial a} = E\frac{\partial S_n(\alpha,\ \beta)}{\partial b} = 0$$

if $a_n \rightarrow \alpha$ and $b_n \rightarrow \beta$ almost surely. But $T(Y_i,\ \alpha) - X_i'\beta = U_i$. Therefore

$$E\frac{\partial S_n(\alpha,\ \beta)}{\partial a} = E\left[\frac{\partial T(Y,\ \alpha)}{\partial a}U\right]$$

and

$$E\frac{\partial S_n(\alpha,\ \beta)}{\partial b} = E(XU).$$

Now, $E(XU) = 0$ because $E(U)=0$ and U and X are independent. But $E\{[\partial T(Y,\ \alpha)/\partial a]U\} \neq 0$ in general because Y is correlated with U. Therefore, the assumption that a_n and b_n are consistent for α and β leads to a contradiction. It follows that the nonlinear least-squares estimators of α and β are inconsistent.

Examination of (6.5) and (6.6) shows that the nonlinear least-squares estimator is an instrumental-variables estimator in which the instruments are X and an estimate of $\partial T(Y,\ \alpha)/\partial a$. As is well known, consistent instrumental-variables estimation requires that the instruments be uncorrelated with U. Viewed from this perspective, the cause of inconsistency of the nonlinear least-squares estimator is that $\partial T(Y,\ \alpha)/\partial a$ is correlated with U and, therefore, is not a valid instrument. This observation suggests that a consistent estimator can be obtained by replacing $\partial T(Y,\ \alpha)/\partial a$ in (6.6) with a valid instrument.

Let W be a column vector of valid instruments. Validity requires that $E(WU) = 0$ and $\dim(W) \geq \dim(\beta) + 1$. Powers, cross-products, and other nonlinear functions of components of X can be used to form W. The choice of instruments is discussed further in Section 6.1.1. Given W, α and β can be estimated by the generalized method of moments (GMM) based on the population moment condition

$$E\{W[T(Y,\ \alpha) - X'\beta]\} = 0, \tag{6.7}$$

provided that this equation uniquely determines α and β. The estimator solves

$$\underset{a,\ b}{\text{minimize}}: \ G_n(a,\ b)'\Omega_n G_n(a,\ b), \tag{6.8}$$

where

$$G_n(a,\ b) = n^{-1}\sum_{i=1}^{n} W_i[T(Y_i,\ a) - X_i'b]$$

and Ω_n is a positive-definite, possibly stochastic matrix. One possible choice of Ω_n is $(WW')^{-1}$, in which case (6.8) gives the nonlinear, two-stage least-squares (NL2SLS) estimator of α and β (Amemiya 1985). Amemiya and Powell (1981) discuss the use of NL2SLS for estimation of (6.2) when T is the Box–Cox transformation.

It is also possible to obtain an estimator of $(\alpha,\ \beta')'$ that is asymptotically efficient for the specified instruments, W, even if U is not independent of X, provided that $E(U|X = x) = 0$. To do this, set Ω_n equal to the following estimator of $\Omega_0 \equiv \{EWW'[T(Y,\ \alpha) - X'\beta]^2\}^{-1}$:

$$\Omega_{n0} = \left\{ n^{-1} \sum_{i=1}^{n} W_i W_i' [T(Y_i,\ \tilde{a}_n) - X_i' \tilde{b}_n]^2 \right\}^{-1}, \tag{6.9}$$

where $(\tilde{a}_n,\ \tilde{b}_n')'$ is a preliminary consistent estimator of $(\alpha,\ \beta')'$ (possibly the NL2SLS estimator).

If U in (6.2) is independent of X, then NL2SLS is the asymptotically efficient estimator based on (6.7), and the second estimation stage is not needed. However, NS2SLS does not fully exploit the implications of the independence assumption. When independence holds, further improvements in asymptotic efficiency may be possible by augmenting (6.7) with moment conditions based on higher-order moments of U. See Newey (1993) for further discussion of this possibility.

The asymptotic distributional properties of GMM estimators were derived by Hansen (1982). Define $\theta = (\alpha,\ \beta')'$ and $\theta_n = (a_n,\ b_n')'$. Hansen (1982) showed that under mild regularity conditions, θ_n is a consistent estimator of θ. Moreover,

$$n^{1/2}(\theta_n - \theta) \xrightarrow{d} N(0,\ V), \tag{6.10}$$

where

$$\begin{aligned} V &= (D'\Omega D)^{-1} D'\Omega\Omega_0^{-1}\Omega D(D'\Omega D)^{-1}, \\ D &= E\frac{\partial}{\partial\theta} W[T(Y,\ \alpha) - X\beta], \end{aligned} \tag{6.11}$$

and

$$\Omega = \operatorname*{plim}_{n \to \infty} \Omega_n$$

V can be estimated consistently by replacing D in (6.11) by

$$D_n = \frac{\partial G_n(\alpha,\ \beta)}{\partial\theta},$$

Ω with Ω_n, and Ω_0 with Ω_{n0}. Thus, (6.10) and (6.11) make it possible to carry out inference about θ in sufficiently large samples.

6.1.1 Choosing the Instruments

It is clear from (6.11) that the covariance matrix of the asymptotic distribution of $n^{1/2}(\theta_n - \theta)$ depends on the choice of instruments, W. This suggests choosing instruments that maximize the asymptotic efficiency of the estimator.

The problem of optimal choice of instruments has been investigated by Newey (1990, 1993) and Robinson (1991). Define $\sigma^2(x) = Var(U|X = x)$ and

$$\Delta(x) = E\left\{\frac{\partial}{\partial\theta}[T(Y,\ \alpha) - X'\beta]|X = x\right\}. \tag{6.12}$$

Then the optimal instruments for estimating θ are

$$W_{opt}(X) = C\Delta(X)/\sigma^2(X),$$

where C is any nonsingular matrix. If U is independent of X, then $\sigma^2(x)$ is a constant and can be dropped from the expression for W_{opt}. If W_{opt} were known, the asymptotic efficiency of an estimator of $(\alpha,\ \beta')'$ would be maximized by solving (6.8) with $W_i = W_{opt}(X_i)$ and $\Omega_n = \Omega_{n0}$.

Of course, this estimator is not feasible because α, β, $\sigma^2(x)$, and the conditional expectation in (6.12) are unknown. However, the estimator remains asymptotically efficient if the unknown quantities are replaced by suitable consistent estimators (Newey 1990, 1993; Robinson 1991). Specifically, α and β can be replaced with consistent but inefficient estimators, such as $\tilde{a}_n$ and $\tilde{b}_n$. The conditional expectation in (6.12) can be replaced by a nonparametric regression estimator of the conditional mean of $(\partial/\partial\theta)[T(Y,\ \tilde{a}_n) - X'\tilde{b}_n]$, and $\sigma^2(x)$ can be replaced by a nonparametric regression estimator of the conditional variance of $T(Y,\ \tilde{a}_n) - X'\tilde{b}_n$. Newey suggests using nearest-neighbor or series nonparametric mean-regression estimators to avoid technical difficulties that are associated with the random denominators of kernel estimators. However, kernel estimators can undoubtedly be made to work as well. See Newey (1990, 1993) for detailed discussions of the nearest-neighbor and series estimation approaches.

6.1.2 The Box–Cox Regression Model

The Box–Cox regression model is the version of model (6.2) that results when $T(y,\ a)$ is given by (6.3). The parameters α and β can be estimated by GMM if they are uniquely determined by the moment condition (6.7). However, Foster et al. (2001) have shown that, depending on the distribution of X, (6.7) may have multiple or even infinitely many solutions. When this happens, GMM does not estimate α and β consistently.

Foster et al. (2001) have proposed a minimum-distance estimator that overcomes this problem if U in (6.2) is independent of X. Define $b_n(a)$ to be the ordinary least-squares estimator of β that would be obtained if α had the value a. That is, $b_n(a)$ is the solution to

$$\underset{b}{\text{minimize}}: \sum_{i=1}^{n} [T(Y_i,\ a) - X_i'b]^2$$

with T given by (6.3). The solution to this problem is

$$b_n(a) = \left(\sum_{i=1}^{n} X_i X_i'\right)^{-1} \sum_{i=1}^{n} X_i T(Y_i,\ a).$$

Define $\hat{U}_i = T(Y_i,\ a) - X_i' b_n(a)$ $(i = 1,\ \ldots,\ n)$ to be the least-squares residuals from estimation of (6.2), and let $F_n[u;a,\ b_n(a)]$ denote the empirical distribution function of these residuals. Thus,

$$F_n[u;\ a,\ b_n(a)] = n^{-1} \sum_{i=1}^{n} I(\hat{U}_i < u),$$

where I is the indicator function. Let F_U denote the CDF of U. Then,

$$P(Y < y) = EI(Y < y) = EF_U[T(y,\ \alpha) - X'\beta].$$

Moreover, $b_n(\alpha)$ is a consistent estimator of β. Therefore, $E\{F_n[T(y,\ \alpha) - X' b_n(\alpha);\alpha,\ b_n(\alpha)]\}$ should be close to $EI(Y < y)$ for any y, but $E\{F_n[T(y,\ a) - X' b_n(a);a,\ b_n(a)]\}$ is likely to be very different from $EI(Y < y)$. This suggests estimating α by solving the following minimum-distance problem:

$$\underset{a}{\text{minimize}} : R_n[a,\ b_n(a)] = n^{-1} \sum_{i=1}^{n} \int_0^\infty \{I(Y_i < u) - F_n[T(y,\ a) - X_i' b_n(a)]\}^2 w(u) du,$$

where w is a positive, deterministic, bounded weight function. Let a_n be the solution to this problem. Foster et al. (2001) show that $[a_n,\ b_n(a_n)']'$ consistently estimates $(\alpha,\ \beta')'$ in the Box–Cox regression model. Specifically, they prove the following theorem.

Theorem 6.1: *Let the data* $\{Y_i,\ X_i : i = 1,\ \ldots,\ n\}$ *be an independent random sample from model (6.2) and (6.3). Assume that* U *is independent of* X *and that* $X'\beta$ *has at least two possible values. Then the joint asymptotic distribution of* $n^{1/2}[b_n(a_n) - \beta]$ *and* $n^{1/2}(a_n - a)$ *is normal with mean 0 and a finite covariance matrix.* ■

The covariance matrix of the asymptotic distribution of the estimator of Foster et al. (2001) is hard to estimate. Foster et al. (2001) present a resampling method that avoids the need for estimating the covariance matrix. To describe this method, let $\{G_i : i = 1,\ \ldots,.\}$ be a random sample generated by a positive, bounded random variable with known mean μ and variance $9\mu^2$. Define

$$\tau_{ijk}(a,\ b) = \int_0^\infty \eta(Y_i,\ X_i,\ Y_j,\ X_j,\ Y_k,\ X_k,\ a,\ b,\ t) w(t) dt,$$

where

$$\eta(Y_i,\ X_i,\ Y_j,\ X_j,\ Y_k,\ X_k,\ a,\ b,\ t) = [I(Y_i \le t) - \phi_{ij}(a,\ b,\ t)][I(Y_i \le t) - \phi_{ik}(a,\ b,\ t)]$$

and

$$\phi_{ij}(a,\ b,\ t) = I[T(Y_j,\ a) - X_j'b \le T(t,\ a) - X_i'b].$$

Define

$$S_n^*(a,\ b) = n^{-3} \sum_{i,\ j,\ k=1}^{n} \tau_{ijk}(a,\ b)(G_i + G_j + G_k)$$

and

$$V_n^*(a,\ b) = n^{-3} \sum_{i,\ j,\ k=1}^{n} X_i[T(Y_i,\ a) - X_i'b](G_i + G_j + G_k).$$

Condition on the data $\{Y_i,\ X_i\}$. The resampling procedure is as follows.

Step 1: Draw a random sample $\{G_i : i = 1,\ \ldots,\ n\}$.
Step 2: Let $b_n^*(a)$ be the solution to $V_n^*(a,\ b) = 0$. Compute

$$a_n^* = \arg\min_a S_n^*[a,\ b_n^*(a)].$$

Step 3: Repeat steps 1 and 2 M times, where M is a large integer. Let $\{a_{nm}^*,\ b_{nm}^*(a_{nm}^*): m = 1,2,\ \ldots,\ M\}$ be the resulting estimates of α and β.

Foster et al. (2001) show that under the assumptions of Theorem 6.1, the joint asymptotic distribution of $n^{1/2}(a_n^* - a_n)$ and $n^{1/2}[b_n^*(a_n^*) - b_n]$ induced by this resampling procedure is the same as that of $n^{1/2}(a_n - a)$ and $n^{1/2}[b_n(a_n) - \beta]$. Therefore, the resampling procedure can be used to obtain confidence intervals for and test hypotheses about α and β.

6.1.3 The Weibull Hazard Model with Unobserved Heterogeneity

The Weibull hazard model with unobserved heterogeneity is a special case of (6.2) that is important in the analysis of duration data and unusually difficult to estimate. To describe this model, define $P(\cdot\,|x)$ to be the CDF of Y conditional on $X = x$ and define $p(\cdot\,|x)$ to be the conditional density of Y. The conditional hazard of Y at the point $(y,\ x)$ is defined as the density of Y at y conditional on $Y \ge y$ and $X = x$. Formally, the conditional hazard function, $\lambda(y|x)$, is

$$\lambda(y|x) = \frac{p(y|x)}{1 - P(y|x)}. \tag{6.13}$$

Let F and f, respectively, denote the CDF and density function of U. Then $P(y|x) = F[T(y,\ \alpha) - X'\beta]$, and

$$\lambda(y, x) = \frac{dT(y, \alpha)}{dy} \frac{f[T(y, \alpha) - X'\beta]}{1 - F[T(y, \alpha) - X'\beta]}. \tag{6.14}$$

The Weibull hazard model is obtained by setting $T(y, \alpha) = \log(y^\alpha)$ for some $\alpha > 0$ and assuming that U has the extreme-value distribution whose CDF is $F(u) = 1 - \exp(-e^u)$. Substituting these functions into (6.14) yields the conditional hazard function

$$\lambda(y|x) = \alpha y^{\alpha - 1} e^{-x'\beta}. \tag{6.15}$$

Substitution of $T(y, \alpha) = \log(y^\alpha)$ into (6.2) gives the equivalent model

$$\alpha \log Y = X'\beta + U, \tag{6.16}$$

where $F(u) = 1 - \exp(-e^u)$. In this model, $E(U)$ is a nonzero constant, rather than zero as assumed in (6.2). However, this change of the location of U can be absorbed in the coefficient of an intercept component of X and, therefore, has no substantive significance.

The Weibull hazard model with unobserved heterogeneity is obtained from (6.15) and (6.16) by assuming that in addition to the observed covariates, X, there is an unobserved covariate, also called unobserved heterogeneity or frailty. For example, if Y is the duration of a spell of unemployment, then the unobserved covariate might represent personal characteristics that affect an individual's attractiveness to employers but are unobserved by the analyst. The unobserved covariate enters the model as an unobserved random variable, V. Thus, in the Weibull hazard model with unobserved heterogeneity, (6.15) and (6.16) become

$$\lambda(y|x) = \alpha y^{\alpha - 1} e^{-x'\beta - V} \tag{6.17}$$

and

$$\alpha \log Y = X'\beta + U + V. \tag{6.18}$$

In this section, it is assumed that V is independent of X and U but that its distribution is otherwise unknown. If the distribution of V were known up to a finite-dimensional parameter, then (6.17) and (6.18) would be a fully parametric model that could be estimated by maximum likelihood. See, for example, Lancaster (1979).

When (6.18) holds, the moment condition (6.7) becomes

$$E[W(\alpha \log Y - X'\beta)] = 0.$$

Equivalently,

$$\alpha E[W(\log Y - X'\gamma)] = 0, \tag{6.19}$$

where $\gamma = \beta/\alpha$. Equation (6.19) reveals why the Weibull hazard model with unobserved heterogeneity is difficult to estimate. Equation (6.19) holds for any value of α. Therefore, (6.19) and (6.7) do not identify α and cannot be used to form estimators of α. Equation (6.19) does identify γ, however. In fact, γ can be estimated consistently by applying ordinary least squares to

$$\log Y = X'\gamma + \nu, \tag{6.20}$$

where ν is a random variable whose mean is zero.

Although (6.7) and (6.19) do not identify α, this parameter is, nonetheless, identified if $e^{-V} < \infty$. The distribution of V is also identified. Elbers and Ridder (1982), Heckman and Singer (1984a), and Ridder (1990) provide detailed discussions of identification in the proportional hazards model with unobserved heterogeneity. The fact that α and the distribution of V are identified suggests that they and $\beta = \alpha\gamma$ should be estimable, though not by GMM based on (6.7) or (6.19).

Before discussing methods for estimating α, β, and the distribution of V, it is useful to consider how rapidly such estimators can be expected to converge. The parameter $\gamma = \beta/\alpha$ can be estimated with a $n^{-1/2}$ rate of convergence by applying ordinary least squares to (6.20). Ishwaran (1996) has shown that the fastest possible rate of convergence of an estimator of α and, therefore, of β is $n^{-d/(2d+1)}$ where $d > 0$ is the largest number such that $Ee^{\pm dV} < \infty$. Thus, α and β cannot be estimated with $n^{-1/2}$ rates of convergence.

Estimating the distribution of V is a problem in deconvolution. The fastest possible rate of convergence of an estimator of the CDF or density of V is a power of $(\log n)^{-1}$. To see why, let Γ denote the CDF of V, and define $W = \alpha \log Y - X'\beta$. Then $W = V + U$, and the distribution of W is the convolution of the distribution of U, which is known, and the unknown distribution of V. If α and β were known, then each observation of Y and X would produce an observation of W. The problem of estimating the distribution of V from observations of W would then be a deconvolution problem of the type discussed in Section 5.1. As was explained in Section 5.1, the rate of convergence of an estimator of Γ is determined by the thickness of the tails of the characteristic function of U. It can be shown that in the Weibull hazard model, where $F(u) = 1 - \exp(-e^u)$, the tails of the characteristic function of U decrease exponentially fast. Therefore, for reasons explained in Section 5.1, an estimator of Γ can have at most a logarithmic rate of convergence. Of course, α and β are not known in applications, but lack of knowledge of these parameters cannot accelerate the convergence of an estimator of Γ. Thus, the rate-of-convergence result for known α and β also holds when these parameters are unknown.

Methods for estimating α, β, and Γ will now be discussed. Heckman and Singer (1984b) suggested estimating α, β, and the distribution of V simultaneously by nonparametric maximum-likelihood estimation. To set up this approach, observe that by (6.18), the density of Y conditional on $X = x$ and $V = v$ is

$$p(y,\ x,\ v,\ \alpha,\ \beta) = \alpha y^{\alpha-1} e^{-x'\beta - v} \exp\left(-y^{\alpha} e^{-x'\beta - v}\right). \tag{6.21}$$

Therefore, the density of Y conditional on $X = x$ is

$$p(y|x,\ \alpha,\ \beta,\ \Gamma) = \int \alpha y^{\alpha-1} e^{-x'\beta-v} \exp\left(-y^{\alpha} e^{-x'\beta-v}\right) d\Gamma(v). \tag{6.22}$$

Now let $\{Y_i,\ X_i : i = 1,\ \ldots,\ n\}$ be a random sample of the joint distribution of $(Y,\ X)$. The log likelihood of the sample at parameter values a, b, and G is

$$\log L_n(a,\ b,\ G) = \sum_{i=1}^{n} p(Y_i|X_i,\ a,\ b,\ G). \tag{6.23}$$

The estimator of Heckman and Singer (1984b) is obtained by maximizing $\log L_n$ over a, b, and G.

The maximum-likelihood estimator of Heckman and Singer (1984b) is unconventional because it entails maximizing over an infinite-dimensional parameter (the function G) as well as the finite-dimensional parameters a and b. Kiefer and Wolfowitz (1956) have given conditions under which maximum-likelihood estimators are consistent in models with infinitely many parameters. Heckman and Singer (1984b) show that their estimator satisfies the conditions of Kiefer and Wolfowitz (1956) and, therefore, is consistent for α, β, and Γ. The rate of convergence and asymptotic distribution of the Heckman–Singer estimator are unknown.

The result of Heckman and Singer (1984b) is stated formally in the following theorem.

Theorem 6.2: *Let* $(a_n,\ b_n,\ G_n)$ *maximize* $\log L_n$ *in* (6.23). *As* $n \rightarrow \infty$, $a_n \rightarrow \alpha$ *almost surely,* $b_n \rightarrow \beta$ *almost surely, and* $G_n(z) \rightarrow \Gamma(z)$ *almost surely for each* z *that is a continuity point of* Γ *if the following conditions hold:*

(a) $\{Y_i,\ X_i : i = 1,\ \ldots,\ n\}$ *is a random sample of* $(Y,\ X)$. *The conditional density of* Y *is given by* (6.22).
(b) α *and the components of* β *are contained in bounded, open intervals.*
(c) The components of X *have finite first absolute moments. The support of the distribution of* X *is not contained in any proper linear subspace of* $\mathbb{R}^d$, *where* d *is the number of components of* X.
(d) The distribution of V *is nondefective. That is, it does not have mass points at* $-\infty$ *or* ∞.
(e) $Ee^{-V} < \infty$.■

This completes the discussion of the Heckman–Singer estimator.

Honoré (1990) has developed an estimator of α that has known asymptotic properties. Honoré considers, first, a model in which there are no covariates. The density of Y in this model can be obtained from (6.22) by setting $\beta = 0$. This gives

$$p(y) = \int \alpha y^{\alpha-1} e^{-v} \exp\left(-y^{\alpha} e^{-v}\right) d\Gamma(v).$$

The CDF of Y can be obtained by integrating $p(y)$ and is

$$P(y) = \int \exp\ (-y^{\alpha}e^{-v})d\Gamma(v).$$

Honoré's estimator is based on the observation that

$$\alpha = \lim_{y \to 0} \frac{\log\{-\log\ [1 - P(y)]\}}{\log y}, \tag{6.24}$$

as can be verified by using l'Hospital's rule. The estimator is obtained by using order statistics of Y to construct a sample analog of the right-hand side of (6.24). The details of the construction are intricate and will not be given here. To state the result, let $Y_{m:n}$ denote the mth-order statistic of $Y_1, \ldots, Y_n$. Define $m_1 = n^{1-\delta_1}$ and $m_2 = n^{1-\delta_2}$, where $0 < \delta_2 < \delta_1 < 1$. Define

$$\rho = 1 - \frac{1}{2}\frac{n^{-\delta_1} - n^{-\delta_2}}{(\delta_1 - \delta_2)\log n}.$$

Honoré's estimator of α is

$$a_n = -\frac{\rho(\delta_1 - \delta_2)\log n}{\log Y_{m_1:n} - \log Y_{m_2:n}}. \tag{6.25}$$

Honoré shows that if $P(e^{-V} > 0) > 0$, $Ee^{-2V} < \infty$, and $\delta_1 + 2\delta_2 > 1$, then the rate of convergence of a_n to α is $(\log n)^{-1}n^{-(1-\delta_1)/2}$. This rate is always slower than $n^{-1/3}$, though it can be made close to $n^{-1/3}$ by choosing δ_1 and δ_2 appropriately. Honoré also shows that the centered and normalized form of a_n is asymptotically normally distributed. Specifically

$$(a_n\sigma)^{-1}(a_n - \alpha) \xrightarrow{d} N(0,1), \tag{6.26}$$

where

$$\sigma^2 = \left[\frac{1}{(\delta_1 - \delta_2)\log n}\right]^2 \frac{n^{\delta_1} - n^{\delta_2}}{n}. \tag{6.27}$$

Equations (6.26) and (6.27) make it possible to carry out statistical inference about α.

Ishwaran (1996) derived an estimator of α whose rate of convergence is $n^{-1/3}$, which is the fastest possible rate when e^{-V} is assumed to have only two moments. Ishwaran (1996) does not give the asymptotic distribution of his estimator.

In models with covariates, α can be estimated by ignoring the covariates (that is, treating them as if they were unobserved) and applying (6.25). Given estimates a_n and γ_n of α and γ, β can be estimated by $b_n = a_n\gamma_n$. Honoré (1990) does not discuss estimation of the distribution of V. This can be done, however, by applying the deconvolution methods of Chapter 5 to the estimates of W_i ($i = 1, \ldots, n$) that are given by $W_{ni} = a_n \log Y_i - X_i'b_n$.

6.2 Estimation with Nonparametric T and Parametric F

This section treats the version of (6.1) in which T is an unknown increasing function but the distribution of U is known or known up to a finite-dimensional parameter. To begin, observe that (6.1) is unchanged if any constant, c, is added to the right-hand side and T is replaced by the function T^* that is defined by $T^*(y) = T(y) + c$. Therefore, a location normalization is needed to make identification possible. Here, location normalization will consist of omitting an intercept component from X. Thus, all components of X are nondegenerate random variables, and all components of β are slope coefficients.

6.2.1 The Proportional Hazards Model

The proportional hazards model of Cox (1972) is widely used for the analysis of duration data. This model is most frequently formulated in terms of the hazard function of the nonnegative random variable Y conditional on covariates X. This form of the model is

$$\lambda(y|x) = \lambda_0(y)e^{-x'\beta}. \tag{6.28}$$

In this model, $\lambda(y|x)$ is the hazard that $Y = y$ conditional on $X = x$. The nonnegative function λ_0 is called the *baseline hazard function*. The essential characteristic of (6.28) that distinguishes it from other models is that $\lambda(y|x)$ is the product of a function of y alone and a function of x alone.

To put (6.28) into the form (6.1), integrate (6.13) with respect to y to obtain

$$\int_0^y \lambda(\tau|x)d\tau = -\log\,[1 - P(y|x)]$$

so that

$$P(y|x) = 1 - \exp\left[-\int_0^y \lambda(\tau|x)d\tau\right]. \tag{6.29}$$

Define the integrated baseline hazard function, Λ_0, by

$$\Lambda_0(y) = \int_0^y \lambda_0(\tau)d\tau.$$

Then substitution of (6.28) into (6.29) gives

$$P(y|x) = 1 - \exp\left[-\Lambda_0(y)e^{-x'\beta}\right] \tag{6.30}$$

under the proportional hazards model. It is easily shown that (6.30) is also obtained by assuming that Y satisfies

$$\log \Lambda_0(Y) = X'\beta + U, \tag{6.31}$$

where U has the CDF $F(u) = 1 - \exp\ (-e^u)$. Therefore, (6.31) is the version of (6.1) that yields the Cox (1972) proportional hazards model.

Equation (6.31) contains two unknown quantities, β and Λ_0. Both can be estimated from data. Consider, first, estimation of β. Define the risk set at y as $R(y) = \{i{:}Y_i \geq y\}$. Cox (1972) proposed estimating β by maximizing the *partial likelihood function* that is defined by

$$L_{np}(b) = \prod_{i=1}^{n} \left[\frac{\exp\ (-X_i'b)}{\sum_{j \in R(Y_i)} \exp\ (-X_j'b)} \right]. \tag{6.32}$$

Equivalently, β can be estimated by maximizing the logarithm of the partial likelihood function. This yields the *partial likelihood estimator* of β

To understand the partial likelihood estimator intuitively, it is useful to think of Y as the duration of some event such as a spell of unemployment. Y then has units of time. Now consider the risk set at time Y_i. Suppose it is known that among the events in this set, exactly one terminates at time Y_i. The probability density that event j terminates at time Y_i given that it is in the risk set is simply the conditional hazard, $\lambda(Y_i|X_j)$. Since the probability that two events terminate simultaneously is zero, the probability density that some event in the risk set terminates at time Y_i is

$$\sum_{j \in R(Y_i)} \lambda(Y_i|X_j)$$

Therefore, the probability density that the terminating event is i is

$$\frac{\lambda(Y_i|X_i)}{\sum_{j \in R(Y_i)} \lambda(Y_i|X_j)}$$

or, by using (6.28),

$$\frac{\exp\ (-X_i'\beta)}{\sum_{j \in R(Y_i)} \exp\ (-X_j'\beta)}.$$

Thus, the partial likelihood function at $b = \beta$ can be interpreted as the probability density of the observed sequence of terminations of events conditional on the observed termination times and risk sets.

The asymptotic properties of the partial likelihood estimator have been investigated by Tsiatis (1981) and by Andersen and Gill (1982). Let b_n denote the partial likelihood estimator. Tsiatis (1981) has shown that under regularity conditions, $b_n \to \beta$ almost surely as $n \to \infty$. Thus, b_n is strongly consistent for β. Tsiatis (1981) has also shown that

$$n^{1/2}(b_n - \beta) \xrightarrow{d} N(0,\ V_b), \tag{6.33}$$

where

$$V_b = -\left[\operatorname*{plim}_{n \to \infty} \frac{1}{n} \frac{\partial^2 \log L_{np}(\beta)}{\partial b \partial b'}\right]^{-1}. \tag{6.34}$$

V_b is estimated consistently by

$$V_{nb} = -\left[\frac{1}{n} \frac{\partial \log L_{np}(b_n)}{\partial b \partial b'}\right]^{-1},$$

thereby making statistical inference about β possible. The proof of asymptotic normality of $n^{1/2}(b_n - \beta)$ is an application of standard Taylor-series methods of asymptotic distribution theory. See Amemiya (1985) or Newey and McFadden (1994) for a discussion of these methods.

The asymptotic normality result may be stated formally as follows:

Theorem 6.3: *Let* $\{Y_i,\ X_i : i = 1,\ \ldots,\ n\}$ *be a random sample of* $(Y,\ X)$. *Assume that the conditional hazard function of* Y *is given by* (6.28) *and that* $E[XX'e^{-2X'\beta}] < \infty$. *Then the equation*

$$\frac{\partial \log L_{np}(b)}{\partial b} = 0$$

has a sequence of solutions $\{b_n\}$ *that converges almost surely to* β *as* $n \to \infty$. *Equations* (6.33) *and* (6.34) *hold for this sequence.* ■

The integrated baseline hazard function, Λ_0, can also be estimated. Let P_X denote the CDF of X. Define $Q(y) = P(Y > y)$. Then

$$\begin{aligned} Q(y) &= 1 - \int P(y|x) dP_X(x) \\ &= \int \exp\left[-\Lambda_0(y) e^{-x'\beta}\right] dP_X(x). \end{aligned}$$

Also define

$$H(y) = \int e^{-x'\beta} \exp\left[-\Lambda_0(y) e^{-x'\beta}\right] dP_X(x).$$

Then some algebra shows that

$$\Lambda_0(y) = -\int_0^y H(\tau)^{-1} dQ(\tau). \tag{6.35}$$

Tsiatis (1981) proposed estimating Λ_0 by replacing the right-hand side of (6.35) with a sample analog. The resulting estimator is

$$\Lambda_{n0}(y) = \sum_{i:Y_i \leq y} \frac{1}{\sum\limits_{j \in R(Y_i)} \exp\ (-X_j' b_n)}, \tag{6.36}$$

where b_n is the partial likelihood estimator of β. Under regularity conditions, $\Lambda_{n0}(y)$ is a consistent estimator of $\Lambda_0(y)$, and $n^{1/2}[\Lambda_{n0}(y) - \Lambda_0(y)]$ is asymptotically normally distributed with mean zero and a variance that can be estimated consistently. See Tsiatis (1981) for the details of the variance and its estimator. In fact, Tsiatis (1981) proves the much stronger result that $n^{1/2}[\Lambda_{n0}(y) - \Lambda_0(y)]$ converges weakly to a mean-zero Gaussian process. A mean-zero Gaussian process is a random function, W, with the property (among others) that the random variables $W(y_1)$, $W(y_2), \ldots, W(y_k)$ for any finite k are multivariate normally distributed with mean zero. See Billingsley (1968) and Pollard (1984) for formal definitions of a Gaussian process and weak convergence and for discussions of other mathematical details that are needed to make the weak convergence results stated here precise.

In many applications, the baseline hazard function, λ_0, is of greater interest than the integrated baseline hazard function Λ_0. However, λ_0 cannot be estimated by differentiating Λ_{n0} in (6.36) because Λ_{n0} is a step function. A method for estimating λ_0 is discussed in Section 6.2.4.

Fan et al. (1997) and Chen and Zhou (2007) considered a nonparametric version of the proportional hazards model in which the conditional hazard function is

$$\lambda(y|x) = \lambda_0(y) \exp [\psi(x)],$$

where ψ is an unknown function. Fan et al. (1997) and Chen and Zhou (2007) show that ψ can be estimated nonparametrically by maximizing localized forms of the partial likelihood function. The estimators are asymptotically normal (though not at $n^{-1/2}$ rates). Not surprisingly, they have a curse of dimensionality, so nonparametric estimates of ψ are likely to be useful only if X is low dimensional.

6.2.2 The Proportional Hazards Model with Unobserved Heterogeneity

In the proportional hazards model with unobserved heterogeneity, an unobserved covariate V enters the conditional hazard function in addition to the observed covariates X. The hazard function of the dependent variable Y conditional on $X = x$ and $V = v$ is

$$\lambda(y|x,\ v) = \lambda_0(y)e^{-x'\beta - v}. \tag{6.37}$$

Model (6.37) is equivalent to

$$\log \Lambda_0(Y) = X'\beta + V + U,$$

where Λ_0 is the integrated baseline hazard function and U has the CDF $F(u) = 1 - \exp(-e^u)$. The Weibull hazard model with unobserved heterogeneity that was discussed in Section 6.1.3 is the special case of (6.37) that is obtained by assuming that $\lambda_0(y) = y^\alpha$ for some $\alpha > 0$. As was discussed in Section 6.1.3, V is often interpreted as representing unobserved attributes of individuals that affect the duration of the event of interest. In Section 6.1.3 it was assumed that λ_0 is known up to the parameter α but that the distribution of V is unknown. In this section the assumptions are reversed. It is assumed that λ_0 is unknown and that the distribution of V is known up to a finite-dimensional parameter.

Most approaches to estimating model (6.37) under these assumptions assume that e^{-V} has a gamma distribution with mean 1 and unknown variance θ. Thus, if $Z = e^{-V}$, the probability density function of Z is

$$p_Z(z) = \frac{\theta^{-1/\theta}}{\Gamma(1/\theta)} z^{1/\theta - 1} e^{-z/\theta},$$

where Γ is the gamma function. Hougaard (1984) and Clayton and Cusick (1985) provide early discussions of this model and its use. Hougaard (1986) and Lam and Kuk (1997) discuss other potentially useful parametric families of distributions of Z. The assumption $E(e^{-V}) = 1$ is a normalization that is needed for identification and has no substantive consequences. This can be seen by noting that if $E(e^{-V}) = \mu$ for some finite $\mu \neq 1$, then an algebraically equivalent model can be obtained by replacing V with $V' = V + \log \mu$ and λ_0 with $\lambda_0' = \lambda_0/\mu$. In the replacement model, $E(e^{-V}) = 1$.

In addition to assuming that e^{-V} is gamma-distributed, most research on model (6.37) assumes that there are no observed covariates X. Only this case will be treated formally here. Models with covariates will be discussed informally. Parner (1997a,b) gives a formal treatment of models with covariates.

The inferential problem to be solved is estimating θ and Λ_0 without assuming that Λ_0 belongs to a known, finite-dimensional parametric family of functions. This problem can be solved by forming a maximum-likelihood estimator of θ and Λ_0.

To form the likelihood function, observe that by arguments identical to those used to derive (6.30), the CDF of Y conditional on $Z = z$ is $P(Y \leq y|Z = z) = 1 - \exp[-z\Lambda_0(y)]$. Therefore, the conditional density of Y is $p(y|z) = z\lambda_0(y)\exp[-z\Lambda_0(y)]$, and the joint density of Y and Z is $p(y|z)p_Z(z)$ or

$$p_{yz}(y, z) = \frac{\theta^{-1/\theta}}{\Gamma(1/\theta)} z^{1/\theta} e^{-z/\theta} \lambda_0(y) \exp[-z\Lambda_0(y)]. \tag{6.38}$$

The marginal density of Y is obtained by integrating $p_{yz}(y, z)$ with respect to z. This yields

$$p_y(y) = \frac{\lambda_0(y)}{[1 + \theta\Lambda_0(y)]^{1+1/\theta}}. \tag{6.39}$$

Equation (6.39) suggests the possibility of estimating θ and Λ_0 by maximizing the likelihood function obtained from p_y. However, the resulting estimator of Λ_0 is a step function with jumps at the observed values of Y. To form a likelihood function that accommodates step functions, let $\varepsilon > 0$ be an arbitrarily small number and let

$\Delta\Lambda_0(y)$ denote the change in Λ_0 over the interval y to $y + \varepsilon$. Then, the probability that Y is observed to be in the interval y to $y + \varepsilon$ is

$$p_y(y)\varepsilon = \frac{\Delta\Lambda_0(y)}{[1 + \theta\Lambda_0(y)]^{1+1/\theta}}.$$

It follows that for observations $\{Y_i : i = 1, \ldots, n\}$ that are a random sample of Y, the log-likelihood function is

$$\log L(t, A) = \sum_{i=1}^{n} \left\{ \log [\Delta A(Y_i)] - \left(1 + \frac{1}{t}\right) \log [1 + t\Delta A(Y_i)] \right\}, \qquad (6.40)$$

where $A(y)$ is the generic parameter for $\Lambda_0(y)$ and $\Delta A(y)$ is the jump in A at the point y. The maximum-likelihood estimator of θ and Λ_0 is obtained by maximizing the right-hand side of (6.39) over t and A.

Maximization of $\log L$ in (6.40) entails computing the estimates of $n + 1$ parameters, namely the estimate of θ and the estimates of the n jumps of $\Delta\Lambda_0$. Nielsen et al. (1992) and Petersen et al. (1996) have pointed out that the computations can be simplified greatly through the use of the EM algorithm of Dempster et al. (1977). To implement this algorithm, suppose for the moment that Z is observable and Z_i is the ith observation. Then Λ_0 can be estimated by (6.36) with Z_j in place of $X_j'b_n$. The EM algorithm replaces the unobservable Z_j with an estimator, Z_{nj}. The estimator of $\Lambda_0(y)$ is then

$$\Lambda_{n0}(y) = \sum_{i:Y_i \le y} \frac{1}{\sum_{j \in R(Y_i)} \exp(-Z_{nj})}. \qquad (6.41)$$

Given this estimator of Λ_0, θ can be estimated by maximizing $\log L$ over t while holding A fixed at Λ_{n0}. Computing the estimate of θ this way is a one-dimensional optimization that is much easier to carry out than the $(n + 1)$-dimensional optimization required to maximize $\log L$ directly. Z_j is estimated by an estimator of $E(Z_j|Y_1, \ldots, Y_n)$. It is not difficult to show that

$$E(Z_j|Y_1, \ldots, Y_n) = \frac{1 + \theta}{1 + \theta\Lambda_0(Y_j)}.$$

This is estimated by

$$E(Z_{nj}|Y_1, \ldots, Y_n) = \frac{1 + \theta_n}{1 + \theta_n\Lambda_{n0}(Y_j)}, \qquad (6.42)$$

where θ_n is an estimate of θ. The EM algorithm consists of iterating (6.41), (6.42), and the one-dimensional maximization of $\log L$ until convergence. Specifically, it consists of repeating the following steps until convergence is achieved (Petersen et al. 1996):

Step 1: Begin with an initial estimate of Λ_0

Step 2: Let $\Lambda_{n0}^{(k)}$ denote the estimate of Λ_0 at iteration k of the algorithm. Obtain $\theta_n^{(k)}$, the iteration k estimate of θ, by maximizing $\log L$ with respect to t while holding A fixed at $\Lambda_{n0}^{(k)}$.

Step 3 (E step): Compute the iteration k estimate of Z_i $(i = 1, \ldots, n)$ by applying (6.42) with $\theta_n^{(k)}$ and $\Lambda_{n0}^{(k)}$ in place of θ_n and Λ_{n0}.

Step 4 (M step): Compute $\Lambda_{n0}^{(k+1)}$ by applying (6.41) with $Z_{nj}^{(k)}$ in place of Z_{nj}. Return to step 2.

Murphy (1994, 1995) has derived the asymptotic properties of the maximum-likelihood estimators of θ and Λ_0. Let θ_n and Λ_{n0} denote the estimators. Murphy (1994) has shown that as $n \to \infty$, $\theta_n \to \theta$ almost surely and $\Lambda_{n0}(y) \to \Lambda_0(y)$ almost surely uniformly over y in bounded intervals. Murphy (1995) has shown that $n^{1/2}(\theta_n - \theta)$ is asymptotically normal with mean zero and that $n^{1/2}(\Lambda_{n0} - \Lambda_0)$ converges weakly to a Gaussian process whose mean is zero. The latter result implies $n^{1/2}[\Lambda_{n0}(y) - \Lambda_0(y)]$ is asymptotically normal with mean zero for any given y. Murphy (1995) gives expressions for the variance of the asymptotic distribution of $n^{1/2}(\theta_n - \theta)$and the covariance function of the limiting Gaussian process for $n^{1/2}(\Lambda_{n0} - \Lambda_0)$.

The extension of the maximum-likelihood estimator to a model with covariates will now be outlined. The model described here is a special case of one considered by Parner (1997a, b) in which V is permitted to be correlated across observations. See Parner (1997a, b) for a formal discussion of the asymptotic properties of the maximum-likelihood estimator.

When (6.37) holds with covariates X and gamma-distributed $Z = e^{-V}$, arguments similar to those leading to (6.38) show that the joint density of Y and Z conditional on $X = x$ is

$$p_{YZ}(y, z|x) = \frac{\theta^{-1/\theta}}{\Gamma(1/\theta)} z^{1/\theta} e^{-z/\theta} \lambda_0(y) x^{-x'\beta} \exp[-z\Lambda_0(y)e^{-x'\beta}].$$

Integration over z gives the density of Y conditional on X = x as

$$p_Y(y|x) = \frac{\lambda_0(y)x^{-x'\beta}}{[1+\theta\Lambda_0(y)e^{-x'\beta}]^{1+1/\theta}}. \tag{6.43}$$

Therefore, the log-likelihood function is

$$\log L(t, b, A) = \sum_{i=1}^{n} \left\{ \log [\Delta A(Y_i)e^{-X_i'b}] - \left(1 + \frac{1}{t}\right) \log [1 + t\Delta A(Y_i)e^{-X_i'b}] \right\}.$$

Maximum-likelihood estimation can now be carried out by using the following modified version of the previously described EM algorithm:

Step 1: Begin with an initial estimate of Λ_0

Step 2′: Let $\Lambda_{n0}^{(k)}$ denote the estimate of Λ_0 at iteration k of the algorithm. Obtain $\theta_n^{(k)}$ and $b_n^{(k)}$, the iteration k estimate of θ and β, by maximizing $\log L(t,b,A)$ with respect to t and b while holding A fixed at $\Lambda_{n0}^{(k)}$.

Step 3′ (E step): Compute the iteration k estimate of Z_i ($i = 1, \ldots, n$) by applying (6.42) with $\theta_n^{(k)}$ and $\Lambda_{n0}^{(k)} \exp\ (-X_i' b_n^{(k)})$ in place of θ_n and Λ_{n0}.

Step 4′ (M step): Compute $\Lambda_{n0}^{(k+1)}$ by applying (6.41) with $Z_{nj}^{(k)} \exp\ (-X_j' b_n^{(k)})$ in place of Z_{nj}. Return to Step 2.

6.2.3 The Case of Discrete Observations of *Y*

The complexity of the estimators of θ, β, and Λ_0 in Section 6.2.2 is due to the need to estimate the function Λ_0, which takes values over a continuum and, therefore, is an infinite-dimensional parameter. The estimation problem can be simplified greatly by assuming that one observes not Y but only which of finitely many intervals of the real line contains Y. This approach was taken by Meyer (1990), who analyzed duration data that were rounded to integer numbers of weeks. See, also, Prentice and Gloeckler (1978). When the interval containing Y is observed but Y is not, $\Lambda_0(y)$ is identified only if y is a boundary point of one of the intervals. Therefore, it is necessary to estimate Λ_0 at only finitely many points. This reduces estimation of θ, β, and Λ_0 to a finite-dimensional problem. The properties of maximum-likelihood estimators of these parameters can be obtained from the standard theory of maximum-likelihood estimation of finite-dimensional parametric models.

To see how estimation can be carried out when Y is observed only in intervals, let $(y_j : j = 0,1, \ldots, K)$ denote the boundaries of the intervals. Define $y_0 = 0$, and assume that $y_K < \infty$. It follows from (6.43) that for $1 \le j \le K$

$$\begin{aligned} P(y_{j-1} < Y \le y_j | X = x) &= \int_{y_{j-1}}^{y_j} p_Y(\xi | x) d\xi \\ &= \left[1 + \theta \Lambda_0(y_{j-1}) e^{-x'\beta}\right]^{-1/\theta} - \left[1 + \theta \Lambda_0(y_j) e^{-x'\beta}\right]^{-1/\theta} \end{aligned}$$

and

$$P(Y > y_K | X = x) = \left[1 + \theta \Lambda_0(y_K) e^{-x'\beta}\right]^{-1/\theta}.$$

Therefore, the log likelihood of a random sample of $(Y,\ X)$ is

$$\begin{aligned} \log L(t,\ b,\ A) = \sum_{i=1}^{n} \sum_{j=1}^{K} I(y_{j-1} < Y_i \le y_j) \log\left[\left(1 + tA_{j-1} e^{-X_i' b}\right)^{1/t}\right. \\ \left. - \left(1 + tA_j e^{-X_i' b}\right)^{1/t}\right] + \sum_{i=1}^{n} I(Y_i > y_K) \log\left(1 + tA_K e^{-X_i' b}\right)^{1/t}, \end{aligned}$$

where $A = (A_0, \ldots, A_K)$ is the generic parameter vector for $[\Lambda_0(y_0), \ldots, \Lambda_0(y_K)]$ and $A_0 = 0$. The unknown parameters of the model are θ, β, and $\Lambda_0(y_j)$ $(1 \leq j \leq K)$. These can be estimated by maximizing $\log L(t, b, A)$ over t, b, and A. The total number of parameters to be estimated is $1 + \dim(X) + K$, regardless of the size of n. Therefore, the estimation problem is finite-dimensional and the theory of maximum-likelihood estimation of finite-dimensional parametric models applies to the resulting estimators.

6.2.4 Estimating λ_0

There are many applications of the proportional hazards model with or without unobserved heterogeneity in which the baseline hazard function λ_0 is of interest. For example, if Y is the duration of a spell of unemployment, λ_0 indicates whether the hazard of terminating unemployment increases, decreases, or varies in a more complicated way as the duration of unemployment increases. This information can be useful for testing substantive explanations of the process of finding new employment. An increasing hazard of terminating unemployment, for example, might be expected if an unemployed individual searches for a job with increasing intensity as the duration of unemployment increases. This section explains how to estimate λ_0.

In the model discussed in Section 6.1.2, $\lambda_0(y) = y^\alpha$, so an estimator of λ_0 can be formed by replacing α with its estimator, a_n, in the expression for λ_0. The situation is more complicated in the models of Sections 6.2.1 and 6.2.2, where Λ_0 is nonparametric. Since $\lambda_0(y) = d\Lambda_0(y)/dy$, one might consider estimating $\lambda_0(y)$ by $d\Lambda_{n0}(y)/dy$, where Λ_{n0} is the estimator of Λ_0 in (6.36). This procedure does not work, however, because Λ_{n0} is a step function.

A similar problem arises in using an empirical distribution function, F_n, to estimate a probability density function f. A density estimator cannot be formed by differentiating F_n because F_n is a step function. In density estimation, this problem is solved by smoothing the empirical distribution function to make it differentiable. The same technique can be applied to Λ_{n0}.

Let K be a kernel function of a scalar argument, possibly a probability density function. Let $\{h_n\}$ be a sequence of positive numbers (bandwidths) that converges to zero as $n \to \infty$. The kernel estimator of $\lambda_0(y)$ is

$$\lambda_{n0}(y) = \frac{1}{h_n} \int K\left(\frac{y - \xi}{h_n}\right) d\Lambda_{n0}(\xi) \tag{6.44}$$

Note the similarity between (6.44) and a kernel density estimator, which is what would be obtained if Λ_{n0} were replaced with F_n in the integral. The remainder of this section provides a heuristic argument showing that $\lambda_{n0}(y)$ has properties that are similar to those of a kernel density estimator. In particular, $\lambda_{n0}(y) \to^p \lambda_0(y)$ as $n \to \infty$ at a rate that is no faster than $n^{-2/5}$ if $y > 0$ and λ_0 is twice continuously differentiable in a neighborhood of y. Similar arguments can be used to show that a faster rate of convergence is possible if λ_0 has more than two derivatives and K

is a higher-order kernel. As in nonparametric density estimation, however, a rate of convergence of $n^{-1/2}$ is not possible.

To begin the analysis of λ_{n0}, write it in the form

$$\lambda_{n0}(y) = \lambda_0(y) + H_{n1}(y) + H_{n2}(y), \tag{6.45}$$

where

$$H_{n1}(y) = \frac{1}{h_n}\int K\left(\frac{y-\xi}{h_n}\right) d\Lambda_0(\xi) - \lambda_0(y)$$

and

$$H_{n2}(y) = \frac{1}{h_n}\int K\left(\frac{y-\xi}{h_n}\right) d[\Lambda_{n0}(y) - \Lambda_0(y)]. \tag{6.46}$$

Now consider H_{n1}. Observe that it can be written as

$$H_{n1}(y) = \frac{1}{h_n}\int K\left(\frac{y-\xi}{h_n}\right) \lambda_0(\xi)d\xi - \lambda_0(y). \tag{6.47}$$

Assume that K is a continuously differentiable probability density function that is symmetrical about zero and whose support is $[-1,1]$. Making the change of variables $\zeta = (\xi - y)/h_n$ in the integral on the right-hand side of (6.47) then yields

$$H_{n1}(y) = \int_{-1}^{1} K(\zeta)\lambda_0(h_n\zeta + y)d\zeta - \lambda_0(y).$$

Now expand $\lambda_0(h_n\zeta + y)$ in a Taylor series to obtain

$$\begin{aligned} H_{n1}(y) &= \int_{-1}^{1} K(\zeta)[\lambda_0(y) + h_n\zeta\lambda_0'(y) + (1/2)h_n^2\zeta^2\lambda_0''(y) + o(h_n^2)]d\zeta - \lambda_0(y) \\ &= (1/2)A_K h_n^2\lambda_0''(y) + o(h_n^2), \end{aligned}$$

where

$$A_K = \int_{-1}^{1} \zeta^2 \; K(\zeta)d\zeta.$$

Substitution of this result into (6.45) yields

$$\lambda_{n0}(y) = \lambda_0(y) + (1/2)A_K h_n^2\lambda_0''(y) + H_{n2}(y) + o(h_n^2). \tag{6.48}$$

Now consider $H_{n2}(y)$. Integrate by parts on the right-hand side of (6.46) to obtain

$$\begin{aligned} H_{n2}(y) &= \frac{1}{h_n^2}\int [\Lambda_{n0}(y) - \Lambda_0(y)]K'\left(\frac{y-\xi}{h_n}\right)d\xi \\ &= \frac{1}{n^{1/2}h_n^2}\int n^{1/2}[\Lambda_{n0}(y) - \Lambda_0(y)]K'\left(\frac{y-\xi}{h_n}\right)d\xi. \end{aligned}$$

As was discussed in Sections 6.2.1 and 6.2.2, $n^{1/2}(\Lambda_{n0} - \Lambda_0)$ converges weakly to a Gaussian process. Let W denote the limiting process. Given any finite, $y_1 > 0$ and $y_2 > 0$, define $V(y_1, y_2) = E[W(y_1)W(y_2)]$. $V(y_1, y_2)$ is the covariance of the jointly normally distributed random variables $W(y_1)$ and $W(y_2)$. Using the theory of empirical processes (see, e.g., Billingsley 1968 or Pollard 1984), it can be shown that

$$H_{n2}(y) = \tilde{H}_{n2}(y) + o_p(n^{-1/2}),$$

where

$$\tilde{H}_{n2}(y) = \frac{1}{n^{1/2}h_n^2}\int W(\xi)K'\left(\frac{y-\xi}{h_n}\right)d\xi.$$

Moreover,

$$\tilde{H}_{n2}(y) \sim N(0, \sigma_{ny}^2),$$

where for any finite $y < 0$

$$\begin{aligned} \sigma_{ny}^2 &= E[\tilde{H}_{n2}(y)^2] \\ &= E\frac{1}{nh_n^4}\int W(\xi)W(\zeta)K'\left(\frac{y-\xi}{h_n}\right)K'\left(\frac{y-\zeta}{h_n}\right)d\xi d\zeta. \\ &= \frac{1}{nh_n^4}\int V(\xi, \zeta)K'\left(\frac{y-\xi}{h_n}\right)K'\left(\frac{y-\zeta}{h_n}\right)d\xi d\zeta \end{aligned}$$

By a change of variables in the integrals

$$\sigma_{ny}^2 = \frac{1}{nh_n^2}\int_{-1}^{1}d\xi\int_{-1}^{1}d\zeta\, V(h_n\xi + y, h_n\zeta + y)K'(\xi)K'(\zeta). \tag{6.49}$$

Because V is a symmetrical function of its arguments, σ_{ny}^2 can also be written in the form

$$\sigma_{ny}^2 = \frac{2}{nh_n^2}\int_{-1}^{1}d\xi\int_{-1}^{\xi}d\zeta\, V(h_n\xi + y, h_n\zeta + y)K'(\xi)K'(\zeta).$$

It is not difficult to show that

$$\int_{-1}^{1}d\xi\int_{-1}^{\xi}d\zeta\, K'(\xi)K'(\zeta) = 0$$

and

$$\int_{-1}^{1} d\xi \int_{-1}^{\xi} d\zeta \xi K'(\xi)K'(\zeta) = -\int_{-1}^{1} d\xi \int_{-1}^{\xi} d\zeta \xi K'(\xi)K'(\zeta) = B_K/2,$$

where

$$B_K = \int_{-1}^{1} K(\xi)^2 d\xi.$$

Therefore, a Taylor-series expansion of the integrand on the right-hand side of (6.49) yields

$$\sigma_{ny}^2 = \frac{B_K}{nh_n} V_1(y,\ y) + o[(nh_n)^{-1}], \tag{6.50}$$

where

$$V_1(y,\ y) = \lim_{\xi \to 0^+} \frac{\partial V(\xi + y,\ y)}{\partial y}.$$

It follows from (6.48) and (6.50) that the asymptotic mean-square error of $\lambda_{n0}(y)$ is minimized when $h_n = cn^{-1/5}$ for some constant $c > 0$. It also follows that with this h_n, $\lambda_{n0}(y) - \lambda_0(y) = O_p(n^{-2/5})$ and

$$(nh_n)^{1/2}[\lambda_{n0}(y) - \lambda_0(y)] \xrightarrow{d} N(\mu_y,\ \sigma_y^2),$$

where $\mu_y = (1/2)c^{5/2}A_K\lambda_0''(y)$ and $\sigma_y^2 = B_K V_1(y,\ y)$. Thus, $n^{-2/5}$-consistency of $\lambda_{n0}(y)$ and asymptotic normality of $(nh_n)^{1/2}[\lambda_{n0}(y) - \lambda_0(y)]$ are established.

Implementing (6.44) requires choosing the value of c. One possible choice is the value of c that minimizes the asymptotic mean-square error of $\lambda_{n0}(y) - \lambda_0(y)$. When $h_n = cn^{-1/5}$, the asymptotic mean-square error is

$$\begin{aligned} AMSE(y) &= \frac{\mu_y^2 + \sigma_y^2}{nh_n} \\ &= \frac{c^4[A_K\lambda_0''(y)]^2}{4n^{4/5}} + \frac{B_K V_1(y,\ y)}{cn^{4/5}}. \end{aligned}$$

$AMSE(y)$ is minimized by setting $c = c_{opt}$, where

$$c_{opt} = \left\{ \frac{B_K V_1(y,\ y)}{[A_K\lambda_0''(y)]^2} \right\}^{1/5}.$$

This value of c can be estimated by the plug-in method, which consists of replacing V_1 and λ_0'' in the expression for c_{opt} with estimators.

6.2.5 Other Models in Which F Is Known

In this section, it is assumed that (6.1) holds with T unknown and F known. In contrast to Section 6.2.1, however, it is not assumed that $F(u) = 1 - \exp(-e^u)$. Instead, F can be any known distribution function that satisfies certain regularity conditions. The aim is to estimate the finite-dimensional parameter β and the transformation function T. The methods described in this section can be applied to the proportional hazards model of Section 6.2.1, although there is no reason to do so. They can also be applied to the proportional odds model (Pettit 1982, Bennett 1983a, b), which is obtained from (6.1) by assuming U to be logistically distributed. The methods described in this section cannot be applied to the proportional hazards model with unobserved heterogeneity described in Section 6.2.2 unless the variance parameter θ is known a priori.

The estimators described in this section are due to Cheng et al. (1995, 1997). These estimators have the advantage that they are applicable to models with a variety of different Fs. If interest centers on a particular F, it may be possible to take advantage of special features of this F to construct estimators that are asymptotically more efficient than those of Cheng et al. (1995, 1997). For example, the partial likelihood estimator of β in the proportional hazards model is asymptotically efficient (Bickel et al. 1993). Murphy et al. (1997) show that a semiparametric maximum-likelihood estimator of β in the proportional odds model is asymptotically efficient. However, an estimator that takes advantage of features of a specific F may not be consistent with other Fs.

Consider, now, the problem of estimating β in (6.1) with a known F. Let $(Y_i,\ X_i)$ and $(Y_j,\ X_j)$ $(i \neq j)$ be two distinct, independent observations of $(Y,\ X)$. Then it follows from (6.1) that

$$E[I(Y_i > Y_j)|X_i = x_i,\ X_j = x_j] = P[U_i - U_j > -(x_i - x_j)'\beta | X_i = x_i,\ X_j = x_j]. \tag{6.51}$$

Let $G(z) = P(U_i - U_j > z)$ for any real z. Then

$$G(z) = \int_{-\infty}^{\infty} [1 - F(u + z)] dF(u).$$

G is a known function because F is assumed known in this section. Substituting G into (6.51) gives

$$E[I(Y_i > Y_j)|X_i = x_i,\ X_j = x_j] = G[-(x_i - x_j)'\beta].$$

Define $X_{ij} = X_i - X_j$. Then it follows that β satisfies the moment condition

$$E\{w(X_{ij}'\beta)X_{ij}[I(Y_i > Y_j) - G(-X_{ij}'\beta)]\} = 0, \tag{6.52}$$

where w is a weight function. Cheng et al. (1995) propose estimating β by replacing the population moment condition (6.52) with the sample analog

$$\sum_{i=1}^{n}\sum_{j=1}^{n}\{w(X'_{ij}b)X_{ij}[I(Y_i > Y_j) - G(-X'_{ij}b)]\} = 0. \tag{6.53}$$

The estimator of β, b_n, is the solution to (6.53). Equation (6.53) has a unique solution if $w(z) = 1$ for all z and the matrix $\sum_{i,\,j} X_{ij}X'_{ij}$ is positive definite. It also has a unique solution asymptotically if w is positive everywhere (Cheng et al. 1995). Moreover, b_n converges almost surely to β. This follows from uniqueness of the solution to (6.53) and almost sure convergence of the left-hand side of (6.53) to $E\{w(X'_{ij}b)X_{ij}[I(Y_i > Y_j) - G(-X'_{ij}b)]\}$.

The asymptotic distribution of $n^{1/2}(b_n - \beta)$ can be obtained by using standard Taylor-series methods of asymptotic distribution theory. To this end, define

$$H_n(b) = \frac{1}{n^2}\sum_{i=1}^{n}\sum_{j=1}^{n}\{w(X'_{ij}b)X_{ij}[I(Y_i > Y_j) - G(-X'_{ij}b)]\}.$$

Then $H_n(b_n) = 0$, and a Taylor-series approximation gives

$$n^{1/2}H_n(\beta) + \frac{\partial H_n(b_n^*)}{\partial b}n^{1/2}(b_n - \beta) = 0, \tag{6.54}$$

where b_n^* is between b_n and β, and $\partial H_n/\partial b$ is the matrix whose $(j,\ k)$ element is the partial derivative of the j th component of H_n with respect to the k th component of b. Cheng et al. (1995) show that $n^{1/2}H_n(\beta)$ is asymptotically normally distributed with mean zero and a covariance matrix equal to the probability limit of

$$Q_n = \frac{1}{n^3}\sum_{i=1}^{n}\sum_{j=1}^{n}\sum_{\substack{k=1\\k\neq j}}^{n}[w(X'_{ij}b_n)e_{ij} - w(X'_{ji}b_n)e_{ji}][w(X'_{ik}b_n)e_{ik} - w(X'_{ki}b_n)e_{ki}]X_{ij}X'_{ik} \tag{6.55}$$

where $e_{ij} = I(Y_i > Y_j) - G(-X'_{ij}\beta)$. Cheng et al. (1995) also show that if G is everywhere differentiable, then $\partial H_n(b_n^*)/\partial b$ converges in probability to the probability limit of

$$R_n = \frac{1}{n^2}\sum_{i=1}^{n}\sum_{j=1}^{n} w(X'_{ij}\beta)G'(-X_{ij}b_n)X_{ij}X'_{ij}. \tag{6.56}$$

Let Q and R be the probability limits of Q_n and R_n, respectively. Then it follows from (6.54) to (6.56) that $n^{1/2}(b_n - \beta) \xrightarrow{d} N(0,\ R^{-1}QR^{-1})$ if w is positive and G is differentiable. The covariance matrix $R^{-1}QR^{-1}$ is estimated consistently by $R_n^{-1}Q_nR_n^{-1}$. This result enables statistical inference about β to be carried out.

Now consider estimation of the transformation function T. This problem is addressed by Cheng et al. (1997). Equation (6.1) implies that for any real y and vector x that is conformable with X, $E[I(Y \leq y)|X = x] - F[T(y) - x'\beta] = 0$. Cheng et al. (1997) propose estimating $T(y)$ by the solution to the sample analog of this equation. That is, the estimator $T_n(y)$ solves

$$n^{-1}\sum_{i=1}^{n}\{I(Y_i \le y) - F[t(y) - X_i'b_n]\} = 0,$$

where b_n is the solution to (6.53). Cheng et al. (1997) show that if F is strictly increasing on its support, then $T_n(y)$ converges to $T(y)$ almost surely uniformly over any interval $[0, \tau]$ such that $P(Y > \tau) > 0$. Moreover, $n^{1/2}(T_n - T)$ converges to a mean-zero Gaussian process over this interval. The covariance function of this process is lengthy and is given in Cheng et al. (1997).

6.3 Estimation When Both T and F Are Nonparametric

This section discusses estimation of (6.1) when neither T nor F is assumed to belong to a known, finite-dimensional parametric family of functions. The aim is to develop $n^{-1/2}$-consistent estimators of β, T, and F. The estimators described here are taken from Horowitz (1996) and Chen (2002). Other approaches to $n^{-1/2}$-consistent estimation are described by Abrevaya (2003) and Ye and Duan (1997). Estimators that are not $n^{-1/2}$-consistent have been described by Breiman and Friedman (1985) and Hastie and Tibshirani (1990). Gørgens and Horowitz (1995) discuss estimation of β, T, and F when observations of Y are censored. Chen's (2002) method can also be applied to censored observations.

When T and F are nonparametric, certain normalizations are needed to make identification of (6.1) possible. First, observe that (6.1) continues to hold if T is replaced with cT, β is replaced with $c\beta$, and U is replaced with cU for any positive constant c. Therefore, a scale normalization is needed to make identification possible. This will be done here by setting $|\beta_1| = 1$, where β_1 is the first component of β. Observe, also, that when T and F are nonparametric, (6.1) is a semiparametric single-index model. Therefore, as was discussed in Chapter 2, identification of β requires X to have at least one component whose distribution conditional on the others is continuous and whose β coefficient is nonzero. Assume without loss of generality that the components of X are ordered so that the first satisfies this condition.

It can also be seen that (6.1) is unchanged if T is replaced with $T + d$ and U is replaced with $U + d$ for any positive or negative constant d. Therefore, a location normalization is also needed to achieve identification when T and F are nonparametric. Location normalization will be carried out here by assuming that $T(y_0) = 0$ for some finite y_0 that satisfies conditions given in Section 6.3.2. With this location normalization, there is no centering assumption on U and no intercept term in X.

The location and scale normalizations in this section are not the same as those of Sections 6.1 and 6.2. When T or F is known up to a finite-dimensional parameter, as is the case in Sections 6.1 and 6.2, location and scale normalization are usually accomplished implicitly through the specification of T or F. This is not possible when T and F are nonparametric. Because of differences in normalization, estimates obtained using the methods described in this section cannot be compared with estimates obtained using the methods of Sections 6.1 and 6.2 without first making adjustments to give all estimates the same location and scale normalizations. To see how this can be done, let T_n, b_n, and F_n denote the estimates of T, β, and F obtained using the methods of this section. Let T_n^*, b_n^*, and F_n^* denote the estimates using another method. Let b_{n1}^* denote the first component of b_n^*. Then T_n^*, b_n^*, and F_n^* can be adjusted to have the location and scale normalization of T_n, b_n, and F_n by replacing $T_n^*(y)$ with $T_n^{**}(y) = [T_n^*(y) - T_n^*(y_0)]/|b_{n1}^*|$, b_n^* with $b_n^{**} = b_n^*/|b_{n1}^*|$, and $F_n^*(u)$ with $F_n^{**}(u) = F_n^*[|b_{n1}^*|u + T_n^*(y_0)]$.

Now consider the problem of estimating T, β, and F with the normalizations $|\beta_1| = 1$ and $T(y_0) = 0$. Because (6.1) with nonparametric T and F is a semiparametric single-index model, β can be estimated using the methods described in Chapter 2. Let b_n denote the estimator of β. It remains to estimate T and F. Horowitz's (1996) estimators of T and F are derived in Section 6.3.1. The statistical properties of these estimators of T and F are described in Section 6.3.2. Chen (2002) provides only an estimator of T. It is discussed in Section 6.3.3. Section 6.3.4 uses these results to obtain an estimator of the proportional hazards model with unobserved heterogeneity when T, F, and the heterogeneity distribution are all nonparametric.

6.3.1 Derivation of Horowitz's Estimators of T *and* F

This section derives Horowitz's (1996) nonparametric estimators of T and F. Consider, first, the estimation of T. This estimator is derived in two steps. In the first step, T is expressed as a functional of the population distribution of (Y, X). In the second step, unknown population quantities in this functional are replaced with sample analogs.

To take the first step, define $Z = X'\beta$. Z is a continuous random variable because X is assumed to have at least one continuously distributed component with a nonzero β coefficient. Let $G(\cdot|z)$ be the CDF of Y conditional on $Z = z$. Assume that G is differentiable with respect to both of its arguments. Define $G_y(y|z) = \partial G(y|z)/\partial y$ and $G_z(y|z) = \partial G(y|z)/\partial z$. Equation (6.1) implies that

$$G(y|z) = F[T(y) - z].$$

Therefore,

$$G_y(y|z) = T'(y)F'[T(y) - z],$$
$$G_z(y|z) = -F'[T(y) - z],$$

and for any (y, z) such that $G_z(y|z) \neq 0$,

$$T'(y) = -\frac{G_y(y|z)}{G_z(y|z)}.$$

It follows that

$$T(y) = -\int_{y_0}^{y} \frac{G_y(v|z)}{G_z(v|z)} dv \tag{6.57}$$

for any z such that the denominator of the integrand is nonzero over the range of integration.

Now let w be a scalar-valued, nonnegative function on $\mathbb{R}$ with compact support S_w such that (a) the denominator of the integrand in (6.57) is nonzero for all $z \in S_w$ and $v \in [y_0, \ y]$ and (b)

$$\int_{S_w} w(v)dv = 1. \tag{6.58}$$

Then

$$T(y) = -\int_{y_0}^{y} \int_{S_w} w(z) \frac{G_y(v|z)}{G_z(v|z)} dz dv. \tag{6.59}$$

Equation (6.59) is the desired expression for T as a functional of the population distribution of $(Y, \ X)$. This completes the first step of the derivation of the estimator of Horowitz (1996).

The second step of the derivation consists of replacing the unknown quantities on the right-hand side of (6.59) with consistent estimators. The unknown parameter β is replaced with b_n. The unknown function $G(y|z)$ is replaced by a nonparametric kernel estimator, $G_n(y|z)$ of the CDF of Y conditional on $X'b_n = z$. G_z in (6.59) is replaced by $G_{nz} = \partial G_n/\partial z$. G_y is replaced by a kernel estimator, G_{ny}, of the probability density function of Y conditional on $X'b_n = z$. The resulting estimator of $T(y)$ is

$$T_n(y) = -\int_{y_0}^{y} \int_{S_w} w(z) \frac{G_{ny}(v|z)}{G_{nz}(v|z)} dz dv. \tag{6.60}$$

To specify the estimators G_{ny} and G_{nz}, let $\{Y_i, \ X_i : i = 1, \ \ldots, \ n\}$ denote a random sample of $(Y, \ X)$. Define $Z_{ni} = X_i'b_n$. Let K_Y and K_Z be kernel functions of a scalar argument. These are required to satisfy conditions that are stated in Section 6.3.2. Among other things, K_Z must be a higher-order kernel. Let $\{h_{ny}\}$ and $\{h_{nz}\}$ be sequences of bandwidths that converge to zero as $n \to \infty$. Estimate p_Z, the probability density function of Z, by

$$p_{nZ}(z) = \frac{1}{nh_{nz}} \sum_{i=1}^{n} K_Z \left(\frac{Z_{ni} - z}{h_{nz}} \right).$$

The estimator of $G(y|z)$ is

$$G_n(y|z) = \frac{1}{nh_{nz} p_{nZ}(z)} \sum_{i=1}^{n} I(Y_i \leq y) K_Z \left(\frac{Z_{ni} - z}{h_{nz}} \right).$$

The estimator of $G(y|z)$ is

$$G_n(y|z) = \frac{1}{nh_{nz}p_{nZ}(z)} \sum_{i=1}^{n} I(Y_i \le y) K_Z\left(\frac{Z_{ni} - z}{h_{nz}}\right). \tag{6.61}$$

The estimator $G_{nz}(y|z)$ is $\partial G_n(y|z)/\partial z$. $G_y(y|z)$ is the probability density function of Y conditional on $Z = z$. It cannot be estimated by $\partial G_n(y|z)/\partial y$ because $G_n(y|z)$ is a step function of y. Instead, the following kernel density estimator can be used:

$$G_{ny}(y|z) = \frac{1}{nh_{ny}h_{nz}p_{nZ}(z)} \sum_{i=1}^{n} K_Y\left(\frac{Y_i - y}{h_{ny}}\right) K_Z\left(\frac{Z_{ni} - z}{h_{nz}}\right). \tag{6.62}$$

T_n is obtained by substituting (6.61) and (6.62) into (6.60).

Kernel estimators converge in probability at rates slower than $n^{-1/2}$ (see the Appendix). Therefore, $G_{ny}(y|z)/G_{nz}(y|z)$ is not $n^{-1/2}$-consistent for $G_y(y|z)/G_z(y|z)$. However, integration over z and v in (6.59) creates an averaging effect that causes the integral and, therefore, T_n to converge at the rate $n^{-1/2}$. This is the reason for basing the estimator on (6.59) instead of (6.57). As was discussed in Chapter 2, a similar averaging effect takes place in density-weighted average-derivative estimation of β in a single-index model and enables density-weighted average-derivative estimators to converge at the rate $n^{-1/2}$. The formal statistical properties of T_n are discussed in Section 6.3.2.

Now consider the estimation of F. As in the estimation of T, the derivation of the estimator takes place in two steps. The first step is to express F as a functional of T and the population distribution of (Y, X). The second step is to replace unknown population quantities in this expression with estimators. To take the first step, observe that because U is independent of X, $P(U \le u | a < Z \le b) = F(u)$ for any u and any a and b in the support of Z. Therefore, in particular, for any points y_1 and y_2 that are in the support of Y and satisfy $y_2 < y_1$,

$$\begin{aligned} F(u) &= P[U \le u | T(y_2) - u < Z \le T(y_1) - u] \\ &= A(u)/B(u), \end{aligned} \tag{6.63}$$

where

$$A(u) = E\{I(U \le u) I[T(y_2) - u < Z \le T(y_1) - u]\} \tag{6.64}$$

and

$$B(u) = E\{I[T(y_2) - u < Z \le T(y_1) - u]\}. \tag{6.65}$$

Equations (6.63)–(6.65) provide the desired expression for F in terms of T and the population distribution of (Y, X).

The estimator of F is obtained by replacing the unknown quantities in (6.63)–(6.65) with sample analogs. To do this, define $U_{ni} = T_n(Y_i) - Z_{ni}$, where $T_n(y)$ is replaced with an arbitrarily large negative number if $y < y_2$ and an arbitrarily large positive number if $y > y_1$. The estimator of $F(u)$ is

$$F_n(u) = A_n(u)/B_n(u), \tag{6.66}$$

where

$$A_n(u) = n^{-1} \sum_{i=1}^{n} I(U_{ni} \le u) I[T_n(y_2) - u < Z_{ni} \le T_n(y_1) - u]$$

and

$$B_n(u) = n^{-1} \sum_{i=1}^{n} I[T_n(y_2) - u < Z_{ni} \le T_n(y_1) - u].$$

The statistical properties of F_n are discussed in Section 6.3.2.

It may seem that F can be estimated more simply by the empirical distribution function of $U_n = T_n(Y) - X'b_n$, but this is not the case. T can be estimated $n^{-1/2}$-consistently only over a compact interval $[y_2, \ y_1]$ that is a proper subset of the support of Y. This is because T may be unbounded at the boundaries of the support of Y (e.g., if the support of Y is $[0, \ \infty)$ and $T(y) = \log y$) and G_z is likely to be zero on the boundaries. Therefore, $T_n(Y)$ and U_n are $n^{-1/2}$-consistently estimated only if $Y \in [y_2, \ y_1]$. In effect, F must be estimated from censored observations of U. The empirical distribution function of U_n is not a consistent estimator of F when there is censoring. Equation (6.66) provides an estimator that is consistent despite censoring.

6.3.2 Asymptotic Properties of $\mathbf{T_n}$ *and* $\mathbf{F_n}$

This section gives conditions under which Horowitz's (1996) T_n and F_n are consistent for T and F, and $n^{1/2}(T_n - T)$ and $n^{1/2}(F_n - F)$ converge weakly to mean-zero Gaussian processes.

The following notation will be used. Let $\tilde{X}$ be a vector consisting of all components of X except the first. Define $d = \dim(X)$. Let β_1 denote the first component of β and $\tilde{\beta}$ denote the $(d-1) \times 1$ vector of the remaining components. Let b_{n1} and $\tilde{b}_n$, respectively, denote the estimators of β_1 and $\tilde{\beta}$. Because $\beta_1 = \pm 1$ and $b_{n1} = \pm 1$ by scale normalization, $b_{n1} = \beta_1$ with probability approaching 1 as $n \to \infty$. Therefore, for purposes of obtaining the asymptotic distributions of $n^{1/2}(T_n - T)$ and $n^{1/2}(F_n - F)$, it can be assumed that $b_{n1} = \beta_1$. Let $p_Z(\cdot|\tilde{x})$ denote the probability density function of Z conditional on $\tilde{X} = \tilde{x}$. Let $r \ge 6$ and $s \ge 2$ be integers. Make the following assumptions:

HT1: $\{Y_i, \ X_i : i = 1, \ \ldots, \ n\}$ is an independent random sample of $(Y, \ X)$ in (6.1).

HT2: (a) $|\beta_1| = 1$. (b) The distribution of the first component of X conditional on $\tilde{X} = \tilde{x}$ has a probability density with respect to Lebesgue measure for every $\tilde{x}$ in the support of $\tilde{X}$. (c) $\tilde{X}$ has bounded support.

HT3: (a) U is independent of X and has a probability density with respect to Lebesgue measure. (b) Let f be the probability density function of U. There is an open subset I_U of the support of U such that $\sup\{f(u):u \in I_U\} < \infty$, $\inf\{f(u):u \in I_U\} > 0$, and the derivatives $d^k f(u)/du^k$ $(k = 1, \ldots, r+s)$ exist and are uniformly bounded over I_U.

HT4: T is a strictly increasing, differentiable function everywhere on the support of Y.

HT5: There are open intervals of the real line, I_Y and I_Z, such that (a) $y_0 \in I_Y$. (b) $y \in I_Y$ and $z \in I_Z$ implies $T(y) - z \in I_U$. (c) $p_Z(z)$ and $p_Z(z|\tilde{x})$ are bounded uniformly over $z \in I_Z$ and $\tilde{x}$ in the support of $\tilde{X}$. Moreover, $\inf\{p_Z(z):z \in I_Z\} > 0$. (d) The derivatives $d^k p_Z(z)/dz^k$ and $\partial^k p_Z(z|\tilde{x})/\partial z^k$ $(k = 1, \ldots, r+1)$ exist and are uniformly bounded for all $z \in I_Z$ and $\tilde{x}$ in the support of $\tilde{X}$. (e) $T(y_0) = 0$, and $\sup\{T(y):y \in I_Y\} < \infty$. For $k = 1, \ldots, r+1$, the derivatives $dT^k(y)/dy^k$ exist and are uniformly bounded over $y \in I_Y$.

HT6: S_w is compact, $S_w \in I_Z$, (6.59) holds, and $d^k w(z)/dz^k$ $(k = 1, \ldots, r+1)$ exists and is bounded for all $z \in I_Z$.

HT7: There is a $(d-1) \times 1$ vector-valued function $\Omega(y, x)$ such that $E\Omega(Y, X) = 0$, the components of $E[\Omega(Y, X)\Omega(Y, X)']$ are finite, and as $n \to \infty$

$$n^{1/2}(\tilde{b}_n - \tilde{\beta}) = n^{-1/2} \sum_{i=1}^{n} \Omega(Y_i, X_i) + o_p(1).$$

HT8: K_Y has support $[-1,1]$, is bounded and symmetrical about 0, has bounded variation, and satisfies

$$\int_{-1}^{1} v^j K_Y(v)dv = \begin{cases} 1 \text{ if } j = 0 \\ 0 \text{ if } 1 \le j \le s-1. \end{cases}$$

K_Z has support $[-1,1]$, is bounded and symmetrical about 0, has bounded variation, and satisfies

$$\int_{-1}^{1} v^j K_Z(v)dv = \begin{cases} 1 \text{ if } j = 0 \\ 0 \text{ if } 1 \le j \le r-1. \end{cases}$$

K_Z is everywhere twice differentiable. The derivatives are bounded and have bounded variation. The second derivative satisfies $|K_Z''(v_1) - K_Z''(v_2)| \le M\,|v_1 - v_2|$ for some $M < \infty$.

HT9: As $n \to \infty$, $nh_{nz}^{2r} \to 0$, $nh_{ny}^{2s} \to 0$, $(nh_{nz}^8)^{-1} \to 0$, and $(\log n)/(n^{1/2}h_{ny}^{1/2}h_{nz}^8) \to 0$.

Assumptions HT1–HT6 specify the model and establish smoothness conditions implying, among other things, that G_y and G_z exist. Assumption HT7 is satisfied by all of the estimators of β discussed in Chapter 2. Assumption HT8 requires K_Z but not K_Y to be a higher-order kernel. A higher-order kernel is needed for K_Z because

G_{nz} is a functional of derivatives of K_Z. Derivative functionals converge relatively slowly, and the higher-order kernel for K_Z is needed to ensure sufficiently rapid convergence. Assumptions HT8 and HT9 are satisfied, for example, if K_Y is a second-order kernel, K_Z is a sixth-order kernel, $h_{ny} \propto n^{-1/3}$, and $h_{nz} \propto n^{-1/10}$.

The following theorems give the asymptotic properties of T_n and F_n:

Theorem 6.4: *Let* $[y_2, y_1] \in I_Y$. *Under assumptions HT1–HT9:*

(a) $\operatorname*{plim}_{n \to \infty} \sup_{y_2 \le y \le y_1} |T_n(y) - T(y)| = 0.$

(b) *For* $y \in [y_2, y_1]$, $n^{1/2}(T_n - T)$ *converges weakly to a tight, mean-zero Gaussian process.* ■

Theorem 6.5: *Let* $[u_0, u_1] \in I_U$ *and* $P[T(y_2) - u < Z \le T(y_1) - u] > 0$ *whenever* $u \in [u_0, u_1]$. *Under assumptions HT1–HT9:*

(a) $\operatorname*{plim}_{n \to \infty} \sup_{u_0 \le u \le u_1} |F_n(u) - F(u)| = 0.$

(b) *For* $u \in [u_0, u_1]$, $n^{1/2}(F_n - F)$ *converges weakly to a tight, mean-zero Gaussian process.* ■

Parts (a) of Theorems 6.3 and 6.4 establish uniform consistency of T_n and F_n. Parts (b) show, among other things, that the rates of convergence in probability of $T_n(y)$ and $F_n(u)$ are $n^{-1/2}$ and that the centered, normalized forms of T_n and F_n are asymptotically normally distributed. The expressions for the covariance functions of the limiting stochastic processes of $n^{1/2}(T_n - T)$ and $n^{1/2}(F_n - F)$ are very lengthy. They are given in Horowitz (1996) together with methods for estimating the covariance functions consistently.

The proofs of Theorems 6.3 and 6.4 are also given in Horowitz (1996). The proofs rely heavily on empirical process methods described by Pollard (1984). Roughly speaking, the proofs begin by using Taylor-series expansions to approximate $T_n - T$ by an integral of a linear functional of kernel estimators and to approximate $F_n - F$ by a linear functional of $A_n - A$ and $B_n - B$. In a second step, it is shown that these approximating functionals can, themselves, be approximated by empirical processes. Finally, uniform laws of large numbers and functional central limit theorems (central limit theorems for sums of random functions instead of sums of random variables) are used to establish the conclusions of the theorem.

6.3.3 Chen's Estimator of T

This section presents Chen's (2002) estimator of T. Chen (2002) does not provide an estimator of F, though it is likely that one can be derived by using methods similar to those used in the derivation of Horowitz's F_n.

As before, normalize T so that $T(y_0) = 0$ for some y_0 in the support of Y. Let $\{Y_i, X_i : i = 1, \ldots, n\}$ be a simple random sample of (Y, X). To motivate

Chen's estimator, define $d_{iy} = I(Y_i \geq y)$ for any y in the support of Y. Define $d_{iy_0} = I(Y_i \geq y_0)$. Then $d_{iy} = I[X_i'\beta + U_i \geq T(y)]$ and $E(d_{iy}|X_i) = 1 - F[T(y) - X_i'\beta]$. Therefore, $E(d_{iy} - d_{jy_0}|X_i, X_j) \geq 0$ if and only if $X_i'\beta - X_j'\beta \geq T(y)$ and $i \neq j$. This suggests that if β were known, $T(y)$ could be estimated by solving the problem

$$\underset{t}{\text{maximize}}: \frac{1}{n(n-1)} \sum_{i=1}^{n} \sum_{\substack{j=1 \\ j \neq i}}^{n} (d_{iy} - d_{jy_0}) I(X_i'\beta - X_j'\beta \geq t).$$

Chen (2002) obtains a feasible estimator by replacing the unknown β with an estimator, b_n, such as one of the estimators described in Chapter 2. Thus, Chen's estimator of $T(y)$ is

$$T_n(y) = \arg \max_{t \in M} \frac{1}{n(n-1)} \sum_{i=1}^{n} \sum_{\substack{j=1 \\ j \neq i}}^{n} (d_{iy} - d_{jy_0}) I(X_i'b_n - X_j'b_n \geq t), \tag{6.67}$$

where M is a suitable compact interval (see Assumption 3 below), $y \in [y_2, y_1]$, and $[y_2, y_1]$ is contained in the support of Y.

To obtain the asymptotic distributional properties of Chen's (2002) estimator, define $Z = X'\beta$, and make the following assumptions.

CT1: $\{Y_i, X_i\}$ is an independent random sample of (Y, X) in (6.1) and U is independent of X.

CT2: (i) $|\beta_1| = 1$. (ii) The distribution of the first component of X conditional on $\tilde{X}$ is absolutely continuous with respect to Lebesgue measure. (iii) The support of the distribution of X is not contained in any proper linear subspace of $\mathbb{R}^d$, where $d = \dim(X)$.

CT3: (i) T is strictly increasing, and $T(y_0) = 0$. (ii) $[T(y_2 - \varepsilon), T(y_1 + \varepsilon)] \in M$ for some $\varepsilon > 0$; compact interval M; and y_0, y_1, and y_2 in the support of Y.

CT4: (i) The density of Z conditional on $\tilde{X} = \tilde{x}$, $p_Z(z|\tilde{x})$, is twice continuously differentiable with respect of z. The derivative is uniformly bounded. (ii) The density of U is twice continuously differentiable with a uniformly bounded derivative. (iii) $\tilde{X}$ has finite third-order moments.

Define

$$h(y^{(1)}, x^{(1)}, y^{(2)}, x^{(2)}, y, t, b) = [I(y^{(1)} \geq y) - I(y^{(2)} \geq y_0)] I(x^{(1)\prime}b - x^{(2)\prime}b \geq t)$$

and

$$\tau(\bar{y}, \bar{x}, y, t, b) = E[h(\bar{y}, \bar{x}, Y, X, y, t, b) - h(Y, X, \bar{y}, \bar{x}, y, t, b)].$$

CT5: $V(y) \equiv 0.5E\{\partial^2 \tau[Y, X, y, T(y), \beta]/\partial t^2\} < 0$, and $V(y)$ is bounded away from 0 for $y \in [y_2, y_1]$.

CT6: $n^{1/2}(b_n - \beta) = O_p(1)$.

Now define $J_{y_0,y}(Y, X) = -V(y)^{-1}\partial^2\tau[Y, X, y, T(y), \beta]/\partial t^2$. The following theorem, which is proved in Chen (2002), gives the asymptotic distributional properties of T_n.

Theorem 6.6: *Let assumptions CT1–CT6 hold. Then*

(a) $\underset{n \to \infty}{\text{plim}} \sup_{y_2 \le y \le y_1} |T_n(y) - T(y)| = 0.$

(b) For $y \in [y_2, y_1]$, $n^{1/2}(T_n - T)$ *converges weakly to a mean-zero Gaussian process,* $H_T(y)$, *whose covariance function is* $EH_T(y)H_T(y') = EJ_{y_0,y}(Y, X) J_{y_0,y'}(Y, X)$.■

Chen (2002) gives a method for estimating the covariance function, thereby making inference with his estimator possible. Chen (2002) also presents the results of Monte Carlo experiments comparing the finite-sample performances of his estimator and several others, including that of Horowitz (1996). Depending on the design and the value of y, either estimator can have the smaller mean-square error. Horowitz's estimator tends to have the smaller mean-square error when y is near the center of the data, and Chen's has the smaller mean-square error further from the center. At present, no known estimator is asymptotically efficient in the sense of minimizing the asymptotic mean-square error uniformly over y.

6.3.4 The Proportional Hazards Model with Unobserved Heterogeneity

This section is concerned with estimating the proportional hazards model with unobserved heterogeneity, model (6.37), when the baseline hazard function, λ_0, and the distribution of the unobserved heterogeneity variable, V, are both unknown. The discussion in this section is based on Horowitz (1999), who shows how to estimate Λ_0, λ_0, and the distribution of V in this model.

As was discussed in Section 6.2.2, (6.37) is equivalent to

$$\log \Lambda_0(Y) = X'\beta + V + U, \tag{6.68}$$

where U is a random variable that is independent of X and V and whose CDF is $F(u) = 1 - \exp\ (e^{-u})$. Because (6.68) continues to hold if a constant is added to both sides, a location normalization is needed to make identification possible. This is accomplished here by setting $\Lambda_0(y_0) = 1$ for some finite $y_0 > 0$. Elbers and Ridder (1982) showed that model (6.68) is identified if $Ee^{-V} < \infty$. For reasons that are explained later in this section, the estimator developed here is based on the stronger assumption that $Ee^{-3V} < \infty$.

Model (6.68) is closely related to the transformation model of Sections 6.3.1–6.3.3. To see the relation, write the transformation model in the form

$$T(Y) = X'\alpha + W, \tag{6.69}$$

where T is an unknown increasing function, the random variable W is independent of X and has an unknown CDF F_W, and α is a vector of parameters whose first component, α_1, is normalized to satisfy $|\alpha_1| = 1$. Models (6.68) and (6.69) are related by $T(y) = (1/\sigma)\log \Lambda_0(y)$ and $W = (V + U)/\sigma$, where $\sigma = |\beta_1|$. Thus, (6.68) is a rescaled version of the transformation model (6.69).

Now observe that $\Lambda_0(y) = \exp[\sigma T(y)]$ and $\lambda_0(y) = \sigma T'(y)\exp[\sigma T(y)]$. Let T_n be a consistent estimator of T_n, such as one of the estimators discussed in Sections 6.3.1, 6.3.2, and 6.3.3. Suppose a consistent estimator of σ, σ_n, is available. Then, Λ_0 is estimated consistently by

$$\Lambda_{n0}(y) = \exp[\sigma_n T_n(y)]. \tag{6.70}$$

If T_n is differentiable, then λ_0 is estimated consistently by

$$\lambda_{n0}(y) = \sigma_n T_n'(y)\exp[\sigma_n T_n(y)]. \tag{6.71}$$

To develop an estimator of σ, define $Z = X'\alpha$ in (6.69). Assume that Z is a continuously distributed random variable with probability density function p_Z. Let $G(\cdot|z)$ be the CDF of Y conditional on $Z = z$. Define $G_z(\cdot|z) = \partial G(\cdot|z)/\partial z$. The estimator of σ will be developed in two steps. The first step is to express σ as a functional of G, G_z, and p_Z. The second step is to replace G, G_z, and p_Z in this functional with consistent estimators.

To express σ as a functional of G, G_z, and p_Z, let $z = x'\alpha$ and F_V denote the CDF of V. Write (6.37) in the form

$$\lambda(y|z,\ v) = \lambda_0(y)\exp[-(\sigma z + v)]. \tag{6.72}$$

Since

$$\lambda(y|z,\ v) = \frac{1}{1 - P(Y \le y|Z = z,\ V = v)}\frac{dP(Y \le y|Z = z,\ V = v)}{dy},$$

it follows from integration of (6.72) that

$$G(y|z) = 1 - \int \exp[-\Lambda_0(y)e^{-(\sigma z + v)}]dF_V(v). \tag{6.73}$$

and

$$G_z(y|z) = -\sigma\Lambda_0(y)\int e^{-(\sigma z + v)}\exp[-\Lambda_0(y)e^{-(\sigma z + v)}]dF_V(v). \tag{6.74}$$

Now define $\sigma(y)$ by

$$\sigma(y) = \frac{\int G_z(y|z)p_Z(z)^2 dz}{\int G(y|z)p_Z(z)^2 dz}. \tag{6.75}$$

By applying l'Hospital's rule to the right-hand side of (6.75), it may be shown that if $\Lambda_0(y) > 0$ for all $y > 0$, then

$$\sigma = \lim_{y \to 0} \sigma(y). \tag{6.76}$$

Equation (6.76) is the desired expression for σ in terms of G, G_z, and p_Z.

The second estimation step consists of replacing G, G_z, and p_Z in (6.76) with consistent estimators. To do this, let K be a kernel function and $\{h_n : n = 1,2, \ldots\}$ be a sequence of bandwidth parameters that converges to 0 as $n \to \infty$. Observe that (6.69) is a single-index model. Accordingly, let α_n be a consistent estimator of α, such as one of the estimators discussed in Chapter 2. Let the data be the random sample $\{Y_j, X_j : j = 1, \ldots, n\}$. In this section, the letter j is used to index observations because i is used later to denote the imaginary number $\sqrt{-1}$. Define $Z_{nj} = X_j'\alpha_n$. Define the following kernel estimators of p_Z, G, and G_z, respectively.

$$p_{nZ}(z) = (nh_n)^{-1} \sum_{j=1}^{n} K\left(\frac{z - Z_{nj}}{h_n}\right), \tag{6.77}$$

$$G_n(y|z) = [nh_n p_{nZ}(z)]^{-1} \sum_{j=1}^{n} I(Y_i \le y) K\left(\frac{z - Z_{nj}}{h_n}\right), \tag{6.78}$$

and

$$G_{nz}(t|z) = \partial G_n(t|z)/\partial z. \tag{6.79}$$

Now define

$$\sigma_n(y) = -\frac{\int G_{nz}(y|z) p_{nZ}(z)^2 dz}{\int G_n(y|z) p_{nZ}(z)^2 dz}. \tag{6.80}$$

Let $\{y_n : n = 1,2, \ldots\}$ be a sequence of positive numbers that converges to 0. If the convergence takes place at a suitable rate, then $\sigma_n(y_n) \xrightarrow{p} \sigma$ (Horowitz 1999). Thus, $\sigma_n(y_n)$ is a consistent estimator of σ. However, the fastest possible rate of convergence of this estimator is $n^{-1/3}$.

Under the assumption that $Ee^{-3V} < \infty$, it is possible to modify the estimator (6.80) so that its rate of convergence is arbitrarily close to $n^{-2/5}$ and its asymptotic distribution is normal with mean 0. Ishwaran (1996) shows that $n^{-2/5}$ is the fastest possible rate of convergence under the assumption that $Ee^{-3V} < \infty$. (Ridder and Woutersen (2003) show that a convergence rate of $n^{-1/2}$ is achievable in at least some cases if $\lambda_0(t)$ is known to be bounded away from 0 and ∞ near $t = 0$. Ishwaran (1996) does not make this assumption, and it is not made here.) The modification is based on a bias-reduction method that was proposed by Schucany and Sommers (1977) for nonparametric density estimation and extended to nonparametric regression by Härdle (1986) and Bierens (1987). To obtain the modified estimator of σ, let q and δ satisfy $1/5 < q < 1/4$ and $1/(2q) - 3/2 < \delta < 1$. Let $\{y_{n1}\}$ and $\{y_{n2}\}$ be sequences such that $\Lambda_0(y_{n1}) = cn^{-q}$ for some finite $c > 0$ and $\Lambda_0(y_{n2}) = cn^{-\delta q}$. The modified estimator is

$$\sigma_n = \frac{\sigma_n(y_{n1}) - n^{-q(1-\delta)}\sigma_n(y_{n2})}{1 - n^{-q(1-\delta)}}. \tag{6.81}$$

Now let Λ_{n0} and λ_{n0} be the estimators of Λ_0 and λ_0 that are obtained by substituting σ_n in (6.81) into (6.70) and (6.71). Let $\tilde{X}$ denote all components of X except the first. To obtain the asymptotic distributional properties of σ_n, Λ_{n0}, and λ_{n0}, make the following assumptions.

PHU1: $\{Y_j, X_j : j = 1, \ldots, n\}$ is an independent random sample of (Y, X) in model (6.37).

PHU2: (i) X has bounded support. (ii) The distribution of the first component of X conditional on $\tilde{X} = \tilde{x}$ has a bounded probability density function for every $\tilde{x}$ in the support of $\tilde{X}$. (iii) The probability density function of Z is seven times continuously differentiable everywhere. The probability density function of Z conditional on $\tilde{X} = \tilde{x}$, $p_Z(z|\tilde{x})$, is everywhere seven times continuously differentiable with respect to z for all $\tilde{x}$ in the support of $\tilde{X}$.

The assumption that X has bounded support can be relaxed at the price of increased technical complexity of the derivation of the asymptotic distributional properties of the estimators.

PHU3: (i) V is independent of X. (ii) $Ee^{-3V} < \infty$.

The weaker assumption $Ee^{-V} < \infty$ ensures identification of σ, Λ_0, and λ_0 (Elbers and Ridder (1982), Heckman and Singer (1984a)), but the fastest possible rate of convergence of an estimator of σ under this assumption is $(\log n)^{-1}$ (Ishwaran 1996), whereas σ_n in (6.81) converges at a rate that is arbitrarily close to $n^{-2/5}$ when Assumption PHU3(ii) holds.

PHU4: (i) $n^{1/2}(\alpha_n - \alpha) = O_p(1)$ as $n \to \infty$. (ii) $\Lambda_0(y) > 0$ for all $y > 0$, $\lambda_0(y) > 0$ for all $y > 0$ in the support of Y, y_0 is an interior point of the support of Y, and Λ_0 has three bounded derivatives on an open interval $I_Y \in (0, \infty)$ containing y_0. (iii) For any $a > 0$ and closed interval $[y_a, y_b] \in I_Y$, $n^{2/5-a}[T_n(y) - T(y)] \to^p 0$ and $n^{2/5-a}[T_n'(y) - T'(y)] \to^p 0$ as $n \to \infty$ uniformly over $y \in [y_a, y_b]$.

PHU5: K has support $[-1,1]$ and is of bounded variation, continuously differentiable everywhere, and symmetrical about 0. In addition

$$\int_{-1}^{1} v^j K(v)dv = \begin{cases} 1 \text{ if } j = 0 \\ 0 \text{ if } 1 \le j \le 3 \end{cases}.$$

PHU6: The bandwidth satisfies $h_n \propto n^{-\kappa}$, where $5/32 < \kappa < 6/32$.

Now define $D(y) = E[G(y|Z)p_Z(Z)]$ and

$$\Omega = \frac{E\{e^{-\sigma Z}[2p_Z'(Z) - \sigma p_Z(Z)]\}}{E[e^{-\sigma Z}p(Z)]}.$$

Assumption PHU4(i) is satisfied by the single-index estimators discussed in Chapter 2. Assumption PHU4(iii) is satisfied by Horowitz's (1996) estimator of T. Assumption PHU5 requires K to be a higher-order kernel.

Define $\tilde{y}$ as the solution to $\Lambda_0(y) = e^{-1}$ and $\tilde{y}_n$ as the solution to $\Lambda_{n0}(y) = e^{-1}$. Let $\{y_{n1}\}$ and $\{y_{n2}\}$ be nonstochastic sequences of positive numbers that satisfy $D(y_{n1}) = cn^{-q}$ and $D(y_{n2}) = cn^{-\delta q}$ for some finite $c > 0$, where $1/5 < q < 1/4$ and $1/(2q) - 3/2 < \delta < 1$.

The following theorem, which is proved in Horowitz (1999), gives the asymptotic distributional properties of σ_n, Λ_{n0}, and λ_{n0}.

Theorem 6.7: *Let assumptions PHU1–PHU6 hold. Then the following hold as* $n \to \infty$.

(a) $n^{(1-q)/2}(\sigma_n - \sigma) \xrightarrow{d} N(0, c^{-1}\Omega)$.

(b) $n^{(1-q)/2}[\Lambda_{n0}(y) - \Lambda_0(y)] = \sigma^{-1}\Lambda_0(y)\log[\Lambda_0(y)]n^{(1-q)/2}(\sigma_n - \sigma) + o_p(1)$ *uniformly over* $y \in [y_a, y_b]$, *and* $\Lambda_{n0}(y_0) = \Lambda_0(y_0) = 1$.

(c) $n^{(1-q)/2}[\lambda_{n0}(y) - \lambda_0(y)] = \sigma^{-1}\lambda_0(y)[1 + \log \Lambda_0(y)]n^{(1-d)/2}(\sigma_n - \sigma) + O_p\{n^{(1-q)/2}[T_n'(y) - T'(y)]\}$ *uniformly over* $y \in [y_a, y_b]$.

(d) $n^{(1-q)/2}(\tilde{y}_n - \tilde{y}) = -[e\sigma\lambda_0(\tilde{y})]^{-1}n^{(1-q)/2}(\sigma_n - \sigma) + o_p(1)$ ■.

Part (a) of Theorem 6.7 implies that the rate of convergence in probability of σ_n to σ can be made arbitrarily close to $n^{-2/5}$ by making q close to $1/5$. Parts (a) and (b) together imply that $n^{(1-q)/2}[\Lambda_{n0}(y) - \Lambda_0(y)]$ is asymptotically normally distributed with mean 0. Parts (a) and (c) imply that the same is true of $n^{(1-q)/2}[\lambda_{n0}(y) - \lambda_0(y)]$ if $y \neq \tilde{y}$. However, $\lambda_{n0}(\tilde{y}) - \lambda_0(\tilde{y})$ converges at the same rate as $T_n'(\tilde{y}) - T(\tilde{y})$, which is typically faster than $n^{-(1-q)/2}$. The singular point is estimated consistently by $\tilde{y}_n$. A confidence interval for $\tilde{y}$ can be obtained by combining parts (a) and (d) of the theorem.

Theorem 6.7 provides a way to obtain uniform confidence bands for Λ_0 and λ_0. To illustrate, consider λ_0. Let $\xi_{a/2}$ be the $1 - a/2$ quantile of the standard normal distribution and let Ω_n be a consistent estimator of Ω. The following is an asymptotic $(1 - a)$ confidence interval for $\lambda_0(y)$ that is uniform over any closed subset of $[y_a, y_b]$ that excludes $\tilde{y}$:

$$\begin{aligned}\lambda_{n0}(y) - \xi_{a/2}\frac{\lambda_{n0}(y)|1 + \log \Lambda_{n0}(y)|\Omega_n^{1/2}}{\sigma_n[cn^{(1-q)/2}]^{1/2}} &\leq \lambda_0(y) \\ \leq \lambda_{n0}(y) + \xi_{a/2}\frac{\lambda_{n0}(y)|1 + \log \Lambda_{n0}(y)|\Omega_n^{1/2}}{\sigma_n[cn^{(1-q)/2}]^{1/2}}&. \end{aligned} \tag{6.82}$$

Inequality (6.82) provides a way to test hypotheses about the shape of λ_0. For example, the hypothesis that λ_0 is strictly increasing is rejected at the asymptotic a level if no strictly increasing function lies completely inside (6.82) for all y in the subset of $[y_a, y_b]$.

The following theorem provides a consistent estimator of Ω.

Theorem 6.8: *Define* $\Omega_n = A_n(y_{n1})/D_n(y_{n1})$, *where*

$$A_n(y) = \int G_n(y|z)[2p'_{nZ}(z) - \sigma_n p_{nZ}(z)]^2 p_{nZ}(z)dz,$$
$$D_n(y) = \int G_n(y|z)p_{nZ}(z)^2 dz, \tag{6.83}$$

and y_{n1} *is as in Theorem* 6.7. *Under assumptions PHU1–PHU6,* $\Omega_n \to^p \Omega$.■

The next theorem provides a data-based method for selecting sequences $\{y_{n1}\}$ and $\{y_{n2}\}$ that satisfy the rate-of-convergence requirements of Theorem 6.7.

Theorem 6.9: *Define* D_n *as in* (6.83). *Let assumptions PHU1–PHU6 hold. Let* c, d, *and* δ *satisfy the assumptions of Theorem* 6.7. *Let* $\hat{y}_{n1}$ *and* $\hat{y}_{n2}$ *satisfy* $\hat{y}_{n1} = \inf\{y{:}D_n(y) \geq cn^{-d}\}$ *and* $\hat{y}_{n2} = \inf\{y{:}D_n(y) \geq cn^{-\delta d}\}$. *Then the conclusions of Theorems 6.7 and 6.8 hold with* $\hat{y}_{n1}$ *and* $\hat{y}_{n2}$ *in place of* y_{n1} *and* y_{n2}.■

Current theory does not provide a method for selecting c, d, and δ in applications. It is likely, however, that these parameters can be selected by using the bootstrap. Specifically, these tuning parameters might be selected by minimizing the estimate of the integrated mean-square error of Λ_0 or λ_0 that is obtained by repeatedly resampling the data randomly with replacement. To illustrate, consider Λ_0. Let $\Lambda_{n0}^{(m)}$ be the estimate of Λ_0 that is obtained from the m th out of M resamples. The estimated integrated mean-square error is

$$EIMSE = M^{-1} \sum_{m=1}^{M} \int_{y_a}^{y_b} [\Lambda_{n0}^{(m)}(y) - \Lambda_0(y)]^2 dy.$$

It is also possible to estimate the density of V, f_V, if V is continuously distributed. To see how this is done, suppose for the moment that Λ_0 and β are known. Define $W = \log \Lambda_0(Y) - X'\beta$. Then $W = V + U$. Let $W_j = \log \Lambda_0(Y_j) - X_j'\beta$ $(j = 1, \ldots, n)$ denote "observations" of W. The distribution of U is known, so estimating f_V is a problem in deconvolution. Deconvolution is discussed in Section 5.1, and the methods of that section can be used to estimate f_V under the (temporary) assumption that W is observable. To do this, let ψ_U denote the characteristic function of U, that is the characteristic function of a random variable whose CDF is $F_U(u) = 1 - \exp(-e^u)$. Let $\tilde{\psi}_{nW}$ denote the empirical characteristic function of W. That is,

$$\tilde{\psi}_{nW}(t) = n^{-1} \sum_{j=1}^{n} \exp(itW_j),$$

where $i = \sqrt{-1}$. Let ψ_ζ be a bounded, real characteristic function with support $[-1,1]$. Finally, let $\{h_n\}$ be a sequence of positive constants that converges to 0 as $n \to \infty$. Then, as is explained in Section 5.1, $f_V(v)$ is estimated consistently by

$$\tilde{f}_{nV}(v) = (2\pi)^{-1} \int_{-\infty}^{\infty} e^{-ivt} [\tilde{\psi}_{nW}(t)\psi_\zeta(h_n t)/\psi_U(t)]dt. \tag{6.84}$$

Now return to model (6.37). Since Λ_0 and β are unknown in this model, the W_js are not observed and $\tilde{\psi}_{nW}$ is not a feasible estimator of the characteristic function of W. W_j can be estimated, however, by $\sigma_n[T_n(Y_j) - Z_{nj}]$. The characteristic function of W can then be estimated by

$$\psi_{nW}(t) = n^{-1}\sum_{j=1}^{n}[\exp(itW_{nj})]I(\tau_{n1} \leq Y_j \leq \tau_{n2}), \tag{6.85}$$

where $0 < \tau_{n1} < \tau_{n2} < \infty$, $\tau_{n1} \to 0$ as $n \to \infty$, and $\tau_{n2} \to \infty$ as $n \to \infty$. The trimming factor $I(\tau_{n1} \leq Y_j \leq \tau_{n2})$ is needed because $T(0) = -\infty$ and $T(\infty) = \infty$ in the proportional hazard model. Therefore, $T(y)$ cannot be estimated consistently uniformly over $0 \leq y < \infty$, and very small and large values of Y must be trimmed away to obtain a consistent estimator of f_V. The resulting estimator is

$$f_{nV}(v) = (2\pi)^{-1}\int_{-\infty}^{\infty} e^{-ivt}[\psi_{nW}(t)\psi_{\zeta}(h_n t)/\psi_U(t)]dt. \tag{6.86}$$

To obtain asymptotic properties of f_{nV}, define $Q = e^{-V}$, and let f_Q be the probability density function of Q. Make the following assumptions in addition to assumptions PHU1–PHU6.

PHU7: ψ_{ζ} is a bounded, real characteristic function with support $[-1,1]$ and two bounded derivatives in a neighborhood of 0.

PHU8: (i) V has a probability density function that is twice continuously differentiable on an open interval $I_V \subset (-\infty, \infty)$. (ii) There are finite constants $q_0 > 0$, $s \geq 0$, $a_1 > 0$, and $a_2 \geq a_1$ such that $a_1 q^s \leq f_Q(q) \leq a_2 q^s$ whenever $0 \leq q \leq q_0$.

Assumption PHU7 is satisfied, for example, by letting ψ_{ζ} be the fourfold convolution of the $U[-1/4,1/4]$ density with itself. Assumption PHU8 is satisfied, for example, if Q has the gamma distribution as is frequently assumed in parametric models of unobserved heterogeneity.

The following theorem, which is proved in Horowitz (1999), establishes the consistency and rate of convergence in probability of f_{nV}.

Theorem 6.10: *Let assumptions PHU1–PHU8 hold. Let* $\tau_{n1} = \inf\{\tau : D_n(\tau) \geq c_1 n^{-2/15}\}$ *for some finite* $c_1 > 0$ *and* $\tau_{n2} = \inf\{\tau : D_n(\tau) \geq 1 - c_2 n^{-2/15}\}$ *for some finite* $c_2 > 0$. *Set* $h_n = (c_3 \log n)^{-1}$, *where* $0 < c_3 < 4/(15\pi)$. *Then* $f_{nV}(v) - f_V(v) = O_p[(\log n)^{-2}]$ *pointwise and uniformly over any compact subset of* I_U.■

Currently available theory does not provide a method for selecting specific values of the c_js in applications. As is often the case in deconvolution (see Section 5.1), the rate of convergence of f_{nV} is slow. Nonetheless, the results of Monte Carlo experiments reported in Horowitz (1999) show that estimates of f_V having the same general shape as the true f_V can be obtained from samples of size 1000, which is smaller than the sample sizes in many economic applications.

6.4 Predicting Y Conditional on X

This section discusses how b_n, T_n, and F_n can be used to make predictions of Y conditional on X. The most familiar predictor of Y conditional on $X = x$ is a consistent estimator of $E(Y|X = x)$. Because (6.1) is a single-index model, an estimator of $E(Y|X = x)$ can always be obtained by carrying out the nonparametric mean regression of Y on $X'b_n$. This estimator converges in probability to the true conditional expectation at a rate that is slower than $n^{-1/2}$. An estimator of the conditional expectation that converges in probability at the rate $n^{-1/2}$ can be obtained if T can be estimated with $n^{-1/2}$ accuracy over the entire support of Y. This is usually possible in the models of Section 6.1.1, where T is known up to a finite-dimensional parameter α. If a_n is a $n^{-1/2}$-consistent estimator of α, T_n^{-1} is the inverse of $T(y, a_n)$, and T is a differentiable function of each of its arguments, then $E(Y|X = x)$ is estimated $n^{-1/2}$-consistently by

$$n^{-1}\sum_{i=1}^{n} T_n^{-1}(U_{ni} + x'b_n),$$

where b_n is a $n^{-1/2}$-consistent estimator of β and $U_{ni} = T(Y_i,a_n) - X_i'b_n$.

Uniform $n^{-1/2}$-consistent estimation of T usually is not possible in models where T is nonparametric, and $E(Y|X = x)$ cannot be estimated $n^{-1/2}$-consistently in such models. A predictor that usually can be estimated $n^{-1/2}$-consistently is the conditional median of Y or, possibly, another conditional quantile. The γ-quantile of Y conditional on $X = x$ $(0 < \gamma < 1)$ is

$$y_\gamma(x) = T^{-1}(x'\beta + u_\gamma),$$

where u_γ is the γ-quantile of the distribution of U. To form a $n^{-1/2}$-consistent estimator of $y_\gamma(x)$, let F_n be an estimator of F that is $n^{-1/2}$-consistent in a neighborhood of u_γ. Let T_n be an estimator of T that is $n^{-1/2}$-consistent in a neighborhood of $y_\gamma(x)$. In models where F is known, F_n can be replaced with F. Estimate u_γ by $u_{n\gamma} = \inf\{u{:}F_n(u) \geq \gamma\}$. Then $y_\gamma(x)$ is estimated $n^{-1/2}$-consistently by $y_{n\gamma}(x) = \inf\{y{:}T_n(y) > x'b_n + u_{n\gamma}\}$. Cheng et al. (1997) and Horowitz (1996) provide detailed discussions of the asymptotic distributional properties of $y_{n\gamma}(x)$ for the models and estimators discussed in Sections 6.2.5, and 6.3.1 and 6.3.2, respectively.

6.5 An Empirical Example

This section presents an empirical example that illustrates some of the techniques described in Sections 6.1, 6.2, 6.3, and 6.4. The data were assembled by Kennan (1985), who studied the relation between the durations of contract strikes and the level of economic activity. The data give the durations, in days, of 566 strikes involving 1000 or more workers in US manufacturing during 1968–1976. The level of economic activity is measured by an index of industrial production in manufacturing

(INDP). In the analysis reported here, high values of INDP indicate low levels of economic activity.

The analysis consists of using the data on strike durations and INDP to estimate three versions of model (6.1). In each version, Y is the duration of strike and X is INDP. The first estimated version of (6.1) is the semiparametric proportional hazards model of Section 6.2.1. In this model, T is nonparametric and $F(u) = 1 - \exp\ (-e^u)$. The second estimated version of (6.1) is a loglinear regression model. In this model, $T(y) = \log y$ and F is nonparametric. Estimation of this model is discussed in Section 6.1. In the third version of (6.1), T and F are both nonparametric. The estimator used here for this version of the model is discussed in Sections 6.3.1 and 6.3.2. The version of (6.1) in which T and F are nonparametric nests both the proportional hazards model and the loglinear regression model. The proportional hazards and loglinear regression models are nonnested, however. There are versions of the proportional hazards model that are not loglinear regressions, specifically any proportional hazards model in which the integrated baseline hazard function does not have the form $\Lambda_0(y) = y^\alpha$ for some $\alpha > 0$. There are also loglinear regressions that are not proportional hazards models, specifically any loglinear model in which U does not have the extreme-value distribution.

The estimation results are summarized in Fig. 6.1, which shows each model's estimates of the conditional first quartile, median, and third quartile of the distribution of strike durations given INDP. All of the models give results that are consistent with Kennan's (1985) finding that strike durations tend to be longer when at low levels of economic activity (high values of INDP) than at high levels. In addition, the conditional first quartiles and medians are similar in all models. The conditional

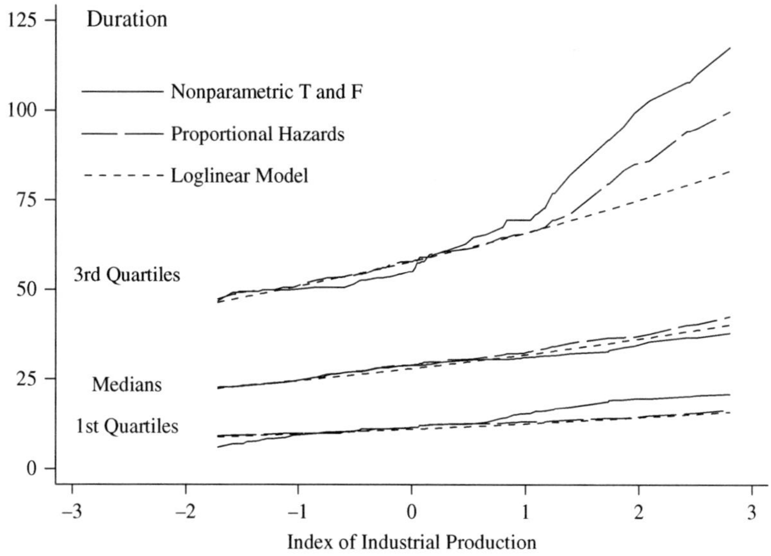

Fig. 6.1 Results of estimating three models of strike duration

third quartiles are similar when INDP ≤ 1.25 but diverge at higher values of INDP. At high values of INDP, the estimated distribution of strike durations is more highly skewed to the right according to the model with nonparametric T and F than according to the proportional hazards model. The distribution of strike durations is less highly skewed to the right according to the loglinear model than according to the proportional hazards model.

Because the model with nonparametric T and F nests the other two models, these results suggest the possibility that the proportional hazards and loglinear models are misspecified, at least for large values of INDP. However, fewer than 7% of the data have values of INDP exceeding 1.25, and a formal test of the proportional hazards and loglinear models against the more general model is not yet available. Therefore, one cannot rule out the possibility that the differences among the estimated third quartiles are artifacts of random sampling error. Nonetheless, the estimation results demonstrate that even a relatively complicated semiparametric estimator such as that of Section 6.3 can yield useful estimates with samples of the sizes found in applications.

Appendix
Nonparametric Density Estimation and Nonparametric Regression

This appendix summarizes properties of nonparametric density, mean-regression, and quantile-regression estimators that are used in the text. Härdle (1990), Silverman (1986), and Fan and Gijbels (1996) provide more detailed presentations of kernel and local polynomial estimators. Newey (1997) provides a detailed discussion of series estimators of conditional mean functions. Bhattacharya and Gangopadhyay (1990), Chaudhuri (1991a), Fan et al. (1994), and Horowitz and Lee (2005) discuss nonparametric quantile estimation.

A.1 Nonparametric Density Estimation

Let X be a random variable with unknown probability density function p. Let $\{X_i: i = 1, \ldots, n\}$ be a random sample of X. The problem addressed in this section is to estimate p consistently from $\{X_i\}$ without assuming that p belongs to a known finite-dimensional parametric family of functions. Assume for now that X is a scalar. The case of multidimensional X is treated in Section A.1.1.

Let P denote the cumulative distribution function (CDF) of X. For any real x, $P(x)$ is estimated consistently by the empirical distribution function of X, which is

$$P_n(x) = n^{-1} \sum_{i=1}^{n} I(X_i \leq x).$$

$P(x)$ and $p(x)$ are related by $p(x) = dP(x)/dx$, but $p(x)$ cannot be estimated by $dP_n(x)/dx$ because P_n is a step function. This problem can be solved by adding to each observation X_i a random number $h_n \varepsilon_i$, where ε_i is sampled randomly from a distribution with known density K and h_n is a scale parameter. The distribution of the resulting random variable, $X_i + h_n \varepsilon_i$, is the convolution of the empirical distribution of X and the distribution of $h_n \varepsilon_i$. The convolution distribution has the density function

J.L. Horowitz, *Semiparametric and Nonparametric Methods in Econometrics*, Springer Series in Statistics, DOI 10.1007/978-0-387-92870-8_7,

$$p_n(x) = \frac{1}{h_n} \int K\left(\frac{x - z}{h_n}\right) dP_n(z)$$
$$= \frac{1}{nh_n} \sum_{i=1}^{n} K\left(\frac{x - X_i}{h_n}\right).$$

The function p_n is called a *kernel nonparametric density estimator. K* is called the *kernel* function. Intuition suggests that $p_n(x)$ should be close to $p(x)$ if n is large (so that P_n is close to P) and h_n is small (so that the convolution X with $h_n\varepsilon$ does not alter the empirical distribution of X too much). Conditions under which this intuition is correct will now be given.

Suppose that K is bounded and satisfies

$$\int_{-\infty}^{\infty} K(v)\, dv = 1,$$
$$\int_{-\infty}^{\infty} vK(v)\, dv = 0,$$
$$\int_{-\infty}^{\infty} v^2 K(v)\, dv = A < \infty,$$

and

$$\int_{-\infty}^{\infty} [K(v)]^2 dv = B < \infty.$$

These conditions are satisfied if, for example, K is a bounded probability density function. Suppose, also, that $h_n \to 0$ and $nh_n / \log n \to \infty$ as $n \to \infty$. Then it can be proved that if p is uniformly continuous,

$$\lim_{n\to\infty} \sup_x |p_n(x) - p(x)| = 0 \tag{A.1}$$

almost surely. See Silverman (1978). Thus, p_n is a strongly uniformly consistent estimator of p.

Now suppose that p is twice continuously differentiable. Then for each x, the fastest possible rate of convergence in probability of $p_n(x)$ to $p(x)$ is $n^{-2/5}$ (Stone 1980). This occurs when $h_n = cn^{-1/5}$ for some $c > 0$. Moreover,

$$n^{2/5}[p_n(x) - p(x)] \xrightarrow{d} N(\mu,\sigma^2), \tag{A.2}$$

where

$$\mu = \frac{1}{2} c^2 A p''(x)$$

and

$$\sigma^2 = \frac{B}{c}p(x).$$

The asymptotic mean-square error (AMSE) of $p_n(x)$ is $\mu^2 + \sigma^2$. Assuming that $p''(x) \neq 0$, the AMSE is minimized by setting

$$c = \left[\frac{Bp(x)}{A^2 p''(x)^2}\right]^{1/5}.$$

The integrated mean-square error of p_n is

$$IMSE = E\int [p_n(x) - p(x)]^2 dx.$$

This is minimized asymptotically by setting

$$c = \left[\frac{B}{A^2 \int p''(v)^2 dv}\right]. \tag{A.3}$$

The uniform rate of convergence of p_n to p is slower than the pointwise rate of $n^{-2/5}$. It can be proved that if p is uniformly continuous, then

$$\left(\frac{nh_n}{\log n}\right)^{1/2} \sup_x |p_n(x) - p(x)| = O(1)$$

almost surely (Silverman 1978).

Equation (A.2) shows that the asymptotic distribution of $n^{2/5}[p_n(x) - p(x)]$ is not centered at 0. Thus $p_n(x)$ is asymptotically biased. The asymptotic bias can be removed at the cost of a slower rate of convergence by setting $h_n \propto n^{-r}$ where $r > 1/5$. This is called *undersmoothing*. With undersmoothing, the pointwise rate of convergence of $p_n(x)$ is $n^{-(1-r)/2}$, and

$$(nh_n)^{1/2}[p_n(x) - p(x)] \xrightarrow{d} N[0, Bp(x)].$$

Asymptotic bias can be removed while keeping the rate of convergence $n^{-2/5}$ by using a jackknife-like method proposed by Schucany and Sommers (1977). To obtain this estimator, let $p_n(x, h_{n1})$ be the kernel density estimator of $p(x)$ based on the bandwidth $h_{n1} = cn^{-1/5}$. Let $p_n(x, h_{n2})$ be the estimator based on bandwidth $h_{n2} = cn^{-\delta/5}$, where $0 < \delta < 1$. Define

$$\hat{p}_n(x) = \frac{p_n(x, h_{n1}) - (h_{n1}/h_{n2})^2 p_n(x, h_{n2})}{1 - (h_{n1}/h_{n2})^2}.$$

Assume that p'' satisfies the Lipschitz condition $|p''(x_1)-p''(x_2)| < c_p|x_1-x_2|^\gamma$ for some constant $c_p < \infty$ and $\gamma > 0$ when x_1 and x_2 are in a neighborhood of x. Then,

$$(nh_{n1})^{1/2}[\hat{p}_n(x) - p(x)] \xrightarrow{d} N[0,Bp(x)].$$

The rate of convergence of p_n can be increased if p has more than two continuous derivatives through the use of a *higher-order kernel*. A kernel K of order s satisfies

$$\int_{-\infty}^{\infty} K(v)dv = 1,$$

$$\int_{-\infty}^{\infty} v^j K(v)dv = 0, \; j = 1,2,\ldots, s-1,$$

$$\int_{-\infty}^{\infty} v^s K(v)dv = A < \infty,$$

and

$$\int_{-\infty}^{\infty} [K(v)]^2 dv = B < \infty.$$

If K is a probability density function, then $s = 2$. A higher-order kernel has $s > 2$. A higher-order kernel must be negative at some values of its argument in order to have a second "moment" of zero. Therefore, a probability density function cannot be a higher-order kernel, but higher-order kernels can be constructed by using formulae provided by Müller (1984). The following is a fourth-order kernel with support $[-1,1]$:

$$K(v) = \frac{105}{64}(1 - 5v^2 + 7v^4 - 3v^6)I(|v| \le 1).$$

Suppose that p has s continuous derivatives, $h_n = cn^{-1/(2s+1)}$, for some $c > 0$, and p_n is the estimator of p that is obtained by using a kernel K of order s and bandwidth h_n. Then the rate of convergence in probability of p_n to p is $n^{-s/(2s+1)}$. This rate increases as s increases, so a faster rate of convergence can be obtained by using a higher-order kernel if p has the required derivatives. If p is s times continuously differentiable, K is an order s kernel, and $h_n = n^{-1/(2s+1)}$, then

$$n^{s/(2s+1)}[p_n(x) - p(x)] \xrightarrow{d} N(\mu,\sigma^2),$$

where

$$\mu = \frac{1}{s!}c^s A p^{(s)}(x)$$

and

$$\sigma^2 = \frac{B}{c}p(x).$$

The AMSE of $p_n(x)$ is minimized by choosing c to minimize $\mu^2 + \sigma^2$. Assuming that $p^{(s)}(x) \neq 0$, the result is

$$c = \left\{ \frac{Bp(x)}{2s} \left[\frac{s!}{Ap^{(s)}(x)} \right]^2 \right\}^{1/(2s+1)}.$$

The asymptotic integrated mean-square error is minimized by setting

$$c = \left\{ \frac{B}{2s} \left(\frac{s!}{A} \right)^2 \frac{1}{\int p^{(s)}(v)^2 dv} \right\}^{1/(2s+1)}.$$

In applications, the bandwidth that minimizes the asymptotic integrated mean-square error, $h_{n,opt}$, can be estimated by the method of least-squares cross-validation. To describe this method, let $p_{nh}(x)$ be the estimate of $p(x)$ that is obtained by using bandwidth h, and let $p_{nhi}(x)$ be the estimate that is obtained by using bandwidth h and omitting observation X_i from the data. Define

$$T(h) = \int_{-\infty}^{\infty} [p_{nh}(x)]^2 dx - \frac{2}{n} \sum_{i=1}^{n} p_{nhi}(X_i).$$

The least-squares cross-validation estimator of $h_{n,opt}$ is the value of h that minimizes $T(h)$.

The least-squares cross-validation estimator, $h_{n,LCV}$, is easy to compute, but it converges to $h_{n,opt}$ at the slow rate of $n^{-1/10}$. That is, $h_{n,LCV}/h_{n,opt} - 1 = O_p(n^{-1/10})$. Consequently, $h_{n,LCV}$ can be noisy and may differ greatly from $h_{n,opt}$ with samples of moderate size. Jones et al. (1996) describe other bandwidth estimators that are more difficult to compute and may require stronger assumptions but have faster rates of convergence and, therefore, are likely to be less noisy in samples of moderate size.

A.1.1 Density Estimation When X Is Multidimensional

In this section, it is assumed that X is a d-dimensional random variable with $d > 1$. Let p be the probability density function of X and K be a kernel function of a d-dimensional argument. Such a function can be a multivariate probability density function or the product of univariate kernel functions. Let $\{h_n\}$ be a sequence of bandwidths. The kernel nonparametric estimator of $p(x)$ is

$$p_n(x) = \frac{1}{nh_n^d} \sum_{i=1}^{n} K\left(\frac{x - X_i}{h_n} \right).$$

It is possible to use different bandwidths for different components of X, but this refinement will not be pursued here.

If $h_n \to 0$ and $nh_n^d/\log n \to \infty$ as $n \to \infty$, then (A.1) holds when X is multidimensional. To obtain the rate of convergence and asymptotic distribution of $p_n(x) - p(x)$, it is necessary to define the multivariate generalization of a kernel of order s. To this end, let $j = (j_1, \ldots, j_d)$ be a d-dimensional vector whose components are all nonnegative integers. Let v be the d-dimensional vector whose components are $(v_1, \ldots, v_d)$. Define

$$v^j = \prod_{k=1}^{d} v_k^{j_k}$$

and

$$|\,j| = \sum_{k=1}^{d} j_k.$$

Let $K(v) = K(v_1, \ldots, v_d)$ and $dv = dv_1 dv_2 \cdots dv_d$. Then K is an order s kernel if

$$\int_{-\infty}^{\infty} K(v)\, dv = 1,$$

$$\int_{-\infty}^{\infty} v^j K(v)\, dv = 0, |\,j| = 1, 2, \ldots, s-1,$$

$$\int_{-\infty}^{\infty} v_k^s K(v)\, dv = A < \infty, \quad \text{for each } k = 1, \ldots, d,$$

and

$$\int_{-\infty}^{\infty} [K(v)]^2 dv = B < \infty.$$

A d-dimensional kernel K of order s can be obtained by setting

$$K(v) = \prod_{k=1}^{d} K_1(v_k),$$

where K_1 is an order s kernel of a one-dimensional argument.

Now assume that the mixed partial derivatives of p of order up to s exist and are continuous. Let K be an order s kernel. Then the fastest possible rate of convergence in probability of $p_n(x)$ to $p(x)$ is $n^{-s/(2s+d)}$. This rate decreases as d increases. As a result, the sample size needed to achieve a given estimation precision increases rapidly as d increases. This is the *curse of dimensionality* (Huber 1985). Silverman (1986) gives an illustrative example in which it is necessary to increase n by a factor of nearly 200 to keep the estimation precision constant when d increases from 1 to 5.

When p is s times continuously differentiable and K is an order s kernel, the fastest possible rate of convergence is achieved when $h_n = cn^{-1/(2s+d)}$ for some $c > 0$ (Stone 1980). Under these conditions,

$$n^{s/(2s+d)}[p_n(x) - p(x)] \xrightarrow{d} N(\mu,\sigma^2),$$

where

$$\mu = \frac{c^s}{s!} A \sum_{k=1}^{d} \frac{\partial^s p(x)}{\partial x_k^s},$$

x_k is the k th component of x, and

$$\sigma^2 = \frac{B}{c^d} p(x).$$

The asymptotic mean-square error of $p_n(x)$ is minimized by setting

$$c = \left\{ \frac{dBp(x)(s!)^2}{2s} \left[A \sum_{k=1}^{d} \frac{\partial^s p(x)}{\partial x_k^s} \right]^{-2} \right\}^{1/(2s+d)}.$$

The asymptotic integrated mean-square error of p_n is minimized by setting

$$c = \left\{ \frac{dB(s!)^2}{2sA^2 \int \left[\sum_{k=1}^{d} \frac{\partial^s p(x)}{\partial x_k^s} \right]^2 dx} \right\}^{1/(2s+d)}.$$

As in the one-dimensional case, the bandwidth that minimizes the asymptotic integrated mean-square error for $d > 1$ can be estimated by least-squares cross-validation, among other ways.

A.1.2 Estimating Derivatives of a Density

Return to the case in which X is a scalar. Let $p^{(k)}(x)$ denote the kth derivative of p at the point x. An obvious estimator of $p^{(k)}(x)$ is the kth derivative of $p_n(x)$ or $p_n^{(k)}(x)$. This section summarizes some important properties of $p_n^{(k)}(x)$.

Differentiation of p_n shows that

$$p_n^{(k)}(x) = \frac{1}{nh_n^{k+1}} \sum_{i=1}^{n} K^{(k)}\left(\frac{x - X_i}{h_n}\right),$$

where $K^{(k)}$ is the kth derivative of K and is assumed to exist everywhere. If K is an order s kernel that is k times continuously differentiable everywhere and if p is $k+s$ times continuously differentiable, then

$$E[p_n^{(k)}(x)] = p^{(k)}(x) + \frac{h_n^s}{s!}Ap^{(k+s)}(x) + o(h_n^s)$$

and

$$\text{Var}[p_n^{(k)}(x)] = \frac{B_k}{nh_n^{2k+1}}p(x) + o[(nh_n^{2k+1})^{-1}]$$

as $n \to \infty$, where

$$B_k = \int [K^{(k)}(v)]^2 dv.$$

It follows from Chebyshev's inequality that $p_n^{(k)}(x)$ converges in probability to $p^{(k)}(x)$ if $h_n \to 0$ and $nh_n^{2k+1} \to \infty$ as $n \to \infty$.

It can be seen that for any given bandwidth sequence and order of kernel, the bias of $p_n^{(k)}(x)$ converges to 0 at the same rate as the bias of $p_n(x)$, but the variance of $p_n^{(k)}(x)$ converges more slowly than the variance of $p_n(x)$. The fastest possible rate of convergence of $p_n^{(k)}(x)$ is achieved when the square of the bias and the variance of $p_n^{(k)}(x)$ converge to zero at the same rate. This occurs when $h_n \propto n^{-1/(2s+2k+1)}$. The resulting rate of convergence is $n^{-s/(2s+2k+1)}$. Thus, estimators of derivatives of densities converge more slowly than estimators of densities themselves and require slower converging bandwidth sequences.

A.2 Nonparametric Mean Regression

Now consider the problem of estimating the conditional mean function $g(x) = E(Y|X = x)$. Assume that X is a scalar, continuously distributed random variable. Let $\{Y_i, X_i : i = 1, \ldots, n\}$ be a random sample of (Y,X). This section describes three different ways to estimate g nonparametrically.

A.2.1 The Nadaraya–Watson Kernel Estimator

Let $p_n(x)$ be the kernel nonparametric estimator of $p(x)$, the probability density of X at x, based on the sample, kernel K, and bandwidth h_n. The Nadaraya–Watson kernel nonparametric estimator of $g(x)$ is

$$g_n(x) = \frac{1}{nh_n p_n(x)} \sum_{i=1}^{n} Y_i K\left(\frac{x - X_i}{h_n}\right).$$

This estimator was first proposed by Nadaraya (1964) and Watson (1964).

Define $\sigma^2(x) = Var(Y|X = x)$. Assume that $\sigma^2(x) < \infty$ for all finite x and that $E\sigma^2(X) < \infty$. If p and g are both s times continuously differentiable and K is an order s kernel, then the fastest possible rate of convergence in probability of $g_n(x)$ to $g(x)$ is $n^{-s/(2s+1)}$. As in nonparametric density estimation, the rate of convergence of a nonparametric mean-regression estimator can be increased by using a higher kernel if the necessary derivatives of p and g exist.

The fastest possible rate of convergence in probability of g_n to g occurs when $h_n = cn^{-1/(2s+1)}$ for some $c > 0$ (Stone 1980, 1982). With this bandwidth, an order s kernel, and assuming existence of the derivatives of p and g through order s,

$$n^{s/(2s+1)}[g_n(x) - g(x)] \xrightarrow{d} N(\mu_R, \sigma_R^2),$$

where

$$\mu_R = \frac{c^s}{p(x)} AD(x),$$
$$D(x) = \sum_{k=1}^{s} \frac{1}{k!} \frac{d^k}{dv^k} \{[g(v+x) - g(x)]p(x)\}_{v=0},$$

and

$$\sigma_R^2 = \frac{B\sigma^2(x)}{cp(x)}.$$

The asymptotic bias of $g_n(x)$ can be removed by using a method analogous to that of Schucany and Sommers (1977) for nonparametric density estimation. See Härdle (1986) and Bierens (1987) for details.

As in nonparametric density estimation, c can be chosen to minimize either the asymptotic mean-square error of $g_n(x)$ or the (asymptotic) integrated mean-square error. The integrated mean-square error is

$$IMSE = E \int w(x)[g_n(x) - g(x)]^2 dx,$$

where w is any nonnegative function satisfying

$$\int w(x) dx = 1$$

and for which the integral in *IMSE* exists. The asymptotic mean-square error of $g_n(x)$ is minimized by setting

$$c = \left[\frac{Bp(x)\sigma^2(x)}{2sA^2 D(x)^2} \right]^{1/(2s+1)}.$$

The asymptotic integrated mean-square error is minimized by setting

$$c = \left\{ \frac{1}{2s} \frac{A^2 \int w(v)[D(v)/p(v)]^2 dv}{B \int w(v)[\sigma^2(v)/p(v)] dv} \right\}^{1/(2s+1)}.$$

The bandwidth that minimizes the asymptotic integrated mean-square error can be estimated by minimizing the following cross-validation criterion function:

$$T_R(h) = n^{-1} \sum_{i=1}^{n} w(X_i)[Y_i - g_{nhi}(X_i)]^2,$$

where $g_{nhi}(x)$ is the kernel estimator of $g(x)$ that is obtained by using bandwidth h and omitting the observation (Y_i, X_i) from the sample.

The uniform rate of convergence of g_n to g is $[(\log n)/(nh_n)]^{1/2}$ almost surely. Specifically,

$$\left(\frac{nh_n}{\log n}\right)^{1/2} \sup_{x \in S} |g_n(x) - g(x)| = O(1),$$

almost surely, where S is any compact subset of the interior of the support of X on which p is bounded away from 0, and p and g are s times continuously differentiable.

If X is d-dimensional with $d > 1$, then $g(x)$ can be estimated by

$$g_n(x) = \frac{1}{nh_n^d p_n(x)} \sum_{i=1}^{n} Y_i K\left(\frac{x - X_i}{h_n}\right),$$

where K is a kernel function of a d-dimensional argument. As nonparametric density estimation, the fastest possible rate of convergence in probability of $g_n(x)$ to $g(x)$ is $n^{-s/(2s+d)}$ when p and g are s times continuously differentiable. Thus, the curse of dimensionality arises in nonparametric mean regression as in nonparametric density estimation. The fastest possible rate of convergence is achieved when $h_n = cn^{-1/(2s+d)}$ for some $c > 0$, in which case $n^{s/(2s+d)}[g_n(x) - g(x)]$ is asymptotically normally distributed.

Derivatives $g(x)$ can be estimated by differentiating $g_n(x)$. As in the case of density estimation, estimators of derivatives of g converge more slowly than the estimator of g itself, and slower converging bandwidth sequences are needed.

A.2.2 Local-Linear Mean Regression

The Nadaraya–Watson estimator of $g(x)$ can be obtained by solving

$$g_n(x) = \arg\min_b \sum_{i=1}^{n} (Y_i - b)^2 K\left(\frac{x - X_i}{h_n}\right).$$

Therefore, the Nadaraya–Watson estimator can be interpreted as approximating $g(X_i)$ by a constant when X_i is close to x. For this reason, the Nadaraya–Watson estimator is also called a local constant estimator.

Another possibility is to approximate g by a linear function near x. This gives

$$g(X_i) \approx b_0 + b_1(X_i - x)$$

when X_i is near x. Now consider choosing (b_0,b_1) by solving the weighted least-squares problem

$$(b_{n0},b_{n1}) = \arg\min_{b_0,b_1} \sum_{i=1}^{n} [Y_i - b_0 - b_1(X_i - x)]^2 K\left(\frac{X_i - x}{h_n}\right).$$

Estimate $g(x)$ by $g_{n,LL}(x) = b_{n0}$. This procedure is called local-linear estimation. The slope parameter b_{n1} estimates $g'(x)$ when this quantity exists. The estimator of $g(x)$ is

$$b_{n0} = g_{n,LL}(x) = \frac{\sum_{i=1}^{n} a_i Y_i}{\sum_{i=1}^{n} a_i},$$

where

$$a_i = \frac{1}{nh_h} K\left(\frac{X_i - x}{h_n}\right) [s_{n2} - s_{n1}(X_i - x)]$$

and

$$s_{nj} = \frac{1}{nh_n^3} \sum_{i=1}^{n} K\left(\frac{X_i - x}{h_n}\right) (X_i - x)^j;\ j = 1,2.$$

Now assume that

(a) $p(x) > 0$ and p and g are twice continuously differentiable in a neighborhood of x.
(b) K is a bounded probability density with support $[-1,1]$ and symmetrical about 0.
(c) $h_n = cn^{-1/5}$ for some positive $c < \infty$.

Then

$$n^{2/5}[g_{n,LL}(x) - g(x)] \xrightarrow{d} N(\mu_{LL},\sigma_{LL}^2),$$

where

$$\mu_{LL} = (1/2)c^2 A g''(x)$$

and

$$\sigma_{LL}^2 = \frac{B\sigma^2(x)}{cp(x)}.$$

As with the Nadaraya–Watson (local constant) estimator, the fastest possible rate of convergence with local-linear estimation is $n^{-2/5}$ when g is twice continuously differentiable. The variance of the asymptotic distribution of the local-linear estimator is the same as that of the Nadaraya–Watson estimator, but the two estimators have different asymptotic biases. Specifically, the asymptotic bias of the Nadaraya–Watson estimator contains the term $g'(x)p'(x)/p(x)$, whereas the asymptotic bias of the local-linear estimator does not contain this term. The term tends to be large if $|g'|$ is large (g is steeply sloped) or $|p'/p|$ is large (the data are highly clustered). In such cases, the local-linear estimator will tend to have a smaller bias and, therefore, smaller mean-square error than the Nadaraya–Watson estimator. Fan (1992) gives examples in which the local-linear estimator outperforms the local constant estimator.

As with the Nadaraya–Watson estimator, the bandwidth for local-linear estimation can be selected by cross-validation. Fan and Gijbels (1996) discuss a variety of other bandwidth selection methods. Local-linear estimation can be extended to vector-valued explanatory variables, X. There is then the usual curse of dimensionality, and the rates of convergence are the same as those of the Nadaraya–Watson estimator.

An important difference between the Nadaraya–Watson and local-linear estimators is their behavior near the boundaries of the support of X. Suppose that $p(x) > 0$ on the boundaries of the support of X. Then the Nadaraya–Watson estimator has a bias whose size is $O(h_n)$ at a boundary, but the local-linear estimator's bias remains $O(h_n^2)$ (although the constants multiplying this rate change) at a boundary. Therefore, the local-linear estimator is likely to be more precise than the Nadaraya–Watson estimator in the vicinity of a boundary at which $p(x)$ is discontinuous.

Local-linear estimation approximates g by a linear function. One can also consider approximating g in the vicinity of x by a higher-degree polynomial:

$$g(X_i) \approx b_0 + b_1(X_i - x) + \cdots + b_q(X_i - x)^q$$

for some integer $q \geq 2$. The coefficients can be estimated by solving

$$\underset{b_0,\cdots,b_q}{\text{minimize}} \sum_{i=1}^{n} [Y_i - b_0 - b_1(X_i - x) - \cdots - b_q(X_i - x)^q]^2 K\left(\frac{X_i - x}{h_n}\right).$$

The resulting value of b_0 is called a *local polynomial* estimator of $g_n(x)$. Fan and Gijbels (1996) show that local polynomial estimation is analogous to using a higher-order kernel, though K here is still a symmetrical probability density function. Specifically, if q is odd and g has $r = q + 1$ continuous derivatives, then the bias of $g_n(x)$ is $O(h_n^r)$. Therefore, the rate of convergence of the estimator is $O[n^{-r/(2r+1)}]$. However, as with a Nadaraya–Watson estimator with a higher-order kernel, the local polynomial estimator with a high-degree polynomial may be highly variable in small samples.

A.2.3 Series Estimation of a Conditional Mean Function

As before, let $g(x) = E(Y|X = x)$. Suppose there is a known set of functions $\{\phi_j : j = 1,2,\ldots\}$ such that

$$g(x) = \sum_{j=1}^{\infty} \beta_j \phi_j(x), \tag{A.4}$$

where the β_js are constant coefficients. Then estimating g amounts to estimating the coefficients β_j. It is not possible to estimate infinitely many coefficients with a finite sample, but one can consider estimating a finite number of them, J_n, by least squares. That is, $\beta_1,\ldots,\beta_{J_n}$ are estimated by

$$\{\hat{b}_1,\ldots,\hat{b}_{J_n}\} = \arg \min_{b_1,\ldots,b_{J_n}} \sum_{i=1}^{n} [Y_i - b_1\phi_1(X_i) - \cdots - b_{J_n}\phi_{J_n}(X_i)]^2,$$

and $g(x)$ is estimated by

$$g_n(x) = \sum_{j=1}^{J_n} \hat{b}_j \phi_j(x).$$

To make sense of this procedure, it is necessary to answer two questions:

1. Under what conditions does the expansion (A.4) exist and what does it mean?
2. What are the properties of the $\hat{b}_j$s and g_n?

The answers to the questions make use of the theory of Hilbert spaces.

A.2.3.1 Hilbert Spaces

A class of functions H is called a Hilbert space if

a. H is a linear space. That is, (i) H contains a zero element; (ii) if $f \in$ H, then $\lambda f \in$ H for any real number λ; and (iii) if $f_1 \in$ H and $f_2 \in$ H, then $\lambda_1 f_1 + \lambda_2 f_2 \in$ H for any real numbers λ_1 and λ_2.
b. Let f_1 and f_2 be any two elements of H. There is a number called the inner product of f_1 and f_2, denoted by $\langle f_1, f_2 \rangle$, with the following properties: (i) $\langle f_1, f_2 \rangle = \langle f_2, f_1 \rangle$. (ii) If $f_3 \in$ H, then $\langle f_1 + f_2, f_3 \rangle = \langle f_1, f_3 \rangle + \langle f_2, f_3 \rangle$. (iii) $\langle \lambda f_1, f_2 \rangle = \lambda \langle f_1, f_2 \rangle$ for any real λ. (iv) For any $f \in$ H, $\langle f, f \rangle \geq 0$ and $\langle f, f \rangle = 0$ only if $f = 0$.

The number $\|f\| \equiv \sqrt{\langle f,f \rangle}$ is called the norm of f. It has the property that $\|f_1 - f_2\|$ is a metric for H.

There are many examples of Hilbert spaces. This section uses the space $L_2[0,1]$ consisting of functions f on $[0,1]$ with the property

$$\int_0^1 f(x)^2 dx < \infty.$$

The inner product in this space is

$$\langle f_1, f_2 \rangle = \int_0^1 f_1(x) f_2(x) dx.$$

Two functions f_1 and f_2 are considered to be equal if

$$\|f_1 - f_2\|^2 = \int_0^1 [f_1(x) - f_2(x)]^2 dx = 0.$$

A set of functions $\{\phi_j \in \mathrm{H}; j = 1,2,\ldots\}$ is called a complete basis for H if for any $f \in \mathrm{H}$ there is a sequence of constants $\{b_j : j = 1,2,\ldots\}$ such that

$$\lim_{J \to \infty} \left\| f - \sum_{j=1}^{J} b_j \phi_j \right\| = 0. \tag{A.5}$$

When this condition holds, one writes

$$f = \sum_{j=1}^{\infty} b_j \phi_j. \tag{A.6}$$

In particular, the meaning of (A.4) is that there are constants $\{\beta_j : j = 1,2,\ldots\}$ such that

$$\lim_{J \to \infty} \left\| g - \sum_{j=1}^{J} \beta_j \phi_j \right\| = 0.$$

A basis $\{\phi_j\}$ is called orthonormal if for any $j,k = 1,2,\ldots$, $\langle \phi_j, \phi_k \rangle = 0$ when $j \neq k$ and $\|\phi_j\| = 1$. If $\{\phi_j\}$ is a complete, orthonormal basis, then $b_j = \langle f, \phi_j \rangle$ in (A.5) and (A.6). Moreover,

$$\|f\|^2 = \sum_{j=1}^{\infty} b_j^2.$$

In addition, if $f_1 = \sum_{j=1}^{\infty} b_j \phi_j$ and $f_2 = \sum_{j=1}^{\infty} c_j \phi_j$, then $\langle f_1, f_2 \rangle = \sum_{j=1}^{\infty} b_j c_j$.

Some examples of complete, orthonormal bases for $L_2[0,1]$ are

1. Cosine functions: $\phi_1(x) = 1$ and $\phi_{j+1}(x) = 2^{1/2}\cos(j\pi x)$ if $j > 1$.
2. Legendre polynomials, $P_j(x)$: Legendre polynomials are usually defined on [–1,1] but can be transformed so that they are orthonormal on [0,1]. After transformation, the first four Legendre polynomials are $P_0(x) = 1$, $P_1(x) = \sqrt{3}(2x-1)$, $P_2(x) = \sqrt{5}(6x^2-6x+1)$, and $P_3(x) = \sqrt{7}(20x^3-30x^2+12x-1)$.

A class of functions called B-splines is an example of a complete basis that is not orthonormal. B-splines are a form of piecewise polynomials. The degree, k, of the polynomials is related to the smoothness of the function space that is spanned. Consider functions on the unit interval [0,1]. For an integer $m > 0$, specify $m + 2k$ points, $\{\xi_j : j = -k, \ldots, m+k\}$, called knots such that

$$\xi_{-k} < \xi_{-k+1} < \cdots < -\xi_{-1} < \xi_0 = 0 < \xi_1 < \cdots < 1 = \xi_m < \xi_{m+1} < \cdots < \xi_{m+k}.$$

Typically, $\xi_0, \ldots, \xi_m$ are equally spaced on [0,1],

$$\xi_j = \xi_0 + j(\xi_1 - \xi_0);\ j = -1, \ldots, -k,$$

and

$$\xi_j = \xi_m + j(\xi_m - \xi_{m-1});\ j = m+1, \ldots, m+k$$

but this is not essential. The pth B-spline ($p = -k, \ldots, m-1$) is defined as

$$B_p(x) = \sum_{j=p}^{p+k+1}\left[\prod_{\substack{i=p\\ i\neq j}}^{p+k-1}\frac{1}{(\xi_i - \xi_j)}\right](x-\xi_j)_+^k;\ 0 \le x \le 1,$$

where $(x-\xi_j)_+^k = (x-\xi_j)^k$ if $x - \xi_j > 0$ and 0 otherwise. B_p is a polynomial function that is nonzero only if $x \in (\xi_p, \xi_{p+k+1})$. The B-spline approximation to a function f is

$$f(x) \approx \sum_{j=-k}^{m-1} b_j B_j(x)$$

for suitable coefficients $\{b_j\}$. B-splines of order $k = 3$ span the space of twice-differentiable functions on [0,1]. Specifically, if f is twice continuously differentiable on [0,1], then the B-spline approximation is twice differentiable and

$$\min_{b_{-k},\ldots,b_{m-1}} \sup_{x\in[0,1]} \left| f(x) - \sum_{j=-k}^{m-1} b_j B_j(x) \right| = Cm^{-2}, \tag{A.7}$$

where $C < \infty$ is a constant. The same result holds for Legendre polynomials. Although B-splines are not orthonormal, they can be made orthonormal by the

Gram–Schmidt orthogonalization procedure. This procedure forms orthonormal linear combinations of the B_js, so orthogonalization by this procedure maintains the approximation property (A.7).

A.2.3.2 Nonparametric Regression

This section describes the use of series approximations to estimate $g(x) = E(Y|X = x)$. Assume for now that X is a scalar and that its support is [0,1]. The support condition can always be satisfied by, if necessary, carrying out the transformation $X \to H(X)$, where H is a smooth, strictly increasing function.

The following notation will be used. Let $\{Y_i,X_i\colon\ i = 1,\ldots,n\}$ be a random sample of (Y,X), and let $\{\phi_j : j = 1,2,\ldots\}$ be a basis for $L_2[0,1]$. Define the $J \times 1$ vector $\phi^J(x) = [\phi_1(x),\ldots,\phi_J(x)]'$ and the $n \times J$ matrix

$$\Phi = [\phi^J(X_1),\ldots,\phi^J(X_n)]'$$

$$= \begin{bmatrix} \phi_1(X_1) & \phi_2(X_1)\ldots\phi_J(X_1) \\ \phi_1(X_2) & \phi_2(X_2)\ldots\phi_J(X_2) \\ & \vdots \\ \phi_1(X_n) & \phi_2(X_n)\ldots\phi_J(X_n) \end{bmatrix}.$$

Define the $n \times 1$ vector $Y = (Y_1,\ldots,Y_n)'$. For any matrix A, define the norm $\|A\|_M = [trace(A'A)]^{1/2}$. Let $\hat{b}$ denote the vector of coefficients that is obtained by ordinary least-squares regression of Y on Φ. That is

$$\hat{b} = (\Phi'\Phi)^{-}\Phi'Y,$$

where $(\Phi'\Phi)^{-}$ is the Moore–Penrose generalized inverse of $\Phi'\Phi$.

The nonparametric series estimator of $g(x)$ is

$$g_{n,S}(x) = \phi^J(x)'\hat{b} = \sum_{j=1}^{J} \hat{b}_j\phi_j(x).$$

To obtain asymptotic distributional properties of $g_{n,S}$, make the following assumptions:

NPS1: (i) $\{Y_i,X_i\colon i = 1,\ldots,n\}$ is a simple random sample of (Y,X). (ii) $Var(Y|X = x) = \sigma^2(x)$ is bounded.

NPS2. The support of X is [0,1]. The density of X, p, satisfies $c_p \le p(x) \le C_p$ for all $x \in [0,1]$, and constants $c_p > 0$ and $C_p < \infty$.

NPS3. g is twice continuously differentiable on [0,1].

NPS4: (i) The smallest eigenvalue of $Q_J = E[\phi^J(X)\phi^J(X)']$ is bounded away from zero uniformly in J. (ii) There is a sequence of constants,

$\{\zeta(J): J = 1,2,\ldots\}$, satisfying $\sup_{x\in[0,1]} \left\|\phi^J(x)\right\|_M \leq \zeta(J)$ and a sequence of constants $\{J_n\}$ such that $\zeta(J_n)^2 J_n/n \to 0$ as $n \to \infty$.

NPS5: For each J, there is a vector β_J such that as $J \to \infty$,

$$\sup_{x\in[0,1]} \left|g(x) - \phi^J(x)'\beta_J\right| = O(J^{-2}).$$

Assumptions NPS1–NPS3 are about the distribution of (Y,X) and are essentially the same as those of the Nadaraya–Watson kernel estimator. Assumption NPS4(ii) is satisfied by orthogonal polynomials with $\zeta(J) \propto J$ and by cosines and B-splines with $\zeta(J) \propto J^{1/2}$. Assumption NPS5 is satisfied by B-splines and orthogonal polynomials. It is also satisfied by cosine bases if g can be extended to be a periodic, even, twice continuously differentiable function on $[-1,1]$. The evenness requirement can be dropped if sine functions are included in the basis in addition to cosines.

Let $\{J_n\}$ be a sequence of positive integers such that $J_n \to \infty$ and $J_n/n \to 0$ as $n \to \infty$. The following theorem, which is proved by Newey (1997), gives the main result of this section.

Theorem A.1: *Let assumptions NPS1–NPS5 hold. Then*

$$\int [g_{n,S}(x) - g(x)]^2 p(x)dx = O_p(J_n/n + J_n^{-4}). \blacksquare$$

Setting $J_n \propto n^{1/5}$ produces the rate $O_p(n^{-4/5})$ in Theorem A.1. This is the fastest possible rate of convergence of the integrated squared error when g has two derivatives. Like the local-linear estimator, the series estimator does not require special treatment of the boundary region of the support of X.

If $n^{1/5}J_n \to \infty$ as $n \to \infty$ (undersmoothing) and certain other conditions hold, it is possible to establish asymptotic normality of a suitably scaled version of $g_n(x) - g(x)$. Andrews (1991), Newey (1997), Zhou et al. (1998), and Huang (2003) provide detailed discussions of conditions for asymptotic normality of series estimators. An important feature of series estimators is that it is easy to impose restrictions such as additivity on them. Sections 3.1.3, 3.2, and 3.3 illustrate the use of this feature of series estimators.

If g has $s \geq 2$ derivatives, the rate in Theorem A.1 is

$$\int [g_n(x) - g(x)]^2 p(x)dx = O_p(J_n/n + J_n^{-2s}).$$

The integrated squared error converges at the usual rate of $n^{-s/(2s+1)}$ when $J_n = n^{1/(2s+1)}$. If $\dim(X) = d > 1$, the rate of convergence of the series estimator is

$$\int [g_n(x) - g(x)]^2 p(x)dx = O_p(J_n/n + J_n^{-2s/d}).$$

The rate of convergence of the integrated squared error is optimized by setting $J_n \propto n^{d/(2s+d)}$, which gives the rate $O_p[n^{-2s/(2s+d)}]$. In applications, the series length, J_n, can be chosen by cross-validation (Li 1987).

A.3 Nonparametric Quantile Regression

Let $F(y|X = x) = P(Y \leq y|X = x)$ denote the CDF of Y conditional on $X = x$. The α-quantile of Y conditional on $X = x$ is defined as

$$q_\alpha(x) = \inf\{y : F(y|x) \geq \alpha\}.$$

If F is a continuous function of y, then $q_\alpha(x)$ solves $F[q_\alpha(x)|x] = \alpha$. This section is concerned with estimating $q_\alpha(x)$ from the simple random sample $\{Y_i, X_i$: i = 1, ..., $n\}$ when X is continuously distributed. Three estimators are described. One is a kernel-type estimator, one is a local-linear estimator, and one is a series estimator. Except when otherwise stated, X is assumed to be a scalar random variable.

A.3.1 A Kernel-Type Estimator of $q_\alpha(x)$

To describe the kernel-type estimator of $q_\alpha(x)$, let p denote the probability density function of X and h_n denote the bandwidth for kernel estimation. Define

$$p_n(x) = \frac{1}{nh_n} \sum_{i=1}^{n} I(|X_i - x| \leq h_n/2)$$

and

$$F_n(y|x) = \frac{1}{nh_n p_n(x)} \sum_{i=1}^{n} I(Y_i \leq y) I(|X_i - x| \leq h_n/2).$$

Then $p_n(x)$ is a kernel estimator of the density $p(x)$ based on the uniform kernel, $K(v) = I(|v| \leq 1/2)$. $F_n(y|x)$ is a kernel estimator $F(y|x)$ based on the same kernel. Define $K_n(x) = nh_n p_n(x)$. The kernel estimator of $q_\alpha(x)$ is

$$q_{n\alpha,K}(x) = \inf\{y : F_n(y|x) \geq \text{int}[\alpha K_n(x)]/K_n(x)\},$$

where int[v] denotes the largest integer that does not exceed v.

Let x_0 be a point in the support of X. Bhattacharya and Gangopadhyay (1990) give conditions under which $q_{n\alpha,K}(x_0)$ converges in probability to $q_\alpha(x_0)$ at the rate $n^{-2/5}$ and $n^{2/5}[q_{n\alpha,K}(x_0) - q_\alpha(x_0)]$ is asymptotically normally distributed. The conditions are

BG1: (i) $p(x_0) > 0$. (ii) $p''(x)$ exists in a neighborhood of x_0. Moreover, there exist $\varepsilon > 0$ and $A < \infty$ such that $|x - x_0| \leq \varepsilon$ implies $\left|p''(x) - p''(x_0)\right| \leq A|x - x_0|$.

BG2: Let $f(y|x) = \partial F(y|x)/\partial x$. Then (i) $F[q_\alpha(x)|x] = \alpha$ and $f[q_\alpha(x)|x] > 0$. (ii) The partial derivatives $f_y(y|x) = \partial f(y|x)/\partial y$, $f_{xx}(y|x) = \partial^2 f(y|x)/\partial x^2$, and $F_{xx}(y|x) = \partial^2 F(y|x)/\partial x^2$ exist in a neighborhood of the point $(q_\alpha(x_0), x_0)$.

Moreover, there exist $\varepsilon > 0$ and $A < \infty$ such that $|x - x_0| \le \varepsilon$ and $|y - q_\alpha(x)| \le \varepsilon$ together imply that $|f_y(y|x)| \le A$, $|f_x(y|x_0)| \le A$, $|f_{xx}(y|x_0)| \le A$, $|f_{xx}(y|x) - f_{xx}(y|x_0)| \le A|x - x_0|$, and $|F_{xx}(y|x) - F_{xx}(y|x_0)| \le A|x - x_0|$.

The following theorem, which is proved by Bhattacharya and Gangopadhyay (1990), establishes $n^{-2/5}$-consistency of $q_{n\alpha,K}(x_0)$ and asymptotic normality of $n^{2/5}[q_{n\alpha,K}(x_0) - q_\alpha(x_0)]$.

Theorem A.2: *Let assumptions BG1 and BG2 hold. Let* $h_n = cn^{-1/5}$ *for some finite* $c > 0$. *Then*

$$n^{2/5}[q_{n\alpha,K}(x_0) - q_\alpha(x_0)] \xrightarrow{d} N(\mu_{\alpha,K}, \sigma^2_{\alpha,K}),$$

where

$$\mu_{\alpha,K} = -c^2\{p(x_0)F_{xx}[q_\alpha(x_0)|x_0] + 2p'(x_0)F_x[q_\alpha(x_0)|x]\}/\{24p(x_0)g\,[q_\alpha(x_0)|x_0]\}$$

and

$$\sigma^2_{\alpha,K} = \frac{\alpha(1-\alpha)}{cp(x_0)f[q_\alpha(x_0)|x_0]^2}. \blacksquare$$

As in nonparametric estimation of a conditional mean function, the asymptotic bias of the conditional quantile estimator can be removed by undersmoothing. Specifically, let $n^{1/5}h_n \to 0$ as $n \to \infty$. Then $(nh_n)^{1/2}[q_{n\alpha,K}(x_0) - q_\alpha(x_0)] \xrightarrow{d} N(0,\tilde{\sigma}^2_{\alpha.K})$, where

$$\tilde{\sigma}^2_{\alpha,K} = \frac{\alpha(1-\alpha)}{p(x_0)f[q_\alpha(x_0)|x_0]^2}.$$

A.3.2 Local-Linear Estimation of $\mathbf{q_\alpha(x)}$

For $\alpha \in (0,1)$, define the check function $\rho_\alpha(t) = |t| + (2\alpha - 1)t$. Suppose for the moment that

$$q_\alpha(x) = \beta_0 + \beta_1 x,$$

where β_0 and β_1 are constants. Then

$$(\beta_0,\beta_1) = \arg\min_{b_0,b_1} E\rho_\alpha(Y - b_0 - b_1 X).$$

Moreover, β_0 and β_1 are estimated consistently by the solution to the problem

$$\underset{b_0,b_1}{\text{minimize}}: \sum_{i=1}^{n} \rho_\alpha(Y_i - b_0 - b_1 X_i),$$

where $\{Y_i,X_i: i = 1, \ldots, n\}$ is a random sample of (Y,X) (Koenker and Bassett 1978).

Now let q_α be nonparametric but smooth so that $q_\alpha(x)$ can be approximated by a linear function in a neighborhood of any fixed point x. Let $\{h_n\}$ denote a sequence of bandwidths. Then a nonparametric local-linear estimator of $q_\alpha(x)$ based on the kernel function K can be formed by solving the problem

$$(b_{n0},b_{n1}) = \arg\min_{b_0,b_1} \sum_{i=1}^{n} \rho_\alpha[Y_i - b_0 - b_1(X_i - x)]K\left(\frac{x - X_i}{h_n}\right).$$

The local-linear estimator of $q_\alpha(x)$ is $q_{n\alpha,L}(x) = b_{n0}$.

Chaudhuri (1991a) and Fan et al. (1994) give conditions under which the local-linear estimator is asymptotically normally distributed. Yu and Jones (1998) give related results and discuss bandwidth selection. Observe that

$$Y = q_\alpha(X) + U, \tag{A.8}$$

where U is a random variable whose α-quantile is 0. Now make the following assumptions.

QLL1: The probability density function of X is continuous and strictly positive in a neighborhood of x.

QLL2: (i) U is independent of X. (ii) The α-quantile of the distribution of U is 0. (iii) U has a differentiable probability density function f_U, and $f_U(u) > 0$ for u in a neighborhood of 0.

QLL3: $q_\alpha(\cdot)$ is twice continuously differentiable in a neighborhood of x, and the second derivative is bounded in this neighborhood.

QLL4: The kernel K is supported on $[-1,1]$ and satisfies

$$\int_{-1}^{1} v^j K(v)\, dv = \begin{cases} 1 & \text{if } j = 0 \\ 0 & \text{if } j = 1 \end{cases}.$$

These assumptions are slightly stronger than those of Chaudhuri (1991a) or Fan et al. (1994) but simpler technically. The following result is a consequence of Theorem 1 of Fan et al. (1994).

Theorem A.3: *Let assumptions QLL1–QLL4 hold. Let $h_n = cn^{-1/5}$, where $c > 0$ is a finite constant. Then*

$$n^{2/5}[q_{n\alpha,L}(x) - q_\alpha(x)] \xrightarrow{d} N(\mu_{\alpha L},\sigma^2_{\alpha L}),$$

where

$$\mu_{\alpha L} = \frac{c^2}{6} q''_\alpha(x)$$

and

$$\sigma_{\alpha L}^2 = \frac{\alpha(1-\alpha)}{2cf_U(0)^2 p(x)}. \blacksquare$$

Under the assumptions made here, $f_U(0) = f[q_\alpha(x)|x]$, so $\sigma_{\alpha L}^2 = \sigma_{\alpha K}^2$ after taking account of the fact that c in $\sigma_{\alpha K}^2$ corresponds to $2c$ in $\sigma_{\alpha L}^2$. As in local-linear estimation of a conditional mean function, the asymptotic bias of the local-linear estimator of a conditional quantile function does not depend on the density of X. The asymptotic bias of $n^{2/5}[q_{n\alpha,L}(x) - q_\alpha(x)]$ can be removed by undersmoothing.

Chaudhuri (1991a) extends the local-linear estimator to local polynomials of degree greater than 1 and vector covariates X. As in nonparametric estimation of a conditional mean function, use of a higher-degree polynomial leads to faster convergence if q_α is sufficiently smooth, and there is a curse of dimensionality associated with higher dimensions of X.

A.3.3 Series Estimation of $q_\alpha(x)$

Let $\{\phi_j\}$ be a complete basis for $L_2[0,1]$. Then if $q_\alpha \in L_2[0,1]$, it can be written

$$q_\alpha(x) = \sum_{j=1}^{\infty} \beta_j \phi_j(x)$$

for suitable coefficients $\{\beta_j\}$. A series estimator of q_α has the form

$$q_{n\alpha,S}(x) = \sum_{j=1}^{J_n} b_{nj}\, \phi_j(x),$$

where the coefficients $\{b_{nj}\}$ are estimated from the data. Various kinds of series estimators have been investigated by He and Shi (1994, 1996), Portnoy (1997), He and Portnoy (2000), and Horowitz and Lee (2005). The discussion in this section is based on Horowitz and Lee (2005). Their estimates of the b_js are the solution to

$$\underset{b_1,\ldots,b_{J_n}}{\text{minimize:}} \sum_{i=1}^{n} \rho_\alpha[Y_i - b_1\phi_1(X_i) - \cdots - b_{J_n}\phi_{J_n}(X_i)],$$

where $\{Y_i, X_i: i = 1, \ldots, n\}$ is a random sample of (Y,X).

Define the random variable U as in (A.8). Let $F_U(\cdot\,|x)$ and $f_U(\cdot\,|x)$ denote the conditional CDF and density of U. For any integer $J > 0$, let $\Phi^J(x)$ be the $J \times 1$ vector whose jth component is $\phi_j(x)$. Horowitz and Lee (2005) make the following assumptions.

HL1: The support of X is [0,1]. The probability density function of X is bounded, bounded away from 0, and twice continuously differentiable on the interior of [0,1]. The one-sided second derivatives are continuous at the boundaries of [0,1].

Horowitz and Lee (2005) assume that the support of X is $[-1,1]$. Here it is assumed that the support is [0,1] to maintain consistency with the discussion in Section A.2.3. The results stated in Theorem A.4 below hold for either support assumption because the support can be changed from $[-1,1]$ to [0,1] by making the strictly monotone transformation $X \to (X+1)/2$.

HL2: (i) $F_U(0|x) = \alpha$ for almost every $x \in [0,1]$. (ii) The density $f_U(\cdot|x)$ exists for every $x \in [0,1]$. (iii) There is a constant $L_f < \infty$ such that $|f_U(u_1|x) - f_U(u_2|x)| \le L_f|u_1 - u_2|$ for all u_1 and u_2 in a neighborhood of 0 and for all $x \in [0,1]$. Also, there are constants $c_f > 0$ and $C_f < \infty$ such that $c_f \le f_U(u|x) \le C_f$ for all u in a neighborhood of 0 and all $x \in [0,1]$.

HL3: $q_\alpha(x)$ is r times continuously differentiable in the interior of [0,1] and has continuous rth-order one-sided derivatives at the boundaries of [0,1] for some $r \ge 2$.

HL4: For any integer $J > 0$, define $Q_J = E[f_U(0|X)\Phi^J(X)\Phi^J(X)']$. The smallest eigenvalue of Q_J is bounded away from 0 for all J and the largest eigenvalue is bounded for all J.

HL5: The basis functions $\{\phi_j\}$ satisfy the following conditions. (i) Each ϕ_j is continuous. (ii) $\phi_1(x) = 1$. (iii) If $j,k \ne 1$

$$\int_0^1 \phi_j(x)dx = 0$$

and

$$\int_0^1 \phi_j(x)\phi_k(x)dx = \begin{cases} 1 \text{ if } j = k \\ 0 \text{ otherwise} \end{cases}.$$

(iv) Define $\zeta_J = \sup_{x \equiv [-1,1]} \left\| \Phi^J(x) \right\|_M$, where $\|\cdot\|_M$ is the matrix norm defined in Section A.2.3. Then $\zeta_J = O(J^{1/2})$ as $J \to \infty$. (v) There are constants $\beta_1, \beta_2, \ldots$ such that

$$\sup_{x \in [0,1]} |q_\alpha(x) - \beta_1\phi_1(x) - \cdots - \beta_J\phi_J(x)| = O(J^{-r})$$

as $J \to \infty$.

Let p denote the probability density function of X. Let $\{J_n\}$ be a sequence of positive integers such that $J_n \to \infty$ and $J_n/n \to 0$ as $n \to \infty$. The following theorem is a consequence of Theorem 2 of Horowitz and Lee (2005).

Theorem A.4: *Let assumptions HL1–HL5 hold. Then*

$$\int_0^1 [q_{n\alpha,S}(x) - q_\alpha(x)]^2 p(x)dx = O_p(J_n/n + J_n^{-4}). \blacksquare$$

As in the estimation of a conditional mean function, series estimators are useful for imposing restrictions such as additivity on conditional quantile functions. Section 3.4 of Chapter 3 provides an illustration.

References

Abrevaya, J. (2003). Pairwise-Difference Rank Estimation of the Transformation Model, *Journal of Business and Economic Statistics*, **21**, 437–447.
Abrevaya, J. and J. Huang (2005). On the Bootstrap of the Maximum Score Estimator, *Econometrica*, **73**, 1175–1204.
Ai, C. (1997). A Semiparametric Maximum Likelihood Estimator, *Econometrica*, **65**, 933–963.
Ai, C. and X. Chen (2003). Efficient Estimation of Models with Conditional Moment Restrictions Containing Unknown Functions, *Econometrica*, **71**, 1795–1843.
Amemiya, T. (1985). *Advanced Econometrics*, Cambridge, MA: Harvard University Press.
Amemiya, T. and J. L. Powell (1981). A Comparison of the Box-Cox Maximum Likelihood Estimator and the Non-Linear Two-Stage Least Squares Estimator, *Journal of Econometrics*, **17**, 351–381.
Andersen, P. K. and R. D. Gill (1982). Cox's Regression Model for Counting Processes: A Large Sample Study, *Annals of Statistics*, **10**, 1100–1120.
Andrews, D. W. K. (1991). Asymptotic Normality of Series Estimators for Nonparametric and Semiparametric Regression Models, *Econometrica*, **59**, 307–345.
Bennett, S. (1983a). Analysis of Survival Data by the Proportional Odds Model, *Statistics in Medicine*, **2**, 273–277.
Bennett, S. (1983b). Log-Logistic Regression Models for Survival Data, *Applied Statistics*, **32**, 165–171.
Beran, R. (1988). Prepivoting Test Statistics: A Bootstrap View of Asymptotic Refinements, *Journal of the American Statistical Association*, **83**, 687–697.
Bhattacharya, P. K. and A. K. Gangopadhyay (1990). Kernel and Nearest-Neighbor Estimation of a Conditional Quantile, *Annals of Statistics*, 18, 1400–1415.
Bickel, P. J. and K. A. Doksum (1981). An Analysis of Transformations Revisited, *Journal of the American Statistical Association*, **76**, 296–311.
Bickel, P. J., C. A. J. Klaassen, Y. Ritov, and J. A. Wellner (1993). *Efficient and Adaptive Estimation for Semiparametric Models*, Baltimore: The Johns Hopkins University Press.
Bierens, H. J. (1987). Kernel Estimators of Regression Functions, in *Advances in Econometrics: 5th World Congress*, Vol. 1, T. F. Bewley, ed., Cambridge: Cambridge University Press.
Bierens, H. J. and J. Hartog (1988). Non-Linear Regression with Discrete Explanatory Variables, with an Application to the Earnings Function, *Journal of Econometrics*, **38**, 269–299.
Billingsley, P. (1968). *Convergence of Probability Measures*, New York: John Wiley & Sons.
Blundell, R., X. Chen, and D. Kristensen (2007). Semi-Nonparametric IV Estimation of Shape-Invariant Engel Curves, *Econometrica*, **75**, 1613–1669.
Box, G. E. P. and D. R. Cox (1964). An Analysis of Transformations, *Journal of the Royal Statistical Society*, Series B, **26**, 211–252.
Breiman, L. and J. H. Friedman (1985). Estimating Optimal Transformations for Multiple Regression and Correlation, *Journal of the American Statistical Association*, **80**, 580–598.

J.L. Horowitz, *Semiparametric and Nonparametric Methods in Econometrics*,
Springer Series in Statistics, DOI 10.1007/978-0-387-92870-8_BM2,

Buja, A., T. J. Hastie, and R. J. Tibshirani (1989). Linear Smoothers and Additive Models, *Annals of Statistics*, **17**, 453–555.

Butucea, C. (2004). Deconvolution of Supersmooth Densities with Smooth Noise, *Canadian Journal of Statistics*, **32**, 181–182.

Butucea, C. and A. B. Tsybakov (2008). Sharp Optimality in Density Deconvolution with Dominating Bias, I, *Theory of Probability and Its Applications*, **52**, 24–39.

Carroll, R. J. (1982). Adapting for Heteroscedasticity in Linear Models, *Annals of Statistics*, **10**, 1224–1233.

Carroll, R. J. and P. Hall (1988). Optimal Rates of Convergence for Deconvolving a Density, *Journal of the American Statistical Association*, **83**, 1184–1186.

Carroll, R. J., J. Fan, I. Gijbels, and M. P. Wand (1997). Generalized Partially Linear Single-Index Models, *Journal of the American Statistical Association*, **92**, 477–489.

Cavanagh, C. L. (1987). *Limiting Behavior of Estimators Defined by Optimization*, unpublished manuscript, Department of Economics, Harvard University, Cambridge, MA.

Cavanagh, C. and R. P. Sherman (1998). Rank Estimators for Monotonic Index Models, *Journal of Econometrics*, **84**, 351–381.

Chamberlain, G. (1986). Asymptotic Efficiency in Semiparametric Models with Censoring, *Journal of Econometrics*, **32**, 189–218.

Chamberlain, G. (1987). Asymptotic Efficiency in Estimation with Conditional Moment Restrictions, *Journal of Econometrics*, **34**, 305–334.

Charlier, E. (1994). *A Smoothed Maximum Score Estimator for the Binary Choice Panel Data Model with Individual Fixed Effects and Application to Labour Force Participation*, discussion paper no. 9481, CentER for Economic Research, Tilburg University, Tilburg, The Netherlands.

Charlier, E., B. Melenberg, and A. van Soest (1995). A Smoothed Maximum Score Estimator for the Binary Choice Panel Data Model with an Application to Labour Force Participation, *Statistica Neerlandica*, **49**, 324–342.

Chaudhuri, P. (1991a). Nonparametric Estimates of Regression Quantiles and Their Local Bahadur Representation, *Annals of Statistics*, **19**, 760–777.

Chaudhuri, P. (1991b). Global Nonparametric Estimation of Conditional Quantile Functions and Their Derivatives, *Journal of Multivariate Analysis*, **39**, 246–269.

Chaudhuri, P., K. Doksum, and A. Samarov (1997). On Average Derivative Quantile Regression, *Annals of Statistics*, **25**, 715–744.

Chen, S. (2002). Rank Estimation of Transformation Models, *Econometrica*, **70**, 1683–1697.

Chen, S. and S. Khan (2003). Rates of Convergence for Estimating Regression Coefficients in Heteroskedastic Discrete Response Models, *Journal of Econometrics*, **117**, 245–278.

Chen, X., O. Linton, and I. Van Keilegom (2003). Estimation of Semiparametric Models when the Criterion Function is Not Smooth, *Econometrica*, **71**, 1591–1608.

Chen, X. and D. Pouzo (2008). *Estimation of Nonparametric Conditional Moment Models with Possibly Nonsmooth Moments*, working paper, Department of Economics, New York University, New York.

Chen, X. and M. Reiss (2007). On Rate Optimality for Ill-Posed Inverse Problems in Econometrics, working paper CWP 20/07, Centre for Microdata Methods and Practice, Department of Economics, University College London.

Chen, S. and L. Zhou (2007). Local Partial Likelihood Estimation in Proportional Hazards Models, *Annals of Statistics*, **35**, 888–916.

Cheng, S. C., L. J. Wei, and Z. Ying (1995). Analysis of Transformation Models with Censored Data, *Biometrika*, **82**, 835–845.

Cheng, S. C., L. J. Wei, and Z. Ying (1997). Predicting Survival Probabilities with Semiparametric Transformation Models, *Journal of the American Statistical Association*, **92**, 227–235.

Chernozhukov, V. and C. Hansen (2005). An IV Model of Quantile Treatment Effects, *Econometrica*, **73**, 245–261.

Clayton, D. and Cuzick, J. (1985). Multivariate Generalizations of the Proportional Hazards Model, *Journal of the Royal Statistical Society*, Series A, **148**, 82–117.

Cosslett, S. R. (1981). Efficient Estimation of Discrete-Choice Models, in *Structural Analysis of Discrete Data with Econometric Applications*, D. F. Manski and D. McFadden, eds., Cambridge, MA: MIT Press.

Cosslett, S. R. (1987). Efficiency Bounds for Distribution-Free Estimators of the Binary Choice and Censored Regression Models, *Econometrica*, **55** 559–586.

Cox, D. R. (1972). Regression Models and Life tables, *Journal of the Royal Statistical Society*, Series B, **34**, 187–220.

Darolles, S., J.-P. Florens, and E. Renault (2006). *Nonparametric Instrumental Regression*, working paper, University of Toulouse, Toulouse, France.

Davidson, R. and J. G. MacKinnon (1993). *Estimation and Inference in Econometrics*, New York: Oxford University Press.

De Gooijer, J.G. and D. Zerom (2003). On Additive Conditional Quantiles with High Dimensional Covariates, *Journal of the American Statistical Association*, **98**, 135–146.

de Jong, R. and T. Woutersen (2007). *Dynamic Time Series Binary Choice*, working paper, Department of Economics, Johns Hopkins University, Baltimore, MD.

Delgado, M. A., J. M. Rodríguez-Póo, and M. Wolf (2001). Subsampling Inference in Cube Root Asymptotics with an Application to Manski's Maximum Score Estimator, *Economics Letters*, **73**, 241–250.

Dempster, A. P., N. M. Laird, and D. R. Rubin (1977). Maximum Likelihood Estimation from Incomplete Data Via the EM Algorithm, *Journal of the Royal Statistical Society*, Series B, **39**, 1–38.

Doksum, K. and J.-Y. Koo (2000). On Spline Estimators and Prediction Intervals in Nonparametric Regression, *Computational Statistics and Data Analysis*, **35**, 76–82.

Elbers, C. and G. Ridder (1982). True and Spurious Duration Dependence: The Identifiability of the Proportional Hazard Model, *Review of Economic Studies*, **49**, 403–409.

Engle, R. F., C. W. J. Granger, J. Rice, and A. Weiss (1986). Semiparametric Estimates of the Relation between Weather and Electricity Sales, *Journal of the American Statistical Association*, **81**, 310–320.

Fan, J. (1991a). On the Optimal Rates of Convergence for Nonparametric Deconvolution Problems, *Annals of Statistics*, **19**, 1257–1272.

Fan, J. (1991b). Asymptotic Normality for Deconvolution Kernel Density Estimators, *Sankhya*, Series A, Part 1, **53**, 97–110.

Fan, J. (1992). Design-Adaptive Nonparametric Regression, *Journal of the American Statistical Association*, **87**, 998–1004.

Fan, J. and I. Gijbels (1996). *Local Polynomial Modelling and Its Applications*, London: Chapman & Hall.

Fan, J. I. Gijbels, and M. King (1997). Local Likelihood and Local Partial Likelihood in Hazard Regression, *Annals of Statistics*, **25**, 1661–1690.

Fan, J., T.-C. Hu, and Y. K. Truong (1994). Robust Nonparametric Function Estimation, *Scandinavian Journal of Statistics*, 21, 433–446.

Fan, J., E. Mammen, and W. Härdle (1998). Direct Estimation of Low Dimensional Components in Additive Models, *Annals of Statistics*, **26**, 943–971.

Fischer, G. W. and D. Nagin (1981). Random Versus Fixed Coefficient Quantal Choice Models, in *Structural Analysis of Discrete Data with Econometric Applications*, D. F. Manski and D. McFadden, eds., Cambridge, MA: MIT Press.

Florios, K. and S. Skouras (2008). Exact Computation of Max Weighted Score Estimates, *Journal of Econometrics*, **146**, 86–91.

Foster, A. M., L. Tian, and L. J. Wei (2001). Estimation for the Box-Cox Transformation Model without Assuming Parametric Error Distribution, *Journal of the American Statistical Association*, **96**, 1097–1101.

Gallant, A. R. (1987). *Nonlinear Statistical Models*, New York: John Wiley & Sons.

Gasser, T., H.-G. Müller, and V. Mammitzsch (1985). Kernels for Nonparametric Curve Estimation, *Journal of the Royal Statistical Society*, Series B, **47**, 238–252.

Gørgens, T. and J. L. Horowitz (1999). Semiparametric Estimation of a Censored Regression Model with an Unknown Transformation of the Dependent Variable, *Journal of Econometrics*, **90**, 155–191.

Gronau, R. (1974). Wage Comparisons – A Selectivity Bias," *Journal of Political Economy*, **82**, 1119–1143.

Härdle, W. (1986). A Note on Jackknifing Kernel Regression Function Estimators, *IEEE Transactions of Information Theory*, **32**, 298–300.

Härdle, W. (1990). *Applied Nonparametric Regression*, Cambridge: Cambridge University Press.

Härdle, W., P. Hall, and H. Ichimura (1993). Optimal Smoothing in Single-Index Models, *Annals of Statistics*, **21**, 157–178.

Härdle, W., H. Liang, and J. Gao (2000). *Partially Linear Models*, New York: Springer.

Härdle, W. and O. Linton (1994). Applied Nonparametric Methods, in *Handbook of Econometrics*, Vol. 4, R. F. Engle and D. F. McFadden, eds., Amsterdam: Elsevier, Ch. 38.

Härdle, W. and T. M. Stoker (1989). Investigating Smooth Multiple Regression by the Method of Average Derivatives, *Journal of the American Statistical Association*, **84**, 986–995.

Härdle, W. and A. B. Tsybakov (1993). How Sensitive Are Average Derivatives? *Journal of Econometrics*, **58**, 31–48.

Hall, P. (1986). On the Bootstrap and Confidence Intervals, *Annals of Statistics*, **14**, 1431–1452.

Hall, P. (1992). *The Bootstrap and Edgeworth Expansion*, New York: Springer-Verlag.

Hall, P. and S. N. Lahiri (2008). Estimation of Distributions, Moments, and Quantiles in Deconvolution Problems, *Annals of Statistics*, **36**, 2110–2134.

Hall, P. and J. L. Horowitz. (2005). Nonparametric Methods for Inference in the Presence of Instrumental Variables, *Annals of Statistics*, **33**, 2904–2929.

Hall, P. and J. L. Horowitz (2007). Methodology and Convergence Rates for Functional Linear Regression, *Annals of Statistics*, **35**, 70–91.

Hall, P. and H. Ichimura (1991). *Optimal Semi-Parametric Estimation in Single-Index Models*, working paper no. CMA-SR5–91, Centre for Mathematics and Its Applications, Australian National University, Canberra, Australia.

Han, A. (1987). Non-Parametric Analysis of a Generalized Regression Model, *Journal of Econometrics*, **35**, 303–316.

Hansen, L. P. (1982). Large Sample Properties of Generalized Method of Moments Estimators, *Econometrica*, **50**, 1029–1054.

Hastie, T. J. and R. J. Tibshirani (1990). *Generalized Additive Models*, London: Chapman and Hall.

Hausman, J. A. and D. A. Wise (1978). A Conditional Probit Model for Qualitative Choice: Discrete Decisions Recognizing Interdependence and Heterogeneous Preferences, *Econometrica*, **46**, 403–426.

He, X. and S. Portnoy (2000). Some Asymptotic Results on Bivariate Quantile Splines, *Journal of Statistical Planning and Inference*, **91**, 341–349.

He, X. and P. Shi (1994). Convergence Rate of B-Spline Estimators of Nonparametric Conditional Quantile Functions, *Journal of Nonparametric Statistics*, **3**, 299–308.

He, X. and P. Shi (1996). Bivariate Tensor-Product B-Splines in a Partly Linear Model, *Journal of Multivariate Analysis*, **58**, 162–181.

Heckman, J. J. (1974). Shadow Prices, Market Wages, and Labor Supply, *Econometrica*, **42**, 679–693.

Heckman, J. J. (1981a). Statistical Models for Discrete Panel Data, in *Structural Analysis of Discrete Data with Econometric Applications*, D. F. Manski and D. McFadden, eds., Cambridge, MA: MIT Press.

Heckman, J. J. (1981b). The Incidental Parameters Problem and the Problem of Initial Conditions in Estimating a Discrete Time-Discrete Data Stochastic Process, in *Structural Analysis of Discrete Data with Econometric Applications*, D. F. Manski and D. McFadden, eds., Cambridge, MA: MIT Press.

Heckman, J. and B. Singer (1984a). The Identifiability of the Proportional Hazard Model, *Review of Economics Studies*, **51**, 231–243.

Heckman, J. and B. Singer (1984b). A Method for Minimizing the Impact of Distributional Assumptions in Econometric Models for Duration Data, *Econometrica*, **52**, 271–320.

Hengartner, N. W. and S. Sperlich (2005). Rate Optimal Estimation with the Integration Method in the Presence of Many Covariates, *Journal of Multivariate Analysis*, **95**, 246–272.

Honoré, B. E. (1990). Simple Estimation of a Duration Model with Unobserved Heterogeneity, *Econometrica*, **58**, 453–473.

Horowitz, J. L. (1992). A Smoothed Maximum Score Estimator for the Binary Response Model, *Econometrica*, **60**, 505–531.

Horowitz, J. L. (1993a). Semiparametric Estimation of a Work-Trip Mode Choice Model, *Journal of Econometrics*, **58**, 49–70.

Horowitz, J. L. (1993b). Semiparametric and Nonparametric Estimation of Quantal Response Models, in *Handbook of Statistics*, Vol. 11, G. S. Maddala, C. R. Rao, and H. D. Vinod, eds., Amsterdam: North-Holland Publishing Company.

Horowitz, J. L. (1993c). Optimal Rates of Convergence of Parameter Estimators in the Binary Response Model with Weak Distributional Assumptions, *Econometric Theory*, **9**, 1–18.

Horowitz (1996). Semiparametric Estimation of a Regression Model with an Unknown Transformation of the Dependent Variable, *Econometrica*, **64**, 103–137.

Horowitz, J. L. (1997). Bootstrap Methods in Econometrics: Theory and Numerical Performance, in *Advances in Economics and Econometrics: Theory and Applications*, Vol. III, D. M. Kreps and K. F. Wallis, eds., Cambridge: Cambridge University Press, Ch. 7.

Horowitz, J. L. (1998). *Semiparametric Methods in Econometrics*, New York: Springer-Verlag.

Horowitz, J. L. (1999). Semiparametric Estimation of a Proportional Hazard Model with Unobserved Heterogeneity, *Econometrica*, **67**, 1001–1028.

Horowitz, J. L. (2001a). Nonparametric Estimation of a Generalized Additive Model with an Unknown Link Function, *Econometrica*, **69**, 499–513.

Horowitz, J. L. (2001b). The Bootstrap, in *Handbook of Econometrics*, Vol. 5, J.J. Heckman and E. Leamer, eds., Amsterdam: Elsevier, pp. 3159–3228.

Horowitz, J. L. (2002). Bootstrap Critical Values for Tests Based on the Smoothed Maximum Score Estimator, *Journal of Econometrics*, **111**, 141–167.

Horowitz, J.L. (2007). Asymptotic Normality of a Nonparametric Instrumental Variables Estimator, *International Economic Review*, **48**, 1329–1349.

Horowitz, J. L. and Härdle, W. (1996). Direct Semiparametric Estimation of Single-Index Models with Discrete Covariates, *Journal of the American Statistical Association*, **91**, 1632–1640.

Horowitz, J. L. and S. Lee (2005). Nonparametric Estimation of an Additive Quantile Regression Model, *Journal of the American Statistical Association*, **100**, 1238–1249.

Horowitz, J. L. and S. Lee (2007). Nonparametric Instrumental Variables Estimation of a Quantile Regression Model, *Econometrica*, **75**, 1191–1208.

Horowitz, J. L. and E. Mammen (2004). Nonparametric Estimation of an Additive Model with a Link Function, *Annals of Statistics*, **32**, 2412–2443.

Horowitz, J. L. and E. Mammen (2007). Rate-Optimal Estimation for a General Class of Nonparametric Regression Models with Unknown Link Functions, *Annals of Statistics*, **35**, 2589–2619.

Horowitz, J. L. and M. Markatou (1996). Semiparametric Estimation of Regression Models for Panel Data, *Review of Economic Studies*, **63**, 145–168.

Hougaard, P. (1984). Life Table Methods for Heterogeneous Populations: Distributions Describing the Heterogeneity, *Biometrika*, **61**, 75–83.

Hougaard, P. (1986). Survival Models for Heterogeneous Populations Derived from Stable Distributions, *Biometrika*, **73**, 387–396.

Hristache, M., A. Juditsky, J. Polzehl, and V. Spokoiny (2001). Structure Adaptive Approach for Dimension Reduction, *Annals of Statistics*, **29**, 1537–1566.

Hristache, M., A. Juditsky, and V. Spokoiny (2001). Direct Estimation of the Index Coefficient in a Single-Index Model, *Annals of Statistics*, **29**, 595–623.

Hsiao, C. (1986). *Analysis of Panel Data*, Cambridge, Cambridge University Press.

Hsieh, D., C. F. Manski, and D. McFadden (1985). Estimation of Response Probabilities from Augmented Retrospective Observations, *Journal of the American Statistical Association*, **80**, 651–662.

Huang, J. (2003). Local Asymptotics for Polynomial Spline Regression, *Annals of Statistics*, **31**, 1600–1635.

Huber, P. J. (1985). Projection Pursuit, *Annals of Statistics*, **13**, 435—475.

Ibragimov, I. A. and R. Z. Has'minskii (1981). *Statistical Estimation: Asymptotic Theory*, New York: Springer-Verlag.

Ichimura, H. (1993). Semiparametric Least Squares (SLS) and Weighted SLS Estimation of Single-Index Models, *Journal of Econometrics*, **58**, 71–120.

Ichimura, H. and L.-F. Lee (1991). Semiparametric Least Squares Estimation of Multiple Index Models: Single Equation Estimation, in *Nonparametric and Semiparametric Methods in Econometrics and Statistics*, W. A. Barnett, J. Powell, and G. Tauchen, eds., Cambridge: Cambridge University Press, Ch. 1.

Imbens, G. (1992). An Efficient Method of Moments Estimator for Discrete Choice Models with Choice-Based Sampling, *Econometrica*, **60**, 1187–1214.

Ishwaran, H. (1996). Identifiability and Rates of Estimation for Scale Parameters in Location Mixture Models, *Annals of Statistics*, **24**, 1560–1571.

Jennrich, R. I. (1969). Asymptotic Properties of Non-Linear Least Squares Estimators, *Annals of Mathematical Statistics*, **40**, 633–643.

John, J. A. and N. R. Draper (1980). An Alternative Family of Transformations, *Applied Statistics*, **29**, 190–197.

Johnson, N. L. (1949). Systems of Frequency Curves Generated by Methods of Translation, *Biometrika*, **36**, 149–176.

Jones, M. C., J. S. Marron, and S. J. Sheather (1996). A Brief Survey of Bandwidth Selection for Density Estimation, *Journal of the American Statistical Association*, 91, 401–407.

Kennan, J. (1985). The Duration of Contract Strikes in U.S. Manufacturing, *Journal of Econometrics*, **28**, 5–28.

Khan, S. (2001). Two-Stage Rank Estimation of Quantile Index Models, *Journal of Econometrics*, **100**, 319–355.

Kiefer, J. and J. Wolfowitz (1956). Consistency of the Maximum Likelihood Estimator in the Presence of Infinitely Many Incidental Parameters, *Annals of Mathematical Statistics*, **27**, 887–906.

Kim, J. and D. Pollard (1990). Cube Root Asymptotics, *Annals of Statistics*, **18**, 191–219.

Kim, W., O. B. Linton, and N. W. Hengartner (1999). A Computationally Efficient Oracle Estimator for Additive Nonparametric Regression with Bootstrap Confidence Intervals, *Journal of Computational and Graphical Statistics*, **8**, 278–297.

Klein, R. W. and R. H. Spady (1993). An Efficient Semiparametric Estimator for Binary Response Models, *Econometrica*, **61**, 387–421.

Koenker, R. and G. S. Bassett (1978). Regression Quantiles, *Econometrica*, 46, 33–50.

Kooreman, P.. and B. Melenberg (1989). *Maximum Score Estimation in the Ordered Response Model*, discussion paper no. 8948, CentER for Economic Research, Tilburg University, Tilburg, The Netherlands.

Kress, R. (1999). *Linear Integral Equations*, 2nd edition, New York: Springer-Verlag.

Lam, K. F. and A. Y. C. Kuk (1997). A Marginal Likelihood Approach to Estimation in Frailty Models, *Journal of the American Statistical Association*, **92**, 985–990.

Lancaster, T. (1979). Econometric Methods for the Duration of Unemployment, *Econometrica*, **47**, 939–956.

Lee, M.-J. (1992). Median Regression for Ordered Discrete Response, *Journal of Econometrics*, **51**, 59–77.

Lee, S. (2003). Efficient Semiparametric Estimation of a Partially Linear Quantile Regression Model, *Econometric Theory*, **19**, 1–31.
Lewbel, A. (2000). Semiparametric Qualitative Response Model Estimation with Unknown Heteroscedasticity or Instrumental Variables, *Journal of Econometrics*, **97**, 145–177.
Li, K.-C. (1987). Asymptotic Optimality for C_P, C_L, Cross-Validation and Generalized Cross-Validation: Discrete Index Set, *Annals of Statistics*, **15**, 958–975.
Li, K.-C. (1991). Sliced Inverse Regression for Dimension Reduction, *Journal of the American Statistical Association*, **86**, 316–342.
Li, Q. and J. S. Racine (2007). *Nonparametric Econometrics: Theory and Practice*, Princeton: Princeton University Press.
Linton, O. B. (1997). Efficient Estimation of Additive Nonparametric Regression Models, *Biometrika*, **84**, 469–473.
Linton, O. B., R. Chen, N. Wang, and W. Härdle (1997). An Analysis of Transformations for Additive Nonparametric Regression, *Journal of the American Statistical Association*, **92**, 1512–1521.
Linton, O. B. and W. Härdle (1996). Estimating Additive Regression Models with Known Links, *Biometrika*, **83**, 529–540.
Linton, O. B. and J. B. Nielsen (1995). A Kernel Method of Estimating Structured Nonparametric Regression Based on Marginal Integration, *Biometrika*, **82**, 93–100.
Linton, O. B., S. Sperlich, and I. Van Keilegom (2008). Estimation of a Semiparametric Transformation Model, *Annals of Statistics*, **36**, 686–718.
Liusternik, L. A. and V. J. Sobolev (1961). *Elements of Functional Analysis*, New York: Ungar Publishing Company.
MacKinnon, J. G. and L. Magee (1990). Transforming the Dependent Variable in Regression Models, *International Economic Review*, **31**, 315–339.
Mammen, E., O. Linton, and J. Nielsen (1999). The Existence and Asymptotic Properties of a Backfitting Projection Algorithm under Weak Conditions, *Annals of Statistics*, **27**, 1443–1490.
Mammen, E. and B.U. Park (2006). A Simple Smooth Backfitting Method for Additive Models, *Annals of Statistics*, **34**, 2252–2271.
Manski, C. F. (1975). Maximum Score Estimation of the Stochastic Utility Model of Choice, *Journal of Econometrics*, **3**, 205–228.
Manski, C. F. (1985). Semiparametric Analysis of Discrete Response: Asymptotic Properties of the Maximum Score Estimator, *Journal of Econometrics*, **27**, 313–334.
Manski, C. F. (1986). Semiparametric Analysis of Binary Response from Response-Based Samples, *Journal of Econometrics*, **31**, 31–40.
Manski, C. F. (1987). Semiparametric Analysis of Random Effects Linear Models from Binary Panel Data, *Econometrica*, **55**, 357–362.
Manski, C. F. (1988). Identification of Binary Response Models, *Journal of the American Statistical Association*, **83**, 729–738.
Manski, C. F. (1994). The Selection Problem, in *Advances in Econometrics: Sixth World Congress*, Vol. 1, C. A. Sims, ed., Cambridge: Cambridge University Press, Ch. 4.
Manski, C. F. (1995). *Identification Problems in the Social Sciences*, Cambridge, MA: Harvard University Press.
Manski, C. F. and S. Lerman (1977). The Estimation of Choice Probabilities from Choice-Based Samples, *Econometrica*, **45**, 1977–1988.
Manski, C. F. and D. McFadden (1981). Alternative Estimators and Sample Designs for Discrete Choice Analysis, in *Structural Analysis of Discrete Data with Econometric Applications*, D. F. Manski and D. McFadden, eds., Cambridge, MA: MIT Press.
Manski, C. F. and T. S. Thomson (1986). Operational Characteristics of Maximum Score Estimation, *Journal of Econometrics*, **32**, 65–108.
Matzkin, R. L. (1992). Nonparametric and Distribution-Free Estimation of the Binary Threshold Crossing and the Binary Choice Models, *Econometrica*, **60**, 239–270.

Matzkin, R. L. (1994). Restrictions of Economic Theory in Nonparametric Methods, in *Handbook of Econometrics*, Vol. 4, R. F. Engle and D. F. McFadden, eds., Amsterdam: Elsevier, Ch. 42.

Melenberg, B. and A. H. O. van Soest (1996). Measuring the Costs of Children: Parametric and Semiparametric Estimators, *Statistica Neerlandica*, **50**, 171–192.

Meyer, B. D. (1990). Unemployment Insurance and Unemployment Spells, *Econometrica*, **58**, 757–782.

Müller, H.-G. (1984). Smooth Optimum Kernel Estimators of Densities, Regression Curves and Modes, *Annals of Statistics*, **12**, 766–774.

Murphy, S. A. (1994). Consistency in a Proportional Hazards Model Incorporating a Random Effect, *Annals of Statistics*, **22**, 712–731.

Murphy, S. A. (1995). Asymptotic Theory for the Frailty Model, *Annals of Statistics*, **23**, 182–198.

Murphy, S. A., A. J. Rossini, and A. W. Van der Vaart (1997). Maximum Likelihood Estimation in the Proportional Odds Model, *Journal of the American Statistical Association*, **92**, 968–976.

Nadaraya, E. A. (1964). On Estimating Regression, *Theory of Probability and Its Applications*, **10**, 186–190.

Newey, W. K. (1990). Efficient Instrumental Variables Estimation of Nonlinear Models, *Econometrica*, **58**, 809–837.

Newey, W. K. (1993). Efficient Estimation of Models with Conditional Moment Restrictions, in *Handbook of Statistics*, Vol. 11, G. S. Maddala, C. R. Rao, and H. D. Vinod, eds., Amsterdam: North-Holland Publishing Company.

Newey, W. K. (1997). Convergence Rates and Asymptotic Normality for Series Estimators, *Journal of Econometrics*, **79**, 147–168.

Newey, W. K. and D. McFadden (1994). Large Sample Estimation and Hypothesis Testing, in *Handbook of Econometrics*, Vol. 4, R. F. Engle and D. L. McFadden, eds., Amsterdam: Elsevier, pp. 2111–2245.

Newey, W. K. and J. L. Powell (2003). Instrumental Variable Estimation of Nonparametric Models, *Econometrica*, **71**, 1565–1578.

Newey, W. K., J. L. Powell, and F. Vella (1999). Nonparametric Estimation of Triangular Simultaneous Equations Models, *Econometrica*, **67**, 565–603.

Newey, W. K. and T. M. Stoker (1993). Efficiency of Weighted Average Derivative Estimators and Index Models, *Econometrica*, **61**, 1199–1223.

Nielsen, G. G., R. D. Gill, P. K. Andersen, and T. I. A. Sørensen (1992). A Counting Process Approach to Maximum Likelihood Estimation in Frailty Models, *Scandinavian Journal of Statistics*, **19**, 25–43, 1992.

Opsomer, J. D. (2000). Asymptotic Properties of Backfitting Estimators, *Journal of Multivariate Analysis*, **73**, 166–179.

Opsomer, J. D. and D. Ruppert (1997). Fitting a Bivariate Additive Model by Local Polynomial Regression, *Annals of Statistics*, **25**, 186–211.

Pagan, A. and A. Ullah (1999). *Nonparametric Econometrics*, Cambridge: Cambridge University Press.

Pakes, A. and D. Pollard (1989). Simulation and the Asymptotics of Optimization Estimators, *Econometrica*, **57**, 1027–1057.

Parner, E. (1997a). *Consistency in the Correlated Gamma-Frailty Model*, unpublished working paper, Department of Theoretical Statistics, University of Aarhus, Aarhus, Denmark.

Parner, E. (1997b). *Asymptotic Normality in the Correlated Gamma-Frailty Model*, unpublished working paper, Department of Theoretical Statistics, University of Aarhus, Aarhus, Denmark.

Petersen, J. H., P. K. Andersen, and R. D. Gill (1996). Variance Components Models for Survival Data, *Statistica Neerlandica*, **50**, 193–211.

Pettit, A. N. (1982). Inference for the Linear Model Using a Likelihood Based on Ranks, *Journal of the Royal Statistical Society*, **44**, 234–243.

Politis, D. N. and J. P. Romano (1994). Large Sample Confidence Regions Based on Subsamples under Minimal Assumptions, *Annals of Statistics*, **22**, 2031–2050.

Politis, D. N., J. P. Romano, and M. Wolf (1999). *Subsampling*, New York: Springer.

Pollard, D. (1984). *Convergence of Stochastic Processes*, New York: Springer-Verlag.

Portnoy, S. (1997). Local Asymptotics for Quantile Smoothing Splines, *Annals of Statistics*, 25, 414–434.

Powell, J. L. (1994). Estimation of Semiparametric Models, in *Handbook of Econometrics*, Vol. 4, R. F. Engle and D. F. McFadden, eds., Amsterdam: Elsevier, Ch. 41.

Powell, J. L., J. H. Stock, and T. M. Stoker (1989). Semiparametric Estimation of Index Coefficients, *Econometrica*, **51**, 1403–1430.

Powell, J. L. and T. M. Stoker (1996). Optimal Bandwidth Choice for Density Weighted Averages, *Journal of Econometrics*, **75**, 291–316.

Powell, M. J. D. (1981). *Approximation Theory and Methods*, Cambridge, UK: Cambridge University Press.

Prentice, R. and L. Gloeckler (1978). Regression Analysis of Grouped Survival Data with Application to Breast Cancer data, *Biometrics*, **34**, 57–67.

Ramsey, J. B. (1969). Tests for Specification Errors in Classical Linear Least-Squares Analysis, *Journal of the Royal Statistical Society*, Series B, **71**, 350–371.

Rao, C. R. (1973). *Linear Statistical Inference and Its Applications*, New York: John Wiley & Sons.

Ridder, G. (1990). The Non-Parametric Identification of Generalized Accelerated Failure-Time Models, *Review of Economic Studies*, **57**, 167–182.

Ridder, G. and T. M. Woutersen (2003). The Singularity of the Information Matrix of the Mixed Proportional Hazard Model, *Econometrica*, **71**, 1579–1589.

Robinson, P. M. (1987). Asymptotically Efficient Estimation in the Presence of Heteroskedasticity of Unknown Form, *Econometrica*, **55**, 875–891.

Robinson, P. M. (1988). Root-N-Consistent Semiparametric Regression, *Econometrica*, **56**, 931–954.

Robinson, P. M. (1991). Best Nonlinear Three Stage Least Squares Estimation of Certain Econometric Models, *Econometrica*, **59**, 755–786.

Schmalensee, R. and T. M. Stoker (1999). Household Gasoline Demand in the United States, *Econometrica*, **67**, 645–662.

Schucany, W. R. and J. P. Sommers (1977). Improvement of Kernel Type Density Estimators, *Journal of the American Statistical Association*, **72**, 420–423.

Serfling, R. J. (1980). *Approximation Theorems of Mathematical Statistics*, New York: John Wiley & Sons.

Sherman, R. P. (1993). The Limiting Distribution of the Maximum Rank Correlation Estimator, *Econometrica*, **61**, 123–137.

Silverman, B. W. (1978). Weak and Strong Uniform Consistency of the Kernel Estimate of a Density and Its Derivatives, *Annals of Statistics*, **6**, 177–184.

Silverman, B. W. (1986). *Density Estimation for Statistics and Data Analysis*, London: Chapman & Hall.

Stefanski, L. and R. J. Carroll (1990). Deconvoluting Kernel Density Estimators, *Statistics*, **2**, 169–184.

Stefanski, L. and R. J. Carroll (1991). Deconvolution-Based Score Tests in Measurement Error Models, *The Annals of Statistics*, **19**, 249–259.

Stoker, T. M. (1986). Consistent Estimation of Scaled Coefficients, *Econometrica*, **54**, 1461–1481.

Stoker, T. M. (1991a). Equivalence of Direct, Indirect and Slope Estimators of Average Derivatives, in *Nonparametric and Semiparametric Methods in Economics and Statistics*, W. A. Barnett, J. Powell, and G. Tauchen, eds., New York: Cambridge University Press.

Stoker, T. M. (1991b). *Lectures on Semiparametric Econometrics*, Louvain-la-Neuve, Belgium: CORE Foundation.

Stone, C. J. (1980). Optimal Rates of Convergence for Nonparametric Estimators, *Annals of Statistics*, **8**, 1348–1360.

Stone, C. J. (1982). Optimal Global Rates of Convergence for Nonparametric Regression, *Annals of Statistics*, **10**, 1040–1053.

Stone, C. J. (1985). Additive Regression and Other Nonparametric Models, *Annals of Statistics*, **13**, 689–705.

Stuart, A. and J. K. Ord (1987). *Kendall's Advanced Theory of Statistics*, Vol. 1, New York: Oxford University Press.

Subbotin, V. (2008). *Essays on the Econometric Theory of Rank Regressions*, Ph.D. dissertation, Department of Economics, Northwestern University, Evanston, IL.

Tjøstheim, D. and B. H. Auestad (1994). Nonparametric Identification of Nonlinear Time Series: Projections, *Journal of the American Statistical Association*, **89**, 1398–1409.

Tsiatis, A. A. (1981). A Large Sample Study of Cox's Regression Model, *Annals of Statistics*, **9**, 93–108.

Watson, G. S. (1964). Smooth Regression Analysis, *Sankhya*, Series A, **26**, 359–372.

White, H. (1982). Maximum Likelihood Estimation of Misspecified Models, *Econometrica*, **50**, 1–25.

Xia, Y. (2006). Asymptotic Distributions for Two Estimators of the Single-Index Model, *Econometric Theory*, **22**, 1112–1137.

Xia, Y., H. Tong, W. K. Li, and L.-X. Zhu (2002). An Adaptive Estimation of Dimension Reduction Space, *Journal of the Royal Statistical Society*, Series B, **64**, 363–410.

Ye, J. and N. Duan (1997). Nonparametric $h^{-1/2}$-Consistent Estimation of the General Transformation Model, *Annals of Statistics*, **25**, 2682–2717.

Yu, K. and M. C. Jones (1998). Local Linear Quantile Regression, *Journal of the American Statistical Association*, 93, 228–237.

Yu, K., B. U. Park, and E. Mammen (2008). Smooth Backfitting in Generalized Additive Models, *Annals of Statistics*, **36**, 228–260.

Zhou, S., X. Shen, and D.A. Wolfe (1998). Local Asymptotics for Regression Splines and Confidence Regions, *Annals of Statistics*, **26**, 1760–1782.

Index